The Curtain Rises

The Curtain Rises

Rethinking Culture, Ideology, and the State in Eastern Europe

Edited by
Hermine G. De Soto
and
David G. Anderson

HUMANITIES PRESS
NEW JERSEY

First published 1993 by Humanities Press International, Inc.,
Atlantic Highlands, New Jersey 07716

©1993 by Humanities Press International, Inc.

Library of Congress Cataloging-in-Publication Data

The Curtain rises : rethinking culture, ideology, and the state in
Eastern Europe / Hermine G. De Soto and David G. Anderson, editors.
p.   cm.
Includes bibliographical references and index.
ISBN 0–391–03771–4 (hard)   ISBN 0–391–03810–9 (pbk)
1. Europe, Eastern—Social conditions.   2. Europe, Eastern—
Politics and government—1989–   3. Post-communism—Europe, Eastern.
I. De Soto, Hermine G.   II. Anderson, David G. (David George), 1965–.
HN380.7.A8C87   1993
306'.0947—dc20   92–13577
CIP

A catalog record for this book is available from the British Library.

Printed in the United States of America

Contents

Acknowledgments

The creation of this volume was a collaborative effort that drew together not only the authors but also countless helpful individuals who patiently guided our research in the field. We hope that these essays will shed some light on the profound changes that are impinging upon their lives.

We would like to specifically commend the effort of our friend and colleague Tahsin Corat for his fine translation of Claude Meillassoux's contribution. Tahsin's swift and detailed work provided great inspiration to us in assembling the volume.

David De Soto deserves special credit for organizing our far-flung correspondence while we were each working in northern Canada or in eastern Europe.

An especially warm acknowledgment is reserved for Susan Hirshberg, who helped collate and proofread the manuscript; and who took time out for dancing when absolutely necessary.

Introduction

For forty years, the analysis of politics and society in Eastern Europe has been anchored in two hollow alternatives. While the Right criticized the evils of "totalitarian society," the Left embraced the vision that state socialism promised—but did not deliver. Yet as these two sides fought rhetorical battles in the universities and the streets of Europe and America, "actually-existing" socialism went about the business of establishing its own institutions and governing everyday life. To the surprise of both sides, Eastern Europe has now erupted into a period of intense transition. As the iron curtain rises, it is evident that the stage has been set with an entirely new scene. Observers have been stunned by the evidence of the frenzied activities carried out quietly behind the scenes during the *entracte*.

The purpose of this volume is to map the contours of recent developments in Eastern Europe. Starting from close observation of the social changes themselves, each contributor rethinks perspectives within the varied disciplines of anthropology, political science, and sociology. While some of the authors reexamine classical theoretical problems, other contributors conduct detailed examinations of the making of the revolutions in the East and their significance for local communities. Although the collection of interpretations presented here is far from conclusive, it illuminates tendencies in the course of the transition. The overall goal is to try to interpret the Eastern European experience in its own terms for a Western audience.

SETTING THE STAGE: THEORETICAL CONTROVERSIES ON EASTERN EUROPE

The volume starts with a theoretical debate regarding the significance of the recent structural changes in Eastern Europe. Unexpected social problems arising in this time of transition challenge old theories; certainly, Marxist theory faces the greatest challenge in explaining the changes in the former state socialist societies. Paradoxes and contradictions play a crucial role in developing theory: Counterposing Marxist theory to the dynamic changes in the East exposes old theoretical limitations and makes possible the construction of new concepts.

The heart of the first section brings to the reader the insights of two distinguished Marxist anthropologists, Claude Meillassoux and Aidan Southall, both of whom have extensive research experience in the first and the third worlds. Working within the Marxist theory of history, they relate this rich experience to the global links that are presently having an impact upon the development (or underdevelopment) of Eastern Europe. Their insights are especially salient considering to what degree the current geopolitical structure will draw Eastern Europe within its influence.

Meillassoux argues that while the fall of the Berlin Wall opens up an unprecedented opportunity for international capitalism, this opportunity is not unambiguous. Through his interpretation of recent overtures of the current political apparatus in the East as courting the agents of power within the Western political economy, he speculates that this union might in fact backfire against the interests of the Eastern administrators. As has happened so commonly in the third world, the momentum of power in the West might lead to a suppression of indigenous sources of power within the arenas of government, science, and the economy.

The most distinctive aspect of Meillassoux's article is his rethinking of the classical Marxist theory of stratification. By arguing that Marxist conceptions of class and the state do not clearly identify the *agents* of oppression within society, he contends that class theory must be refocused upon the discrete *social corps* that operate at the behest of class forces. Meillassoux addresses the problem of class reductionism by arguing that the varied political and civil institutions such as the army, the technocratic corps, or the trade unions can shift alliances within this time of transition. By drawing attention to how these institutions are restructured, Meillassoux provides stimulating criteria for deducing the direction of future changes.

Aidan Southall's call for a critical rereading of the texts of Marx and Engels to better understand how Lenin interpreted and applied Marxist theory to the grand social experiment of this century—socialism in Eastern Europe—points to a dilemma that arises continually in social processes: the question of the relationship of theory, politics, and practice. Southall raises the fundamental question of whether the Marxist theory of history was ever meant to address the actual conditions of tzarist Russia during Lenin's political engagements. In particular, he closely examines Lenin's theory that "socialist" institutions might be governed either through socialist competition or through centralized accounting and control. His analysis discloses a missed opportunity for constructing the type of utopia that Marx and Engels envisioned: He questions the wisdom of destroying the Russian commune, which might have provided a protective foundation for a civil society. Southall's analysis suggests that a distinctive path of political development might have been possible if the first leader of the Soviet state had had a greater sensitivity to the dynamics of local institutions.

THE POLITICS OF DECOLLECTIVIZATION

As a complement to the analyses of the theoretical contradictions presented in the first section, the contributors in this section examine how these contradictions unfold on a local level. In particular, these case studies direct us to a detailed understanding of local political institutions, especially that distinctive experiment for which Eastern Europe is famous: collectivization. In many ways the phenomena of decollectivization are symbolic of the controversial nature of the recent reforms. While the demand for the elimination of state-administered agriculture often is lauded as a natural evolution toward pluralistic political institutions *and* private property, it is overlooked that the rural people of the East are in fact defending aspects of collective property. The contributors in this section examine how the goals of rural activists for new agricultural institutions are being actualized within the legal framework left by state socialism.

David Kideckel warns that it is premature for Western critics to judge the movement *against* state-controlled collective agriculture as a movement *for* individual landownership. Starting from the observation that the formal actions taken by Romanian peasants against the collective farms have been limited to spontaneous reactions against the administrative control of party cadres and centrally administered land allocations, Kideckel discovers a reluctance to jettison the specific rights and securities of collective agriculture. This phenomenon is not specific to Romania, as the other contributors in this section note. At the same time that Romanian peasants fight to preserve the principles of egalitarian pay and labor control, Siberian hunters lobby for appropriate types of guaranteed education and employment, and Hungarian farmers defend the freedom from taxation that their collective gives them. While Kideckel notes that there is a residue of rights that rural populations will fight to protect, he does not find an impassioned defense of collective institutions. He concludes that support for collective agriculture is produced from indecision in the face of conflicting visions over the direction that reform should take.

David Anderson argues that mere de facto support for collective institutions for want of a clear vision of the future does not invalidate the exercise of sorting among the contradictory set of norms and expectations of the rural population. He maintains that a detailed analysis of the statements of rural activists can rescue the few shining moments of wisdom that the tragic experiment of collectivization has produced. Through an analysis of Siberian social movements, Anderson illustrates that demands for education and guaranteed "appropriate" occupations are rights that can only be understood within the context of state socialism. The positive results of Soviet modernization are highlighted through his examination of the history of the Soviet state in a decidedly non-Western and nonindustrial region of the U.S.S.R. While Anderson concurs with other contributors in this volume that the stampede toward reform threatens to remove rights that the local population accepts as their right of citizenship, he takes a critical look at the practice of holding Euro-American institutions as the standard for a "modern" civil society. He shows that Siberian activists reserve the right to institute their *own* model of reform and to not uncritically appropriate a model from another socioeconomic context.

Christopher Hann captures the multitude of options for the reform of collective agriculture through a theoretical reflection upon his fifteen years of ethnographic research in Hungary. He argues that the diverse visions of reform can be best understood through the concept of a "hierarchy of ownership structures." By focusing on the history of the specialist cooperatives in Hungary that "enabled private ownership to develop within a socialist framework," he recognizes a property institution that lies in between the false alternatives of private *or* collective property. Hann's analysis presents an account of the complex nature of rights that existed under state socialism. This varied institutional foundation in turn generates sophisticated proposals to reform. Hann warns that to ignore the fabric of rights existing in the villages is to court economic disaster.

FRACTURED SOCIALISM AND THE RISE OF NATIONALISMS

While the first two sections of the book explore conflicts arising within political economy, this section extends the analysis of structural changes to their dramatic impact on national identities. Although for many years Eastern Europe was reputed to be welded together by the dictatorship of the proletariat, recent events have exposed the fragile nature of that proletarian identity. The authors in this section illustrate the conflicting process by which vibrant and often chauvinistic nationalisms create a contradictory sense of unity as the old state socialist identities crumble.

Continuing in the critical spirit of Southall and Meillassoux, Fahrünnisa Kulluk examines classical Marxist scholarship on national identities, nation-states, and national(ist) movements. She concludes that the century-old writings of Marx and Engels are inadequate for explaining ethnic struggles in late capitalist societies, let alone in Eastern Europe.

These inadequacies stem not only from the distant era in which they wrote but also from Marx and Engels's vision of communism as a conflict-free social mode. Their theory, according to Kulluk, prevented Marx and Engels from developing concepts in which the (re)emergence of nationalism in socialist societies could be understood.

In agreement with the theories of Wallerstein and Meillassoux, Kulluk connects the problem of nationalism to the context of the global capitalist system. She advances the striking hypothesis that national(ist) movements actually transform power relationships regardless of the class and ideological orientations of actors. The lesson to be drawn from Kulluk's conclusion is that the political impact or potentials of national(ist) movements cannot be precisely determined because of the unpredictable fluidity of identities in revolutionary periods.

The conjunctural nature of national(ist) movements is illustrated masterfully in Dejan Trickovic's anthropological study of the fracturing of national identity in Yugoslavia. Like Kulluk, Trickovic emphasizes the dynamic process by which identity changes are fed by geopolitical and structural changes. To underscore his point, he outlines the specific historical conditions that made Yugoslavian national unity possible—a capitalization upon its strategic position betwixt and between NATO and the Warsaw Pact—and recaptures the different meaning that the *rise* of a Berlin wall had for this strategically defined socialist Yugoslavian identity. The contrast to the instability of the present day emphasizes that the collapse of the cold war has not meant, as many people assume, joy and celebration for all Eastern Europeans.

The changes in post-Tito Yugoslavia suggest that colonial techniques of forceful suppression cannot solve the nationality problem. Anatoly Khazanov's analysis begins with the dynamics of this technique and with the premise that the Soviet state is an *imperial* state in the sense that force has been the cornerstone of state control over annexed ethnic groups. Khazanov's political-anthropological interpretation thus approaches the question of Soviet state hegemony from a different angle than does Kulluk, who emphasizes the socioeconomic roots of current social movements. While both authors offer differing views on the fundamental organizing principle of the Soviet state, their analyses converge through an accounting of the contradictory role that state-granted privileges play in stabilizing the empire's ethnic frontiers. As Khazanov explains, one of the key policy goals of the Soviet state was the recruitment of "cadres" in ethnic areas through specific recruiting quotas in educational and state institutions. During the apogee of Soviet state hegemony, these cadres would publicly denounce their own nationality and repudiate their native tongue. However, as the reform movement gained momentum, those individuals who were courted and compromised by lucrative positions in the state apparatus were conveniently well placed to become the leaders of nationalist movements. Thus there can be seen a melding of economic and political imperatives in the current reform movement.

Whereas Trickovic and Khazanov emphasize that nationalism separates ethnic groups and tends toward civil war, Graf et al. describe how the collapse of socialism in the German Democratic Republic has resulted in a different form of nationalism. The absence of distinct German ethnic groups, along with the lack of different language groups and religious traditions, has not favored the development of separatism within Germany. On the contrary, Graf et al. describe how within the transitional period, the fear of unemployment and insecurity about the new future has led to an identification with an all-German Volk. This shift not only obscures socioeconomic inequities but also buries the momentum of the preexisting East German solidarity against the state. The analysis of Graf et al. makes the important and tragic observation that the nationalist revival has prevented the possibility of the creation of a "Third Path" that would combine the best features of both the GDR and the FRG. In their terms, economic powers from the West have "hijacked" the revolution through the lack of a responsive political organization among the Left in East Germany.

As the above case studies indicate, the "new" nationalism in the East remains an extremely contradictory force. While, on the one hand, this force empowers local groups to establish their own definitions and priorities, on the other hand, it takes on its political agenda out of opposition to the preceding order. Khazanov describes this dynamic as "colonial ingratitude" of the educated elites, whom the Soviet state had once helped foster. While the new nationalism is felt most intensively in ethnic villages, it feeds off of the larger imperial framework in which it is embedded (Khazanov) as well as the position occupied by these ethnic movements in a worldwide division of labor (Kulluk).

THE TRANSITION: IDENTITIES, IDEOLOGIES, AND NEW UTOPIAS

The transition in Eastern Europe can be characterized as an explosion of new utopias in dramatic opposition to reigning state ideologies. As Karl Mannheim foresaw earlier in this century, the self-affirming and creative aspect of *utopias* is in constant struggle with *ideologies* that serve to preserve and enforce political power. As many of the contributors herein emphasize, while social movements bear the unmistakable mark of preexisting state administrations, in their own way they have an impact upon previous power structures. While movements centered on nationalism often have an ethnocentric and reactionary orientation, the ferment in the East also carries the promise of new perspectives for future social organization. The authors in this section examine the demands among particular groups within the new civil society for forms of democratic participation within the construction of that new society.

The transition from a passive and atomized political stability to a turbulent, revolutionary crisis is captured by Sam Beck in his firsthand ethnographic account of the struggles following the Romanian revolution. Beck demonstrates how the Romanian state "fused" itself to civil society by outlawing and meticulously policing all public opposition. The revolution presented the opportunity for Romanian citizens to experiment with a "new discourse"—a discourse that was leading to a new form of "political literacy." The dark side of this blossoming of utopian dialogue was the absence of institutionalized means to structure dissent. This led the "new" state to crush the opposition movement in the university square with the same brutal means employed by the "old" state.

This paradox illustrates, as Beck phrases it, "the dialectical link" between the state and civil society in post-Communist nations. Here again we are reminded that during the reign of the iron regimes of Eastern Europe the independent agency of social actors was not absent. Even in Romania, the umbrella of the Securitate and Ceauşescu's state provided a stable foundation for multitudinous informal networks. The sheer pervasiveness of these fractured channels of commerce and information should lead even the casual observer to expect that they will persist following the crumbling of the state edifice. Indeed, Beck sees Romanian public behavior trapped in the role of ritually reproducing the types of action that the Ceauşescu state supported. While this should not be a cause for fatalistic pessimism, the Romanian case points to the need for detailed analysis of social behavior in the aftermath of state socialism rather than the assumption that a new society will be inscribed upon a "clean slate."

The blossoming of new utopias in the East does not always yield progressive results. As both Laszlo Kürti and Hermine De Soto describe, the collapse of the old institutional structure threatens real guarantees for Hungarian and German women. Women in Eastern Europe are threatened in two ways. On the one hand, equality guaranteed under the socialist state is presently being dismantled under the "new" republican states. On the other hand, patriarchal elements within the "new" society are taking advantage of political liberalizations to place women back in the domestic sphere.

Laszlo Kürti demonstrates how notions of love and gender identity are culturally constructed and how such constructions are ideologically manipulated. He juxtaposes such myths to everyday life experiences of working women and men in the former "socialist" Hungary, and to Alexandra Kollontai's vision of a new socialist love, or "winged eros." Kürti's ethnographically oriented analysis reveals that a winged eros was never achieved. On the contrary, the ideologies of socialism created unforeseen gender confusions.

However, while the former system was hardly successful in creating new gender and love relations, the transition from socialism to "westernization," according to Kürti, develops concurrently into different mythologies regarding work, body, and gender. Kürti contends that the "springtime of the nation" in 1989, and the turn toward the West, created ideological expressions that are embedded in nationalistic and political rhetoric and he outlines postrevolutionary political leaders' propositions in which republics of Eastern Europe ought to be "built of a myriad of creches and kitchens."

Like the previous authors, Hermine De Soto points to theoretical limitations of Marxist scholarship, arguing that the Marxist emphasis on class analysis left unexamined the problems of gender equality and inequality. This theoretical blind spot had severe consequences for women living under the authority of the former rational redistributive administrations. She also argues that due to the logic of patriarchal and economic structures, neither the former rational redistributive system nor the late capitalist system favor equality for women at the workplace and in the domestic sphere.

In her analysis, De Soto traces the experience of East German women prior to the revolution and after the revolution. Like Graf, she argues that the women's movement, although successful in the transitional period in regard to negotiating demands for their autonomy and for a "Third Way," failed in the first elections (1990) to participate in the major political decision-making process. East German women are now entering into a fully formed late-capitalist welfare state. However, whereas the former regime repressed human agency and women's contestations, the latter state has to refrain from such dictatorial procedures because the late-capitalist welfare state's powers are limited vis à vis civil society. De Soto's suggestion is that the high unemployment rate for Eastern German women today will be a contested terrain for the future.

While activists in the East struggle to express their utopian visions and to bring these visions into practice, it is important to realize that this transition is not the *first* such transition from authoritarian state structures to a more loosely structured society. As Pi-Sunyer noted during his fieldwork in Spain, Spanish activists have felt a strange kinship for the struggles that the East Europeans are only just launching. Pi-Sunyer's provocative comparative analysis of Franco Spain's and East Europe's march to "democracy" offers the Spanish experience as a signpost toward a possible East European future.

Unlike the analysis suggested by Meillassoux, that of Pi-Sunyer suggests a more optimistic trajectory for Eastern Europe. According to Pi-Sunyer, two important political processes develop during transitional periods. The first process melds old structures of power and new leadership, producing a repressive reflection of the old order (as in Yugoslavia). The second process includes a reemergence of minority demands for participation in the political process. Real crises arise when political systems only allow *partial* reforms and political freedoms; the incomplete restructuring noted by Khazanov in the U.S.S.R. seems to meet this criteria. For Pi-Sunyer and Trickovic, a possible escape from the trauma of civil war would be a "united" Europe that addresses regionalism, ethnonationalism, and separatism. However this goal must first clear the real economic and political hurdles of the global political system noted by Meillassoux and Kulluk.

As this book goes to press, the true depth of the challenges facing the peoples of Eastern Europe remains obscured. Through firsthand ethnographic accounts and the rethinking of old theories, the contributors present images of everyday life in Eastern Europe that will, it is hoped, stimulate interest for further research. As the iron curtain rises, we are presented with both an intriguing spectacle and an unprecedented opportunity for the constructing of new solidarities between the critical scholars of East *and* West, who are no longer constrained by the confrontational politics of the cold war. This book is a contribution toward such a process.

DAVID G. ANDERSON
HERMINE G. DE SOTO

PART I
Setting the Stage:
Theoretical Controversies
on Eastern Europe

Toward a Theory of the "Social Corps"

CLAUDE MEILLASSOUX

The business press properly refers to the economic system in which we live as capitalism, whereas under the pen of an intellectual the term seems incongruous and outdated, if not derogating. We are invited to be blind to the existence of capitalism at the very moment of its triumph over the Stalinist states and while it is expanding at a prodigious rate in Asia. One wonders whether the social sciences have come to the point where they are no longer capable of grasping concretely their object through the current vocabulary, but instead only in an abstract way, if not metaphysically, through meaningless categories that reduce their object to immaterial nonexistence.

Just like we are told that capitalism is bogus, so we are told of the "social classes." Yet the press informs us daily of the whereabouts of billionaires. Who are these people whose earnings could be twice the budget of an African state?[1] Who are the people belonging to boards of trustees? Why are we not allowed to think that those large corporations and their tycoons are unable to influence world events, even though they proved their power and know-how by such a capacity for accumulation? Does the business world consist only of sound and fury? Or could this world be seen as the result of competitive, often hostile, but nevertheless converging policies of so many capitalist fractions? We have before our eyes the unprecedented organization of the world, steered by international institutions such as the World Bank and the IMF, which under the control of the richest capitalist countries are dominating the governments of the rest of the planet with the supreme means of power: money. But in the name of anti-Marxism, this decisive aspect of the organization of our world, along with the power of the class that dominates it, is kept outside the boundaries of mainstream research.

As for the proletariat, because its great majority is somewhere out of sight in southern and eastern countries, it sinks in the abyss of history. The misery of the third world seems to some to be not the result of overexploitation but caused by the flaws of these people: laziness, native incapacity, corruption, if not uncontrollable salaciousness, and so on. These are populations that have been drawn for two generations to

2

crowded cities of the third world, where, fed on imported food products, they multiply in order to provide cheap labor to expatriated foreign businesses. It is hypocrisy that these people should not be considered proletarians! And what of the migrant workers in our own cities? Who are they? Are they aliens who are not counted as belonging to "our" working classes? Or are they benighted members of our civilization who only deserve the charity of some food and contraceptives? Although we know that people of the South are the victims of a ruthless policy advocated by the International Monetary Fund, we accept its rationale with a sigh as we are told that this is for their own good. We disregard as trivial the policies of perpetual industrial delocalization, which continually create, abandon, and re-create working classes all over the world.

Capitalism has undergone deep transformations since its inception. One is the emergence and development of *social corps*—the term I use for bodies of people *serving* the social classes, either the bourgeoisie or the proletariat (with the largest number serving the former)—often labeled as "classes" in current sociology. Excepting the capitalist class, the social corps account for almost all of the educated and knowledge-producing population. The ensuing bias amongst intellectuals might explain the current misconceptions of prevalent social relations. Most social corps are the instruments of the organization and domination of a comparatively small but powerful capitalist class that uses them to exploit an expanding working class across the world.

The prodigious development of techniques in industries and the service sector since the late 1970s has increased the productivity of labor to such an extent and at such a rate that it may not ever be reabsorbed through capitalist expansion. The relative overpopulation of the third world generated by the implantation of expatriated industries since the 1950s is now extending itself to the heart of the "developed" countries (Meillassoux 1991a). Partly because workers are continuously deskilled by technological progress and partly because of the policies of delocalization, fewer and fewer workers all over the world can find buyers for their labor power. In this conjuncture, unemployment grows because of the structural incapacity of the capitalist system to set a balanced redistribution of the profits coming from an increase in the productivity of labor. Since monetarist economists claim that wealthy people are more likely to save and invest than the needy classes—which consume any additional income—they advocate that money be channeled to the rich. This means that one should expect that the normal effect of capitalism, which is a continuous and growing disparity of income, will be accentuated instead of alleviated. Despite being a perpetual object of complaints from the business world, the state is used as an instrument in the matter of unemployment to revert the maintenance of unemployed people to the unemployed themselves or, at best, to society at large. In this manner the business world escapes its responsibility. In such a conjuncture, the proletariat is less likely than ever before to buy the fruits of its own production.[2]

The fall of the Berlin wall gives international business the opportunity to exploit a new labor force that is better qualified than the third world proletariat. Although this newly available proletariat is supported by a developed, albeit degraded, industrial infrastructure, it fulfills the current technological requirements of international business. According to the greedy formula of Pierre Bérégovoy, the French minister of finance, the Eastern market presents itself as a deposit of twenty-five years of growth. One could only be pleased by the political liberalization of the Eastern European countries. However (as of December 1989) it seems that this liberalization will be simultaneous with a submission to a new Western imperialism, which is facilitated by the complicity of the existing nomenklatura. These events, however sudden, seem to corroborate the theory of class and social corps presented further on.

The purpose of this chapter is to extend the theory of social classes by the introduction of a complementary notion of social corps.

While two social classes polarize the development of capitalist society as a whole—the capitalist (or bourgeois) class and the proletariat—each one generates a social corps that is distinct from its class but entrusted with some of the essential functions of maintaining the existence of that class. For the bourgeois class these functions would include the management of enterprises, education, politics, supervision and containment of the working classes, repression, and so on. For the proletariat, these functions would consist mainly of the leadership and organization of trade unions and political parties. The exercise of such functions may induce some social corps, under certain circumstances, to try to substitute themselves for the class they serve.

In order to achieve an initial approximation of the concept social *corps*, it is useful to clarify the concept of social *class* to which it is linked. I will proceed by contrasting the taxonomic approach of classical sociology with an organic approach. I will first try to define these social corps on the basis of their emergence, the nature of their relations with the social classes from which they had sprung initially, the specificity of their ideology, and the extent of their political potentiality. As the development will show, this approach leads to an interesting analysis of the Stalinist bureaucratic regime as avatar of a social corps.

THE SOCIAL CLASSES

There are two opposing approaches to the study of social classes. The first one is taxonomy, which classifies people on the formal basis of one criterion (for instance, the level of income or occupation or education). The second approach defines classes in their historical context through their organic relationship to each other.

The taxonomical approach of mainstream sociology leads to a hierarchical representation of society as made up of strata presumed homogeneous (in that they are defined by variants of the same criterion). These strata are ordered relatively to one another on the basis of quantitative or qualitative gradation. This hierarchical ordering is generally qualified by relative notions that are not very telling, such as upper, middle, and low.

To be strict, a taxonomic classification should rely on a single discriminatory criterion selected in such a way as to characterize relatively each category and exclude unequivocally what does not belong in that group. However, criteria such as income or education are situated on an inorganic continuum that does not indicate when one leaves one class to move on to the next one. They cannot therefore delineate a social category with any precision. Moreover, this method does not allow cross-checking of several criteria: For instance, people with the same occupation may not have the same income or the same behavior; or people with the same education level will be classified in different occupations or in different income brackets, and so on. Thus it is not possible to combine several of these criteria without creating a confusion that can only be solved through the arbitrary subordination of one to another. In short, they cannot be combined without undermining the scientific claim of the taxonomic approach.

The most shapeless (and yet the most convenient) notion of this sociology is the category of middle class. This class includes, rather incongruously, groups such as professionals (who receive fees), executives and officials (who receive salaries), and army officers (and their pay). These are all lumped together with "middle" capitalists such as businessmen (who make profits), traders (who receive markups), and stockholders (who "earn" revenue) or with groups that are the remnants of a precapitalist economy, such as artisans or artists (whether they are independent or subsidized by a public or private patron). The variety of this vocabulary of remuneration suggests that these groups may have different functions and interests in society and that such notions as high, middle, and low are a bit too narrow to capture these functions and interests.

To increase the confusion, mainstream sociology sometimes uses the term *bourgeoisie* to designate a class with a high income level without actually distinguishing income from capital. The distinction mainstream sociology sustains between middle and petty bourgeoisie does not express the difference either. The notion of a middle bourgeoisie may be that of the previously mentioned middle class, which is a rather blurry concept, or it may refer to a fraction of the bourgeois class disposing of an average-size capital. However, it seems that the petty bourgeois is not understood in this sociology as a segment of the bourgeois class with "petty" capital (unable to employ wage labor) but as people who work close to the bourgeois and who try to imitate its attitudes and political behavior and to maintain their distance from the working class.

Contrary to the taxonomic approach, the dialectical method defines social components according to the organic relations they have with one another. It analyzes these components as belonging to a comprehensive set of relations within a defined social context. Classes are those components articulated around a central relationship, that of exploitation. They are a historical product of the development of the social system, with each class existing in relation to the other but in a conflicting opposition. Accordingly, social classes are neither homologous nor symmetrical.

The dominant class owes its existence to the exploitation of the other class, which remains subordinated to the former for the fulfilling of its basic needs. The dominant class cannot be rid of its exploited class without losing the social basis of its own existence. The dominated class can only liberate itself from the exploiting class by changing the entire structure of society.

Thus, the process of exploitation polarizes capitalist society around these two classes that exist through one another. In the organic sense, the dominant class, which is usually called the bourgeoisie, controls and owns the *social* means of production and exchange,[3] that is, all the means that are used to satisfy the material and cultural needs of a society. To run this apparatus of production and circulation, the dominant class depends on the use of a proletariat made of men and women who have no other resources than the sale of their labor power, as they have no access to the ownership and control of the means of production.

I propose to extend this basic analysis in order to define other components of capitalist society based on these two crucial social classes. I designate these components as social corps. Mainstream sociology may count them as classes unless they stuff them in the catchall categories of middle classes and petty bourgeoisie.

A proper definition of *social corps* has to start with a review of the concept of social class from which it emanates.

THE BOURGEOISIE

The capitalist system presupposes the private appropriation of the social means of production and allows the unlimited enrichment of those who control it through profit accumulation.

According to our extensive approach, people who enjoy the ownership of productive or distributive capital and who temporarily or permanently employ wage earners belong to the bourgeoisie. Historically, national bourgeoisies developed within the boundaries of the aristocratic states the nations inherited after the bourgeois revolutions. Each national bourgeoisie tried to protect those territories and their populations in order to create their own domestic markets as a springboard for the conquest of foreign outlets. The most advanced national capitalisms wanted to impose a free trade regime on weaker countries, which in turn wanted a protectionist arrangement.

The quest for raw materials, land, and labor through the colonization of noncapitalist countries has extended the rivalry of national bourgeoisies to a global level. The most devastating conquests and the most ruthless massacres were the result of that expansion. The two world wars that pitted the national bourgeoisies against one another were also the bloodiest in human history. The main goal of these wars was to solve through violence the expansionist competition of rival national capitalist classes. The wars ended up establishing the leadership of the United States over world capitalism, eliminating thereby the possibility of its having recourse to wars to solve its *internal* problems.[4] Since then, capitalism has been restructuring itself as a new international political order within the hegemonic framework provided by the United States in which nationality takes a back seat to the concentration of capital. At the same time, nevertheless, the efforts of newly forming bourgeoisies to establish their presence, either in the underdeveloped continents or now in the former Eastern block, take again the form of ethnic, regional, or nationalist conflicts. The nationalist conflicts are of limited scope, and more often than not they are exploited indirectly by the superpowers.

Immediately after the Second World War, the United States, which was no longer threatened by other capitalist powers, feared that the Soviet Union was capable of pulling out too large a segment of the world from the free market either through propaganda or armed subversion. U.S. policy was dictated by the concern to contain, if not to destroy, the Soviet Union. The fact that Japan and Germany were located at the two ends of the USSR was an incentive to start restoring a strong capitalism in these two countries. With obstacles at both ends, "socialism" could at least be contained in its existing boundaries. The MacArthur plan in

Japan and the Marshall Plan in Europe had this parallel objective. Everything was done to develop in these two spatial poles the conditions for the development of powerful capitalist economies, even at the risk of creating dangerous competitors in the process, as is the case today. In contrast, in the Latin American countries, where local existing bourgeoisies were strengthening around the new development opportunities created by the war (and where Soviet influence was rather negligible at the time), the United States pursued a policy of destructuring these potential competitors. Democratic governments were systematically destabilized in favor of more servile military dictatorships. The national bourgeoisies of these countries were undermined, and progressive parties were physically destroyed.

Thus, two contradictory policies were implemented across the world. One was to encourage "democracy" and to assist the economic and political development of existing bourgeoisies in position in order to contain communism. The other, on the contrary, was to subvert over-competitive national bourgeoisies through military dictatorships where such a threat was not present. The Cuban revolution and its extension to Central America, most notably to Nicaragua, somewhat motivated the United States to modify, at last, this contradictory policy and to experiment in the 1980s with a more "democratic" approach in South America.[5]

Besides being divided by national differences, the bourgeois class in any country is divided into several fractions around a variety of cleavages. Parallel to the concentration of grand capital, the capitalist class is itself in the process of a transformation (Meillassoux 1984). One fraction, still dominated by family structures, continues to exist in its original hereditary form. Its capital, which is more or less interpenetrated with its estate, is passed down either through inheritance or by affinity. Capitalist dynasties still exist and are continuously recreated. But a more modern fraction, which grew with the centralization of large corporations, is recruiting less through birth than by co-option. This modern capitalist class legally owns a comparatively small but critical percentage of the total stocks of its enterprises, which, along with financial skill, gives it de facto control over the totality of the capital. I will call the first fraction the hereditary bourgeoisie and the second the co-optative bourgeoisie.

The capitalist class altogether is further divided up into diverse and changing fractions depending on the nature of the capital they each handle (trading, landed, industrial, financial capital, etc.). Their interests may be violently opposed but alleviated through the constant vertical concentration of capital that integrates financial, productive, and distributive units. Concentration also affects the organizational forms of capitalist production, which range from large transnational capitalism to microcapitalism. Due to its vast economic and political presence, big capital is a de facto social force that can count on state protection when needed, even in the temple of liberal economics (e.g., the financial aid given to the private corporation Chrysler by the government of the United States under Ronald Reagan in the 1980s). International capital is also divided among large international consortiums whose alternating strategy of competition and collision may cause new levels of concentration.

In addition, each branch and every fraction of capitalism, depending on its level of concentration and specific history, may have in its midst different types of capitalist classes, such as hereditary or co-optative, contracting or subcontracting, with large or small capital, and so on. These various forms of capital shape themselves into different configurations in each capitalist country.

The concentration process does not necessarily lead to monopoly. While large corporations strive to destroy their most immediate competitors, at the same time banks belonging to the same group may provide subordinated forms of capital with loans. These loans are profitable in the short run but may also transform lesser forms into future competitors.

Continuously renewed competition, while ensuring the dynamism of the system, also divides the capitalist class both economically and politically. Although the fractions of the capitalist class in a country may display political solidarity when facing the working class or at certain other critical moments, they remain antagonistic among themselves.

This division of the bourgeoisie compels each of its competitive fractions, in their striving for political control, to seek alliances with other social components, especially the people of working classes whose support remains decisive in parliamentary democracies. While on the economical level the class relationship is one of exploitation, politically it must be one of alliance. The mediation of political parties manipulated by professional politicians under ideological labels contributes to overcome this contradiction by blurring the class origin of the bourgeois fractions involved.

On the international level, one observes that *economic* power and the direct or indirect control of political affairs tend to be captured by a high cosmopolitan bourgeoisie and used not simply against the working class but also against rival capitalists, either to take advantage of them or to restrain their development.

THE PROLETARIAT

In Rome, the *proletarius* was a person who had no other wealth but his own and his progeny's capacity to work. By *proletariat*, Marx designated a class composed of people whose access to income is through the sale of their labor power to an owner of capital. The proletariat includes all who are in this situation of dependence regardless of whether they are employed. But this definition is incomplete. The condition of the modern proletarian is linked to the *gauged* sale of his or her labor power, either directly by measuring the time of work or indirectly by measuring the volume of production (piecework). In its "pure" form, capitalism only remunerates those who own the means of production and distribution in one form or another and those who sell their labor power or services to the owners. It excludes the nonproducers. The care of children, the sick or disabled, the old or the unemployed is done through transfers that are not in the logic of capitalism. Such redistribution, when it exists, operates through institutions such as kinship, charities, and social security, which are foreign to pure capitalism. Within the bourgeois class, where income is made up of unlimited profit, kinship ties can accommodate the nonproductive members. But in the case of the proletariat, wages are limited to the number of working hours. Even when they are based on the cost of living, which is not the general case, hourly wages are not computed to compensate for unforeseen sickness or unemployment, for the "downtime" of old age, or according to the number of children one has to feed.[6] The workers, therefore, have to have access to resources other than their wages if they are to have security and take care of their progeny.

In the first stages of capitalist development, the relationship of the proletariat with another class of producers, that is, the peasant community, gave them access to additional resources. As the peasantry disappeared, society had to take charge of part or all of the costs involved in the reproduction and maintenance of workers and their families, either through charity, mutual help, or social security.[7] When institutionalized, social transfers are, at best, calculated according to specific measured needs (days of sickness, of unemployment, number of children, etc.), therefore according to norms that are alien to capitalism.

Still it might be in the interest of some employers to form and maintain a stable and qualified working class of their own. Historically such a policy was designed by early capitalists when a qualified labor force was comparatively scarce as, for instance, in Bismarck's Prussia, Krupp's factories, or in the textile sector of northern France. But in the conjuncture of underemployment and lowly qualified labor, employers enjoy an extra profit when they don't pay for the maintenance and reproduction of labor power. The policy of colonial domination, having created a global capitalist economy, allows business to make use of an immense reserve of semirural labor. Thus the conjuncture of underemployment and less qualified labor is generalized the world over, enabling employers to obtain cheap labor, either by hiring seasonal and migrant labor from abroad or by settling factories in countries that offer a semirural proletariat. In both cases, the resulting profit is made of *labor rent* that is added to the regular surplus value, thanks to the employment of workers whose maintenance and reproduction are left mostly to themselves or their families (Meillassoux 1981).

At the lowest end of exploitation, child labor is gaining ground every day. In countries where unemployment is highest, and capital the least productive, children represent a large demographic class; they are cheaper than their elders, quickly replaced, expendable, docile, and unorganized. The rate of accident and death among this juvenile laboring population illustrates tragically what we mean by overexploitation, that is, a destructive exploitation that weakens reproduction. This form of exploitation, which condemns unemployed adults to depend on the labor of their offspring, is also at the root of an unbalanced demographic growth and of drastic social decay.

Furthermore, the fractions of the working class that are on the verge of unemployment are most susceptible to the call of ideologies of hatred, which identify the poorest as threatening competitors for their jobs. This is not without reason, since this internal competition for jobs is a deliberate policy of the employers.

The geographical dispersion of the present international proletariat, the countless forms of exploitation and overexploitation to which they are submitted, the differences in culture and educational levels, the misery in which millions of unemployed are often deliberately left in order to suppress their capacity to revolt—all these circumstances severely undermine the proletariat's ability to start a militant organization. Circumstances rather run in favor of the substitution of charity for political action and of religious sects for political parties. Contemporary ideology tries to rub out the subversive notion of proletariat by substituting the idea of the Christian "poor"; thus the proletariat is removed from its own context (that is, labor). This view is further facilitated by massive layoffs and unemployment. Workers are ejected from the mills and the destitute are thrown in the streets. The organic and revolting phenomenon of exploitation thus disappears behind this touching vision of misery that, taken out of its context, seems to have been caused by destiny alone, with charity as the sole solution.

If the various types of income paid by the capitalist class to its employees do not all bear the name of "wage," it is because they refer to social components distinct from the proletariat. The role of remuneration depends on whether it is for labor power or services rendered, whether the worker is directly exploited or whether he or she is supervising and organizing exploitation. A qualitative difference becomes evident beyond a certain level of remuneration between wage-earning workers and salaried "cadres," or executives. People whose *wages* are gauged by the hour or by the piece fulfill a different function than those who, at a higher level in the same enterprise, are paid on a monthly or a yearly base to manage, organize, or control the production. The *salaries* paid to high-level executives are justifiable not so much in terms of their knowledge or amount of work as in terms of their loyalty.

THE SOCIAL CORPS

The organic and functional criteria that define capitalist society point to the primacy of its two polarizing classes: the bourgeoisie and the proletariat. Classes are identified according to the primary forms of revenue (profits and wages) that stem from the unlimited capacity to accumulate for one class and from the precise measurement of labor power for the other. But an increasing fraction of the population, particularly in the economically dominant countries, does not actually belong to either class. This fraction falls into what mainstream sociology calls the middle class. My contention is that the majority of this middle class is made of various and distinctive social corps. Each class *secretes*[8] such social corps to fulfill functions that the class finds itself unavailable or unfit to exert partly or fully. These corps are, for the bourgeoisie, such groups as the army and police, managers and cadres, professional politicians, and educational bodies. For the proletariat the social corps are for all practical purposes limited to the apparatuses of the trade unions and the workers' political parties. While the vocation of the social corps generated by the bourgeoisie is to assist this class to exercise its domination, the task of the corps that issue from the proletariat is—or should be—to protect the dominated classes from exploitation and to fight against the political domination of the bourgeoisie.

Unlike the social classes that establish their historical destiny through the implementation of a societal political project, social corps are primarily motivated by the preservation of their own existence, even to the detriment of the class from which they proceed. In a crisis situation, some corps may even try to divert their essential function and make use of the crisis in an effort to substitute themselves for the originating class or to gain more autonomy from it. Such attempts are limited, nevertheless, because of any corps' structural inability to carry a political project beyond a restricted political aspiration. The historical destiny of a social corps is bound by the limited vision provided by its specialized functions. The specific social conditions surrounding the emergence of a social corps—such as its restricted understanding of the social system and the limited nature of its ideology, which is borrowed from its parent class—make it incapable of implementing a political project that will not eventually be taken over by one or the other classes that polarize the social system.

SOCIAL CORPS THAT EMANATE FROM THE CAPITALIST CLASS

In its rising years, the bourgeoisie handled by itself production management and the exercise of political power. Family members of the owners ran the enterprises. Parliamentarians were from bourgeois families. However, since the bourgeoisie was a minority, as is the case for all dominant classes, it became increasingly difficult for it to handle by itself all the tasks necessary to maintain its domination. The concentration of capital on the one hand and the globalization of capitalism on the other have widened the gap between the number of people in the bourgeois class and the size of the populations submitted to its economic hegemony. Presently, the members of the capitalist class can hardly let themselves be involved in administrative, repressive, educational, technological, and even political functions. These tasks are either too demanding or too demeaning or they require more personnel than are available within the bourgeoisie.

At the end of the twentieth century, the capitalist class, strictly speaking, includes only those who have the decision-making power by virtue of their control over capital within the enterprises. This class is made of all the members of the boards of corporations of all sizes. Among the members is a restricted group, or "high" bourgeoisie, that sits in the boardroom of large multinational corporations and controls the means of international economic power. The members of this high class tend to be more and more restricted in number, but also more powerful with the gradual concentration of corporations and political centralization.

The real power of the capitalist class is essentially in the hands of this latter fraction, which is linked to concentrated capital. This high class relies on high-level organizational and financial management skills. The size of private capital and its insertion in the national and global economies enable this international fraction to influence rather decisively the internal and external policies of states and international institutions. The small and medium capitalists are excluded from these functions of high politics. Therefore, unable to assume all the tasks that help maintain its domination, the bourgeoisie has to recruit a majority of people *outside of its ranks* to handle these tasks on its behalf, under its direct or indirect supervision.

The easiest way to discern among these corps is to identify the ones allocated to functions of repression, to the management of companies, to government, and to "social reproduction."

THE REPRESSIVE CORPS

The repressive social corps consist of the army and the police, or private militia (such as the ones in the German Nazi party in charge of the implementation of openly criminal political tasks).

The Professional Army

Even in the midst of a capitalist democracy, the military remains the antithesis to that system. It is a hierarchic body appointed from the top down, with no representational forms. This hierarchy is based on the notion of the indisputable ability of the superior or senior over the inferior or cadet. The remuneration reflects only this hierarchy: It is independent from the duration of work, as the underlying principle assumes that a soldier is on duty at all times. Economically, this is a nonproductive corps with a destructive vocation. As such, it is a vast consumer of the means of destruction that the dominant class provides. Politically, this is an authoritarian corps whose objective is to solve the problems of humanity by suppressing life. The bourgeois armies have been the bloody instrument of international competition between capitalist nations and of global imperialist exploitation. The bourgeois nations have succeeded in building a "patriotic" ideology that eliminates any distinction between the interests of the dominant class and those of their dependent populations.[9] As contemporary capitalism is more unified, armies are no longer maintained to make wars among bourgeois nations. Instead, the military organization has become important in other fields. Nationally, the infantries are nowadays targeting the elimination of the "enemy from within." Internationally, armies serve to preserve imperialist interests and domination in the dependent countries. In other words, the army is now involved less in national warfare than in class struggle, which is perceived under the guise of a new form of patriotism. Hence, modern professional armies are devoted mostly to police operations. They usually face disarmed civilians in operations to maintain law and order. The most serious potential danger for professional repressive soldiers has become the confrontation with other armies—especially popular armies. In such a situation, as in Algeria or in Vietnam, the army professionals try to limit the dangers for themselves by claiming the need for a bigger contingent of military personnel, and they send drafted civilians into combat. Fighting other professional and repressive armies is far less risky, as the Gulf War has shown.

Since the professional army is the only corps authorized to permanently deploy weapons at home, and since its cadres may have an extraordinary range of special powers given to them (martial law, martial court, etc.), this army also represents a constant threat to its own nationals and to civilian institutions, despite its constant pledges of loyalty. The army in democratic bourgeois states has always been considered, indeed, as a potential threat for the civilian government, so much so that constitutional dispositions place the military under the latter's authority. But in neocolonial countries, being materially dependent on foreign "aid," the army represents a permanent lethal danger for the local government. The sublimation of the army is accomplished through the negation of everything civilian, citizens or government, including the class from which it emanates. Although there was a time when it was honorable for the members of the bourgeoisie to join the officer corps and fight for their country, the army's contemporary functions are such that it rather attracts embittered people from fractions of disappearing classes such as the aristocracy, the destitute small bourgeoisie, or from a proletariat on the verge of becoming lumpen.

The Police

If the army tends to assume high police functions, internationally and nationally, the police proper still operate nationally. In a well-managed democracy the police forces are segmented into fractions that are kept separately dependent on the civilian authority so that they can be used against each other and, if need be, against the army. Police forces undertake the functions of protecting private property, maintaining law and social and political order, and repressing criminals and the working classes. These corps enjoy little prestige, even among bourgeois circles, and their remuneration is low. This group recruits from the dominant class even less than the army. Instead it recruits from disappearing classes such as the foreclosed peasantry, the bankrupt and proletarianized small entrepreneurs, and the racist proletariat.

THE CADRES AND EXECUTIVES

The specific function of the capitalist class is the management of businesses at the highest decision-making level; it preserves its authority there.

For a time, in the era of the "rising bourgeoisie" (*la bourgeoisie conquérante*), business-owning families assumed for themselves managerial tasks and technical responsibilities. But industrial concentration comparatively reduced the number of family members with respect to the scope of functions to fulfill. Industrial accounting, management techniques, and engineering became more complicated and required longer and more specialized education. The recruitment of executives, engineers, administrators, and other educated cadres became indispensable to fulfill managerial tasks, while the proprietory families kept leadership functions—especially that of trustees. But the incapacity of prodigal sons led eventually to the opening up of these family councils to selected competent executives. At long last, the way was paved for the formation of a co-optive capitalist class, as was mentioned previously. This latter class has developed primarily in large enterprises that require sophisticated managerial skills and where capital owning has disengaged itself from patrimonial property. Financial control rests on another kind of property—transferable securities, stocks, and shares—whose ownership delineates the modern capitalist class. Wherever this class managed to supplant the hereditary bourgeoisie, it established a co-optive system of recruitment to the boards of trustees, the class barrier of the modern bourgeoisie. I would say that executives, of whatever level, who are not admitted to board membership do not actually belong to the capitalist class.[10] Executives, along with other cadres, engineers, or technicians—regardless of their income, culture, and level of knowledge—constitute a social corps. This is the case even if they own some shares of the company or attain a life-style similar to that of their employers.

Today, the comparatively privileged position of the managerial social corps is already under threat. The proletarianization of the cadres continues up the hierarchy as the proletariat this corps controls shrinks in numbers. The cost of the proletariat's labor-time, in turn, comes to be gauged more and more accurately in the anticipation of labor-time's coming exploitation.[11]

PROFESSIONAL POLITICIANS

The field of politics would seem to be the main arena of action for the dominant class. But in a capitalist society, where politics is subordinate to the "laws of the market," the dominant class prefers to keep control of the economic field. The parliamentary system is convenient for the bourgeoisie insofar as it provides a "forum of reconciliation" that preserves the freedom of action of each of its fractions and enables them to put up a political defense against competition until one of them dominates the others. But persuasion is a subtle art. Elections and ministerial and parliamentary positions take up a lot of time. Although members of the grand bourgeoisie, such as the Kennedys and the Rockefellers in the United States, or Giscard d'Estaing in France, are still found in ministerial, parliamentary, or even presidential positions, they are now joined by increasingly numerous professional politicians. Truman, Nixon, Reagan, Pompidou, Chirac, Barre, Mitterand, and such others do not belong to the high bourgeoisie as we define it. Many are professionals, lawyers, scholars, or civil servants or have modest origins. They are present in political positions more on the basis of their training than because of their birth.

Professionalism in politics is common to all countries with a parliamentary democracy. One of the more telling examples is the case of the Institutionalized Revolutionary party (PRI) of Mexico, which has been in government under successive names since 1935. This party co-opts its cadres and trains them within itself; it imposes a system of rotation on the candidates to offices and designates a new nominee to the presidency of the United States of Mexico every four years who is invariably elected, thanks to the PRI's machine. The party staff, which is both competent and corrupt, is typically recruited from university positions and liberal professions. These members owe their wealth to their political position rather than the other way around. They may end up belonging to the bourgeois class if they manage to accumulate a level of capital high enough to give them access to positions of decision-making in businesses.

The professionalization of politics grows from the necessity to arbitrate the conflicts that exist both between classes and among the dominant class. These conflicts paralyze the latter's ability to govern. For instance, the repeated attempts of the Indian bourgeoisie to govern through its own Janatha party failed repeatedly because of the immense heterogeneity of this class, whose members range from fiercely reactionary estate owners to socially progressive industrialists. Since no single fraction or coalition of fractions is capable of mediating these opposing positions, the Indian bourgeoisie was obliged to hand over the power to the professional politicians of the Congress party and to the arbitration of the Gandhi "dynasty."

In South Africa, the National party (NP), which has been in office since 1948, was formed initially by Afrikaan politicians without links to South African capital, if not against it. The National party had to create a governmental economic sector. However, the NP has eventually become (and now is) the indispensable political agent of the business circles. It arbitrates between blacks and whites by keeping racial struggle alive. For half a century the NP knew that its policy of provocation against Africans brought it the support of most white voters in proportion with the intensity of the racial conflict. However, the NP arbitrates between more or less fictitious "ethnic" fractions maintained in the midst of the black populations, among administratively invented Bantustans, between the inhabitants of black townships and Bantustans, between African classes in the process of formation, or between governmental bureaucracies and black bourgeoisie (Meillassoux and Messiant 1991).

The professional politician knows how to seduce electoral populations and, once elected, discreetly and adroitly become the agent of one of the fractions of the ruling classes. Under these conditions, the professional politician should not be viewed as carrying out the mandate of the electorate. He does not get elected because of his program but because his personality inspires confidence in the electorate. The parties no longer conduct political debate to elaborate policies but are electoral machines where the militants (whose only qualification is their partiality to the charisma of the candidate) are led by "communications" and electoral campaign finance experts. The use of a *language of competence* by the professional politician and the affirmation that politics is a profession (and not a function) deprives the electorate of initiative and hides the interest-oriented choices behind the appearance of technocratic objectivity (Posel 1991, 31–61). Still, professional politicians are not the mere spokespeople of the dominant class, for their ability to preserve their position does not stem from their devotion to the bourgeoisie but from their skill in arbitrating between its various fractions. The preservation of the parliamentary system and "democracy" protects their existence and positively acts in favor of democratic institutions. If faced by a threat against these, many professional politicians would become the champions of the "democratic" ideal (i.e., parliamentary ideal) of which they are the prime beneficiaries after all.

THE INTELLECTUAL PROFESSIONS

"The bourgeoisie has played an eminently revolutionary role in history. It cannot exist without constantly revolutionizing the instruments of production, that is the conditions of production, that is, all social relations" (Marx and Engels 1948). This permanent bourgeois revolution was put in motion by scientific discoveries and by the teaching given by a trained educative social corps. This has been the main instrument of the reproduction of bourgeois society. Its ambiguity stems from its function: to revolutionize the bourgeois universe permanently without ever changing its class character. The bourgeoisie survives through revolution but within its own system. Consequently, it requires that professional intellectuals position themselves at the margins of criticism and subversion. From one end of the capitalist world to the other, the level of tolerance is inversely proportional with development. In dependent countries where the exploitation of international capitalism is patent, scientific research is stuck. The technological monopoly of the international bourgeoisies will be preserved. The social sciences, which are considered too subversive, will be ignored or banned. In advanced "democratic" countries, where "freedom of thought" is less consequential because its diversity makes it easier to neutralize, the dominant class, in order not to be blinded to its own problems, has to take the risk of letting criticism become subversive. But the most reactionary fractions of the bourgeoisie, those that recoil even before the necessary transformation of capitalism, ally themselves to those who wish to hide their foul, dubious activities in order to limit the scope of freedom of thought. Such people periodically succeed in limiting that scope even though this leads to limiting the foresight of the dominant class and opening it up to severe crises. For instance, under the pressure exerted by the reactionary fractions of the bourgeoisie and that high-level mob (*pegre*), the level of economic knowledge has become so restricted that liberal economists are now incapable of predicting a stock market crash even in the very short run. Liberal economists' wooden or indecipherable theoretical discourse amounts to repeated and contradictory "demonstrations" that wages are too high. But the tolerance of the state toward dubious stock market transactions, the general corruption that pervades international trade, the huge sums of money from criminal activities reinjected into legal business by money-laundering banks, the existence of tax evasion and tax havens where bankers and mafioso cannot be distinguished, the use of hit men in industrial espionage—all these facts are considered marginal phenomena by conventional economists and are prudently ignored (Walter 1986; Couvrat and Plessis 1989).

After burning themselves when encountering the walls of the mental jail erected by the dominant class, many intellectuals tend to react as under the effect of a conditioned reflex: They come up with the most obscure, anodyne, or fashionable research topics.

Since the material conditions of intellectuals are diverse and changing, their activities cannot be associated with a definite standard of living or with particular working conditions. The university corps is even more of a client than all other social corps: The relationship between its remuneration and its work time is very flexible, and it is the object of a comparatively detached surveillance. Professors or researchers can devote a portion of their time to writing books whose revenues are theirs. They may obtain subsidies by participating in research programs. More generally, the intellectual does not find immediate justification for political choices in his or her strict material conditions. This choice may rather depend on the degree of acknowledgment he or she receives from worldly circles and on his or her propensity to flatter their whims.

At the lowest pay level of this intellectual hierarchy are the schoolteachers. Although education is incessantly celebrated as the best of professions, their work load remains the heaviest. They share the conditions of the wage-earning class: The boundaries of the social corps stop here.

Both academics and schoolteachers, however, contribute to the education of other social corps. Their educational function is all the more crucial in that skill will come above birth in the future hierarchy of the young people they are given to train. The checks on creativity are equal to their pedagogical capacity. However, these checks work to the detriment of intellectual curiosity and scientific imagination that are indispensable to the dominant class if it is to maintain its potentialities to continue to revolutionize itself.

Thus, nearly each new generation of pupils and students who come to the threshold of this system of conditioning express periodically a gesture of retreat (May 1968, December 1988). The revolutionary inclinations of youth seem to have been perceived as a potential danger to be averted. Just as alcohol was the means to daze the workers in the nineteenth century and to divert them from political action, drugs might have been directed to these young generations with the same goals. Certain obscure activities and alliances of the CIA, the success of some strange literature, such as the faked ethnology of a shadowy author, the assimilation of drugs into "revolution" by other "thinkers," the amazingly relaxed attitude of U.S. diplomacy toward certain drug-producing countries raise some questions in that respect.

The list of social corps is not limited. One should add, for instance, the category formed by international bureaucrats, who, despite their multiple nationalities, have acquired a uniform perspective that has been provided for most by their U.S. education and the very significant emoluments of their posts.

The social corps of the United States may undertake actions of an international dimension. For example, agents of the CIA and similar organizations present their governments with faits accomplis dictated by obscure and occultlike goals. Blinded by the "cult of intelligence" and by a reactionary ideology, they do not hesitate to produce fake documents that are circulated widely and accorded credibility even in governmental circles.

Even though the *salaries* paid to the bourgeois social corps are apparently similar to *wages*, the difference, as was pointed out, is that salaries are not strictly proportional to labor time. This is obviously the case for the military corps (see previous discussion). It is also the case in relation to cadres and executives. Ideological notions of professional conscience, loyalty, duty, company spirit, and so on transform employment into a relationship with a moral content. Although these corps may in extreme cases resort to striking, it is considered an unbecoming practice, frequently banned or limited by customary or actual rules of the profession.

Individuals drawn into these social corps are, to a certain extent, in the position of clients.[12] Their labor is not actually strictly gauged as with the proletariat. There is a tacit understanding according to which the administration will take charge of the cadres or executives in exchange for indefinite availability on their part. This type of relationship creates loyalty and a belief that this corps belongs to the dominant class.

The social corps of the bourgeoisie are not direct sources of surplus value. This is evident in the case of sterile and costly corps such as the repressive army. Their primary function is not to be exploited but to help to exploit. This is even the case for cadres and teachers, who prepare people more or less directly for those activities that create surplus value, even though these cadres and teachers can be pushed to become workaholics by their employers.

As we have seen, the "labor" of the bourgeois social corps is not precisely measured and their retribution is not commensurate with their production: There is no labor exploitation without measurements. One understands that for political reasons, the parties of the Left would like to assimilate the social corps into the wage-earning class, but neither the social practice of these groups nor a theoretical analysis would support this notion. The fact that their remunerations are not rigorously linked to labor time creates a distinction between social corps and exploited classes, both in general and within the same branch. Between the high executive in an industry and the worker, the university professor and the schoolteacher, the physician and the nurse, retribution is disproportionate. All sorts of economic rationalizations have been put forward to explain these gaps, in particular the level of education. But even though they have an element of truth, the quantitative gap betrays a qualitative difference.

The social corps emanating from the bourgeoisie is financed through public or private sectors. In the first case, the dominant class rewards this corps through the mediation of the state budget, declaring its functions to be in the "public interest," implying that all the bourgeoisie's fractions are the beneficiaries of those functions. Other social corps are directly remunerated from capitalist profits. Now, professionals such as physicians or architects are paid by the job and not with an institutionalized salary. In that capacity they would not be directly subordinated to the bourgeoisie, although their activities still keep them financially dependent on that class. Their classification as a social corps is a matter of debate.

In the perspective outlined thus far, social corps are not to be considered as the same kinds of social components as the classes from which they emanate. Unlike classes, social corps do not proceed from a dialectical contradiction that shapes the totality of the society and that would irreducibly put social corps in opposition to social classes. Social corps are the products of the contradictions internal to the development of each of the social classes. When these social corps are in a position to play a major political role, as happens in certain conjunctures, only exceptionally do they reach the social and political dimensions of a social class.[13]

THE POLITICAL INTRUSION OF THESE SOCIAL CORPS

Since the capitalist class is the dominant class, it does not struggle to win power but to maintain it. It uses the social corps, and in particular the repressive corps, as a means to perpetuate its domination or as ramparts against threats. For this dominant class, the social corps are a conservative means to maintain, to transform, and to defend the economic power the dominant class holds. Hence each function entrusted to each corps can be considered as an essential one. The army is convinced of the grandeur of its national mission; the police see themselves as necessary ramparts of law and order; the executives, engineers, and cadres know that without their skills the economy will collapse; and the intellectuals demonstrate that they are the "aristocracy of reproduction."

In each of these social corps, the individuals that compose it have, in varying degrees, a feeling of identification stemming from the awareness of fulfilling a common function—one that defines their relationship with the bourgeoisie. Since this function serves the dominant class, each corps is permeated by a diffuse and contradictory ideology borrowed from its originating class but adjusted and altered to fit the narrowness of its specialization. This ideology becomes more or less pronounced depending on the political conjuncture. A corps may start to see itself as a possible replacement for the bourgeois class if it is convinced that its function is above others in maintaining power.

Partly because of its social responsibility but mostly because it is kept from decision-making positions, each of these corps may be tempted to distance itself from the originating bourgeoisie to act in its own interest. Each is thus capable of posing a serious threat to the bourgeoisie. However, besides every corps' initial dependence on the bourgeoisie, the fact that each is the agent of a single function deprives it, as opposed to a class, of the capacity to fulfill a transcending political project. The weakness of secondhand ideology and the difficulty of dominating other social corps (some of which may have similar aspirations) limit the viability of such attempts, even when they are violent in nature.

THE ARMY IN POWER

Under certain historical circumstances, repressive corps may be in a position to implement decisive political functions. This can occur when the bourgeoisie or one of its fractions, in order to overcome a severe crisis, entrusts, at its own risk, a part or the totality of government functions to the repressive corps. Often this is done if the bourgeoisie is losing ground because it is limited within the bounds of democratic legality. The bourgeoisie may choose a legal corps (such as the army or the police) or an illegal corps (such as a paramilitary party or the "militia"). Thus, the professional fraction of the army is almost always in a position of accessibility to power. The fact that it deploys a military arsenal is both its political strength and its economic weakness. This arsenal is a strength because the army can use it against the civilian authorities. It is a weakness because the army does not have the economic capacity to produce its own weaponry.

When the army is entrusted with special authority for warfare, one calls on its loyalty to dissuade it from using violence for its own goals. But the object of this loyalty may vacillate between the administration and the "fatherland." It is tempting for the military to persuade itself that the first may have betrayed the latter in order to legitimate the military's own betrayal in the name of patriotism. To prevent the possibility of the armed forces operating for its own profit or for the profit of any other illegitimate force, democratic states have had to promulgate constitutional arrangements that place the army under the final authority of the civilian power.

Regardless of their nature, whether they are national, colonial, or social, wars create a favorable set of circumstances for the takeover of power by the army. In such situations, constitutional guarantees are weakened or suspended by martial law, "war measures," "security rules," and so on. The protection mechanism put in place by civilian authority may not be operational. In Japan, for example, during the imperialist expansionist policy of the post-Meiji period, colonial wars followed by national war against the United States had given so much power to the army that it succeeded in imposing a military dictatorship on the Japanese bourgeoisie and bureaucracy, both of which were the instigators of that belligerent foreign policy. The army also dictated the continuation of the war (that is, the prolongation of its own power) after 1942 even though at that point, virtually all the goals of the Japanese bourgeoisie were reached. However, this insistence to go until the bitter end led to the nuclear disaster and meant a loss of credibility for the army in postwar Japan. When, as in such a case, the army becomes autonomous, it does not have any perspective or means of action other than the military ones. Thus, if the army is left to initiate a war or a repressive action on its own initiative, it can only continue its military actions to the point of exhaustion. From a military perspective, negotiations are equated with defeat and the negation of the raison d'être of the army as a social corps whose existence is restricted to the narrow military function. An army as such cannot initiate peace without in the process denying itself.

Lebanon is an illustration of those cases where the militia has become a sort of nongovernmental organization searching for sponsors and using different ideological covers. In that country, where social classes are constitutionally divided into denominational fractions incapable of political expression, the armed groups are also without a class-based political vocation. Their representation is weak and without any institutional basis that might measure it. They exist only through the war and its prolongation. This is a "war" that kills civilians in bombardments. These losses are played up as casualties of these militia, though, in reality, the members of the militia and their leaders are rarely victims. The negation and the disintegration of civilian authority, which are conditions of the militia's perpetuation as a social corps, are extended to the destruction of the civilian population.

Despite all this, the army, which is the only corps along with the police to use weapons and to enjoy extraconstitutional powers over the population (who gave them the weapons in the first place), cannot maintain itself in power exclusively for its own goals and through its own means. As we know, the army is a sterile organism. It destroys but does not produce anything. Its consumption is considerable. Being a nonproductive organism, it can only remain in power with the support of a productive class or some of the components of such a class (bourgeois or proletarian, national or foreign) that are in a position to supply the army with its weapons and take care of its personnel. This dependency is what enables the bourgeois classes to ultimately control armies, whether at home or abroad. This dependency also means that armies cannot be reliable and cannot be loyal to any cause that does not include military supply capability.

THE PARAMILITARY CORPS

The risk of losing control of an armed corps is larger when the bourgeoisie, to defend its status, creates a paramilitary corps capable of political, ideological, and repressive actions. Such was the Nazi party in Germany.

After the First World War, the German bourgeoisie thought that its legal system and parliamentary democracy would prevent it from attaining the following goals: stopping the rise of the working classes; containing the Bolshevik revolution knocking on its door; and convincing the German people to wage another international war to reclaim its economic losses. In order to eliminate its external and internal enemies, it chose to accept the services of an organization of demagogues and professional killers with no democratic and legal scruples. The Nazis, recruited from every stratum of the population, gave themselves an ideology that is a perverse form of what is most reactionary in bourgeois ideology. Racial superiority—which could be endowed to the great majority of Germans—was a substitute for the superiority of class, as this cannot be claimed openly without alienating the working class and risking the alliance with them, which was critically important at that patriotic juncture. The notion of a German race was the ultimate form of nationalism. This racist ideology could also be used to push capitalist exploitation of citizen by citizen to an absolute level as it designated a portion of the population as undeserving to live. The economics of total war required total mobilization of the labor force and the total elimination of the useless ones. The labor camps and extermination camps fulfilled that double function. Nonproductive people were exterminated using industrial methods. They started with physically handicapped people. Next, all children and aged people and most women of the so-called inferior races were systematically destroyed. At the same time, the still "valid" persons, along with political opponents and Russian war prisoners (who were considered as totally expendable), were exploited to death in the service of big corporations such as Krupp, Thyssen, and I. G. Farben.[14]

After having served the German bourgeoisie by militarily defeating rival capitalist countries, the Nazi corps, which existed only through repression and warfare, by its very nature could not conclude the war without disappearing. The Nazis wanted to extend their fatal fate to the German people as a whole. However, this Wagnerian desire to survive in the Wahalla did not suit the German industrial bourgeoisie. This was all the more true since its productive potential was more seriously threatened by the suicidal scorched-earth policy of Hitler than it ever was by the Allies. The industrial bourgeoisie managed to take the power back with the help of the competitive corps of the army but at the price of a crushing military defeat. The last service that the Nazis rendered to their masters was to stand to be condemned and executed in place of the bourgeoisie. This allowed the latter to maintain its domination in post-war Germany.

Unlike the military people and their like, other social corps do not have the use of arms that they can use against the class from which they emanate. Civil servants, justice officers, and professional politicians whose existence is linked to the parliamentary democracy are not so much of a threat. This may not be as true of the managerial corps. The bourgeoisie is even more suspicious of the intellectual corps than it is of the military, which are, after all, agents of law and order, while intellectuals, on the contrary, are capable of "transforming ideas into material forces."

TECHNOCRATS AS BACK-SEAT DRIVERS

The growing functions of company cadres, engineers, and managers led writers like James Burnham (1941) to announce that a new social class made up of "managers" was in the process of replacing the bourgeoisie. As we have seen, this social corps is not in a position to participate as such in the highest decision-making despite its obvious technical skills. Those few who manage to make it to the board of directors do not sit as representatives of the cadres but as co-opted members of the bourgeoisie. At their own social level, company cadres are excluded from decisions that involve long-term financial and political strategies that do not rely on sheer technical rationality and that even go against it. But this may be misunderstood by managers as contempt for their capacity. The frustration that ensues is nurtured by the belief that their know-how qualifies them better than the bourgeoisie to run businesses and the economy in general. The idea is latent that their own rationality would be better adapted to solve both economic and social problems and that "experts" should replace corrupt and incompetent politicians. They believe that with their methods they could eliminate inequalities, waste, and the incoherence of certain financial and political decisions.

In France, some of the high civil servants and executives proposed a peaceful transition to socialism after the May 1968 events. They thought that the pressure from the masses would suffice to expropriate the bourgeoisie from its productive capital and to democratize the state, which they could run intelligently (cf. Alphandéry et al. 1968).

But given their education and their ideological formation, the majority of technocrats in most situations remain loyal agents of capitalism. Despite their culture (or perhaps because of it) they are easily deluded into believing the scientist ideology of psycho- or biosociology that they belong to the dominant class. To the extent that capitalism offers to a very few the opportunity of social mobility on the basis of merit and work, sociobiology provides them with an ideological justification: Intellectual capacities are not hereditary but randomly distributed. Diplomas, degrees, and tests are the proof that one belongs to this new naturally gifted but select elite, and, as such, that person is in a position to be hired as the right arm of an eminent tycoon or to start his or her own business. This ideology moves this new elite to accept the system fully and exposes its members to an intense mobilization. Their devotion to the company should be total and their availability absolute. They must accept being put in competition with their colleagues and being fired if at a certain age they have not been co-opted by the ruling class. To succeed, they copy the upper-class life-style, and they greedily submit themselves to the "efficient lies" or "performing truths" of advertising, which squarely target them and constantly activate "their anxiety of being unable to keep up with the appearances of life-style, the shame of failing to consume and the anguish of worldly poverty" (Anonymous 1989, 16).

LE MIROIR AUX INTELLECTUELS[15]

Since Plato, intellectuals have had a rational dream: that intelligence be in power. Ever since, they have been looking for allies to construct that utopia. Some of them see the solution in social democratic parties, which send us back to political professionalism. But many among them are aware that the dominant class can use its intellectual skills only to further its own interests. The perspectives of either thinking in the terms of a materialist class or remaining in a subordinate condition revolt them. Some think that they should bring to the dominated classes the education these classes are deprived of and the reflection they are not given the leisure to practice. Their expectation is to side with exploited classes and peoples and gain some influence on them. But although their ears have been stuck to the ground since the end of World War II to detect the grumbling of an upcoming revolution from the favellas and the factories, they have heard nothing coming. The endlessly predicted final crisis of capitalism is not happening. Just the opposite is occurring. Long before the triumph of capitalism, in November 1989 (the fall of the Berlin Wall), the intellectuals of the Left were already discouraged by the bureaucratic idiocy of the Communist apparatuses, by the economic incapacities and the corruption of the nomenklatura, by the dictatorships in the third world, by the apparent passivity of the oppressed people, and by racism in the working classes. Disheartened by the revolutionary apathy of classes that were believed to be revolutionary by nature, some intellectuals thought that the revolution could take place through their own initiative, without awaiting a problematic political consciousness in the exploited classes. A handful of them were convinced that bloody and direct action could create a mass movement. They represent an extreme and criminal caricature of this antirevolutionary pessimism that manifests itself in murderous acts, discrediting every cause their name is associated with. They justify in the "public opinion" the repression of all forms of subversive action.[16]

Intellectual specialization may be the limit to the exercise of power. Knowledge and reflection are confined to areas delineated by philosophical, or almost metaphysical, limits. For the most part, academics (even economists) have little experience in industrial management. They are ignorant of the problems of production and distribution. They are not knowledgeable enough to invent new modes of management even if a revolution were to take place. They may not be able to orient the technicians in such a situation. They do not constitute a social corps capable of controlling the productive apparatus long enough to take it away from the hands of the dominant class. The hierarchical conception existing in France that makes knowledge proportional to rank works against the democratization of the production process. Were intellectuals in power, would they not continue to govern from above? Worse, they might prove to be incapable of exchanging "ideas," fearing that they would be plagiarized. Ideologically, as the bourgeois class strengthened itself, its desire to replace the dominant class was gradually taken over by the temptation to join it and to fit into its way of thinking. While previously the intellectuals' attempt to identify themselves with exploited peoples was generous, it is now admitted that the misery of these peoples is due to their incapacity to control their demography or due to their corrupt leaders (implying that these leaders are truly representative of their people), if not to some "racial" incapacity. The improvement in their standard of living means that by now intellectuals may have too much to lose if exploitation ends. Along with this, politics has given way to charity as the means to face a morally uncomfortable situation. It would become uncomfortable for intellectuals to accept the class theory of Marx, which establishes a direct organic opposition between the exploited and exploiters, that is, between poverty and wealth, since it would part them from a rather cozy capitalism, after all. Thus, exploitation is preferably considered out of its context, its determinations are deliberately blurred or leveled through the convenient theses of postmodernity. The existence of classes is denied or diluted in new taxonomic categories that are not organically linked to one another.

THE BUREAUCRATIZATION OF THE SOCIAL CORPS OF THE BOURGEOISIE

The dominant class now has the initiative. In the exercise of its functions, the social corps act on instructions. When the employers make a mistake, it is within the outlook that they themselves established: They are responsible only to themselves. The executive, even entrusted with delegated power, always comes to a turning point when his deputation ends and when initiative may jeopardize his job. The lower the cadres, the less knowledge they have of the circumstances that command the choices and the more precise instructions they need. The more numerous and detailed those instructions are, the less room for initiative they leave and the greater chance there is of an inadequate response to an unspecified situation. If the boss wants to eliminate human mistakes, he has to withdraw initiative from his employees. The further concentration of the dominant class makes these channels between decision and execution more rigid. The number of people who execute decisions increases faster than the number of decision-makers, who tend therefore to resort to more rigid rules in order to keep their control. The bureaucratic process permeates private business just as it does public administration.

Regarding this point, if the corps of the professional politicians is, as stated, the ultimate power, then despite all appearances ultimate power is not in their hands. The bourgeois state, which is not at the heart of political initiative—as this is ultimately held by the business circles—is condemned to bureaucratization with no recourse. The postmodern intellectuals, possibly because they wish to be blind, or to blind others to the existence of social classes, consider the bourgeois state a sort of *deus ex machina* that secretes bureaucracies as a matter of fact: It is the "logic of the organization" that imposes itself on the citizens and oppresses them. So the existence that postmodern intellectuals deny to living classes, they concede to inert constructs! There is no exploiting bourgeois class, but there is an oppressive state. These intellectuals bestow the responsibility of oppression on the abstract institutional structures they are occupying themselves on behalf of a master whose existence they openly deny, all the while trying to assimilate themselves into the master structure. Caught in these logical contradictions, they can only express themselves in confusion.

THE SOCIAL CORPS OF THE PROLETARIAT

The proletariat as the dominated class does not have the same consciousness-raising opportunities as the bourgeoisie, or the latter's means to affirm its political existence. The proletariat's education level is lower. The workers' unions and parties only cover a limited percentage of the working class. Consequently, the union finds itself in the position of not being capable of fulfilling entirely its tasks of organization. Its representation, politically or at work, is handled by an educated minority that itself is a minority in the politically conscious group. The leadership of unions and workers' political parties is made of men and women from various social origins; they are intellectuals or sometimes members of the bourgeoisie. The leadership used to be composed of devoted and committed people, often with no pay at the beginning. It is when an organization acquires the means to employ a *permanent staff* that it tends to act like a social corps.

This is how the proletariat in capitalist society also generates its own social corps, which is also endowed with functions essential to its achievement as a social class. But since the proletariat in its subordinated situation is not responsible to the society at large, its social corps are primarily responsible to themselves in handling the confrontation with the dominant class. This, in turn, implies less specialization and division of the corps than in the case of the bourgeoisie. This still gives the social corps of the proletariat more of a political function and the prospect of forming a government.

We will see how these social corps evolve in their relations with the working class through a dialectical unfolding analogous to the one discussed in the case of the bourgeoisie, although opposite in content.

THE WORKERS' BUREAUCRACY

The social corps of the working class has the responsibility to organize and lead this class toward better positions in bourgeois society. It is composed of working-class parties and trade unions. While the role of the *unions* is to fight against exploitation, the historical vocation of working-class *parties* is, or should be, to prepare the proletariat for power. Whether this eventuality is very distant or imminent, it is the sole justification of their existence. Since the proletarian class does not dispose within itself sufficient means and personnel to carry out these social and political tasks, it is forced to admit as cadres individuals of various social origins.

Because social classes are not symmetrically positioned, the relations of the social corps toward their respective classes are inverted. Unlike the social corps of the bourgeoisie, which are generated to preserve the power of the dominant class, those of the working class are supposed to be the leadership stratum in the class struggle and the vanguard in the conquest of power. Therefore, these corps find themselves right away in a leadership position, which they justify through the myth of their absolute identification with the working class and its aspirations. The trust they demand on this basis has put them in position to maintain their distance from the rank and file, to manage to stay permanently in leadership positions, and to conspire underhandedly with the "class enemy."

The process by which the proletarian corps become more distant from their class cannot be analyzed without first discussing their relationship to this class.

The personnel of the working-class apparatus, being in a position of leadership with respect to the proletariat, stand opposed to the bourgeoisie and its representatives. But even though they display themselves as the adversaries of the bourgeoisie and the employers, they tend to downplay this opposition to a position of intermediaries, and soon to that of a broker between the employers and the working class. The preservation of their influence is further guaranteed if they act for the benefit of both parties rather than as the exposed vanguard of one party. As go-betweens, they are both the champions of the working class as they announce a strike or a revolution and the heroes to the employers as they negotiate a settlement and social order.

The relationship of the working class vis-à-vis its social corps is totally different from the relationship of the bourgeoisie with its own corps. While the danger for the bourgeoisie is in its own corps' escaping its authority in an attempt to substitute itself for this class, the proletariat is on the contrary threatened by its corps' relinquishing power and conspiring with the dominant class.

Most Communist parties, in France, Spain, Italy or Portugal, partly owe their political existence to their role as social moderators, which the bourgeoisie expects of them. Given the corrupting influence of the bourgeoisie, the betrayal of these corps is probable if the circumstances are right.[17] The workers' bureaucracies that grow in the midst of bourgeois society are not qualified to lead the working class to revolution. The sclerosis of these apparatuses is evident in the constant reelection of the same leaders (on the basis of their "competence") and the aging of those officers in highly responsible positions. It is difficult indeed for modest people who have been elected to a position of power to accept a return to the rank and file. They are aware that if revolutionary circumstances were to present themselves, they would be swept away by new leaders who would emerge from the movement. Hence, they show a resistance to what may lead to such an outcome, which objectively makes them accomplices of the dominant class.

THE NOMENKLATURA

According to the previous analysis, one could consider the social fraction that held power in the former Soviet Union as a social corps that was the executor of an authentic but aborted revolution. The preservation of this corps depended upon its capacity to relate to the capitalist powers.

At the time of the Russian revolution, the aristocratic class was in power. A landed and industrial bourgeoisie, although comparatively weak, was gaining strength nevertheless. The bourgeois parties were the first instruments of the revolution. The socialist parties, Bolsheviks and Mensheviks, came as necessary allies to rally the peasant and the working classes. For the first time in history, the working-class organizations were led by intellectuals and scholars fed on the scientific approach of economics and politics. They were capable of overcoming the bourgeois revolution and driving the country toward what they wanted, which was, now and then, to be a proletarian revolution. Trotsky was aware, nevertheless, that the move was anticipated. In *The Permanent Revolution* (1931) he sees that the proletarian revolution will have to complete a bourgeois revolution first in both the economic and democratic senses to prepare the ground for a proletarian revolution. Given this situation, the proletarian parties had to accomplish a task that could not be entrusted right away to the rank and file but had to be accomplished by competent people capable of substituting themselves for a time for the failing bourgeoisie.

Historically, the Soviet bureaucracy constituted itself to fulfill successive functions *on behalf of* the working class. When it became obvious that the revolution could not possibly extend itself to Europe, and that Lenin's strategy was condemned, a new turn was initiated from internationalism to nationalism through the *mot d'ordre* "revolution within one country." But instead of achieving the bourgeois revolution, Stalin eliminated Trotsky in order to fight the bourgeoisie as the "internal enemy." He invented a Russian bourgeoisie supposedly capable of constantly renewing itself and whose never-ending liquidation justified the party's protective function, that is, internal and permanent repression. The Russian peoples were given "protectors" instead of revolutionaries. The new bureaucracy increased the scope and intensity of the repressive war measures put in place by Lenin and Trotsky during the conflict with Europe. This exaggerated class struggle was the pretext to eliminate physically all democratically inclined revolutionaries. Economically, this was the basis for the creation of a primitive accumulation system through the gulag labor camps.

After Khrushchev, the third function of this bureaucracy was to act as a broker between the Soviet people and international capitalism. The notion of peaceful coexistence at this international level between the Stalinist apparatus and the capitalist states is the flip side of national "class collaboration" of working-class bureaucracies with their own bourgeoisie. While the first transition from Lenin to Stalin was bloody, the second, from the "protectors" to the "brokers" (Khrushchev and Gorbachev—with a Stalinist relapse with Brezhnev) was done through internal bureaucratic coups, as no fraction wanted to be under the dictatorship of another one.

The nomenklatura was a part neither of the bourgeoisie nor of the proletariat. Frozen in time by the forcibly national character of the revolution, the bureaucracy took capital away from the bourgeoisie without ever passing it on to the working class. It withheld the property of the bourgeoisie over the means of production without modifying the relations of labor that this ownership relation generates. The nomenklatura administered the production apparatus without actually appropriating it. This economic project remained in between the bourgeoisie and the working class, immobilized by a corps deprived of the energy of a class to give it vitality. Although the nomenklatura was materially privileged, the practices of its members were not similar to those of the bourgeoisie. They preserved themselves *as a corps* only if they refrained from individually owning the means of production (which are consequently out of the market). They disclaimed heredity and birth privileges and condemned nepotism and corruption (all the while trying to cheat) to prevent their disintegration as a corps. Through this "renunciation" they gave the people the appearance of their representativeness and their legitimacy. The Soviet bureaucracy pretended to be attached to "Marxism," but as to a "dead ideology" made deliberately dull to deprive it of its subversive potential. But this misshapen acknowledgment of historical materialism was insufficient to sterilize Marxism completely. Its subversive force will find a way to eliminate sooner or later those who falsely claim to be its legatees.

If this bureaucracy (nomenklatura) was not a class but a corps, it did not have an autonomous political destiny despite its distant revolutionary roots. Like the proletarian bureaucracies in bourgeois countries, it survived only because of the intermediary role it had given itself between two antagonistic forces, which are the distorted global counterparts of the two main classes in society: "proletarian peoples," of whom the Soviet population looms foremost, and "big international capital." The disappearance of capitalism as interlocutor would eliminate this mediating function.

As a social corps without an independent political destiny, the nomenklatura was hardly capable of innovating beyond the economic policy initiated during the revolutionary period. It proved unable to compete with the capitalist economy, or even to disengage from it. This is evidenced by the economic stagnation of the USSR and by its dependence on U.S. agriculture, on Western technology, and even on foreign currency.[18] This is further evidenced by its present demand for foreign investments and aid. Finally, the current professional politicians seem to embrace the sale of the population of the former USSR to international capitalism as Gorbachev did with the East German people.

The ideological about-face in 1989 was not a radical departure for the nomenklatura. It could afford to abandon a Marxism it always scoffed. What drives it is not ideology but opportunism. The main present concern of the bureaucrats is to preserve their domestic political position and to receive the protection of international capitalism against the people they have been persecuting (just like the Red Khmers gained the international support of the major capitalist powers). To this purpose they are ready to surrender the Russian industrial sector and to deliver the labor power of their population to the "market economy." The ambition of party bureaucrats is to be kept as agents of this transformation in the position of a new professional "democratic" political corps. By confessing their past "mistakes" and crimes, they try to convince others that they are the least susceptible to relapse into the same errors and therefore best fit to rule a market economy. They are ready to take advantage of the euphoria of the political liberalization to inflict upon their own citizens the sacrifices required by this new colonization project.

The social corps of the Russian proletariat, faithful to itself more than to the class it emanated from, has accomplished its "revolution" and moved as such to the side of the other class. Such a transformation, which deprived the nomenklatura of its base as a consolidated corps, introduces the germ of partition within itself. The dissolution of the Communist party in the USSR, the introduction of the capitalist economy, and the merging of the former Soviet bureaucracy into a class system tends to transform its functional fractions into rival social corps. Already the repressive fractions (the army and the KGB) and the professional politicians are competing for power.

This internal conflict within the decaying bureaucratic corps is taking place while a new business class is emerging on their side. This new capitalist class is itself made of many components, some of them (and not the least) originated from bureaucratic corruption, others from petty business. As a class in formation, it has been restrained in its capacity for expansion. Against its willingness to exist, it still finds the political field occupied by converted bureaucrats. Against the bureaucratic attempt to maintain centralization at the highest level, local business classes propose nationalism, that is, the making of each federated state into a protected domestic market susceptible to support for the start of its new enterprises. This would form the base for national diplomacy to attract foreign economic and military aid. To the extent that these fractions are neither politically strong nor organized, and that Western powers will be tempted to take advantage of this opposition to play their own underhanded game (as in Yugoslavia), the struggle for power among these fractions and the emerging bourgeoisies is bound to continue.

CHINESE BUREAUCRATIC "PROLETARIAT"

In China (as in the former Soviet Union), popular mobilization was realized through wars against foreign powers. More so than was the case in Russia, the Chinese Communist Party had to rely on the peasantry. Therefore the party had all the incentives to remove the dependency of the peasants on landlords and to give them a cause to fight for in order to mobilize a popular national army. One must note, however, that the support of the peasantry did not come about through the party's own structures. The party relied instead on young people extracted from the peasant social milieu and drafted into the Red Army. The peasantry is not revolutionary in essence, although it can be driven to revolt. It cultivates a deferential attitude toward agrarian dominant classes. The peasant's ambition is to become a landowner. The values of the peasantry include the domination of the older generation, male authority, religious terrorism, and superstition that bends the individual to the morale and virtues of the reproduction of the family and community. In fact, it was the young peasants, mobilized in the Red Army and freed from this restrictive value system, who constituted the revolutionary regiments. In that new military milieu, in the hands of political instructors, among a young male population, these peasants experimented with a different kind of social relationship ignoring kinship and age.

Maoist ideology, to which these soldier-peasants were submitted, was not peasant in essence but was a peculiar variety of Marxism. Maoism is a doctrine built on a theory of the *industrial* working class more or less adapted to a largely *agrarian* society. The relationship between the peasants and this theory is historically not the same as that of the working class. As peasants, they can only submit to it—the theory of a proletarian revolution is beyond their experiential perspective. They have no hold on the theory, nor do they have any practical basis that would allow them to criticize it or to contribute to it. By appointing themselves the guardians of this ideology, the leaders of the revolution also put themselves in the position to be the only ones who could produce or interpret it. The "revolution" was thus bestowed upon the peasantry by a military-type bureaucracy. As the ultimate interpreters of the orthodoxy, the bureaucracy placed the peasantry under its tutelage. Later, this ideologically (but not socially) proletarianized peasantry was opposed to the urban workers. Too much political power in the hands of the working class would have threatened this construction and weakened the political foundation of Maoism.

To preserve the social basis of his rule, Mao implemented several measures to stop the rural exodus and the emergence of a powerful urban working class. He tried to keep the production of steel in rural communes. He restricted contacts between the peasantry and the industrial working class. But he also sent the young urban youth to the "school of the peasants."

Mao opposed Liu Shao Shi on the problem of industrialization. He might have feared that a rival fraction in the bureaucracy would use the support of the industrial working class to challenge him. When the conflict became acute, Mao tried to reenact an operation similar to that of the making of the Red Army, that is, to build an internal force devoted to his rule: the Red Guards. But now unable to mobilize the peasantry (since the war against foreign powers was over), he relied this time on the urban youth, rebellious and having difficulty with accepting the authority of the bureaucrats. The motto was "fight bureaucracy," that is, the fractions hostile to Mao.

The Red Guards came from a social background that was quite different from that of the peasantry. They had received a revolutionary education that included notions of class struggle and social justice. It is possible that their claims went beyond what Mao was prepared to accept. Moreover, hoodlums recruited by adverse fractions discredited the democratic aspirations of the Red Guards by committing many atrocities. To control the situation, Mao ordered the creation of tripartite committees in which the Red Army, now a professional body, was to arbitrate between the party and the Red Guards. The army tried to exploit this position to become the major bureaucratic fraction. Eventually, it was the "industrialist" camp, perhaps in better control of the party apparatus, that managed to eliminate Lin Piao and to discredit the army by an amalgam with the Red Guards. Since then, successive bureaucratic factions (cliques) have come to power in a succession of coups. Each one grants the people the right to criticize provided that it is used against the previous faction in power. In essence, the bureaucratic system does not change; it functions to preserve itself and its fractions. As for the economy, unlike its Soviet counterpart, the Chinese bureaucracy inherited a weak capitalism. The Chinese "revolution" thus had to invent a modern economic system from scratch. For a period, when the population was invited to contribute to daily economics by learning elementary thinking in the "little red book," the impression was that an original development was in process. But everything that encourages initiatives is a danger for the bureaucratic power. The solution of the bureaucracy was in its own image: uniformity in everything, conformity to its decisions, bureaucratic authoritarianism in production and distribution through huge centralized projects and massive physical liquidation of rebellious people. The pinnacle of the bureaucratic imagination was the institution of labor camps and of the "special zones" in China open to Western corporations where the exploitation of labor, including child labor, is the fiercest.

The main opposition between the two so-called socialist countries, that is, the Soviet Union and China, came from their rival intention to occupy the position of a necessary intermediary between capitalist states and "proletarian" peoples. In that regard, neither the Soviet Union nor China ever hesitated to align themselves with the ugliest dictatorships from the "free world" as long as those dictatorships were opposed to their rival. When the USSR aligned itself with the Argentine military junta, China became the ally of Ugarte Pinochet. Chinese diplomats invited to their country the most conservative politicians, such as Strauss and Nixon, even after they were retired from office. Besides the diplomatic advantages expected from this position of go-between, it provided the bureaucracy with a new economic opportunity: the sale at low cost of the labor power of its citizens to foreign investors. At that point, its role as an intermediary favors capitalist interests quite openly. The ideology of class origin vanishes to reveal the bureaucracy's true nature: that of a social corps that has no goal other than its own preservation.

Is the bureaucracy a social corps capable of creating other social corps? My working hypothesis at this point is that only social classes generate social corps. The bureaucracy is one entity whose diverse functions, handled by several corps in capitalist societies, are fulfilled within itself. The army, the state, the administration, the managers, and so on all belong to the nomenklatura. The nomenklatura is a unique organism, as indicated by its strict hierarchical structure and the regulated access to distinct sets of material privileges. This hierarchical community has also an esprit de corps that does not exclude strong diverging interests and brutal conflicts between its various components, or the changes in their respective influence depending on the conjuncture. The single-party system is designed to resolve those tensions, however violent they may be, *within the bureaucracy* and to not let them be politically exploited by the population.[19]

CONCLUSIONS

The theory of social corps allows us to differentiate between various components of a social system and to classify them in an organic fashion, that is, according to the relations that link them to the classes that generated them and to each other. The qualitative distinction between social classes and social corps underlines the unabated relevance of the polar positioning of classes—though this was blurred in the late historic transformation of capitalist society whereby the dominant class was reduced to a small minority.

Because of this reduction, and also because this dominant minority's exploitation was extended to a worldwide scale, class relations became less evident. The populations of the large industrial countries of Europe and North America, as well as Japan, are mostly made of the dominant capitalist classes and their numerous social corps. The local proletariat, which is relatively privileged, is also comparatively small compared to the huge disorganized, exposed, and defenseless proletariat exploited in third world countries and now in Eastern Europe. The social transformations visible in the dominant nations reflect very imperfectly the nature of the general evolution of capitalist society as a whole. Western observers who are too narrowly focused on domestic developments periodically announce the disappearance of the proletariat (and/or of the social classes) and diagnose their nearsightedness as a trend inherent to capitalism.

To put the social corps in perspective, I suggest the following schematic configuration of international capitalism. A comparatively small minority of national and international businessmen (i.e., the dominant class in its diversity) collects surplus value extracted from the proletariat on a world scale and disposes of it any way it sees fit. Chief among the costs of this huge enterprise is the remuneration of the social corps, who directly or indirectly manage this exploitation or prepare the conditions to make it possible. This activity is correctly labeled as "service" and not "labor," as the social corps are not introduced into the capitalist system to be exploited but to assist the hegemonic class in its tasks. The mode of remuneration is not strictly based on measured labor time as for the proletariat. The specialized functions of the bourgeois social corps and the content of their material relation with their employers make their political aspirations appear as deviant variations of bourgeois ideology. If one applies the same analysis to the proletariat (although it cannot obviously be symmetrical), one finds its social corps more political than technocratic but somehow frozen in a bureaucratic and conservative form. This form encompasses the bureaucratic hierarchies of the former USSR and China and their satellites in a coherent global arrangement. These bureaucracies have revealed their ultimate vocation of driving their citizens into international capitalism to become its modern proletariat. This subordination relativizes the East-West opposition and reveals their actual complicity against the population that they govern.

This global model goes beyond the perspective of capitalist societies limited to "national" levels. It reveals the naïveté of the classification arrangement of the mainstream sociology consisting of strata or layers piled on top of each other according to a meaningless criterion. These criteria are spatial for the anglophones (high/middle/low) and hierarchical for the francophones (*supérieur/moyen/inférieur*)—and both criteria contain no information. In contrast, our configuration, which starts from an empirical grasp of the socio-*institutional* (and not professional) categories of modern society, organically links classes and social corps to one another according to their specificity, function, and historical perspectives. This configuration allows us to evaluate the extent of their intervention in politics, not on the basis of their presumed "motivations" but on the examination of the historical and economic conditions of their existence and perpetuation.

Politically, the social corps generated by the bourgeoisie in dominant capitalist countries more than counterbalance proletarian votes. Social corps are concerned with the electoral process without being radical. There are individuals among them who are sensitive to social justice and wish for changes—although they would not want to lose anything in that process. Other members of these social corps simply refuse to take that risk. Since they are products of the system and of the class of capitalists, such members are congenitally incapable of questioning domination fundamentally, even when they themselves are its target. The individual political position of the members of these social corps varies depending on their belief of being accepted or rejected by the bourgeoisie. This is the basis of what is known as a "left" or "right" inclination among them.

The median position occupied by social corps in our capitalist society, and their discovery of not belonging to any class, fuel their conviction that social classes, if they ever existed, are now forever gone. Social corps are the real "social actors" of our "postmodern" society.

This analysis stops in 1991 at the stage of the international social evolution. It hints at two transformations of major importance, the evidence of which is already apparent:

One is the gradual and deliberate elimination of the "surplus laboring population" starting in regions considered as overpopulated through the deterioration of the conditions of life. This deterioration can be seen in the increase in the price of subsistence and other necessities; in the removal of public services devoted to the maintenance and reproduction of life (hospitals, maternity wards, social security systems, etc.); in restrictions on the means to fight against epidemic diseases and other large-scale calamities; and in the growing flexibility of labor regulations—particularly in relation to child employment (Meillassoux 1991b). Sub-Saharan Africa seems to be the first designated victim, to be apparently followed by Latin America. A contrast to this process of immiseration is the expansion of the Asian proletariat as a result of the development of the satellite economies of Japanese capitalism and the extension of this chain effect to the satellites of these first-tier satellites.

The second transformation is the extension to executives and cadres of the *systematic* form of exploitation that prevailed with the exploitation of manual labor. Now that the supply of manual labor is shrinking, the social corps whose function was to assist the capitalist class in the exploitation of the working classes are running the very real risk of being exploited themselves in a similar way—of becoming the new proletariat of the "postmodern" epoch.

This chapter refers, therefore, to a historical period already in the process of transformation. Still, it is essential to contribute to the understanding of both the ending period and the coming one, to sharpen our view of the constitutive part of the capitalist world at a time that might be its historical apogee.

Translated by Tahsin Corat

Notes

1. The largest individual fortunes in the world amount to $15 billion.
2. This policy and the preference given on exportation is depleting the domestic market of each country and preventing a national *reprise*. Only Japan and, to a lesser extent Germany, seem concerned with the refueling of their domestic markets.
3. Social means of production are those that operate within a social division of labor and whose products satisfy a demand exceeding that of the producers themselves. They may be private or public according to the destination of the profits.
4. War, in all its forms, is used now only by the big powers against the dominated countries.
5. The systematic execution of leftist leaders by the local armed forces also made a return to "democracy" less risky.
6. The French minimum wage is officially computed on the basis of the needs of a bachelor working every working hour of his active life and dying on the day of his retirement.
7. Marx (1970, 172) makes the correct assumption that "the sum of the means of subsistence necessary for the production of labor power must include the means necessary for the laborer's substitutes, i.e. his children" but wages

are computed in terms of hours of labor, while the number of children of each laborer varies. Earnings based on hourly wages cannot fulfill the needs for reproduction of the wage earners as a social class without some form of redistribution of income.

8. I use the verb "to secrete" in order to express the fact that social corps are not a deliberate creation of the classes but rather the result of a half-reluctant process undertaken as a response of the class to an unwanted situation that forces it to delegate power. Tasks such as management, war, politics, and education were at first fulfilled by the bourgeois themselves.

9. The bourgeois classes have been the first since the American Revolution to mobilize millions of unpaid soldiers to their service.

10. One of the longest-standing requests of the unions of business cadres in France is the right to participate as full-fledged members on the board of trustees from which they are institutionally excluded. An executive can join the board on his or her own only if he or she is a shareholder with a standing comparable to that of the other members of the board.

11. The constant check of the whereabouts of cadres by an electronic card manufactured by Delta Protection is the beginning of this trend. Such a card, worn by supervisors at all times, measures labor time more accurately than the punch clock. It not only monitors entrances and exits at the doors of the enterprise but inside it as well. It follows every step of the wearers to check their moves and identify the people they meet. Used as keys to workshops and offices, it limits access to certain zones at certain times and to authorized individuals. The intellectual labor of conception, management, or supervision may still be too subtle to be fully measured this way, but new gadgets to "evaluate" it quantitatively are on the drawing board.

12. I call a "client" one who owes one's services to his patron in return for material protection, with no equivalence being involved (Meillassoux 1973).

13. The clerics of organized religions, originally a corps of the aristocratic classes, may transform themselves into a class, as the Indian Brahmans did, for instance.

14. Besides the "rationale" of war economics, there was the willingness to exterminate blindly and madly people labeled as noxious and offered as victims to a common "German" hatred in an attempt to implicate the people in a binding collective "national" crime.

15. [Editor's note] This is a turn of the French *miroir aux alouettes*, the device used as a decoy for larks. It figuratively refers to any deception or delusion.

16. Whatever the initial intentions of terrorism, it too often ends up in the hands of special agencies who use it as a means of provocation or to carry on their dirty jobs. (See in Italy the case of the secret but official organization Gladio, inspired by the CIA, which planned political murders entrusted to the Red Brigades as a mean of provocation and destabilization.)

17. It is known, for instance, that Irving Brown of the American Federation of Labor, one of the two most powerful trade unions in the United States, was used as an agent by the U.S. administration to instigate the split of the French trade union movement after World War II.

18. The former organization COMECON was cleared for trading in dollars. The best goods in Eastern Europe can be purchased only in special stores accepting only foreign currencies. Even Soviet peasants have received promises to be partly paid in American money.

19. An exception to this rule was the Cultural Revolution by which Mao made an internal party conflict public and thus put the entire bureaucracy at risk. However, the attitude of the Chinese government during the student revolts in July 1989 showed that it had learned its lesson: The internal purge should come before the repression.

References

Alphandéry, C., Bernard, Y., Bloch-Lainé, F., and Chevrillon, O. 1968. *Pour nationaliser l'État*. Paris: Éditions du Seuil.

Anonymous. "Qu'est-ce que c'est la publicité?" *Delenda*. no. 2: 16–23.

Burnham, J. 1941. *The Managerial Revolution*. New York: John Day.

Couvrat, J. F., and Plessis, N. 1989. *La face caché de l'économie mondiale*. Paris: Hâtier.

Marx, K., and Engels, F. 1948. *Manifesto of the Communist Party*. New York: International Publishers.

Marx, K. 1970. *Capital*. London: Lawrence and Wishart.

Meillassoux, C. 1973. "Are There Castes in India?" *Economy and Society* (2) no. 1: 89–101.

———. 1981. *Maidens, Meals and Money*. Oxford: Oxford University Press.

———. 1984. "La reproduction sociale." *Cahiers Internationaux de Sociologie* (77): 383–395.

———. 1991a. "La leçon de Malthus" in F. Gendreau, C. Meillassoux et al. (eds.). *Les spectres de Malthus*, Paris: Études et documentation internationales (EDI), Institut français de recherche pour le développement en coopération (ORSTOM), Centre français sur la population et le développement (CEPED). pp. 15–32.

———. 1991b. "A Paradoxical Growth." International Conference: Development and Rapid Population Growth: A New Look into the Future of Africa. Paris: Institut national d'études démographiques (INED), Ministère de la Coopération, United Nations Organization (UNO).

Meillassoux, C., and Messiant, C. (eds) 1991. *Génie social et manipulations culturelles en Afrique du Sud*. Paris: Arcantère.

Posel, D. 1991. "Un nouveau discours de légitimation" in C. Meillassoux and C. Messiant (eds.). *Génie social et manipulations culturelles en Afrique du Sud*. Paris: Arcantère, pp. 31–61.

Trotsky, L. 1931. *The Permanent Revolution*. New York: Pioneer.

Walter, I. 1986. *L'argent secret*. Paris: J. C. Lattés.

The Problems of Socialism: A Reappraisal of the Orthodox Texts

AIDAN SOUTHALL

The general aim of this analysis is to examine the degree of consistency between the theory of social change and the revolutionary transformation worked out by Marx and Engels. I will specifically examine the attempts to implement the theory in the Paris Commune, and the way in which the October revolution was conducted, bringing the Soviet Union into existence as a grand experiment to test the feasibility of these ideas.

It has been obvious for at least twenty years, if not much longer, that the Soviet Union was not fulfilling its promises and that many of its claims were false. Scholars noted that what happened during and after the revolution seemed utterly remote from the plans and principles of Lenin's *The State and Revolution* (SW 2, 238–327).[1] This work, which was regarded as one of his most utopian writings, is also one of his most theoretical writings, laying claim to Marxist orthodoxy in explicit detail. Criticism of the Soviet Union by Marxists was very muted until recently. Until the death of Stalin, members of Communist parties in all countries were actually under orders from the Soviet Union. There was also a reluctance to criticize the Soviet Union when it was felt that public opinion on the subject was already prejudiced. But the matter is too important to be veiled in silence. If the Soviet experiment failed in major respects, as even its leaders now seem to feel, it is of vital importance to know whether it failed because it deviated from Marxist principles or whether those principles themselves are proved deficient by the experiment. It is therefore necessary to relate the views of Lenin to those of Marx and Engels, and all of them to the practice of the former Soviet Union.

MARX AND ENGELS

Engels's brief "Draft of a Communist Confession of Faith" (MECW, 96–103), written in June 1847, already specified the elimination of private property and its replacement by communal property, defined the proletariat, and declared that revolutions are not made deliberately or

43

arbitrarily but are the consequence of circumstances "not in any way whatever dependent either on the will or on the leadership of individual parties or whole classes." Nonetheless, the proletariat is forcibly repressed and "thus a revolution is being forcibly worked *by the opponents of communism* [my emphasis]" so that the proletariat is being driven into revolution (MECW, 101–102).

According to Engels, replacement of the existing social order will have to be gradual. First, there will be "political liberation of the proletariat through a democratic constitution, followed by limiting private property, employing workers in national workshops and factories and on national estates" and "educating all children at the expense of the state" (MECW, 101–102).

All these points remained fundamental, with some elaboration and change of emphasis. Engels's somewhat longer catechism "Principles of Communism" (MECW, 341–357) followed four months later on October 1847. It specified that the proletariat depends "entirely and solely from the *sale* of its labor [my emphasis]," thus making clear that the proletariat cannot include peasants. The new social order will be "run by society as a whole, for the social good, according to a social plan and with the *participation* of all members of society [my emphasis]" (MECW, 348). Peaceful methods of revolution were desirable, but the oppressed proletariat might be "goaded into a revolution." The democratic constitution, with the political rule of the proletariat, would be inaugurated directly in England, indirectly in France and Germany, because their small peasants and urban petty bourgeois were not yet fully proletarianized—but soon would have to conform to the demands of the proletariat. "This will perhaps involve a second fight, but one that can end only in the victory of the proletariat. Industrial armies will be formed, especially in agriculture, and large palaces erected on national estates as common dwellings for communities of citizens engaged in industry as well as agriculture, combining the advantages of both urban and rural life without the onesidedness and disadvantages of either" (MECW, 341). Credit and banking would be centralized in the hands of the state. The proletariat would be compelled to go always further, to concentrate all capital, all agriculture, all industry, all transport, and all exchange more and more in the hands of the state. Thus, "private ownership will automatically have ceased to exist, money will have become superfluous, and production will have so increased and men will be so much changed that the last forms of the old social relations will also be able to fall away" (MECW, 341). This amounts to the achievement of full communism, and the process appears here sharply telescoped, although it was said it would be gradual. For Lenin, the sequence appears somewhat different.

According to Marx and Engels, the revolution cannot take place in one country alone. "It will be a revolution taking place simultaneously in all civilized countries" (at least England, the United States, France, and Germany—Russia is not mentioned). All three groups of so-called socialists, the reactionary, the bourgeois, and the democratic were found wanting and were rejected.

The much longer *Manifesto of the Communist Party* (MECW, 477–519), written by Marx and Engels in December 1847 and January 1848, retains all the above principles but drops the catechistic form by adding much detail. It engages the reader with powerful arguments, vivid aphorisms, and clarion calls to triumphant revolution: "The history of all hitherto existing society is the history of class struggles" (MECW, 482).

Although "the theory of the Communists may be summed up in the single sentence: Abolition of private property," in fact it was not the abolition of property generally, but the abolition of *bourgeois* property. The idea of abolishing the hard-won self-earned property of the petty artisan or small peasant (a form of property that *preceded* the bourgeois form) was ridiculed. There was no need to abolish that, although the development of industry was destroying it anyway:

> Communism deprives no man of the power to appropriate the product of society; all that it does is to deprive him of the power to subjugate the labor of others by means of such appropriation. (MECW, 500)

> If the proletariat is compelled by force of circumstances, to organize itself as a class, if, by means of a revolution, it makes itself the ruling class, and, as such, sweeps away by force the old conditions of production, [it will] have swept away the conditions for the existence of class antagonisms and of classes generally, and will thereby *have abolished its own supremacy as a class.* . . . [In its place,] we shall have an *association* in which the free development of each is the condition for the free development of all [my emphasis]. (MECW, 506)

Finally, they conclude with the ringing peroration:

> The Communists disdain to conceal their views and aims. They openly declare that their ends can be attained only by the forcible overthrow of all existing social conditions. Let the ruling classes tremble at a Communistic revolution. The proletarians have nothing to lose but their chains. They have a world to win. Working men of all countries unite! (MECW, 519)

Here the peaceful option, previously stated as desirable though unlikely, has faded entirely in favor of aggressive polemic. Great were the hopes for the uprising thought to be already imminent, and great was the disappointment when the beginning of the western revolution (as exemplified in the Paris Commune) was crushed. If ever words could perform, here Marx and Engels yearned, even against their materialistic principles, to breathe fire into them and speed them on as swords in the hands of the exploding insurrection.

In contrast to Marx and Engels, Lenin was to put it more strongly in "Can the Bolsheviks Retain State Power?" which he wrote in a desperate attempt to persuade the Bolsheviks to action in 1917:

> The state, dear people, is a class concept. The state is an organ or instrument of violence exercised by one class against another. So long as it is an instrument of violence exercised by the bourgeoisie against the proletariat, the proletariat can have only one slogan: *destruction* of this state. But when the state will be a proletarian state, when it will be an instrument of violence exercised by the proletariat against the bourgeoisie, we shall be fully and unreservedly in favor of a strong state power and of centralism. (SW 2, 374)

THE PARIS COMMUNE

The Paris Commune of 1871 aroused Marx and Engels's hopes. Surviving for a bare two months, it can hardly be seen as the successful establishment of a model new society. To the dominant bourgeois press it was a frightening outburst of bloodthirsty savagery, menacing the very roots of civilization and requiring all decent men and enlightened nations to suppress it immediately at whatever cost. False hearsay reports of brutalities and horrors supposedly perpetuated by the communards were constantly promulgated by the press. In fact, the chief brutality lay in its suppression when 25,000 citizens were callously shot in the streets by the bourgeois government.

Brief as the episode seems, its symbolic importance is impossible to exaggerate, and many of its actual achievements were significant, however fleeting; the commune did, under Marx's powerful pen, become a model and standard by which all socialist efforts were to be judged for the next half-century. It remained a sacred inviolable model for Lenin, who constantly invoked it as if for legitimacy, while in practice he picked some aspects to follow while seeming to ignore others that might seem equally fundamental.

The Paris Commune was a self-government of the producers. It featured universal suffrage; all of its deputies and officials were elected and, moreover, were paid only laborers' wages and were subject to recall at any moment. The commune was to provide the model for even the smallest country hamlet. All of France was to be organized into self-working and self-governing communes created by the laborers themselves. Rural communes of every district were to administer their common affairs by an assembly of delegates in the central town, which would again send deputies to the national delegation in Paris. The commune was the political form under which the emancipation of labor was to be worked out. Every person was to become a working person. Members wanted to make a *truth out of individual property* by transforming the means of production, namely, land and capital, now chiefly the means of enslaving and exploiting labor, into mere instruments of free and associated labor. Cooperative producers would supersede the capitalist system by uniting to regulate national production. Cooperative production does not do away with class struggles but provides the rational medium in which that class struggle can run through its different phases in the most rational and *humane* way. The working class would know they had to pass through different phases of class struggle. From the moment the working person's class struggle became real, the fantastic utopias of Marx and Engels would evanesce. This would not follow because the working class had given up the ends aimed at by these utopists, but because they had found the real means to realize them (Draper 1971, 76–77).

In his "Marginal Notes to the Program of the German Workers' Party" in the *Critique of the Gotha Program 1875* (SW 3, 13–30), Marx gives some further explanation of how society would work. He says he is dealing with

> a communist society, not as it has *developed* on its own foundations, but on the contrary, just as it *emerges* from capitalist society; which is thus in every respect, economically, morally and intellectually, still stamped with the birth marks of the old society from whose womb it emerges. Accordingly, the individual producer receives back from society—after the deductions have been made—exactly what he gives to it. What he has given to it is his individual quantum of labor. . . . He receives a certificate from society that he has furnished such and such an amount of labor (after deducting his labor for the common funds), and with this certificate he draws from the social stock of means of consumption as much as costs the same amount of labor (MESW, 17–18).

Here we are left to imagine vast storehouses, the corruption of those who make out and distribute the certificates, the common practice of inflating the payroll with imaginary names, and the withholding, the hoarding, and even the black market. One could imagine (but still very idealistically) this system improving fairness and raising standards for the most deprived. But the idea that such a system could provide "to each according to his need" was totally unrealistic.

What is need anyway? While fully recognizing the absurdity and harmfulness of many needs satisfied in contemporary capitalism, it is still inconceivable that Marx's system could allocate leisure goods, concerts, and art galleries. It presupposes a vast planning bureaucracy with no safeguards against corruption, and the whole sad development of *exactly what happened* in the USSR. Even the very weak socialism of nationalized key industries has failed to show productive efficiency improvement. Such a system is only conceivable if run at the grass roots by incorruptible beings, hardened to resist temptation by long experience with egalitarian workers' management systems.

LENIN AND THE REVOLUTION

In April 1917 Lenin (SW 2, 29–33) declared in Thesis 8: "It is not our immediate task to 'introduce' socialism, but only to bring social production and the distribution of products at once under the control of the Soviets of Workers' Deputies." Thesis 9 emphasizes the party's demand for a "commune state" on the model of the Paris Commune.

The Communist principle of "from each according to his ability, to each according to his needs" is achieved only when "labor has become not only a livelihood but *life's prime want*, after the productive forces have increased with the all-round development of the individual, and all the springs of *cooperative wealth* flow more abundantly [my emphasis]." By this time, of course, human beings have somehow been redeemed and converted into new creatures.

Lenin follows Engels's *Anti-Dühring*, on the Marxist theory of the state. According to Lenin (SW 2, 248–249), the proletariat will first seize state power and turn the means of production into state property. The workers thereby abolish themselves as proletariat, abolish all class distinctions and class antagonisms, and abolish *the state as state*, or build a state "which is no longer a state in the strict sense of the word." The first act by which the state really comes forward as the representative of the whole society—the taking possession of the means of production in the name of society—is also its last independent act as a state. State interference in social relations becomes, in one domain after another, superfluous, and then dies down of itself. The government of *persons* is replaced by the administration of *things* and by the conduct of the process of production. The state is not "abolished." It withers away. (It was the anarchists who demanded that the state be abolished overnight.)

Later, Lenin returns to the same theme, reiterating that

destruction of the State Power is the aim set by all socialists, including Marx above all. Genuine democracy, i.e., *liberty and equality*, is unrealizable unless this aim is achieved. But its practical achievement is possible only through Soviet or proletarian democracy, for by *enlisting the class organizations of the working people in constant and unfailing participation in the administration of the state, it immediately begins to prepare the complete withering away of the state.* (SW 2, 105–106)

Lenin then follows Marx's *Poverty of Philosophy* to the effect that

the working class will substitute for the old bourgeois society an *association* (in which the free development of each is the condition for the free development of all) which will preclude classes and their antagonism and there will be no more political power proper, since political power is precisely the expression of class antagonism in bourgeois society. . . . The proletarian will . . . centralize all instruments of production in the hands of the state, i.e. of the proletariat organized as the ruling class. (SW 2, 253–255)

Lenin sees this as the "dictatorship of the proletariat," as Marx and Engels called it after the Paris Commune: "This proletarian state will begin to wither away immediately after its victory (after one day), because it is unnecessary" (SW 2, 257).

Let us compare this with Lenin's own comments on the actual progress of the revolution in May 1917:

In many provincial areas the revolution is progressing in the following way: the proletariat and the peasantry, on their own initiative, are organizing Soviets and dismissing the old authorities; a proletariat and peasant militia is being set up; all lands are being transferred to the peasants; workers' control over the factories and the eight-hour day have been introduced and wages have been increased; production is being maintained, and workers control the distribution of food, etc. (SW 2, 104)

The growth of the revolution in the provinces in depth and scope is, on the one hand, the growth of a movement for transferring *all power to the Soviets* and putting the workers and peasants themselves in control of production. On the other hand, it serves as a guarantee for the buildup of forces, on a national scale, for the *second stage* of the revolution, which must transfer *all state power to the Soviets* or to other organs *directly expressing* the will of the majority of the nation (organs of *local self-government*, the Constituent Assembly, etc.).

Lenin's view was different, and less facile, after the revolution, when he reported to the First Congress of the Communist International in March 1919:

> In no civilized capitalist country does "democracy in general" exist; all that exists is bourgeois democracy; and it is not a question of "dictatorship in general," but of the dictatorship of the oppressed class, i.e., the proletariat, over its oppressors and exploiters, i.e., the bourgeoisie, in order to overcome the resistance offered by the exploiters in their fight to maintain their domination. . . . History teaches us that no oppressed class [i.e., including the bourgeoisie] ever did, or could, achieve power without going through a period of dictatorship, i.e., the conquest of political power and forcible suppression of the resistance always offered by the exploiters—a resistance that is most desperate, most furious, and that stops at nothing. (SW 3, 98–99)

At the same time Lenin also realized that "to compel a whole section of the population to work under coercion is impossible" (SW 3, 124). In April 1920 Lenin recognized in "From the Destruction of the Old Social System to the Creation of the New" that each stage of transformation was going to take far longer than had been implied (SW 3, 288–290). "The problem of communist labor . . . is the paramount problem in the building of socialism." Lenin had to replace the idea of Communist labor with

> socialist labor, for we are dealing not with the higher, but the lower, the primary stage of development of the new social system that is growing out of capitalism. Communist labor in the narrower and stricter sense of the term is labor performed gratis for the benefit of society, not for the purpose of obtaining a right to certain products, . . . but voluntary labor, . . . labor performed because it has become a habit to work for the common good—labor as the requirement of a healthy organism.

In his last writings, Lenin had to confront an even more bitter realization that not only was progress slow but he had been forced into an actual reversal, almost a betrayal, in restoring the modified capitalism of the New Economic Policy (NEP): "We are now retreating, going back, as it were; but we are doing so in order, after first retreating, to take a running start and make a bigger leap forward" (SW 3, 673). These were brave words. All Lenin could do was to express confidence that "in a few years, . . . NEP Russia will become socialist Russia" (SW 3, 678).

For Lenin, the masses had to recognize that the Soviets of Workers' Deputies were the only possible form of revolutionary government. As long as the Bolsheviks were in the minority in the soviets, they would carry on the work of criticizing and exposing errors and at the same time they would preach the necessity of transferring state power to the Soviets of Workers' Deputies.

Lenin envisioned a state that would not be a parliamentary republic (which would be a retrograde step in his view) but a republic of soviets of workers, agricultural laborers, and peasant deputies. The abolition of the police, the army, and the bureaucracy would be the primary task. The standing army would be replaced by the arming of the whole people. The salaries of all officials, all of whom were elective and displaceable at any time, would not exceed the average income of a worker. Thus his vision of a "commune state" was based on the model of the Paris Commune (SW 2, 32ff.).

Lenin proposed that responsibility for the agrarian policy be shifted to the Soviets of Agricultural Laborers' Deputies. The main feature of the agrarian program would be the nationalization of *all* lands in the country. Public land would be disposed of by the local Soviets of Agricultural Laborers' and Peasants' Deputies. In addition, the agrarian program would include the establishment of separate soviets of deputies of poor peasants and the setting up of a *model farm* on each of the large estates under the control of the Soviets of Agricultural Laborers' Deputies.

At this important transitional juncture, Lenin developed unique ideas on "socialist competition." In "How to Organize Competition" (SW 2, 467–474), he expounds on the paradox that while capitalists always praise competition and private enterprise and accuse socialists of refusing to understand the importance of these virtues, in fact capitalists do the opposite:

Capitalism long ago replaced small, independent commodity production, under which competition could develop enterprise, energy and bold initiative to any *considerable* extent, by large- and very-large factory production, joint-stock companies, syndicates and other monopolies. Under such capitalism, competition means the incredibly brutal suppression of the enterprise, energy and bold initiative of the *mass* of the population. . . . Far from extinguishing competition, socialism, on the contrary, for the first time creates the opportunity for employing it on a really *wide* and on a really *mass* scale, for actually drawing the majority of working people into a field of labor in which they can display their abilities, develop their capacities, and reveal those talents, so abundant among the people whom capitalism crushed, suppressed and strangled in thousands and millions. Now that a socialist government is in power *our task is to organize competition* [my emphases].

Accounting and control—this is the main economic task (the

essence of socialist transformation) of every Soviet of Workers', Soldiers' and Peasants' Deputies (as the supreme state power, or on the instructions, on the authority, of this power), of every consumers' society, of every union or committee of suppliers, of every factory committee or organ of workers' control in general. . . . The accounting and control essential for the transition to socialism can be exercised only by the people. Only the voluntary and conscientious cooperation of the *mass* of the workers and peasants . . . The land, the banks and the factories have now become the property of the entire people. . . . Competition must be arranged between practical organizers from among the workers and peasants. Every attempt to establish stereotyped forms and to impose uniformity from above, as intellectuals are so inclined to do, must be combated. . . . The Paris Commune gave a great example of how to combine initiative, independence, freedom of action and vigor from below with voluntary centralism free from stereotyped forms. Our Soviets are following the same road. . . . All Communes—factories, villages, consumers' societies and committees of supplies—must *compete* with each other as practical organizers of accounting and control of labor and distribution of products.

In "A Great Beginning" (July 28, 1919; SW 3, 164–183) Lenin optimistically lists the successes of his twenty-month-old regime, but he still harps upon the essential part played by large-scale production.

The communist organization of social labor, the first step towards which is socialism, rests, and will do so more and more as time goes on, on the free and conscious discipline of the working people themselves who have thrown off the yoke both of the landowners and capitalists. This new discipline does not drop from the skies . . . it grows out of the material conditions of large scale capitalist production, and out of them alone. Without them it is impossible. (SW 3, 17)

It is the very growth of large-scale production and capitalist cartels, trusts, and finance capital that provides the principal foundation for the advent of socialism: Capitalist-trained workers become the intellectual and moral force as well as the physical executor by means of dictatorship of the proletariat; this leads to the means of production becoming the property of society. Marx had already regarded the bourgeois as a revolutionary class—as the bearer of large-scale industry—relative to the feudal lords and the lower middle class (MESW, 20).

In giving his interpretation of Marx's concept of socialism, Lenin (SW 1, 15–43) had already emphasized the ever more rapid socialization of labor that had occurred since Marx's death. This included the growth of large-scale capitalist production and capitalistic cartels, syndicates, and trusts and the gigantic increase in the dimensions and power of finance capital, which provided the principal foundation for the inevitable advent of socialism.

Capitalism breaks for all time the ties between agriculture and industry, but at the same time, through its highest development, it prepares new elements of those ties, a union between industry and agriculture based on the conscious application of science and the concentration of collective labor, and on a redistribution of the human population (thus putting an end both to rural backwardness, isolation and barbarism, and to the unnatural concentration of vast masses of people in big cities). Democracy is a form of the state . . . on the one hand the organized, systematic use of force against persons; on the other, the formal recognition of equality of citizens, the equal right of all to determine the structure of, and to administer, the state. . . . It welds together the proletariat, and enables it to crush . . . the bourgeois state machine . . . and to substitute a more democratic state machine, but a state machine nevertheless, in the shape of armed workers who proceed to form a militia involving the entire population. Here "quantity turns into quality": *such* a degree of democracy implies overstepping the boundaries of bourgeois society and beginning its socialist reorganization. If really *all* take part in the administration of the state, capitalism cannot retain its hold. The development of capitalism, in turn, creates the *preconditions* that *enable* really "all" to take part in the administration of the state . . . (universal literacy . . . already achieved in the most advanced capitalist countries), then the "training and disciplining" of millions of workers by the huge, complex, socialized apparatus of the postal service, railways, big factories, large scale commerce, banking, etc., etc. (SW 1, 36–37)

Accounting and control—that is *mainly* what is needed for the "smooth working," . . . of the *first* phase of communist society. *All* citizens are transformed into hired employees of the state, which consists of the armed workers. *All* citizens become employees and workers of a *single* countrywide state "syndicate." . . . The accounting and control necessary for this have been *simplified* by capitalism to the utmost and reduced to the extraordinarily simple operations— which any literate person can perform—of supervising and recording, knowledge of the four rules of arithmetic, and issuing appropriate receipts. . . . The whole of society will have become a single office and a single factory, with equality of labor and pay. (SW 2, 37)

But this "factory discipline" . . . is by no means our ideal, or our ultimate goal. It is only a necessary *step* for thoroughly cleansing society of all the infamies . . . of capitalist exploitation. . . . From the moment all members of society, or at least the vast majority, have learned to administer the state *themselves*, have taken this work into their own hands, . . . the need for government of any kind begins to disappear altogether. The more complete the democracy, the nearer the moment when it becomes unnecessary. The more democratic the "state" which consists of the armed workers, and which is "no longer a state in the proper sense of the word" the more rapidly *every form of state* begins to wither away. (SW 2, 311–313)

Were they *mesmerized* by their own dialectic? Did they think that the development of a factor x (say, democracy), was *bound* to lead to its own negation *automatically*? Was their idea that the *development* of democratic government will *inevitably* lead to the *disappearance* of democratic government, which *will be socialism*? Since this democratic government took the form of the dictatorship of the proletariat (an oxymoron in which the contradiction failed to lead to any transformation), it resulted not in socialism but in permanent tyranny.

All power to the people! This was the terrifying thought that haunted even the founding fathers of the U.S. constitution. They were genuinely inspired by an idealistic yearning to achieve a government of the people, by the people, for the people—as it was later to be defined—but at the same time they were scared out of their wits at the idea that the wrong people (poor people, uneducated people, uncultured people, and un-gentlemanly people) might really take power. They hoped to devise a constitution that would give a convincing appearance of giving power to ordinary people, without ever allowing it actually to happen. Lenin achieved the same end by the opposite method; Instead of concealing the issue, he confronted it so outrageously that no one would dare challenge it.

CONCLUSIONS

As we have seen, Marx and Engels established the theory of socialist and Communist transformation through their intense efforts culminating in the *Manifesto of the Communist Party*. Lenin accepted this and subsequent elaborations such as that of Engels in *Anti-Dühring* as *authoritative* without explicitly suggesting any changes. But the original theory envisaged revolution occurring in England, France, and Germany, not tsarist Russia. However, Russia was beginning to boil over into revolution even before Lenin began to take charge. It would seem that a revolutionary Marxist party could not possibly have escaped from the conclusion that this was a ripe revolutionary situation presented to it by the working out of the forces of history, as its theory had foretold, except that revolution was not occurring where the contradictions of capitalism had reached their most advanced, acute stage. This was already a major, not a minor, deviation from the theory, yet the theory has never been refined or reformulated to take account of it.

The question had been obliquely addressed in the debate over the transformational possibilities of the Russian commune. Marx concluded that the commune could provide a base for the direct transition to socialism only if it was supported and carried by the revolution in Western Europe, which was still imminently expected (MESW, 152–161). This revolution never did occur, and the commune never was used as a base of revolutionary transformation but was swept away, first by Lenin's equivocal centralizing system of soviets, then by the chaos of war communism and NEP laissez-faire, and finally by Stalin's brutal collectivization. Since Marxism is fundamentally a theory of history, it cannot survive unless it is reformulated to make sense of history as it has actually occurred. Such critical reappraisals as have so far appeared from within the Marxist fold fail to do this.

The theory of revolution, which derives from Marx's theory of history, requires that men (and we must now explicitly add women) act consciously from within the forces of history, making their small yet vital contribution from inside this tumultuous stream at precisely the correct moment of ripeness. Was this indeed what Lenin did? What went wrong? I think that an adequate Marxist analysis of this has never been made.

Lenin forced the hands of the Mensheviks, uncompromisingly splitting the Bolsheviks off from them. He forced the hands of reluctant Bolsheviks, wearing down the Central Committee till it agreed to overturn Kerensky's government. He forced the hands of the Petrograd Soviet, which had handed power back to Kerensky's government. Given developments since 1989, it is legitimate to wonder whether Plekhanov, the Mensheviks, and the Petrograd Soviet were all correct, and closer to Marx, in their view that the bourgeois revolution and full development of capitalism had to come first. Admiration for Lenin's insistence that all power must go to the people without further delay is matched by disgust that it never did so.

Lenin was clearly autocratic and dictatorial, with an almost incredible capacity for verbal coercion. The blinding force of his personality, the overwhelming intensity of his commitment, and the unwavering decisive clarity of the goals he had set could sway his colleagues and win them over to momentous courses of action of which they had previously all disapproved. Yet there is no sign that Lenin was corrupted by power as such. Perhaps that compounded his blindness to this factor in ordinary men. He fought relentlessly to get his way, but he accepted the majority decision, having usually made it his own. Are we then forced to conclude that the revolution Lenin brought about and the channel into which he steered it was a deviation from the revolution actually ripening in the womb of history (to use Marx's favorite metaphor)? Did he transgress and violate a fundamental tenet of the Marxist theory of historical process and the proper course of revolutionary transformations? Was it indeed a bourgeois revolution that the contradiction between the forces and the relations of production was precipitating and that Lenin's overbearing will forced out of its proper course with the direst consequences?

This is indeed a thoroughly tenable, logical conclusion. Lenin was theoretically incorrect in his intransigent, scornful opposition to the Mensheviks, his determination to split off the Bolsheviks, and his browbeating them into forcing a revolution upon a proletariat that hardly existed except in Petrograd. Even the Petrograd Soviet was theoretically correct in handing over power to the provisional bourgeois government.

The fateful consequences of these theoretically incorrect decisions by Lenin may be followed in the tortured sequence of events and in Lenin's frenzied reiteration of scintillating contradictions. For if Lenin's revolutionary strategy was deviant, some of the difficulties it ran into go back to flaws inherent in the original theory of Marx and Engels.

As Lenin was forced to put theory into practice, latent contradictions became overwhelming. In 1914 he had summarized Marx's theories with evident approval, reinforcing the idea that capitalism "provides the principal material foundation for the inevitable advent of socialism" (SW 1, 37). But did he think this had already happened in Russia? Even in 1919 he still attributes the "free and conscious discipline of the working people," on which socialism depends, to the preparation provided by capitalism. The first of all Marxist revolutionary principles is that "revolutions are not made deliberately or arbitrarily" but are the consequence of circumstances "not in any way dependent either on the will or on the leadership of individual parties or whole classes" (MECW, 349–350). How can Lenin possibly escape conviction for violating this principle? According to Marx, the revolution is forced upon the proletariat by the *opponents* of communism, and the proletariat is driven and goaded into it by them. Even so, "replacement of the existing social order will have to be 'gradual' and first will be 'political' liberation of the proletariat through a democratic constitution."

It is true that Marx and Engels became more belligerent in the final manifesto, but in Lenin all trace of the original expression of preference for peaceful transformation is completely lost. Lenin was not averse to violence. He welcomed it if it was to be used by the proletariat against the bourgeoisie. No oppressed class could achieve power without "dictatorship" and forcible suppression of resistance. The masses, too, had to be made to see things the way Lenin saw them, and the whole population had to be *compulsorily* organized in consumers' societies.

Splendid as it sounds in rhetoric, how could the dictatorship of the proletariat possibly bring about the withering of the state? Was there, indeed, ever a dictatorship of the proletariat under Lenin? Some critics have suggested that there was only a dictatorship *over* the proletariat. The issue is raised again and again, and one is forced to conclude that Lenin really was deadly serious about popular participation, at least in principle. Some favorite phrases are indeed ambiguous. "The new social order will be run by *society as a whole*." Private property would be replaced by *community* of property. There would be participation of *all members of society*.

Surely Lenin did not mean the participation ridiculed in parliamentary democracy, where every four years or so the people choose which of their oppressors shall rule them? Even that illusory right was more than Lenin's Soviet Union was ever to obtain, except in the most narrowly artificial, ritual form.

Against the insistence on popular participation of all members of society is the equal insistence on centralism, centralization, and the virtue and necessity of the large scale, one of the bitter gifts of capitalism itself. Marx and Engels already spoke of industrial armies, national workshops, and "palaces" as common dwellings for workers (a bitterly prophetic comment on the drab, overcrowded, mass housing of the Soviet Union). Yet this enormous accretion of centralized power is at the same time the very process of the state's withering away. Private property, and money, would cease, production would rise, men would be changed, and old social relations would fall away. Did this assume a parliamentary democracy as the state, or was "the state envisioned" somewhere beyond this dimension?

Lenin regarded parliamentary democracy as a retrograde step when compared with his vision of a democracy of soviets inspired by the Paris Commune. This has to be taken seriously, although events never gave Lenin a chance to work it out in any realistic way. It could only have been a kind of indirect, pyramidal democracy, which, ironically, was the form that colonial governments always favored as a delaying tactic in the face of agitators' demands for direct, parliamentary democracy. The crucial feature of a pyramidal democracy is that it restrains the role of political parties, focusing on the choice of individuals at several successive levels, which appears to result in the ultimate selection of moderate, elite candidates. It is, incidentally, the form chosen by Yoweri Museveni in Uganda, after twenty years of disastrous experience of the failure of attempted parliamentary democracy.

Lenin added a fascinating new note to the idea of democracy, in addition to his obsession with the virtues of the large scale delivered by capitalism, with his idea that the whole system could be run as an administration of things, not persons, by an extraordinarily simple system of accounting, easily accessible to every literate person, and, as Lenin's most unexpected revolutionary idea, that it could all be run on the basis of competition between its component units. Competition had been ruled out by Marx and Engels as inseparable from capitalist private property. But this is still a very serious idea of tremendous potential, part of the key to a possible solution of socialist contradictions, which, unfortunately, history denied Lenin any opportunity to implement.

This extraordinary combination of large-scale popular participation, competition, and simple accounting for the administration of things rather than persons comes somewhat nearer to a realistic idea for the possible achievement of socialist goals, although it was never put into practice. Perhaps the withering away of the state seems such a beguiling achievement of the impossible that we are predisposed to believe any authoritative formula.

Yet the Marxist statements are singularly contradictory and also involve an element of vacillation. The proletariat, forced to become a class, seizes the state and becomes the ruling class, thus sweeping away class antagonisms and abolishing its own supremacy as a class (since there is nothing left to be supreme over). The proletariat makes *state property*, the means of production, thus abolishing itself as a class and the state as a state. This seems to be a non sequitur but may be a flashback to Hegel's negation of the negation. The state becomes, for the first time, the representative of the whole society and takes possession of the means of production in the name of the whole society. This is the state's last independent act, after which it begins to become superfluous and dies away. The only realistic aspect of this is Lenin's idea that the state becomes the administration of things instead of people and therefore can be administered by *all* the people from top to bottom by simple accounting methods. There is no more politics, only administration! If Max Weber's interpretation of the development of bureaucracy in the modern capitalist state is exaggerated, Lenin's idea of the happy, egalitarian, efficient running of a vast state with simple arithmetic seems impossibly naive. He goes on, "There will be a single state syndicate, a single office and a single factory, for the whole nation. The more democracy, the more unnecessary it becomes. It is a state consisting of the armed workers, which is no longer a state in the proper sense of the word" (SW 2, 312–312). Such a state is still the dream of millions, but it has never yet been implemented in reality. There are two central flaws that seem to run all through Lenin's work, both theory and practice: failure to comprehend the inevitably corrupting force of concentrations of power and, in light of this, failure to develop appropriate grass-roots organizations of local production, distribution, and exchange, with appropriate systems for coordinating them into larger entities through which overall goals are achieved.

People in the former Soviet Union have now actually begun to ask whether the USSR was socialist! Such a question would have been sacrilegious until very recently, yet now it is openly asked in Moscow. If Lenin himself went astray, the look at his works will have to be very critical. Any truly radical rethinking and reformulation will have to consider very seriously the counterproductive effects of revolutionary violence, which may encourage a momentary solidarity and esprit de corps but in the long run discourages the development of those organizational and working habits necessary for the emergence of true socialism. Lenin was somewhat confused about "the great change from working under compulsion to working for oneself," thinking too much of the military measures to suppress resistance and the need to organize on a "gigantic national if not international scale" (SW 2, 468). Lenin did not think sufficiently of the lower cellular structure of his organization, which is more important than the gigantic level he set as his goal. No socialism will ever be achieved by gigantism. The early beginnings with the grass-roots Soviets were quite promising in themselves, but they were bureaucratized and their essential quality of local, egalitarian initiative was destroyed. The desperate military fighting for one's life against resistance, in which Lenin found himself, is not the best way of promoting proper socialist labor and productive organization. It promotes command, discipline, and obedience, as the Soviet Union proved, rather than equality, reciprocity, and initiative. Lenin was closer to the mark when he saw the ultimate goal of Communist labor as "labor performed gratis for the benefit of society, not for the purpose of obtaining a right to certain products, but voluntary labor, labor performed because it has become a habit to work for the common good, labor as the requirement of a healthy organism" (SW 3, 289). That goal will certainly take a long time to reach, as he foresaw, but at least one must move in the right direction and not away from it. It will also be necessary to ensure that power and authority is distributed as widely as possible to reduce its corrupting temptations. It will probably be necessary to build up from the ground level, from the grass roots, not from the top down, as revolutions have slipped into doing so far. Socialism is indeed only just beginning.

Socialism as conventionally practiced has become stuck. It is no progressive transition to anything but has become a stagnant means of state oppression and exploitation. The solution will have to be some form of cooperation, however negative that word has become. By far the longest relevant experiment carried out to date is that of Yugoslavia, for almost forty years. The acute current difficulties of the Yugoslav economy and society are by no means all to be related to his experiment, which has in fact achieved notable successes both in raising productivity and in pioneering the popular democratic organization of production itself. Some of the current problems are due to ethnic conflicts exacerbated, if not caused by, as yet unsolved regional economic inequalities. They are in part a demonstration of the fact that the Yugoslav peoples are free to express themselves. Such ethnic conflicts are ubiquitous today, and any socialist experiment in the future will have to confront and solve them. Nowhere is this more true than in Africa, where the failure of socialism so far is simply an expression of the fact that it has not been socialism at all.

Note

1. All references to Marx and Engels from their Collected Works (1976), Volume 6 will be cited with the abbreviation MECW. All references from the Selected Works of Marx and Engels, (1977), Volume 3 will be referenced with the abbreviation MESW. All references to Lenin are from his three-volume Selected Works (1967). Citations will appear with the abbreviation SW as well as with the volume number.

References

Draper, H. (ed.). 1971. *Karl Marx and Friedrich Engels' writings on the Paris Commune*. New York: Monthly Review.

Edwards, S. (ed.). 1973. *The communards of Paris, 1871*. Ithaca, NY: Cornell University Press.

Lenin, V. 1977. *Selected works* (in three volumes). Moscow: Progress.

Marx, K., and Engels, F. 1976. *Collected works*, vol. 6. Moscow: Progress.

———. 1977. *Selected works*, vol. 3. Moscow: Progress.

PART II
The Politics of Decollectivization

Once Again, the Land: Decollectivization and Social Conflict in Rural Romania

DAVID A. KIDECKEL

In this chapter I consider the ongoing process of agricultural transformation in postrevolutionary Romania with an eye to describing the variety of forces shaping this process and to explaining the diversity of local responses to it. Specifically I examine the meaning of the rural transformation for the organization and social life of local communities. I suggest how the rural transformation contributes to maintaining social differentiation and heightens political conflict in the local community while preserving state power and abetting the frailty of civil society in the postsocialist community.

THE SIGNIFICANCE AND DECLINE OF COLLECTIVIZATION AT STATE AND LOCAL LEVELS

Collective agricultural practices are fast waning in rural East Europe in general and in Romania in particular. However, to understand, if not predict, the future of rural East Europe it is not enough to assume the automatic rejection of collectivization in East European communities. In fact, as considerable questions remain about the extent to which collectivization was accepted and integrated into East European rural life and culture, we must understand the complex role of the collective farms to better understand the current period of change.

Of all the institutions developed by the East European socialist states, the agricultural production cooperatives, or collective farms, especially highlighted the contradictions between the ideals and realities of these states. This contradictory quality is mirrored in their history. Thus, the East European state placed extraordinary emphasis on collectivization as a strategy for the development of socialist society, charging it with two essential missions: (1) to rationalize and expand agricultural production to free labor and provide capital for national development, and (2) to develop the socialist consciousness of the notoriously individualist peasantry while ensuring state control through socialist agricultural practice and bureaucratic-based, party-controlled organization. These two goals were effected by a wide variety of policies in the diverse socialist states, though these policies generally mandated such principles and practices as large-scale mechanization under state direction if not outright control, land amalgamation and joint ownership, collectivized team production, remuneration by team results, consensual decision-making guided by party activists, and creation of special funds for widows, orphans, and the impaired, as well as vacations, pensions, and health benefits for members.

Despite these lofty goals, much of the East European rural populations only partially took to collectivization, and the farms rarely reached the level of achievement originally foreseen for them by socialist planners and ideologues. Each East European state had its own set of conditions that limited the success and development of the collectives and shaped local orientations to the farms. For example, in Poland and Yugoslavia the existence of alternate sources of social power (the church in Poland and the ethnic republics in Yugoslavia) facilitated the political organization and vitality of the private peasantry and restricted the implementation of collectivization throughout the socialist period. Hungary reduced her commitment to the collectives in the wake of the 1956 rebellion and instead focused on the development of agricultural service and marketing cooperatives and on the private sector. Czechoslovakia and the GDR retained a strong collective farm system, though they were enabled only by extensive subsidies, high rural wages, and the relative success of state industry, which provided the rural population with the perception of a high standard of living. In Albania, Bulgaria, and Romania centrally directed agriculture was implemented in a large-scale way. The first two placed the greatest emphasis on the development of state farms (Albania) and agroindustrial communes (Bulgaria), while Romanian agriculture relied on multivillage collective farms on about 60 percent of its terrain. However, in all cases the intensely collectivized farms were a constant source of local discontent and critique about the nature of socialism, even though they remained in force until revolutionary 1989.

The limited successes and jaundiced perceptions of collectivization by East European rural populations were based on a combination of factors both general to East European socialism and specific to the local communities in which collectives were found. Generally, as socialist ideology and investment policies often downgraded agriculture as a livelihood, the farms became the refuge of the least capable workers, who were treated and paid accordingly (cf. Mitrany 1951). Bureaucratism in agriculture and the constant experimentation with agriculture to address the chronic labor and capital shortfalls in socialist society also provoked a near-permanent sense of separation and alienation between collective farm labor and management. The farms were often seen by their work force as exploitative places where there was no choice but to steal from them before they robbed you (cf. Sampson 1984). Local factors were as numerous as collectivized communities. Given the collectives' multifaceted role in local rural communities, it was impossible for them not to serve as the context for the typical and constant interpersonal and interfamilial conflicts that characterize small communities the world over. Also, local ecological conditions, demographic factors, ethnic differences, and class hierarchies all potentially affected the successful operation of the farms and the identity and productivity of its work force.

The unsteady relationship of East European peasantries and agricultural collectivization readily became a tool of cold war rhetoric and competition and was used as one argument for the blanket condemnation of socialism by Western critics. Uncertainty about collectivization was thus mistakenly generalized into a universal desire for private agriculture on the part of the East European peasantry. However, nothing could be further from the truth. In fact, to accept this blanket Western condemnation not only is a hasty generalization but also obscures the complex sociocultural and political economic realities of rural East and Central European communities and thus prevents the likelihood of our understanding the wrenching process of change and transformation that such communities are currently experiencing. The collectives had and have their success stories and their supporters. To understand what and who these are is thus also to understand the potential process and problematic of change in the postsocialist world.

For one thing it must be noted that the farms achieved a measure of success in forming a socialist peasantry, in rationalizing agricultural production, and in improving rural standards of living. Studies of collectivized communities report a pervasive acceptance of egalitarian principles of pay and labor control among the collectivized peasantry (Bell 1983, Hann 1979, Hollos 1983, Humphrey 1983, Salzmann and Scheuffler 1974, Swain 1985) and also suggest a number of direct and indirect societywide benefits of collectivization like the professionalization of agricultural labor, the expansion of education and rural services (Swain 1985, Ratner 1980), an improved though difficult status of women (Cernea 1975, 1978), and improved health via a reduced labor regime for collective farmers generally. Other features of the collectivized economy with strong support among East European rural populations included predictable salaries and urban amenities like roads, electrification, and continuing education.

The overly generalized Western critique of collectivization also ignores the diversity of social groups in East European communities and their diverse responses to collectivization and its postrevolutionary transformation. For all their difficulties, socialism and collectivization certainly contributed to diversification in the East European rural community. Through them separate strata of administrators, office workers, legal officials, technocrats, service workers, and agricultural extension agents were created in communities previously characterized by diversity mainly in terms of landed wealth and related household status. Thus, the experience of both collectivization and decollectivization, of political conflagration and transformation, must be filtered through these diverse group consciousnesses to arrive at any meaningful interpretation of East European change. Such diversity of response and its meaning for the postsocialist future is particularly visible in the Romanian Olt Land region of southern Transylvania in which I carried out fieldwork over the past two decades, the case to which I now turn.

THE ROMANIAN REVOLUTION, POSTREVOLUTIONARY POLITICS, AND THE ORIGINS OF DECOLLECTIVIZATION AND RECOLLECTIVIZATION

The Romanian revolution that toppled the hated Ceauşescus was an urban phenomenon. Though intimations of revolution were seen in sporadic outbreaks of worker unrest in the late 1970s and early 1980s, the overthrow of the government was accomplished by students, office workers, and even housewives, whose loss of life ultimately convinced the army to take their side and complete the removal of the Ceauşescu clique. Beginning in Timişoara in western Romania on December 15, 1989, the revolution quickly spread to Bucharest, Sibiu, Braşov, and Iaşi, with demonstrations in a host of lesser cities as well. By December 22 the Ceauşescus had fled and on Christmas Day they were executed in the ancient city of Tîrgovişte.[1]

As demonstrations and riot spread in the cities, there were only sporadic instances of violence and rebellion in village communities throughout the country, mainly where there had been particularly severe local leadership. In fact, I heard of no instances where collective farm or state-owned tractor station property was attacked, removed, or threatened in any way. When villagers did participate in the revolution it was largely as part of contingents of workers from the urban and suburban factories where they were employed. In other instances rural youth outside primary and secondary cities barricaded main roads to check the identity of passing motorists in order to detain fleeing security agents or party bigwigs. Other than participating in these activities, however, villagers clung to their TV sets and Voice of America and Radio Free Europe broadcasts to hear of the revolution's progress.

Postrevolutionary attitudes to collectivization at first were shaped by the intense euphoria and social unity that the toppling of the Ceauşescus promoted. Thus, in the immediate aftermath of the revolution the diversity of opinions regarding collectivization was obscured (and the Western critique of collectivization supported) by the postrevolutionary tendency to get rid of any and all things tainted by identification with socialism and the Ceauşescus. Action to dissolve the farms and distribute their assets was especially common. Throughout the country, simultaneous with the transfer of power to the provisional government and the dismissal of party cadres, farm headquarters were taken over by groups of rural citizens, and ad hoc village assemblies voted unanimously to dissolve the farms and make their resources available on an equal basis to all who wanted them. As would later come out, such meetings included both members and nonmembers of the farms as well as those who had and had not contributed private land resources when the farms were founded (cf. Pop 1990).

In a portent of things to come, the anticollective fervor was also a spin-off of the quest for power among those seeking political office in the vacuum of the postrevolutionary moment. For example, in Hîrseni commune of the Olt Land region, an assembly of delegates from the four villages that made up the local collective farm was held at the end of January in which a number of nonmember industrial workers from collective households also participated. At that meeting a majority of the participants voted to severely curtail the size of the collective by allowing households to claim as much land as they could work themselves. They also voted to dismiss the farm president, who doubled as Communist party secretary and who had been in office since 1979. According to some informants, opinion in favor of decollectivization was especially swayed by the local head of the provisional National Salvation Front (NSF) government, who had appointed himself to this position days after Ceauşescu's execution and who sought to retain his position by pandering to local demands.

The questionable political legitimacy of the National Salvation Front provisional government also contributed to postrevolutionary anticollectivism. Before the May 1990 election the NSF government attacked the farms, seemingly to curry rural favor. A law it enacted in late winter 1990 provided one-half hectare use plots to all collective farm members and to nonmembers who fulfilled minimal farm work requirements in 1989. In great contrast to Ceauşescuite policies where fifteen-are use plots (one are equals 1/100 of a hectare) were given farm members but often only in exchange for hay or other produce, these plots were given regardless of the size of a household's gardens or courtyard and without demand for other compensation. Though no formal land law was passed until February 1991, the provisional government also looked the other way as some farms were summarily dissolved, allowed other farms to nullify agricultural and animal produce contracts with the state, encouraged collectives to distribute their animal stock to private households, freed them to establish their own contractual relations with the formerly state-owned and -controlled tractor parks, and raised pensions for collective farm members.

This official anticollectivism in Romania was short-lived. As the NSF consolidated its power through spring 1990, its ultimate suspicion of privatization surfaced. Though sizable anticollectivist sentiment persisted in the villages, the NSF political platform called for neutrality regarding all forms of property; its huge electoral plurality, especially in the rural areas, further dissipated its support for private agriculture.[2] Further, the government's refusal to articulate a clear-cut agricultural and land tenure policy was a clear signal for many villagers to reinvigorate their support for collectivism, while other villagers were overcome with confusion about the farm and their role on it.

For example, in Hîrseni commune by early spring 1990, the anticollectivism of the postrevolutionary period was heatedly contested by a number of local householders who questioned the validity of the original vote to decollectivize. They said the vote was invalid since only farm members had the right to dissolve the farm, they demanded the farm be reconstituted, and they also reappointed the dismissed president. As a result of this meeting about half the households in two of the four villages (Sebeş and Mărgineni) elected to stay in the collective and half chose to privatize and reclaim some amount of land (from four to ten hectares). In one of the other commune villages (Copăcel) nearly all farm households went private, and the collective was disestablished. And in Hîrseni village itself, the administrative center of the commune, over 90 percent voted to stay in the collective.

As I see it, this diversity of responses grew from two factors. First was the uncertainty over the future of Romanian agriculture and questions about privatization itself. The NSF government, after all, had only taken half-measures regarding agriculture. Though it intimated widespread privatization was just around the corner[3] it hesitated to act on this. Even its more benign policy toward the use plots was equivocal. The plots were still considered collective farm property and could be diminished in size at any moment.[4] Given the absence of a clear agricultural policy and the lack of state investment in a private agricultural sector, Romanian rural villagers could only respond in this jumbled and uncertain manner.

More than agricultural uncertainty, however, was the very fact of village socioeconomic differentiation, which oriented individuals and households to different economic possibilities and promoted such a diversity of response. Such diversity, of course, is not harmful in and of itself. In more settled political economic conditions it would illustrate a healthy variability and inform democratic political processes. However, in the postrevolutionary Romanian political economic climate character-ized by persisting questions about the true nature of the revolution, the continued role of high Communist party functionaries in the NSF-led state, and the intractability of Romania's economic problems, such di-verse strategies easily provoked dissension, derision, and charges and countercharges of capitalist profiteering or Communist fellow-traveling.

Even passage of new land tenure legislation has not clarified villagers' choices about their economic futures. Certainly dissolution of the agri-cultural cooperatives and a vigorous private agriculture is allowed. The law, in fact, legalizes ownership of up to ten hectares of arable land per family[5] and also allows sale and purchase of land up to one hundred hectares per family, so long as that land is worked by those who own it. However, along with private agriculture, the law also allows (some would even say encourages) the creation of new agricultural associa-tions and the reestablishment of cooperative farms as common-stock associations. If such associations are established in place of the collective farms, they are given the right to take over the former farm buildings, orchards, agricultural inventories, and animal stock not distributed to former cooperative farm members. Given the range of possibilities for both private and cooperative agriculture to persist in Romania today, villagers are confronted with critical personal decision-making about their economic futures. It is thus partially the task of social science to lay bare that decision-making to see what it implies about the East European present and future.

STRATEGIES OF AGRICULTURAL UNCERTAINTY

What then explains the various approaches of rural citizens to collecti-vization or privatization? The adoption of any one particular agricultural strategy appears to depend on a range of factors particular to each rural household in relation to the general socioeconomic environment of the region where it is found. Elsewhere I have elaborated a more complex model of rural household economic strategy that takes into considera-tion household history, political connections, educational background, demographic structure and its possibilities, kindred size, and even serendipity to explain particular economic choice-making.[6] These factors can be simplified to five household agricultural strategies which varied from unabashed continued support of collectivized production to an intense desire to accumulate private land. Between these two polar strategies there were also an orientation to a limited private agriculture (i.e., taking only the half-hectare plot originally offered by the government), a mixed strategy of working both for the collective and on the household use plot, and a rejection of agriculture entirely.

Before the land law was passed, most of those electing to "go private" were households extensively involved in collective farm production before the revolution. As they had long depended on agriculture, many had accumulated sufficient tools, draft animals, and other resources through the years of collectivization to make private agriculture a reasonable option. Paradoxically, however, other households electing to go private in a large way by taking as much land as possible from the collective farm were from an elite, though nonagricultural, stratum with both the financial and demographic wherewithal, though not necessarily the agricultural acumen, to support extensive private agriculture. This group's response seems first to be related to the threat to their political standing that the antisocialist revolution represented. Furthermore, they wouldn't particularly profit by maintaining the collective farm, and they had few other economic skills on which to depend. For example, the president of an Olt Land commune, Consumers Cooperative, whose late father had been a past president of its collective farm but who had little or no agricultural experience himself, nonetheless decided to claim ten hectares of collective land even before the land law was passed. When I asked him how he planned to work the land, his response, "we'll find a way," suggested to me, perhaps wrongly, that he was counting on the use of his connections and large cash reserves to manipulate the demand that one work all private land oneself. Except for a few "intense privatizers," the greatest number of local households opted for a return to small-scale private agriculture and claimed from two to five hectares of land from the farms. Fed up with things socialist and the bureaucratic interference the farm represented, they preferred to depend on themselves and to combine moderate industrial incomes and land resources for their subsistence. Still, these households were limited because they faced a number of daunting issues that threatened their ability to successfully develop their newly private estates. First, of course, were the actual legal and financial implications of their decision. As the NSF-led government had yet to pass a privatization law, their very action was on shaky legal ground. In interviews conducted in April 1990, most of this group firmly believed that some kind of private agriculture would be allowed. To defend their interest in privatization, however, many of these households supported the Liberal party due to its clearer policy regarding privatization rather than supporting the NSF or even the Peasant party, which in some ways favored private agriculture too strongly. Privatizing households also questioned the cost of either repurchasing land or renting it from the state and, in the latter case, questioned how long leases would be operable.

Even more problematic than these legal and financial issues were those concerning access to necessary agricultural knowledge and technology, problems that didn't so much concern getting the land back as learning how to work it. Regarding the former, as discussed previously, agriculture had been treated so poorly in the Ceauşescu years that many had rejected it entirely. Even graduates from agricultural high schools attempted to avoid agricultural careers at any cost, so few young people in the Olt Land region had either the necessary knowledge to work in agriculture or a passion for it. Accessing adequate production technologies was (and is) an even greater problem, as most collectives refused to give up control over their draft animals; only those with privately owned horses and water buffalo, sufficient hay to keep them, the equipment like plows, harrows, and carts, would be able to make a go of private production. While another recent law enabled private ownership of tractors, these are also in very short supply and prohibitively expensive. In Sebeş village, Hîrseni commune, eleven households applied to purchase tractors from a regional tractor factory at a cost of about 120,000 lei, but most imagine the wait for them will be longer than two years.

In contrast to privatizing households (and to the Western critique of collectivization), as post-Ceauşescu revolutionary fervor declined, many households actually supported maintaining the collective farm and its landed base. The largest number of farm supporters derived from that group of households whose members occupied one or another mid-range salaried position on the farm in both production and administration (e.g., brigade and team leaders, quartermasters, accountants, agronomists). The overwhelming vote of citizens of Hîrseni village, the administrative center of Hîrseni commune, to keep the collective of course reflects the greater participation of this type of village in the farm bureaucracy. But not only bureaucrats voted for the farm. Many other households had concerns about the economic risks and additional labor associated with private farming. These people often had incomes that derived mainly from industry and lacked access to means of production for private agriculture, but nonetheless sought a steady and predictable quantity of agricultural resources for their household. In fact, some younger households more committed to industrial careers actually feared a return to private agriculture. For example, one couple in their early forties, both workers whose respective households had owned about twenty hectares of arable land before World War Two, spoke of their horror at a rumor that people were to be required to take back and work the amount of land that their parents had registered in the collective. They had no desire to work in agriculture at all, considered even the half-hectare to which they were entitled somewhat of a burden, and saw some sort of occasional collective production where they could make use of the resources of the larger organization as a more reasonable solution to their particular circumstances. Some few "collectivists" also believed in the social democratic legacy of the collective, though mainly as an afterthought to these larger political economic interests.[7]

Those who favored neither large-scale private agriculture nor continued collectivization but preferred to take their half-hectare or one-hectare plots (for two farm members) were often late middle-aged couples close to retirement or recently pensioned. To them private agriculture was not worth the effort and the collective would continue to make too many demands on their time and energy. They could easily satisfy their own subsistence needs and, supplemented by their pensions, spend their remaining years as independent smallholders.

Thus, the diversity of village strategies toward private agriculture, decollectivization, and recollectivization appears more related to household history, demography, occupation, and past economic practice than to any overwhelming desire to overturn socialism. Nonetheless, because the land was the main issue over which rural political debate was centered, attitudes to land tenure also forced people to take stands on sensitive political questions and exposed them to land-based conflict.

DECOLLECTIVIZATION AND LOCAL LIFE

Much as collectivization set loose an intense political struggle for power and advantage in the 1960s, decollectivization performs the same role in post-Ceauşescu Romania. Though the issue of property rights has been somewhat clarified by the new land law, actually putting the law into effect and organizing a productive private agriculture while preserving and encouraging a strong cooperative sector has created a host of problems and contradictions, not only for Romania but throughout Eastern Europe (cf. Szelenyi and Szelenyi 1991).

As much as at the national level, the struggle over decollectivization informs local community life. Despite the new land law, serious rifts have developed between those who favored the farm and now favor the formation of agricultural associations, and those who favored complete privatization. Though these diverse economic strategies are not necessarily incompatible, the political and economic uncertainties and problems of post-Ceauşescu Romania make conflict between decollectivizers and recollectivizers over access to agricultural means of production somewhat inevitable. In Olt Land villages, for example, the great variability in soils from one locale and one field to the next have already provoked legal battles between the diminished collectives and newly privatized households over the land returned to the latter. Similarly, until privatized households are provided with sufficient traction power and/or draft animals, there will continue to be trouble over their access and the cost of these services as well (cf. Camasoiu and Sasu 1991). In Hîrseni commune questions over land rights have generated a number of legal claims and petitions to state authorities by newly private farmers and have spilled over into community social discourse as well. Gossip about those who favored maintaining the collective was particularly vicious. According to many informants, such people hoped to protect the farm's integrity only to save their own sinecures and predictable monthly salaries without having to be too involved in actual agricultural production. Collectivists were also criticized in the same antibureaucratic terms as farm administrators were in the Ceauşescu years when people characterized collective farm labor as "seven with briefcases and one with a hoe" (şapte cu mapă şi unu cu sapă). Echoing the rejection of bureaucratism, one informant laughingly said that "those with the long nails should come and use them to harvest our potatoes." Pejorative remarks about the few favoring an unbridled private agriculture were also common and focused on their desire to exploit others. Though some of these statements were said with humor, they nonetheless betrayed a continued disorganization in local life and an inability and unwillingness to recognize and allow for differences in working for common social goals, a definite legacy of the vicious competitiveness of the last decade of the Ceauşescu epoch.

Of course, the most significant result of this conflict is its continued, though unintended, support for a large state presence in rural community life. The struggle over resources has demanded that the state remain the ultimate arbiter of community relationships and the ultimate source of potential well-being for those sorely in need of basic agricultural resources. Recollectivizers defer to state power as the chief prop of their treasured institution while privatizers look to the state to assist them in their quest for reasonable land and means of production. If by civil society we mean "people's organizing themselves outside the structures of the party-state, in multifarious independent social groupings" (Ash 1986), then the post-Ceauşescu local community is decidedly lacking in this quality and fearful of its development.

In an earlier version of this chapter I spoke of some causes for optimism about the future of Romanian village life and agriculture. In the midst of the recriminations about land policy, there appeared the possibility for a real cooperativism to grow from community efforts independent of national institutions. In most instances these efforts developed out of necessity, as was the case of the related households who contracted to purchase tractors together or that of households on the same street who pastured their sheep and cattle together. This developing cooperativism was incredibly frail, however, and though one possible answer for Romanian agriculture, as well as a potential harbinger of civil society in the Romanian community, it is now tainted red by its collectivist implications. Furthermore, the large-scale privatization underway in a society wracked by suspicion and material shortages has created even more difficult problems of production and helps reproduce the suspicions and recriminations of the Ceauşescu years.

Thus, since the revolution, the situation in Romania has gone from bad to worse with a proportionate decline in an already tense social and political discourse. A recent letter from a friend suggests the difficulties faced by all:

> Here in the villages the biggest problem now is the land. The collective farm has been dissolved, but nothing has replaced it. Some people can no longer work the land because they are old or sick and we don't know how they will survive. Uncultivated land will destroy both the country and the village. It is also very difficult for those who are young and healthy because they must work only with horses and primitive agricultural tools. How can we begin to grow enough for the market? We can't? And then what?

Good question!

Notes

The present version of this paper has benefited by commentary from participants at the conference Anthropology and Politics in Post-Communist Europe, held in Zaborow, Poland, September 30 to October 4, 1990. Special thanks to Steve Sampson, Katherine Verdery, and Mieke Meurs for their comments and especially to Sam Beck for his extensive comments and suggestions.

1. For the best written accounts of the events of the Romanian revolution and its immediate aftermath see Cullen 1990 and Macpherson 1990.
2. In the Făgăraş region, including both villages and towns, the NSF received about 78 percent of the vote. This percentage was higher if the villages alone are taken into consideration.
3. One recent joke commented on the failure of the government to be fully forthcoming regarding agricultural privatization: "Now they are giving land to

the peasant . . . and if the peasant isn't home they leave it at his doorstep."

4. Some observers consider NSF's waffling on agriculture to be purposeful and designed to keep the rural population off-balance, uncertain, and hence politically disorganized and ineffective.

5. Family is understood as a nuclear family comprised of spouses and unmarried children who reside with them. Multigenerational peasant stem family households could thus qualify for double or even triple the amount of land.

6. This work, forthcoming from Cornell University Press, will be titled *The solitude of collectivism: Romanian villagers to the revolution and beyond.*

7. Katherine Verdery suggests that support for the collective might be due to limited available land in any particular community. In Hîrseni commune, however, this wasn't the case. For example, Copăcel village households unanimously opted for private agriculture. Yet this village has the smallest amount of arable land relative to the number of households in the commune. It does, however, have extensive pastureland and, perhaps most important, a long tradition of opposition to the farm and the socialist state.

References

Ash, T. 1986. "Does central Europe exist." *New York Review of Books* (October 9):45–52.

Bell, P. 1983. *Peasants in socialist transition: Life in a collectivized Hungarian village.* Berkeley: University of California Press.

Camasoiu, I., and Sasu, E. 1991. "Statul nea compărat griul cu 1,90 lei kg. şi ne vinde tăriţă cu 2, 50 lei kg." *România Liberga* (January 17):3a.

Cernea, M. 1975. "The large-scale formal organization and the family primary group." *Journal of Marriage and the Family* 37(4): 927–936.

———. 1978. "Macrosocial change, feminization of agriculture, and peasant women's threefold economic role." *Sociologia Ruralis* 18(2–3):107–124.

Cullen, R. 1990. "Report from Romania." *The New Yorker* (April 2):94–112.

Hann, C. 1979. *Tazlar: A village in Hungary.* London: Cambridge University Press.

Hollos, M. 1983. "Ideology and economics: Cooperative organization and attitudes toward collectivization in two Hungarian communities." In *New Hungarian peasants: An east central European experience with collectivization,* eds. M. Hollos and B. Maday, pp. 93–122. East European monographs, No. 134, New York: Columbia University Press.

Humphrey, C. 1983. *Karl Marx collective: Economy, society, and religion in a Siberian collective farm.* Cambridge: Cambridge University Press.

Macpherson, W. 1990. "In Romania." *Granta* 33 (summer):9–58.

Mitrany, D. 1951. *Marx against the peasant: A study in social dogmatism.* Chapel Hill: University of North Carolina Press.

Pop, I. 1990. "Împărtireă pămîntului—dereaptă, după, lege!" *Adevărul* 1(40 February 10):1–2.

Ratner, M. 1980. "Educational and occupational selection in contemporary Romania: A social anthropological account." Ph.D. dissertation, anthropology, American University (Ann Arbor, university microfilms).

Salzman, Z., and Scheuffler, V. 1974. *Komarov: A Czech farming village.* New York: Holt, Rinehart, and Winston.

Sampson, S. 1984. "Rich families and poor collectives." *Bidrag til Oststatsforskning* (Nordic Journal of Soviet and East European Studies) 10(2).

Swain, N. 1985. *Collective farms which work?* London: Cambridge University Press.

Szelnyi, I., and Szelenyi, B. 1991. "The social impact of agrarian reform: Social and political conflicts in the post-communist transformation of Hungarian agriculture." *Anthropology of East Europe Review* 10(1):12–24.

Civil Society in Siberia: The Institutional Legacy of the Soviet State

DAVID G. ANDERSON

In an attempt to categorize the rapid changes in Eastern Europe and the former Soviet Union, many scholars have been drawn to the concept of civil society. This concept, long familiar to classical political theorists in the West, seems to evocatively capture the demands of contemporary Russian activists for civil rights and the rule of law. However, while the term is empowered by its historical connotations, it is also compromised by its past.[1] It is often tempting to read the changes in the former Soviet Union as a mere recapitulation of the struggles fought in the West centuries ago. While many political analyses of Eastern Europe and Russia concern themselves with identifying the *genesis* of civil society, in this chapter I will take the opposite tack of trying to locate unique civil institutions that are the legacy of Soviet state socialism and that are *still* defended by contemporary activists.

It is undeniable that central planning and collectivized property gave the Soviet state a large scope for oppression of tragic dimensions. Yet one cannot help but wonder what specific experiences under seventy years of state socialism inspire the architects of a "new" civil society. Notwithstanding all claims to the contrary, reformers in the former USSR cannot inscribe new institutions on a clean slate but must design their reforms upon the base of heavily centralized state political and economic institutions. Through the analysis of the proposals for political and economic reform from a nation of hunters and herders far from the center of Soviet hegemony, I will demonstrate that a sufficient account of social movements in the former USSR must take into consideration the legacy of the Soviet state.

The case examined here is that of the Evenki of southeastern Siberia. The analysis of Evenk civil society on the same theoretical terrain as other European societies is particularly illuminating. By approaching questions of institutional reform through the critical eyes of Evenk activists, we can cast the history of Soviet state-building in a new light. Since Evenk experiences with the discourse of rights and institutional forms were restricted to their collective experience with the Soviet state, their reasoning about rights and institutions focused upon nuances within the turbulent history of institutional change in the Soviet period. Political lobbying for the respect of codified and uncodified rights, as well as critical evaluations of various collective farm institutions, can be read as historical sociological analyses of institutional life within the former Soviet Union generally.

This chapter will commence with a brief introduction to the concept of civil society as it is applied in European contexts in the Marxist litera-ture. The balance of the chapter will be an analysis of the elements of civil society that were *already* existing as of 1989 among the Evenki based on my meetings with Evenk political activists. The contours of Evenk civil society will be negatively illustrated by enumerating some of the rights and institutions the Evenki felt they had lost due to relatively recent centralizations of power in the Soviet state. Finally, through an examination of Evenk proposals for reform, the positive legacy of Soviet state socialism will be outlined.

ON "MODERN" CIVIL SOCIETIES AND THEIR COLONIZATION

In the Marxist tradition, the rediscovery of civil society is credited to Gramsci. Writing during the apogee of Fascism in Italy and as Stalin sharpened the powers of the Bolshevik state, Gramsci was preoccupied with the politics of constraining the modern state. In order to prescribe a political strategy that avoided state idolatry or fatalistic economism, Gramsci defended the positive aspects of civic associations and institu-tions. Thus in his military metaphor, the state is only an "outer ditch" supported by the "powerful system of fortresses and earthworks" of civil society (Gramsci 1971, 238). In his view, people are not spurred into action by sagacious state managers or by the faceless logic of economic necessity but instead act upon their *interpretations* of what is necessary. The key factor that triggers the resolve to act are the ideologies that are freely formed in independent association. The burden of analysis for Gramsci thus falls upon a civil society that is distinct from economic and political spheres of social action. According to Bobbio (1988, 84), Gram-sci's notion of civil society is distinct from that of Hegel or Marx since it "includes not only the sphere of economic relations but also their spon-taneous or voluntary forms of organization."

While the Gramscian framework indicates that the organizational logic of civil society is distinct from the laws of motion of commodity markets and state bureaucracies, it sheds little light on the origin of these three spheres. A theoretical understanding of the development of civil societies is crucial when trying to understand systems in transition—

such as the USSR. In *Prison Notebooks*, Gramsci indicates that strong civil societies arise out of the histories in particular nations. For example, "In Russia, the State was everything, civil society was primordial and gelatinous; in the West, there was a proper relation between state and civil society, and when the State trembled a sturdy structure of civil society was at once revealed" (Gramsci 1971, 238). Gramsci was by far not the first to calibrate the "proper" relationship between state and civil society on the example of the West. From the admonishments of the Russian Westernizers to the numerous pathologies of "oriental despotism," there is a long tradition that has established the political "distinctiveness" (or often "backwardness") of the East.[2] Contemporary accounts seem to concur with this assessment.[3] However, in this time of transition, it is not sufficient to locate weaknesses within the political traditions of a society, but it is important to identify strategies for building constructively on existing traditions to establish a liberating alternative. In order to add a critical edge to the analysis of national political traditions, it is necessary to supplement Gramsci's analysis.

One interesting theoretical contribution to the analysis of civil society in the East had been made by Andrew Arato and Jean Cohen (Arato and Cohen 1988; Cohen and Arato 1989; Arato 1989). To fill in the contours of the Gramscian definition of civil society, they rely upon an adaptation of Jürgen Habermas's (1987) blending of "system" and "lifeworld." They argue that civil society can be defined as a set of *institutions* existing within a *modernized lifeworld* that are in turn protected from the destructive influence of the political power and commodity markets by *sets of rights*. Their use of Habermas gives their theory two strengths. First, by equating civil society with a lifeworld, they are able to recall a rich literature that analyzes the full symbolic and integrative dimensions of a sphere of popular associations. Second, by counterpoising a modernized lifeworld to other systemic dynamics within society they can give an account of what processes derail the development of a "healthy" civil society. Each aspect will be briefly outlined in turn.

Habermas's definition of the lifeworld has its roots in Alfred Shutz and Thomas Luckmann's (1973) phenomenology. In broad strokes, "lifeworld" refers to a set of symbols and understandings by which groups integrate themselves socially. It specifically identifies the normative content of values and institutions that are crucial in order to gauge pathological forms of social integration as well to understand political resistance. As Habermas (1987, 139) writes, "The life world is . . . not measured against criticizable validity claims or standards of rationality, but against standards for the solidarity of members and for the identity of socialized individuals." Arato and Cohen's (1988, 44) definition of civil society focuses on that aspect of the lifeworld that is no longer intuitive and "sacred" but is formally codified in institutions that can bear the brunt of "questioning and discursive adjudication."

Arato and Cohen also adopt Habermas's view of the evolution of societies. Habermas distinguishes societies by the degree to which the lifeworld becomes rationalized through the development of formal subsystems that govern political and economic affairs. In tribal societies all political and economic matters are "coextensive" with the lifeworld. Political and economic decisions are reached through patterns of symbols and communication that are unique to each particular society (Habermas 1987, 164–165). Modern societies are distinguished by political and economic spheres that are no longer guided by "communicative action" but are "steered" by "delinguistified" media that are independent of the patterns of integration existing in each particular lifeworld. Two media are specifically identified: the medium of power that governs administrations, and the medium of money that steers the market.

Habermas does not give a rosy account of the gradual decoupling of systems and lifeworld as societies become more complex. The process of modernization is open to the threat of damaging distortions. Modernization can produce the "irresistible irony" that as societies become more complex, efficient, and rationalized, they erode the logic of the lifeworld to the extent of "bursting" it (Habermas 1987, 155, 186). This process is labeled "colonization." According to Cohen and Arato (1989, 498), colonization of civil society occurs whenever the institutions of an incompletely modernized lifeworld are overwhelmed by the imperatives of money and/or power to the extent that indigenous imperatives are suffocated.

Arato and Cohen's adaptation of Habermas supplements Gramsci's schematic framework in a manner that is particularly useful for conceptualizing social change in complicated social formations such as the Soviet Union. By carefully distinguishing the logics of social and system integration from substantive institutions, they develop a framework that can be equally critical of state socialism as monopoly capitalism. Through the emphasis of the ambivalent nature of institutions, one is able to identify pathological forms of social organization while simultaneously searching for positive forms that protect the sources of social integration.

The expanded definition of civil society that Arato and Cohen achieve through dialogue with Habermas also makes it possible to examine the development of civil society empirically. Arato and Cohen argue that a "modern" civil society is indicated by certain institutional and legal guarantees that protect autonomous civil associations from colonization by the state or by the market.

> Every society develops institutions which assure the transmission of culture, integration and socialization. *Civil* societies, whatever their form, presuppose a juridical structure, a constitution, that articulates the principles underlying their internal organization. Within the context of a *modernized* lifeworld . . . civil society exists *only* where there is a juridical guarantee of the reproduction of the various spheres in the form of *sets of rights*. (Arato and Cohen 1988, 42)

The indicators of a modern civil society are thus:

1. A range of public institutions that function independently from the demands of the market or the state
2. The presence of legal guarantees that carefully and rationally circumscribe the activities of the market or state
3. The presence of vibrant social movements that coordinate civil institutions through communicative action (rather than the steering imperatives of money or power)

By means of these criteria, Cohen and Arato (1989, 502) argue that social movements in the USSR represented civil society only "in formation" since they lacked independent bases for mobilization. This conclusion recalls the analyses of many Western scholars that the foundations for a healthy civil society have not been laid in the East. To challenge this axiom, the empirical case of Siberian social movements will be presented to provide evidence that some institutions of (even) Soviet socialism have provided a basis for social reproduction. The complaint of Siberian activists is that the postrevolutionary institutions that they had once recognized as their own have been colonized by more recent centralizations of power. Moreover, they fear that recent market liberalizations will in turn colonize their institutions even further.

AN EVENK CIVIL SOCIETY

By the end of the 1930s, the traditional society of the Zabaikal'skie Evenki had been radically transformed by the actions of the Soviet state.[4] Although this group of seminomadic hunters and herders has engaged in trade with its neighbors since the seventh century, the Soviet administration distinguished itself in its considerable investment of resources for "developing" this previously "backward" people (Anderson 1991). Following the conclusion of the Russian civil war, various waves of activists came to the Evenki to transform their indigenous institutions. Under the auspices of the Committee of the North (Komitet Severa), young activists came into the district with literacy brigades to conduct classes in the summer months. Some of the brightest Evenk children were sent on to continue their education in boarding schools or even to the prestigious Institute of Native Peoples in Leningrad.

Indigenous economic institutions were transformed at an equally rapid pace. Family-controlled reindeer herds were formally collectivized into artels (*arteli*) and later into collective farms (*kolkhozi*). Although collectivization was *formally* complete by the late 1930s, elders maintain that the Evenki retained a large degree of control over their lives in the collective farms until the late 1960s and 1970s. In these more recent decades, two major changes rocked Evenk society. Locally controlled collective farms were sublimated into one of two types of centrally directed farms: state farms (*sovkhozi*) or state economic enterprises (*gos-promkhozi*). Furthermore, the construction of a massive railway line with its associated workers' settlements, hydroelectric dams, and mines has led to a complete restructuring of the traditional economy.

The variety of the socioeconomic impacts on Evenk society and the intense pace of change make this area an interesting case. As Habermas himself notes in a Western context, it is possible to test the thesis of internal colonization sociologically "wherever the traditionalist padding of capitalist [sic] modernization has worn through and central areas of cultural reproduction, social integration, and socialization have been openly drawn into the vortex of economic growth" (Habermas 1987, 367–368). As Soviet planners themselves admitted, the "explosive" impact of *socialist* economic development on these people has had profoundly negative effects (Boiko 1979, 5).

In what manner can the contemporary struggles of Siberian activists in Zabaikal'e be understood as the activities of a *civil* society? According to Cohen and Arato (1989, 502), Siberian social movements would likely be disqualified as civil societies on two counts. First, it could be argued that the Evenki do not have *institutions* independent of the state (and the steering medium of power) that are in turn protected by a solid "set of rights" (Arato and Cohen 1989, 42). Second, since intellectuals drawn from the ranks of hunters and herders are the active participants in Evenk political associations, one could argue that Evenk social imperatives are not "modernized" but seek to fight a rearguard battle against economic modernization.

The results of fieldwork in Siberia reveal that aboriginal activists had distinctively modern attitudes toward their struggle. Although codified sets of rights protecting Evenk civil society did not exist in Soviet jurisprudence, the Evenk activists designed their political program around the defense of a small number of "rights" that were provided administratively through various government departments.[5] Further, they most emphatically recommended institutional reform to secure their projects. These two elements illustrate that Siberian activists did not wish "to turn the clock back" through the reinstatement of an autarchic community of nomads. Instead they sought reform through the contemporary political and legal structure and especially within the current semi-industrial occupational structure. While it might be debatable that Evenk society achieved a greater or lesser *degree* of "modernity," the fact that activists rallied behind specific rights and institutional reforms distances them from the ideal type of a "premodern" society.

The field data will be organized in three parts. An overview of the national Siberian aboriginal rights movement will be presented at the outset with emphasis given to how it constitutes itself within the language of rights and institutions. By commencing with Siberian social movements writ large, we can show the general nature of the many complaints brought forth by local activists. Next, two distinctive sets of rights will be documented: rights to education and rights to an appropriate occupation. Both of these themes illustrate quite well the dialectical interrelation of Evenk civil society with the Soviet state. Through the words of Evenk activists, it will be shown how local Evenk educational and economic institutions came to be colonized by the state. The proposals for reform hark back to the memory of previously existing *uncolonized* civil institutions that constitute the legacy of Soviet modernization. While the negative side of Soviet modernization will be portrayed through the experience of the Evenki with education and formalized employment, the positive side will be illustrated through Evenk proposals for institutional reform.

SIBERIAN SOCIAL MOVEMENTS AND THE CONCEPT OF RIGHTS

The rhetoric of Evenk activists reflects the recent renaissance of political activity by native peoples across Siberia. Siberian native peoples have a long history of resisting the various injustices of both Tsarist and Soviet bureaucracies. This resistance has usually been coordinated either informally at the village level or equally sporadically on the national level by a growing aboriginal intelligentsia. It has only been in the mid-1980s that these disparate groups began to consolidate themselves into a united political movement. Indeed, the year 1989 seems to have been a watershed in the development of unionwide Siberian political movements. In early 1989 Vladimir Sangi formed an umbrella organization in Moscow known as the Association of Native Peoples to raise funds and to coordinate the activities of the various regional groups. The summer of 1989 also saw native delegates from all over the former Soviet Union gather in Yakutsk for the first All-Union Festival of Native Youth.

The Siberian aboriginal rights movement illustrates two differing approaches to the problem of rights: one that focuses on existing codified laws and one that affirms the legitimacy of uncodified practices. In general, these approaches distinguish the national movement from local movements. The national movements produced formal documents that were steeped in the language of Soviet jurisprudence. Local hunters and herders, by contrast, tended to ground their political demands within lengthy reflections on their own concrete experiences.

The first approach looks beyond the administrative apparatus of the Soviet state toward a legal system that respects the rule of law. There are two good examples of this in the documents of the national aboriginal rights movement. On the one hand, the legitimacy of the Soviet state was questioned by appealing to the more universal legitimacy of the United Nations and international law. Of the two forums, the Association of Native Peoples had the most international orientation. Their declaration directly focused upon the protection of statutes of the United Nations (Association 1990, 46, 56). This position underscored the unique constitutional position of aboriginal people as nations existing within large states. On the other hand, the Soviet state was chided for not respecting its own laws. The documents from the Festival of Native Youth were particularly eloquent in calling for the codified, constitutional protection of linguistic and educational rights within current autonomous *okrugi* (districts).[6] In a section on environmental law, the festival indirectly addressed the question of the rule of law:

> [We call for] the suspension of the blatant (*frontal'noe*) industrial exploitation of the North under the complete dominating economic and bureaucratic (*vedomstvennye*) interests of Soviet Ministries and Departments. In our country there should be no "conquerors (pokoriteli) of the North." [We propose to] call the attention of the Supreme Soviet to the pressing (*napriazhennoe*) condition of the environment of the Siberian districts, . . . and to the extremely unsatisfactory fulfillment or [even] disregard for the [environmental] law of the U.S.S.R. by Soviet Ministries and Departments. (Seminar "Molodezh' i Sever" 1989, 2)

This tact illustrated a respect for law by faulting both the economic state apparatus for breaking the legal code and the political state apparatus for not enforcing its own statutes. In both examples, the national aboriginal rights movement stripped legitimacy from existing bureaucratic practices by pointing to rights existing within a body of codified law.

The second approach toward the articulation of discrete "sets of rights" searches the past for experiences with Soviet institutions that provided workable models of self-government. Unlike the highly analytical documents of the national organizations, the proposals of local hunters for change are wrapped within extremely perceptive critiques of the processes of socioeconomic change as instigated by governing institutions. In Zabaikal'e most informants singled out the transition of 1969–1973 from locally administered collective farms (*kolkhozi*) to centrally administered state enterprises (*sovkhozi* and *gospromkhozi*) as a key regressive change. Informants universally tied this administrative shift to a loss of opportunities for employment and education. While this observation is a comparison of existing conditions to a past that may be imperfectly remembered, the comparison itself underscores a normative message that informs contemporary movements. Evenk activists stressed that the Soviet state had a moral duty to support the economic and social development of native peoples by maintaining or increasing state subsidies for education or for traditional occupations. The weight of this critique lies in its appeals to the momentum of past *uncodified* practices. Attempts by the state managers to trim their budgets is seen as a betrayal of a tacit social contract,[7] or worse, as a predatory failure to return to local citizens value that is earned by selling natural resources for foreign currency.

The strategy of affirming modern rights guaranteed within preexisting practices in Zabaikal'e can be best illustrated by two "sets" of rights: (1) rights to education and (2) rights to an appropriate occupation.[8] I will first demonstrate why these rights can be thought of as "modern" and second, give some examples of how these rights both modernized and colonized the traditional Evenk lifeworld.

RIGHTS TO EDUCATION

The heart of the Siberian civil society is the small but active strata of aboriginal intelligentsia in Siberian communities. The existence of this strata is almost entirely credited to the impact of state-sponsored education. One of the first mandates of the postrevolutionary "Committee of the North" was the formation of a pool of cadres who would "educate the aboriginal population in the Soviet community spirit and socialist culture" (Dolgikh 1967, quoted in Kuoljok 1985, 63). By 1927, twelve state boarding schools and forty locally administered schools existed across the North (Komitet Severa 1927, 79). In Leningrad, a special academy was established for pedagogical training that hosted 1,303 aboriginal students by 1933 (Kuoljok 1985, 63). The cumulative effect of education on shaping an intelligentsia is seen in the biographies of

Siberian activists today (Bartels and Bartels 1984). All the present-day Evenk activists of the various political associations in Zabaikal'e were professionals with a higher education. Many were educated in the prestigious Institute for Native Peoples in Leningrad. The uniqueness of the Soviet state's educational legacy cannot be overemphasized. In other circumpolar countries, including Canada and the United States, there is not as high a proportion of native peoples attaining a higher education.

The effects of education in forming a modernized lifeworld were both negative and positive. In the early days of collectivization, the boarding schools isolated children from their nomadic families, simultaneously disrupting socialization within the family and the transmission of traditional skills. As one Evenk elder noted:

> When they brought me to Tungokochen from Yumurchen I didn't speak a single Russian word. I had long hair and Evenki boots. They just brought me directly [from the taiga]. I had never seen a village or never had been in a house. It was very strange for me to live a life where you couldn't hear the sound that the bells make on the deer. I missed the smell of smoke in the yurt. This was native and close to me. . . . I was about 10 then. That would be about 1931. This was the mistake. They alienated (*otarvali*) us [from the land] and then they suggested (*vnushat'*) that our [old] life was dirty. . . . At the beginning I couldn't sleep. I would sleep on the floor. But after a while I got used to it and I thought "how could I ever have lived like that." I had the impression that life on the taiga was dark, without any hope. The new generation is completely alienated from what [we] had earlier longed for. It is for this reason that our deer herders are [now] becoming fewer in number. From childhood they are alienated from the language and the culture. In my opinion, when I came back from [the Institute of Native Peoples in] Leningrad I should have been sent back to the deer pasture to teach them. They shouldn't have kept me among the Russians. I should have been helping form a new culture—a nomadic culture. It was the alienation of children from their parents that was the mistake. (Tape B, side A)

Despite the considerable extent to which education penetrated the traditional lifeworld of the Evenki, our informants displayed a universal respect for it. Formal education was seen as having an important role to play in forming "a new culture." They did not call for an end to the classroom but for the creation of more schools. The key difference is that they wish to have schools established on their own terms; that is, in a manner that does not colonize traditional imperatives.

In Tungokochenskii district of Zabaikal'e there were small primary schools in each Evenk settlement and a large boarding school (*internat*)

in the former district capital, Tungokochen. The boarding school recently hired an instructor to teach the Evenk language for three hours per
week. The Tungokochen initiative group wished to expand education to
provide a base for cultural reproduction but also to ensure that Evenk
children find work in the highly professionalized collective farm occupational structure:

> In the last few years not one Evenk [male] child has finished an eighth
> grade education. In the last few years even the army will not accept
> them insofar as the army requires an eighth grade education [this
> cuts them off from the most easily available trade education]. . . .
> Although the Tungokochen boarding school (*internat*) pretends to
> provide full state services (*obespechenie*)—this is not true. There are in
> fact only meals there. The children wear their own clothes. Before
> parents send their children to the school they must dress them from
> head to foot. Meanwhile the supervisor of the warehouse sells off
> printed scarfs and housecoats to whoever bring her fish from home.
> [This has gone on so long] that it has already become an institution
> (*voshlo v sistemu*)! (Petition 2)

This quotation underscores the key elements of the informal social
contract that the initiative group was defending. Public education was
expected to provide free of charge both a solid occupational training and
a certain standard of living for native children including transportation,
room and board, and clothing.

The Evenk initiative group in Tungokochen faulted the centrally developed school curriculum for the lack of interest in education by Evenk
students. It pointed out the irony that Evenk students were forced to
drop out of school for the failure to pass courses in the English language
when their own language was given so little emphasis (Petition 2). The
problem with teaching the Evenk language was compounded by the fact
that the textbooks that did exist were printed in the dialect of the Evenk
language spoken in the Evenk Autonomous District [*okrug*]. There has
been an attempt to rectify the shortage of written material by printing a
page of the district newspaper in the Evenk language. The first issue of
this paper, entitled *Sovetskii Sever*, with the Evenk section came out on
July 22, 1989. The direct interest that local pedagogues have in reforming
the curriculum and in using new media for language education illustrates their interest in using modern techniques of social integration to
strengthen their lifeworld.

In Kalarskii district in 1989 there was one school in the village of
Chapo Ologo where the Evenk language has been taught from the first
to third grades for the past ten years. The initiative group there hoped to
capitalize upon overtures by the state-owned railway construction cor-

poration to build another two new primary schools in Kiust'-Kemda in 1991. There is a plan to extend Evenk language classes in Chapo Ologo to the eighth grade by 1995 (Tape 2, Side A). In a fashion similar to the activists in Tungokochenskii district, the Kalarskie Evenki stressed the importance of establishing schools that meet local needs:

> We have all sorts of opportunities to study at the Institute of Native Peoples in Leningrad, at the Krasnoiarsk Pedagogical Institute, at our own forestry institute or the institute of culture or that of trade, but the fact remains that there is not one Evenk student that has finished the eighth grade. . . . The general problem is a low level of social development. . . . The social milieu is poor. The students start with a handicap. Then they can't succeed because the curriculum is not suited to them. They sit through the fourth grade for a couple of years and all this time they are growing taller. Then they say "what am I doing here with these children?! It's better for me to drop out." It would have been better to put him out along with the deer herders. We want to start a training workshop out with the deer brigades. Students will spend two whole days with deer and then will return to the village for an academic education. That way by the time they finish they will have a solid primary education and qualifications to work as deer herders. (Tape 2, side A)

The Evenki of this district stressed also the need for programs that take into account the social conditions of families and the future employment goals of the students.

In the previous quotation, the speaker stresses the colonizing effects of formal education by pointing out that employment in traditional occupations is precluded by participation in the education system. The speaker subtly underscores this problem by pointing to the irony that a variety of educational opportunities exist for the Evenki at special institutions but that they are in practice unavailable to local students due to the barriers posed in local schools. The proposals of the Kalarskie Evenki went further than those of Tungokochenskii district by advocating the extension of formal education into training for positions as traditional herders. Perhaps due to the Kalarskii district's longer experience with education and the corresponding greater number of intelligentsia, we found a stress on combining formal education with the social reproduction of traditional occupations.[9]

In both examples from Tungokochenskii and Kalarskii districts, there is a consciousness of the negative and positive impacts of formal education. The negative examples emphasize the destructive impact that boarding schools and centrally formulated curricula had on local processes of social integration. The positive statements present concrete proposals for how formal education might play a vibrant role in strengthening the local community. In this latter instance, an education in state-sponsored schools without tuition and with the provision of room, board, and a clothing allowance was defended as an implicit right.[10]

RIGHTS TO AN APPROPRIATE OCCUPATION

One of the most pernicious problems confronted by Evenk activists was the problem of unemployment. By Western standards, the absolute unemployment rates in Soviet times were almost insignificant. In each village that we visited there were between five and ten Evenk adults who could not find any work (approximately 1 percent of the Evenk population). However, this issue became framed within a central tenet of the Soviet social contract that full employment was guaranteed (Kagarlitsky 1989, 211–212). Thus, the presence of *any* level of unemployment became a sign of bad faith on the part of state managers. The problem of unemployment became amplified when it was coupled to the problem of Evenk adults being *excluded* from work in their specialty. According to the activists, adults with both traditional skills and those with higher occupational training often were unable to find work in their home villages while nonnatives from other areas of the Soviet Union were imported to fill in these places. The tragedy of this situation was double-edged. Not only were some families denied a livelihood, but the hiring practices of centrally administered state farms made a higher education appear superfluous while simultaneously undermining the reproduction of traditional skills. Evenk activists drew attention to the need for an employment structure that was meaningful for the reproduction of Evenk civil society.

It was difficult to establish the exact parameters of the problem of "functional unemployment."[11] Most of our informants could give us information at the level of their own villages, while district party officials were not willing to discuss the problem.[12] However, the importance of this issue is unequivocally captured by this statement at a Tungokochen public meeting:

> We have heard [the excuse from the district first secretary] that few Evenki finish the tenth grade [and thus very few are employable]. The following should be considered.
>   Look at Sergei A. He finished the tenth grade two years ago. And such he remained. He is not a hunter. This is how we use cadres! We train cadres and they become unemployed!
>   Tamorov K. finished veterinary college. They found no work for him. Now he works in Bauntovskii district [Buriatskaia Autonomous Republic] with the cattle herders.

Viktor K. also returned from the army. A hunter. One must find work for him. Again! A work place could not be found. And so what? [He hears,] "All the places are full, you won't become a hunter because all the trapping sections are occupied. . . . The Evenki can't hunt."

Its just bureaucratic attitudes that have initiated these horrors. Already things have degraded to the point that we are not far from a situation like that in Armenia.

There's a difficult situation in [the village of] Zelenoe Ozero on this count. There *are* deer herders. A [Party] commission found that people want to work. The commission even decided to establish a second [reindeer] herd. Therefore it's important that we PAY MORE ATTENTION to what is going on locally, unlike what those who sit at their desks have done. [Otherwise] deer herders will no longer exist. . . . Before speaking you have to know the conditions. You have to be at Zelenoe Ozero to speak with deer herders. You have to be in Tungokochen to speak with people. This is all for now. (Notebook 1, 88)

There are two issues entwined in the previous quotation. The first is a criticism that the expectation that work be "found" for "educated cadres" is not fulfilled due to the "bureaucratic attitudes" of those who "sit at their desks." The second is that those who were *not* considered cadres, that is, hunters or herders, were prevented from exercising their skills either because the state manager did not know that they exist or because "work places" were "occupied" by proper cadres. A tragic portrait is rendered wherein those who invested in the state system were spurned while those that remained exclusively anchored within their lifeworld were brushed aside. The results of such a policy, according to this lifelong Evenk party activist, can be a loss of legitimacy like "that in Armenia" or the complete disintegration of the Evenk lifeworld—"the deer herders will no longer exist."

The Russian directors of the state farms (*sovkhozi*) and the state economic enterprises (*gospromkhozi*) denied that the Evenki were being deliberately excluded from employment. They insisted that strict meritocratic standards of recruitment were employed—standards that the Evenki often did not meet.[13] These meritocratic standards followed from the statutes that governed the highly centralized consolidated farms. In contrast to collective farms (*kolkhozi*), *gospromkhozi* and *sovkhozi* required directors with a higher education and workers with a variety of qualifications. In the case of the state hunter (*shtatnoe okhotnik, okhotnik-promyslovnik*), the worker was expected to hunt only in the winter months and for the rest of the year he or she was expected to perform house construction or to harvest hay. Often the Evenki were the best hunters but the worst *workers*.[14]

This tangle of job descriptions was made more complicated by the high turnover of directors. The Vitimskii *gospromkhoz* hosted thirteen directors in twenty years. A "transient" (*priezhii*) director was usually not sensitive to the history of his or her adopted community. If he or she perceived that there was a shortage of qualified employees, it was very easy to import outside workers. During the period in the mid-1970s when the turnover of directors in Ust'-Karenga was very high, nine Russians were given the lucrative positions of state hunters.[15]

The interesting aspect about this conflict is that although Evenk activists used exclusive terms such as "transient," or made comparisons with the ethnic conflict in Armenia, the debate was not styled exclusively in nationalist terms. The proposals presented in petitions and at public gatherings did not aim at allocating posts according to the nationality printed in the passport of each applicant. Instead, both the activists and the directors of state enterprises grounded their defense in the norms of operation of specific institutions. The Evenki wished to dovetail recruitment norms to the occupational structure of local communities. Directors, by contrast, spoke of the virtues of a worker with more general, industrial skills.

It can be further argued that the meritocratic rules governing consolidated state farms also did not specifically aim to discriminate against the Evenki but instead to indirectly colonize their lifeworld by systematically removing local controls over the way that labor was divided and rationalized. The fact that these rules treated all applicants equally did not compensate for the fact that appropriate employment for local applicants was not ensured. Because of the barriers within the educational system discussed previously, a strange outcome was created wherein many of the best Evenk hunters were unemployed.

The problems created by centralized recruitment norms compound over time if they are not rectified. The majority of the Russian state hunters were attracted by a high salary and a taste of freedom that was produced by their isolation from the reach of the bureaucracy. The longer "transients" worked within the state farm, the more seniority they accumulated, making it impossible to dismiss them under the statutes governing their employment. The desire of the "transients" for a high-paying and adventurous life-style was quite costly when one considers the erosion of the sense of stewardship for the land. The fact that they were relatively free from state regulation unfortunately overlapped with their freedom from the local, uncodified limits on overhunting that were "naturally" exercised by indigenous residents of Zabaikal'e. This element of stewardship was captured well by an exchange between an official from the district Party committee (*raikom*) and the leader of the Evenk initiative group at a public meeting in Chara:

Evenk leader (initiative group). Although in Srednyi Kalar we have enough of our own [Evenk] state hunters, for some reason the leadership is hiring from all corners other [nonnative] hunters. This infringes on the rights of native residents.

Representative, (raikom). Why *should* we hire native hunters? The State Plan demands that each hunter produce 3,000 rubles of fur. But some of the Evenki only produce 1,700 rubles or 2,000 rubles. Last year only two hunters fulfilled the plan!

Evenk leader (initiative group). That is completely misleading! When we are talking about a [transient] hunter, he will try to shoot everything he can. If there are thirty sable there he will shoot them all. Everybody around this table will confirm this. Ours [Evenk hunters] will never take them all. They will never shoot just because "the plan isn't fulfilled." . . . Before hunters used to take only what was necessary for their own suppers. Extra animals were never taken (*ubrali*) (Tape 2, Side B).

The destruction of stewardship through the standardized job descriptions demanded by state farms cycled back to produce more unemployment as wildlife stocks decrease. In Tungokochenskii district, where the sable have almost been trapped out of existence, Evenk hunters were no longer able to find work even as temporary amateur (*liubiteli*) hunters. All the sable quotas were reserved for the salaried state-hunter positions.[16] These positions were most likely to be given to a nonnative individual.

CONCLUSION—REBUILDING SOCIALIST INSTITUTIONS

In their petitions and during our interviews, Evenk activists insisted that the right to an appropriate occupation be institutionalized within the state-farm structure. This guarantee, in their view, should also reflect the skills offered by local residents. In their statements, they demanded that those individuals who had become "cadres" through participation in formal training programs be provided with guaranteed employment in their home villages. They recognized that this could not be achieved within the current structure of state farms. They instead proposed institutional change.

Two main proposals for reform could be singled out. The first was to transform the existing *gospromkhozi* into *sovkhozi*. The second was to create a special "national" village council (*natsionalnyi sel'sovet*) in which the local political institution (*sovet*) overlapped with the economic institution (*sovkhoz*).

The decentralization advocated by the first proposal implied a number of institutional shifts that would give the Evenki the capacity to control the division of labor and the recruitment of cadres within traditional sectors. Although both state farms (*sovkhozi*) and state productive enterprises (*gospromkhozi*) embraced the same broad principle of property, the *gospromkhoz* had a number of features that placed it closer to the state.[17] The *gospromkhoz* was teamed directly with an industrial enterprise (in this case, fur-tanning factories) that gave it access to favorable wholesale prices for both inputs and produced goods. More significantly, production quotas in *gospromkhozi* were set directly by the Provincial Executive Committee (*obispolkom*) while the *sovkhozi* were regulated by the less powerful (but more responsive) provincial agricultural committees. This jurisdictional difference gave the *gospromkhoz* much more power in negotiating with the state for subsidies and favorable prices, but it also implies that this institution had to accept the structural conditions dictated by the state. Furthermore, the *gospromkhozi* in Zabaikal'e in 1989 were regulated by the Ministry of Hunting of the Russian Republic (Glavokhota) while the *sovkhozi* were governed by the Federal (All-Union) Ministry of Agriculture (Gosagroprom). Those institutions that were more closely tied to the Russian republic ironically seemed to be much more bureaucratized and starved for hard currency than those linked to the union-level department.[18] Thus, the simple proposal by activists to change the affiliation of their economic enterprises implies very complicated changes in the way that these enterprises were administered. The expectation of the activists was that these institutional shifts would give them the power to hire local cadres and to administer production in a manner sympathetic to local needs.

The second proposal was to create a village soviet in which the Evenki form the majority (*natsionalnyi sel'sovet*). Such a project had been proposed for the village of Zelenoe Ozero (Tape 7, Side B) and had actually been attempted in the village of Chapo Ologo. Through the unity of a local political apparatus and an economic enterprise, the activists felt that they would be able to shape employment practices in a manner consonant with the need to reproduce their lifeworld. By ensuring that Evenk residents were the majority in one village and in one *sovkhoz* it became legally possible to control the recruitment of cadres and hiring and employment practices. In Chapo Ologo Evenk activists sought to further strengthen their control over production by declaring that their village *sovkhoz* had the exclusive responsibility for the issuance of hunting licenses and for the exploitation of mineral resources. If this act found support, it would place production relations under the guidance of a locally regulated institution instead of a colonizing state institution.[19] Constitutionally, this act would have given the *sovkhoz* equivalent power over the dispositions of natural resources as currently possessed by North American native reservations. The difference here was that these institutions would still be on the same legal terrain as other institutions within the Soviet state. Although this second proposal was more nationalistic in content, its form stopped short of absolute autonomy.

The urgency of these proposals for reform was underscored by the recent course of reform in the Soviet Union. The reigning proposals for decollectivization and decentralization revolved around wholesale privatization of *existing* institutions. It is conceivable that if the highly centralized state economic enterprises (*gospromkhozi*) were sold to stockholders as a single unreformed entity, huge oligopolies would be created overnight. While this contingency was not mentioned by our informants in Zabaikal'e in 1989, many hunters and herders were concerned about the implications of the reforms for land-leasing (*arenda*) that allowed producers to purchase whole hunting areas. Although the land-leasing reforms were met with great enthusiasm in the European parts of the former Soviet Union, in Siberia only the wealthiest can afford to purchase the hundreds of hectares of land required to hunt or herd. In Zabaikal'e the wealthiest individuals were precisely those transient workers who had been saving money from their lucrative jobs within the state farms. If the course of land-leasing was not regulated, the Evenk hunters and herders feared that they would be permanently excluded from their traditional lands through the sale of collectivized territory.

The proposals for institutional reform by Siberian activists revealed the contradictory nature of Soviet state-building. While activists in Siberia universally exposed the colonizing and exploitative nature of centralized state institutions, they proposed reforms that fit within the then institutional structure of the Soviet state. In framing their proposals, activists referred to universal principles, or "rights," that they demanded their state adhere to in order to preserve its legitimacy. However, they also more concretely examined over seventy years of experience with state socialism for evidence of institutions that were not as colonizing. The fact that the experience of the Evenki with the language of institution-building is limited strictly to their contact with the Soviet state reveals that there was a foundation within the structure of the Soviet state upon which new institutions could be constructed. The message of the Zabaikal'skie Evenki can thus be placed within a broader context as the former Soviet Union enters an accelerated period of reform. Instead of importing institutional models that have evolved in a Western context, as many reformers currently advocate in the Soviet Union, it may be both desirable and practical to search for indigenous examples to guide the process of reform. The example of institutional reform within Zabaikal'e gives a provocative example of how this process might be carried out.

Notes

This chapter is based on two months of fieldwork and library research in the Soviet Union during June and July of 1989. This research could not have been conducted without the enthusiastic help of Vasilii Valerionovich Belikov at the Buriat Filial of the Academy of Sciences of the USSR. Equally indispensable was the assistance of numerous Evenk scholars and professionals who hosted us in their villages. I would especially like to thank Liuba Bodukina, who generously sought out potential hosts for our research at the First Festival of Native Youth in Yakutsk. Of our hosts in Zabaikal'e I would like to thank Anna Taskerova, Gilton Aruneev, Vladimir Torgonov, and Vladimir Kozulov.

1. A history of the modern concept of civil society is given by John Keane (1988). Keane's account has been critiqued by Andrew Arato (1989). Cohen (1982) discusses the interrelation of Hegelian and Marxist notions of civil society. Cohen and Arato (1989) situate the modern concept of civil society in opposition to the ancient concept. Szücs (1988) sketches the history of relations between the state and civil society in Russia, Western Europe, and Eastern Europe.
2. For interpretations that emphasize the impact of Western ideas on Russian history see the essays by Kahan and Cherniavsky in Cherniavsky (1970) and the book by Valentine Bill (1959). Karl Wittfogel (1973) makes the classic link between oriental despotism and Soviet politics. Recent reinterpretations and critiques can be found in Anderson (1974, 462–549) and Wolf (1983, 75–82).
3. Andrew Arato's forthcoming article (in press) makes the stronger claim that the Soviet state completely destroyed indigenous civil institutions, leaving nothing positive in its wake. Jacques Rupnik (1988) makes a similar claim. In this volume, David Kideckel and Sam Beck argue in the Romanian context that the momentum of preexisting state administrations limits the chances for the formation of a civil society.
4. Zabaikal'e is a region lying to the northeast of Lake Baikal just to the north of the Mongolian and Chinese borders. It is composed of three political districts: the Buriatskaia Autonomous Republic, Chitinskaia Province and Irkutskaia Province. Fieldwork was conducted in eight villages located in Tungokochenskii and Kalarskii districts of Chitinskaia Province and in Bauntovskii district of the Buriatskaia Autonomous Republic. Formal open-ended interviews were tape-recorded with Evenk and Russian informants. Public meetings were also recorded. Oral statements were corroborated with local petitions, documents in local archives, and with articles from local newspapers. Material from the field will be quoted as (Tape #, Side #) (Notebook #, p. #) (Petition #).
5. There has recently been evidence that these uncodified rights will be put into legislation. The Supreme Soviet of the Russian Federation was (June 1991) examining five draft laws that would legalize the creation of new

ethnic enclaves on a provincial, district, or village level; provide guarantees for language education; allow for free cultural "associations"; and create areas of priority land use for native peoples (V. I. Boiko, 1991).

6. The documents from the Festival of Native Youth are all unpublished open letters or petitions. The document that I am referring to here is addressed to the Central Committee of the Communist Party, the Supreme Soviet of the USSR and the Soviet of Ministers of the USSR. During the festival, delegates were asked to join discussion groups (*seminari*) to draft petitions to central authorities.

7. The political stability generated by the Brezhnev apparatus through guaranteed employment, the provision of consumer goods, and a minimum standard of living is referred to by some authors as a type of social contract. Victor Zaslavsky (1982) refers to legitimizing effects of the "historic compromise" (pp. 132–135) or the promises of a "soviet way of life" (pp. 86–90). Boris Kagarlitsky (1989, 211–212) analyzes Soviet literature on the construction of "the new social contract."

8. In addition to these two rights, the Zabaikalsk'ie Evenki also called for locally controlled use rights to state lands and the direct control of mineral extraction by local state farms. In this chapter, I will emphasize rights to education and employment since this particular bundle has more in common with the European parts of the former Soviet Union and with Eastern Europe than the unique case of land rights in Siberia. For a complementary analysis of land tenure and property rights see Anderson (1992).

9. There were three qualified Evenk language teachers in Kalarskii district as opposed to only one in Tungokochenskii district. One more specialist was to be trained from Tungokochen in 1990 (Tape B).

10. It was unclear to me the extent to which these liberal provisions for education were a codified guarantee by the state or an uncodified expectation of native people. My feeling was that provisions for affirmative action at the institutes in Leningrad and Krasnoiarsk, and the subsidies for education at boarding schools, followed from administrative statutes within the Department of Education.

11. The mismatch between education levels and job opportunities was a common problem throughout the former Soviet Union—so much so that Soviet sociology coined the term "functional unemployment" to describe it. The problem, however, was particularly damaging in native communities because of their small populations and the dramatic impact of industrial life on their cultures. For the first treatment of this problem in the Siberian context see Zolotrubovii (1979).

12. Documents from each village state farm (*sovkhoz*) and state productive enterprise (*gospromkhoz*) shed some light on the problem. Out of a total of twenty-three state hunters in the Karengskii gospromkhoz (Ust'-Karenga), only five were Evenk. In the Vitimskii gospromkhoz thirteen Evenki were employed only as manual laborers while there were six Russian state hunters (Petition 1). In the Kalarskii sovkhoz (Srednyi Kalar) out of sixteen hunter-workers (*okhotnik-promyslovnki*) nine were Evenki. Similar statistics exist in the Buriatskaia Autonomous Republic (Belikov 1988).

13. There is evidence that in Tungokochenskii district, the directors were not that innocent. The unemployment levels were much higher until a special provincial Party commission was formed in 1988 to investigate complaints of

discrimination. Several Evenk hunters were immediately hired. The Party commission was formed at the request of the Evenk initiative group (Petition 1).

14. Another regulation that hindered native employment was the requirement that all individuals who bore arms be certified as "sane" by a psychiatrist or the police. Any infraction involving a firearm—even if it did not involve injury—indirectly unemployed a hunter.

15. This was a very lucrative salaried position. The state hunter earned 400–500 rubles for five months of intensive work in 1989. In addition to these official earnings, the hunter could make additional money on the black market. Petition 1 claims that many Russian immigrant hunters killed as many as 80–90 sables in a season. The existence of high wages and a criminalized (but vibrant) black market revealed the importance of the fur industry for the state. The sale of furs to foreign markets was a source of foreign currency.

16. The ecological crisis in Tungokochenskii district was made more severe by a series of forest fires in 1987 and 1988 that destroyed the lichen (*yagel'*) pastures. Reindeer lichen takes almost a full decade to recover from such a catastrophe. The lack of fodder made the Party officials reluctant to increase deer stocks, contributing further to Evenk unemployment. The initiative group claimed that fires were set by careless immigrant workers. It also asserted that the destruction of the pastures was not as severe as the "specialists" claimed. They reported that the specialists surveyed the district from the air and did not speak to herders or examine specific pastures closely.

17. In Soviet textbooks the history of economic institutions is described as an evolution between differing forms of property. The most progressive forms of property are those that are embraced most completely by the state (Hegedus 1976, VII). In collective farms (*kolkhozi*), the members collectively own the assets of the farms and receive their income as a portion of the income of the collective. State farms (*sovkhozi*) and state productive enterprises (*gospromkhozi*) are founded upon state property. Their workers receive salaries and state pensions from the coffers of the general civil service.

18. The reasons for this discrepancy are not clear to me. A possible hypothesis might be that the union-level bureaucracies responded much more quickly to the decentralizing reforms initiated by the central government. The republic-level ministries may have been much more conservative and resistant to change from the center.

19. Immediately after this zone was declared in May 1989 by district Party officials, it was legally challenged by provincial Party officials. As of July 1990 this court challenge had not yet been settled.

References

Anderson, D. G. 1991. "Turning hunters into herders: a critical examination of Soviet development policy among the Evenki of southeastern Siberia." *Arctic* 22(1):12–22.

———. 1992. "Property rights and civil society in Siberia: An analysis of the social movements of the Zabaikal'skie Evenki." *Praxis International* 12(1): 83–105.

Anderson, P. 1974. *Lineages of the absolutist state.* London: New Left Books.

Arato, A. in press. "Civil society and social movements in the Soviet Union." in *Perestroika from below,* eds. Jim Butterfield and Judith Sedaitis. Boulder, CO: Westview Press.

———. 1989. "Civil society, history and socialism: Reply to John Keane." *Praxis International* 9(1–2):133–151.

Arato, A., and Cohen, J. 1988. "Civil society and social theory." *Thesis Eleven* (21):40–64.

Association of the Small Peoples of the North of the Soviet Union. 1990. "Programme of the association of the small peoples of the north of the Soviet Union." in *Indigenous peoples of the Soviet north,* International Workgroup for Indigenous Affairs, 48–53. Copenhagen: International Secretariat of IWGIA.

Bartels, D., and Bartels, A. 1984. "Affirmative action programmes for Siberian native peoples." *Canadian Journal of Native Education* 11(2):27–53.

Belikov, V. V. 1988. "Uvoleny iz . . . Taiga" (Dismissed from . . . the Taiga). *Komsomol'skai Pravda* (Truth of the Komsomol') July 15:1.

Bill, V. T. 1959. *The forgotten class: The Russian bourgeosie from earliest beginnings to 1900.* New York: Praeger.

Bobbio, N. 1988. "Gramsci and the concept of civil society." in *Civil society and the state: New European perspectives,* ed. John Keane, 73–100. New York: Verso.

Boiko, V. I. 1979. "Predislovie [Introduction]." in *BAM i narody severa* (BAM and the peoples of the north), eds. V. I. Boiko et al., 3–7. Novosibirsk: Nauka.

Cherniavsky, M. 1970. *The structure of Russian history.* New York: Random House.

Cohen, J. 1982. *Class and civil society.* Amherst: University of Massachusetts Press.

Cohen, J., and Arato, A. 1989. "Politics and the reconstruction of civil society." in *Zwischenbetrachtungen: Im prozeß der aufklärung,* 482–503. Frankfurt am Main: Suhrkamp Verlag.

Dolgikh, B. O. 1967. "Obrazovanie sovremennykh narodnostei severa SSSR (The formation of modern northern nationalities of the U.S.S.R.)." *Sovetskaia etnografia (Soviet Ethnography)* 3:3–15.

Gramsci, A. 1971. *Selections from the prison notebooks.* New York: International Publishers.

Habermas, J. 1987. *The theory of communicative action* (vol. 2), *Lifeworld and system: A critique of functionalist reason.* Boston: Beacon Press.

Hegedus, A. 1976. *Socialism and Bureaucracy.* London: Allison & Busby.

Kagarlitsky, B. 1989. *The thinking reed.* New York: Verso.

Keane, J. 1988. *Democracy and civil society.* New York: Verso.

Komitet Severa. 1927. "Sovetskoe stroitel'stvo: rasshirennyi plenum komiteta severa pri prezidiume VTsIK (Soviet structuring: The General Assembly of the Committee of the North of the Presidium of the All Russian Central Committee [from February 28 to March 3, 1927])." *Severnaia Azia* 3:76–91.

Kuoljok, K. E. 1985. *The revolution in the North: Soviet ethnography and nationality policy.* Uppsala: Almqvist & Wiksell International.

Rupnik, J. 1988. "Totalitarianism revisited." in *Civil society and the state: New European perspectives,* ed. J. Keane, 263–290. London: Verso.

Seminar "Molodezh' i Sever." 1989. "Pismo k Tsentral'nomu Komitetu KPSS, Verkhovnomu Sovetu SSSR, i Sovetu Ministrov SSSR (Letter to the Central Committee of the CPSU, the Supreme Soviet of the USSR, and the Soviet of Ministers of the USSR)." Unpublished open letter.

Shutz, A., and Luckmann, T. 1973. *The structures of the lifeworld.* Evanston: Northwestern University Press.

Szücs, J. 1988. "Three historical regions of Europe." in *Civil society and the state: New European perspectives,* ed. John Keane, 291–332. New York: Verso.

Wittfogel, K. 1973. *Oriental despotism: A comparative study of total power.* New Haven: Yale University Press.

Wolf, E. 1983. *Europe and the peoples without history.* Berkeley: University of California Press.

Zaslavsky, V. 1982. *The neo-Stalinist state.* White Plains, NY: M.E. Sharpe.

Zolototrubovii, V. S. 1979. "Sotsialnye aspekty problem trudovoi zaniatnosti" (The social aspects of employment problems). In *BAM i narody severa* (BAM and the peoples of the North), eds. V. I. Boiko et al., 79–91. Moscow: Nauka.

Property Relations in the New Eastern Europe: The Case of Specialist Cooperatives in Hungary

CHRISTOPHER HANN

> All revolutions until now have been revolutions for the
> protection of one kind of property against another kind
> of property (Engels 1972, 114).

The theme of property relations is central to most understandings of socialism, and it is widely assumed (both by participants in Eastern European societal changes and by external commentators) that following the demise of socialism a new basis for property ownership must be established. Some see this as a straightforward matter of reestablishing capitalist private property, but even where this view prevails among policymakers, the political, economic, and legal complications of restoring ownership rights that have been ineffective for forty years have turned out to be formidable. It is widely reported that problems in this area are having adverse effects on Western willingness to invest in what was formerly the German Democratic Republic and in other parts of Eastern Europe.

In this chapter I shall focus upon Hungary, within Hungary upon the rural sector and debates concerning the decollectivization of socialist agriculture, and within this sector upon the region in which I have carried out fieldwork over the past fifteen years, a region in which a distinctive form of cooperative is common. My general argument is that it is unhelpful to think in terms of "rewinding the entire film reel," to use a metaphor of János Kornai (1990, 73), since there is plenty of evidence that people do not want this and that it would probably lead to economic disaster. Rather, we should look closely at some of the hybrid institutions of János Kádár's Hungary and recognize that an eclectic hierarchy of ownership structures offers the most satisfactory developmental path. Contrary to those who announce the death of communism and promote capitalist triumphalism, I argue that ordinary villagers have come to see beyond these mesmerizing ideological ideas. They see both state and market for the abstractions they are, whereas to many East European intellectuals as well as to Westerners, these terms identify active historical agents. The villagers are interested in pragmatic compromises, including diverse forms of property consistent with both economic efficiency and social equity, that cannot be pigeonholed as *either* socialist *or* capitalist. The theories and policy recommendations of the social scientists studying Eastern Europe in this unique period may both be improved by a closer consideration of these grass roots.

Both in Marxism and in Western liberal-conservative theory, the question of property plays a role of quite central significance. For the Marxist tradition the private ownership of the means of production establishes the foundation for the exploitative class relations of capitalist industrial society. As Marx and Engels themselves put it in the *Communist Manifesto*, "The theory of the Communists may be summed up in the single sentence: Abolition of private property" (1968, 47). Thus a central theme of communism is the complete suppression of private property rights and the reinstatement of the communal forms of property characteristic of early mankind ("primitive communism").[1]

For the liberal-conservative tradition private property rights are of course central not only to political freedom but also to economic efficiency, thanks to the incentives they provide for accumulation. This is the tradition explicitly invoked by so many intellectuals in Eastern Europe at the present time. They see the collectivist and egalitarian emphases of the socialist period as incompatible with efficiency and freedom.[2]

Thus both the Marxist and the liberal-conservative traditions attach central importance to property relations. Moreover they seem to share the same sharp opposition between individual (private) and collective (public) forms of property. However, the usefulness of this opposition, and of the focus upon property rights generally, can be questioned from many angles.

First, there is a strand of argument maintaining that in a mature industrial economy, property relations lose their former significance. On this argument it may be more appropriate to analyze the behavior of the managers of joint-stock companies than to study the structure of ownership. Economic efficiency no longer requires that entrepreneurs be owners: it is more a technical matter of devising adequate incentives.[3]

Second, there is a need to look again at the socialist demand to replace private property rights with collective rights. Social anthropologists, as we shall see further on, have long since pointed out the errors in early analyses of communalism in tribal land tenure and elsewhere. Following their insights, we can recognize that the nominal conversion of private property into state or cooperative ownership does not in itself bring about any improvement in democratic controls over resources. The implication is that we need to look much more carefully at how property rights can be truly socialized (Brus 1975), and the work of C. B. Macpherson may be instructive here. I shall return to these theoretical considerations in the concluding section.

PRIVATE PROPERTY IN LAND AND THE FATE OF THE SMALLHOLDERS

Marx and most Marxists paid relatively little attention to the specific features of the countryside. Like other contemporary social theorists they tended to assume that large-scale operations dependent upon wage labor would sooner or later come to dominate in agriculture as in industry (Newby 1983). The vitality of family farming in even the most advanced Western countries shows the limitations of this view. Today it is easy for economists to show why the family should retain an economic edge in activities that require high supervision costs and that are highly seasonal. Hence our familiarity in the West with agrarian structures based on private property rights, highly capitalized but still reliant primarily upon family labor. In contrast to this pattern, the complex division of labor on a Soviet-style collective farm is widely and correctly seen to have led to great economic dislocation as well as to social and ecological disaster (Shanin 1990, 188–206). The call for a restoration of private property rights in this sector therefore has great intuitive attractions.

The strength of the call for a private property basis in the rural sector in contemporary Eastern Europe is increased by the widespread view that a high degree of property consciousness is deeply secreted in the peasant community. Since many East European villagers were in fact subsistence-oriented peasants rather than market-oriented farmers until the recent past, it might be held that restoring ownership rights would not only provide the incentives essential for a strong economic performance but would also reinstate a valued principle of culture. For example, in his analysis of a peasant "general type" Teodor Shanin has noted the importance of a direct peasant-land link, though he avoids the error of equating peasant ownership with modern bourgeois property rights.[4]

Following fieldwork in Hungary and Poland, I have tried to explore the *complexity* of property rights in socialist Eastern Europe. To summarize an earlier discussion (Hann 1985, 167–176), I found that rural dwellers in Hungary were substantively better off than their counterparts in Poland, even though the latter had escaped socialist collectivization and had been more successful in maintaining formal legal property rights. The socialist state in Poland had failed to modernize the rural sector and was profoundly suspicious of independent farmers for ideological reasons. The nominal persistence of private property was decisively outweighed by the power of the state to determine the conditions in which those rights were exercised. In Hungary, in contrast, within a few years of mass collectivization the state began pragmatically to promote ways of integrating family-labor farms into large-scale collective operations. Essentially what took shape was a symbiosis (Hann 1980; Swain 1985), a mutually beneficial collaboration that enabled the standard of living of the whole rural population to improve very dramatically and that conferred further substantial benefits upon the wider society (not to mention a high degree of legitimacy upon the government). This collaboration can be seen also as a synthesis of left- and right-wing political elements. If we use the terms Alec Nove (1983, 143) borrows from Peter Wiles, we can readily appreciate that although collectivized lands could produce certain "left wing" crops (for example, most cereals) very efficiently, there were other "right wing" branches of production in which it would have been extremely costly and inefficient to attempt to impose socialist principles. In these activities, for example, most animal breeding and dairy production, it made sense to encourage rural households to produce commodities in response to changing price signals (over which the authorities, as in most other countries, always exercised careful control).

In a strict legal sense the members of collective farms (*termelő szövetkezetek*—literally "producers' cooperatives") did not lose their property rights. But in practice their character was certainly transformed as the peasants saw their lands swallowed up into the collective; they were paid a low rental in return. They were entitled to a "private plot," but they had no control over its location. Initially intended to meet subsistence needs of rural families, these plots were increasingly oriented to market production as the Kádárist social compromise unfolded. In some villages the right to a plot was commuted to a cash payment or other benefits. But whether or not the rural family had any direct access to land, it was comparatively easy to engage in small-scale commodity production: pigs could be fattened in every backyard with cheap feed available from the collective sector. Thus many small farmers in rural Hungary maintained significant levels of commodity production without having any direct personal access to land. Many no longer worked on the land at all but commuted to urban jobs or were employed in ancillary activities of their collective farm.

Serious criticisms can be leveled at this strategy. In most regions the policies facilitated a massive exodus of unskilled labor from the rural sector, and they did nothing to raise the status of the poorest layers of village society (Márkus 1980). Those who benefited in the Kádár period tended to be the descendants of those who were already beginning an embourgeoisement trajectory before the socialist period, as Iván Szelényi has recently argued (1988), and in this respect the Hungarian path can be condemned from a fundamentalist Marxist-Leninist standpoint.[5]

Equally strong objections may be forthcoming from the liberal-conservative perspective. For example, high subsidies were paid out to farms with a poor natural endowment when it might have been more rational to encourage a contraction of activities in such regions. More generally, it can be argued that the power of the state to determine the conditions of farming were every bit as great in Hungary as in Poland. Property-holders at all levels were always liable to political interference, and they had no legal protection against interference by state or party officials.

In spite of such reservations there can be little doubt that compared with the rest of the socialist world, the experience of Hungarian collectivization was remarkably positive. As Nigel Swain has convincingly argued, these collective farms really did *work*, and the secret lay in large measure in their successful mobilization of family labor. Moreover, this successful economic performance continued in the much less favorable economic environment of the 1980s, when government supports were reduced (Swain 1987). There was a new boom in small enterprises in the countryside and rural living standards in many regions continued to improve dynamically even after most of the Hungarian economy had fallen into recession.

A successful collectivization was thus part of the background against which the Communist party gave up its monopoly of power and a new Independent Smallholders' party, a reincarnation of the strongest of Hungary's political parties of the 1940s, emerged to call for a restitution of the property relations of 1947.[6] Obviously the Smallholders could not hope to match their impact on an earlier generation, when they had won an outright majority in the free elections of 1945. But they ran very aggressive electoral campaigns in 1990 and formed a coalition government with the right-of-center Hungarian Democratic Forum and the Christian Democratic People's party. Smallholders' party representatives took the Ministry of Agriculture and other key positions and set about trying to implement their commitment to decollectivization. However, it very soon became apparent that even their own coalition partners would not countenance such a radical upheaval. It was argued that restoring the property relations of 1947 would jeopardize all the economic progress made in the rural sector. Smallholders claimed that a firm framework of private property rights would guarantee the security needed for sensible planning and investment by farmers, but their opponents maintained that even to raise the possibility of decollectivization was to introduce a fatal measure of uncertainty into the sector. Many people were reminded of the slogans of land reform in the 1940s, particularly Land to the Tiller! and felt uncomfortable at the thought of large estates passing back to families who no longer lived in the countryside, or even in the country at all. Discussions about how to compensate such former owners soon became bogged down. At the time of writing in early 1991, a solution to what has become known as the "land question" seems as far off as ever, but support for the Smallholders seems to have waned considerably. In order to assess the significance of their demands and of the ambivalent responses these demands evoked, I shall now turn to a specific region before returning to consider more general implications of this case study in the conclusion.

PROPERTY RELATIONS AND THE SPECIALIST COOPERATIVES

The distinctive feature of specialist cooperatives in Hungary was the possibility they allowed for the organic development of independent family farms by peasants who were not significantly incorporated into the vertical structures of any collective. This type of cooperative came to account for some 10 percent of the country's total vineyard area, and about 45 percent of this area in the county of Bács-Kiskun, where my fieldwork took place.[7]

From their inception in the early 1960s, it was emphasized that these cooperatives were a transitional form that would in due course be converted into regular collective farms. Pressure was applied in the later 1970s to increase the area of collective cultivation, and these policies involved some dislocation of family farms. However, any villagers who wished to remain independent farmers were able to do so. Membership in the specialist cooperative was virtually obligatory, but members were not required to work in the collective sector, and few of them did so. As elsewhere in rural Hungary, many families sought to supplement farming with other sources of income outside the villages, or with other wage-labor activities within their village. Marketing of produce was generally through the cooperative, though other options, including the "free market" in towns as far away as Budapest, were also available.

In this way the specialist cooperatives came to form an extreme variant of the integration outlined in the previous section. The small farmers of many villages in Bács-Kiskun County maintained their mixed farming (vineyards were the usual mainstay) with the aid and active support of their cooperatives. They exercised a higher degree of control over their work than most collective farm members, and unlike the latter, most retained a direct link to at least some of their inherited fields. Formally and legally, property rights in the specialist cooperatives were no different from those prevailing in the collective farms. Villagers did not have the right to buy and sell land as in the presocialist period, and they certainly felt that the *quality* of their ownership had been transformed everywhere. The point was clearly made whenever the cooperative expanded its collective operations at the expense of one of its members. Compensation could usually be offered elsewhere, for there was no shortage of land, but the offer was often declined by the peasant. In general people did not talk much about the exact legal status of the land they farmed and might not themselves be clear whether a particular plot was nominally their private property, on which they paid the council a small sum in tax, or whether it was the property of the collective farm, to which they paid a small rental for its use. When a farmer sold his produce and was paid through the cooperative, the nature of his property rights in the land he farmed was quite irrelevant. Indeed, many producers of agricultural commodities did not have direct access to land at all, as noted previously.

By the 1980s the general political climate had changed profoundly. Many specialist cooperatives brought in complex schemes to promote "private ownership" *within* a socialist framework. The most widespread example concerned the establishment of new vineyards to the specifications of large-scale farms (i.e., with wide gaps between rows to facilitate mechanized spraying, etc.) but with property rights, including the right to alienate, allocated to individuals and their families. The family took prime responsibility for the management of each plot and the organization of the harvest. Results showed that where vineyards were set up in this mixed way, the yields were up to twice as high as when pure "social ownership" was adhered to and the rural family was not mobilized (Simó 1987, 85).

In other cases where the pursuit of pure collectivist ideals had led to inefficiency, the solutions devised in the 1980s were more radical. For example, in the village I know best, the leadership of the specialist cooperative decided that previous efforts to maintain a collective machine park had not been profitable. They therefore sold off the machines (at giveaway prices, according to some critics) to their own workers, who were then able to use them to compete with already established private tractor owners. One of the ex-employees gave the following account of what happened:

The cooperative sold off its tractors and the nine of us drivers bought them. They cost about 80,000—140,000 forints, but we could pay in installments. We formed a so-called "machinists' specialist group" and worked both for the collective and for the individual members. But there was so much administration involved that we got tired of it, so we simplified matters: we rejoined the cooperative as members and now we're contracted to work 1500 hours for it annually. The branch leader tells us what to do and I just pass word on to the guy who's been doing it in the past. The wage is fixed, and so is the cost of fuel, maintenance etc. Each owner has to repair and look after his own machine, it's not the specialist cooperative which has to worry about these jobs. The advantage of this is the machine has got an owner (*gazda*) and not just a user, and that's a big difference.

Why is it better like this? Because this work is not rigid shift work, and we don't have to look at our watches, we just concentrate on the job. You feel free. If you want to work at night you can, or if you want to you can do just a few hours in a day. Of course it's essential that you get jobs done by the deadline, and do the work to the proper standard. (Pavlovits 1990, 56)

In this situation the change of political climate in 1990 raised further hopes, but it also created new anxieties.[8] Some villagers were enthusiastically in favor of the Smallholders' party's program to restore the property relations of 1947 to the letter. This implied the dissolution of all forms of cooperatives and state farms. It also implied the allocation of land to millions of people who had never farmed and did not live in the countryside rather than to those who had actually been working the land. Cynics commented that to implement such a program would be next to impossible, and it was mainly designed to bring business for lawyers for decades to come (lawyers were prominent among the leaders of the Smallholders' party, for example, in the new parliament that was elected in May 1990).

In many villages in Bács-Kiskun the problem took a special form because the radical call for restoration threatened to upset the established farming patterns of the specialist cooperatives. Some activists favored this course, but some cooperative leaders won support when they argued that to abolish the cooperatives altogether would leave many smaller farmers vulnerable. Without the services and backup of the cooperative, they might not survive at all. Much discussion focused on the inevitable decline in output that would follow if land passed to absentee owners who would take no steps to ensure that it would be efficiently cultivated. Some villagers also expressed deeper ethical worries about transferring property back to people who had never worked it, particularly if that property had been transformed beyond recognition in the socialist period. In some cases, for example, it was suggested that land allocated to a farmer in compensation for a plot appropriated from him elsewhere and then converted to vineyards by him at great expense should simply revert back to the original owner—even when that owner had migrated to Budapest forty years earlier and the windfall legacy would accrue to grandchildren who had never even seen the village.

To assuage intuitive anxieties concerning cases such as this, one local branch of the Independent Smallholders' party suggested the following modifications to the party's national policy:

> In what follows we will give our opinion about the land question, since numerous rumors and mistaken pieces of information have been circulating in our community.
>
> Our daily bread comes directly from productive land, and therefore the fate of that land is a life and death question. Only a small percentage of the productive area of our country is in private hands, whilst at the same time a significant part of food output derives from private farms. It follows that the privatization of productive land is a question of life and death.
>
> Two questions have to be posed in connection with the ownership of land. Who should get the land, those people who pulled the country's cart out of trouble after 1945 and were then vilified for doing so? Or those who have the capital to purchase it? On this point justice apparently comes into conflict with economic interests, because in 1947 there were no large estates and land ownership was in the hands of the people. The Hungarian peasantry was not able to enjoy its thousand year patrimony for long because the land was confiscated. But that land is still there and if it is claimed by its owner then he must get it back (that's what the rule of law means). Of course that does not exclude the possibility that legislators should require by decree that all land should be cultivated.
>
> Someone who held land in 1947 can only claim it back if he asks for it. It is probable that we would still have enough surplus for a fresh distribution, so that those who were not owners in 1947 could gain access to land. But there are areas where private farms have taken shape, and for this reason the distribution of land can only proceed on the "collectivized" areas. Naturally such land cannot be taken away from its present tenants, especially not when it has been converted to vineyard or orchard. In this sort of case the former owner will get his land back in some other site where there is a realistic possibility of reallocation. (*Vadkerti Ujsag* (2) No. 7 1990, 12)

The debate that broke out on the land question in 1990 divided opinion within communities, within the Smallholders' party, and between that party and its coalition partners. It may well have increased uncertainty in the agricultural sector, with obvious adverse consequences if, for example, some farmers who were not 1947 owners began to reduce investments. My impression is that after some initial euphoria, when many villagers were enamored of the idea of becoming fully fledged capitalist owners and in several parts of the country the Smallholders initiated "spontaneous" land redistribution, the local activists had great difficulty in convincing farmers of the importance of becoming "owners" in the usual capitalist sense. Many villagers were worried about increasing tax liabilities if they claimed more land, and these villagers preferred to retain a looser link to a specialist cooperative through which they would always be able to gain access to more land if they wanted it, in line with changing household circumstances.[9]

DISCUSSION

As we have noted, according to dominant ideological strands in socialism, which can justifiably be seen as central to its very definition, private property rights establish the basic source of social injustice and must therefore be replaced by social or collective ownership. Rural Eastern Europe after 1950 witnessed the emergence of a very clear hierarchy in forms of property ownership. At the top was property that belonged to the state and was worked by wage-labor employees in the manner of the Soviet *sovkhoz*. In second place stood a cooperative form of property (cf. the Soviet *kolkhoz*) according to which the farm was said to belong to its members collectively, though as time went by, working conditions in the collective sectors of such farms came to resemble those of the state farms. Private farming, including the so-called household plot element within collective farms, came at the bottom of the hierarchy for ideological reasons even though it was abundantly clear that the household plot was everywhere crucial to the overall performance of agriculture.[10] In the Hungarian context the specialist cooperatives were frequently criticized as a "lower form." In spite of the fact that the members' nominal legal rights were not specified as different from those of collective farm members, the fact that most members of specialist cooperatives remained highly independent in practice was a source of irritation to ideologues.

But this ideological approach to property rights was repeatedly and successfully contested. As noted previously, from the outset Hungarian collectivization took more account of distinctive local conditions than was possible in most other socialist countries. Gradually the specialist cooperatives were able to diversify the forms of property they embodied, as illustrated earlier with the partnership schemes in vineyards and the privatization of tractors.[11] In Bács-Kiskun County there were even cases of collective farms that broke with the Marxist laws of history by dropping back to the status of specialist cooperative, theoretically a lower form of property. In spite of some significant reversals in the 1970s, the overall trend of Kadar's Hungary was to break down ideological prescriptions governing property relations and to subvert old dogmas by the subtle introduction of radically new content into apparently familiar institutions.

Following the demise of Communist government in Hungary, calls for a simple inversion of the old socialist hierarchy of property forms are only to be expected. The Smallholders are only the most extreme among many voices presently calling for a restitution of what they see as the classical forms of private property. Other forms may be allowed to persist out of sheer necessity on a temporary basis, but they are now alleged to be decidedly inferior. Even the specialist cooperatives have come under fire from the new wave of liberal-conservative ideologues: The compromise they represent is no more satisfactory in the eyes of the new Right than it was to the old Left.

I was told by one specialist cooperative chairman in summer 1990 of his great satisfaction in now being able to go to county and national meetings without the stigma of representing an inferior form of property holding. The leaders of state farms and collective farms were consulting him in an effort to see what they might learn from the specialist cooperatives. In my view there is a good deal to be learned, but it is emphatically not reducible to a lesson about the virtues of private property of the classical bourgeois recipe. Rather I see these cooperatives as offering a model for transcending the old antinomies of private and collective. A hierarchy of property rights in which some activities and tools are owned and controlled by individuals and households while many other property rights remain subject to the controls of larger groups and a wider political community is compatible with both economic efficiency and a greater measure of democracy throughout social life (including production). Certainly these democratic controls have been slower to mature than the productive dynamic these cooperatives have fostered. There should be no illusions about how unwelcome these institutions were to peasants when they were first imposed. However, their development was never a simple "top-down" phenomenon, and at the local level I was given the impression that by the late 1980s the specialist cooperatives had become much more responsive to their members and democratic in their procedures.

In more theoretical terms I suggest that the evidence from this corner of rural Hungary can be placed in context by drawing on a number of scholarly traditions both inside and outside social anthropology. In anthropology it is above all thanks to the work of Max Gluckman that we know how to treat property relations: as social relations between people and not, as modern capitalist society would often seem to imply, as relations between people and the material things they own.[12] Contrary to some of the most powerful assumptions of the colonial period in which his work was carried out, Gluckman argued that African tribal land tenure was organized through a complex hierarchy of estates of administration that were tied in with social and political status. Africans did not hold land as private property in the modern Western sense, but it was equally misleading to state that traditional tenure systems were simply communal. Rather, all members of society had both rights and obligations, and the estates of production were farmed by individuals and households. All group members had a right to the means of production, that is, to adequate land, which was typically allocated to them by a village headman whose own rights derived from his position of allegiance to a chief or king in a status hierarchy. Status superiors did not interfere in the day-to-day management of the estates of production, though they did exercise rights over their revenues. No one had the right to alienate property, which in this specific sense could be regarded validly as communal. Claims not enforced (for example, following migration) would simply revert back to the next level of the social hierarchy.

In order to translate some of the arguments made by Gluckman for a status-dominated society (in Maine's sense) into the age of the modern industrial "contract," it may be useful to bring in the work of C. B. Macpherson, who has done much to remind modern audiences of Marx's old point that the meaning of property has undergone major changes in history.[13] In particular, the identification of property rights with *private* property and the right to exclude others is very much a product of early capitalist, market-dominated economies. Macpherson's critique of "possessive individualism" is accompanied by a powerful plea for the revival of a notion of *common* property. Rather than absolute rights to exclude others, Macpherson, like Gluckman, seems aware that many persons and corporations can have overlapping rights in the same property. In a mature industrial society individuals should possess rights *not to be excluded* from various benefits of society, such as the right to work. This does not commit Macpherson to a simplistic endorsement of collectivism and central planning. I shall argue below that his emphasis upon common property is best viewed as one element in combinations of property rights that can only be determined by careful consideration of local conditions and that it is consistent with extensive reliance on markets for economic efficiency.

It may of course be suggested that, even if Macpherson is right about the changing character of property rights in developed capitalist societies (and recent trends in the West cast doubt on some of his basic assumptions), in Eastern Europe it is still appropriate to aim at introducing the most absolute and exclusive forms of private property. This in essence is the Kornai position, according to which the whole history of possessive individualism and market expansion must be relaunched. However, a more subtle and realistic perspective on property rights in the region is that provided recently by Ellen Comisso, the last theorist I shall consider in this brief discussion and who shares Kornai's fundamental concern with economic efficiency.

Comisso takes a broad approach to property rights, as do Gluckman and Macpherson, emphasizing social relations, but takes more trouble to distinguish "property rights systems" from what she terms "the allocation system" (1991, 167). The latter is a realm in which the principle of competitive markets is undeniably the most effective, according to Comisso. However, in the tradition of Wlodzimierz Brus and Alec Nove, she does not accept Kornai's equation of market with private ownership and sees no a priori theoretical or practical objections to "market socialism," that is, a combination of a market mechanism for allocative efficiency with a socialist property-rights system. Comisso argues that this combination has not really been tested up to now in Eastern Europe, not even in post-1968 Hungary. Rather, Eastern Europe was characterized by communal ownership which may plausibly be seen as analogous to Macpherson's common property. But whereas Macpherson saw only virtues in the principle of nonexclusion, Comisso highlights all the economic problems that flow from failure to protect economic decision-makers from politically motivated interference. Her solution is to insist, in the traditional liberal-conservative manner, on clear boundaries between the spheres of economics, politics, and law, between what she terms proprietary as opposed to communal space. Where she differs from most liberal-conservatives is in her demonstration that "lodging property rights in the hands of economic actors" does not necessarily mean handing them over to only private individuals or joint-stock companies. Cooperatives and the state itself may be equally appropriate as ownership units, provided that their property rights are genuinely free of political interference and enforced by an independent judiciary.

Comisso's analysis goes beyond a reformulation of the observations of many other critics of "weak property rights" under socialism.[14] In the light of East European experience in recent decades, she is surely right to insist on the necessity for improved allocative efficiency. Her critique of communal property has serious implications for Macpherson's position. Whatever the exact scope of communal rights in a "status" society, such as those studied by Gluckman, surely in modern industrial society there is no proven alternative to a rigorous separation of economic managers from politicians, with the whole system backed up by the rule of law. However, it might be argued that Comisso, like the liberal-conservatives, exaggerates the importance of the legal dimension and goes further than is necessary or desirable in seeking to insulate economic from social and political factors. Alongside the need to ensure objective calculation of precise costs by economic actors is the need to remember that property rights as social and political phenomena will always be embedded in concrete local institutions. These institutions are concerned not only with economic output but also with democratic controls over production, with its wider social consequences, and with the basic needs and security of a population that may be much larger than the immediate work force. Rather than argue for a new socialist property-rights system, as opposed to the system usually preferred by other Westerners, the private system, Comisso would do well to pay more attention to local practice. She would find in Hungary in the late Kadar period the potential for establishing a creative mixture of property forms within more democratic frameworks. At this point I must return to the specialist cooperatives of Bács-Kiskun. I believe these provide an example of institutional flexibility that shows how Comisso's main complaints about communal property can be partially overcome at the local level without the wholesale Americanization required by the presently dominant versions of the liberal-conservative paradigm.

In the environment of Bács-Kiskun, given the existing settlement pattern and other conditions in 1961, it made sense to devolve greater autonomy to family farms than would have been economically warranted in other, more fertile and densely populated regions. Hungarian agriculture as a whole has shown itself to be highly successful in responding flexibly to changing conditions: Behind the lip service that had to be paid to socialism, a sophisticated structure of rights and entitlements was negotiated. Because of the need to maintain the ideological facade of socialism, there was a great deal of imprecision concerning the property arrangements of the Kádár period. This has been almost universally criticized, and even the Hungarian Communist party when it was still in government had committed itself to a more rigorous legalistic specification of property rights. In the case of the specialist cooperatives, for example, there was discussion of how to regulate a market in land and how to ensure equal social security entitlements for work carried out on one's own farm rather than on collective land (Romány 1987, 16). Undoubtedly there was a need for clarification of questions such as these, but I want to suggest that the very vagueness that characterized so many deleterious social practices under socialism may also have had positive effects. I think that far from leaving ordinary people feeling powerless in the absence of unambiguous statute law, it left many rural citizens with a *greater* sense of control and personal autonomy. They were secure in the knowledge that basic welfare guarantees were underwritten by the cooperative, and they could choose for themselves in what type of labor process they wished to participate and could readily expand or contract the dimensions of their family farming by prompt negotiation with the cooperative without needing to find a lawyer in town to draw up private contracts. Villagers in cooperatives were also increasingly able to play a part in controlling land that they did not farm themselves but that might still be important to their own activities (for example, in producing fodder for their own use in animal breeding). In such ways the specialist cooperatives were able to reconcile the requirement for economic efficiency with the need for basic security for all members while at the same time introducing a significant element of self-management previously entirely missing in socialist cooperatives.

It should be clear that many, probably most, property rights held by villagers in this kind of framework would have to be private and exclusive. In other words, not only houses, cars, and consumer goods but also large house plots and particularly high-value plots such as vineyards should be owned by individuals who are not obliged to share these goods with other individuals, and these rights must of course be protected under law. But it could be decided to limit the area of land that could be held in this way, for example, to the size that can be farmed by two full-time adult workers, and to limit also the number of houses and cars. All these goods could be alienated, with a proviso perhaps that village land should not pass to nonresidents. If a family migrated, its landholdings would pass to the cooperative, which would, of course, be required to pay compensation to the family.

Some agricultural land might appropriately be left in state ownership on the understanding that state farms were organized along strict business lines as in Western agribusiness. But in the Hungarian countryside, much agricultural land could remain in cooperative ownership and be farmed by a variety of methods, as indicated previously, ranging from high-tech agribusiness to labor-intensive family farms operating on a much smaller scale. There can be little doubt, above all because of the high costs of supervising labor, that the family-labor farm will remain a major economic force in the rural sector for many years to come. It is therefore important to establish exclusive rights for individuals and families over particular estates of production, the revenues of which they would not have to share with other economic actors. This can be achieved through leasing arrangements between the cooperative and its members. The duration of the lease could be highly variable to allow for the variability in the family labor force over the course of the life cycle. For example, a family could choose to give up land for a few years while its young men were carrying out military service but then to increase its acreage when funds were urgently needed a few years later to finance new house-building. Families wishing to make a long-term investment, in an orchard, for example, should be allowed to do so, if they so wish, by adding such plots to their "private" holdings—provided that these do not infringe on the norms suggested above.

Where there might be grounds to fear that some lessees of land would degrade the soil through excessive short-term exploitation, it should not be beyond the wit of the expert advisers of the cooperative (who should certainly include environmental economists as well as agronomists) to come up with appropriate guidelines and to impose sanctions if these are broken. In this way the "externalities" of any farming operation could be better "internalized" through the workings of such a community cooperative than through any conceivable alternative. The government would still be able, through taxes and subsidies, to assist villages with less favorable natural endowments. Such village cooperatives would be charged with providing basic property rights, that is, access to sufficient land or alternative means of labor in the cooperative, corresponding to Macpherson's notion of common property, for all members of the community. But in meeting this objective it would be essential to allow extensive space for competitive markets. The rents paid by farmers, the fees they would pay to the providers of machine services on their plots, and the prices that they would pay for their inputs and that they receive for their outputs would all be determined by the market principle. Only competitive markets would ensure that the agricultural sector did not experience the kind of degeneration observed in the Soviet Union, where the basic guarantee of subsistence welfare to all members was accompanied by endless informal manipulation of a status hierarchy and not by a structure of effective economic incentives.[15]

All this is not another utopian vision, not an academic fantasy, but a close approximation of the reality that was emerging in the specialist cooperatives of Bács-Kiskun County. Although I have no space to explore the issues here, I would argue that broadly similar structures were emerging in other parts of the Hungarian countryside and in industrial sectors in the 1980s. Of course there were many differences. Above all, the greater concentration of capital in modern factories makes it impossible to devolve to many urban workers the sort of property rights most

family farmers can enjoy. But numerous experiments with small cooperatives and "economic work partnerships" showed that it was possible
to move in the same direction in other sectors, for example, to create
urban industrial equivalents of agriculture's "private plot" (Stark 1989;
Hann 1990). Where large factories cannot be split up, it is at least
possible to allow the workers more control over their activities and to
give them a say (votes) in the decisions made by "managers." Again it is
a question of complementing Macpherson's notion of common property
with a closer specification of exclusive rights exercised by individuals.[16]

We do not really know if steps taken in this direction in Hungary in
the 1980s were successful. For example, some observers found that
measures to democratize industrial management were well received by
workers (Kürti 1990), while others were distinctly unimpressed (Hankiss
1990). My own view is that the kind of syncretic diversity that emerged
in Hungary in the 1980s allowed institutions like the specialist cooperative to meet the human needs of its members in an ultimately fruitful
way. This diversity allowed progress toward considerable material afflu-
ence, albeit unevenly distributed, while limiting the exploitation of wage
labor and affording most members a high degree of choice and control
over their work. These forms of property rights were very far from
perfect, mainly due to their awkward genesis in the period of authoritarian socialism. It is important to remember that even in the late 1980s
numerous Communist party members and large sectors of the economy
were resistant to reform. Nevertheless, I would argue that in the case of
Hungary there was every prospect for a continuation of pragmatic
reforms until events elsewhere in the region late in 1989 dramatically
altered the balance of power both externally and internally.

From this perspective the alternative promised for the 1990s, that is,
capitalism in something like its classical form, is a rather unattractive
proposition to many Hungarians—even to many of those who complained most during the late Kádár period. To borrow the metaphor in
the title of this volume, I am arguing that in Hungary the curtain was
being raised in a gradualist, pragmatic, and creative way from the
mid-1960s onward. In response to pressures "from below" and in order
to improve economic efficiency, policymakers in Hungary promoted a
search for diverse and flexible forms of property rights. In doing so they
moved beyond the familiar dichotomy between the poles of private
property on the one hand and communal property on the other. Their
synthesis has some affinity with the hierarchies of property rights identified by Gluckman in tribal land tenure, and also with the enriched and
deeply humanist vision of property rights put forward by Macpherson.

It respected the need for allocative efficiency emphasized by Comisso while placing greater weight than she does on the flexibility of local economic institutions and less on legal structures.

Today, the organic process of transformation that became well established in the Kádár period is apparently over, and in its place we have a new set of dogmas and invitations to relaunch bourgeois society from stage one. To judge from the most influential elite spokespersons and the declarations of policymakers, it would seem that the revolutions throughout Eastern Europe are concerned with the protection of bourgeois private property against all other forms of property rights. But one hears less of this sort of thing at the grass roots. In particular, in the specialist cooperative villages few are seeking the demise of this institution. Even the local activists of the Independent Smallholders' party admit that restoring the property relations forcibly disrupted around 1950 is neither feasible nor equitable in 1990. For most of the rural population, property rights are certainly of the greatest importance. Most of them do own their houses, and consumerist aspirations to possess more material goods have propelled the economic transformation of the whole country. But the villagers I know are *not* preoccupied with land ownership in the way that most of their grandparents had to be. They seem to be more receptive to a hierarchy of rights such as that pioneered by the specialist cooperatives, which provides a better combination of security, democratic control, and economic efficiency than any other system of property rights known to them, either individualist or collectivist. It is possible that many other East European citizens have similarly transcended (or would like to transcend) crude antinomies of classical capitalism and socialism. It is high time our theories took account of this grass-roots maturity (and time Professor Kornai stopped dreaming about rewinding old reels).

Notes

1. This is the position of Jean-Jacques Rousseau in the eighteenth century, as well as Marx and Engels in the nineteenth. The *Communist Manifesto* called explicitly for the "abolition of property in land." It also made a clear distinction between "the property of the petty artisan and of the small peasant" on the one hand, and "the bourgeois form," on the other.
2. The theorists of the liberal-conservative economic tradition would include Mill, Weber, and Schumpeter. However, the more profoundly conservative variants of Hayek and Friedman provide probably the best-known strands of the tradition among Eastern European intellectuals at the present time.
3. Influential accounts of such trends in the twentieth century have been provided by Burnham (1941) and Galbraith (1990). The latter has recently

proclaimed: "It does not seem to me greatly important as to where the ultimate ownership resides" (Galbraith 1990, 9).

4. See Shanin (1990, 24–25; 112–113). I am presently preparing a paper on the strength of the family-land relationship in Eastern Europe in the context of decollectivization.

5. Thus there were in the media, particularly in the early 1970s, frequent harsh words about peasants getting rich overnight and about "petty bourgeois elements," etc.

6. The Independent Smallholders' party was reestablished in November 1988. The reason for specifying 1947 was simple: By this time the egalitarian postwar land reform had been implemented and many former large estates broken up, while Communist attempts to promote collective farms had not yet made any impact.

7. For background on the specialist cooperatives of this region see Molnár (1987).

8. My fieldwork in this region began in 1976 and has continued intermittently. Only a brief visit was possible in August 1990—see Hann (forthcoming). I am aware that much further research is needed to sustain the arguments developed here.

9. Similar problems have been reported from other socialist countries now pursuing partial decollectivization. See Pryor (1991). See also two forthcoming articles by Tamara Dragadze at the Centre for Soviet and East European Studies at the University of London. The first, coauthored with J. Tsagardi, is called "Rural Perestroika in the Republic of Georgia." The second, coauthored with A. Ismailova, is "Family, Village and Nation in Soviet Azerbaijan."

10. I should make it clear that I reject the view that the limited success of Hungarian collectivization is entirely due to the private sector. The success stems from the integration of the small farmers into the socialized sector, as Swain (1985; 1987) had demonstrated. However, many Western observers have consistently argued that any successes in socialist agriculture must be in spite of, rather than thanks to, the socialist sector; and this is the predictable line taken by many in the Smallholders' party.

11. It is worth noting that local Communist officials are thought to have played the key role in ensuring a pragmatic collectivization policy in Bács-Kiskun, among them Tibor Simó and Pál Romány (Simó 1987; Romány 1987).

12. Gluckman's views are set out in numerous publications over many years. Two works (1943; 1965) are particularly useful.

13. Macpherson's views on property are best summarized in Macpherson (1973, chap. VI). See also his contributions to Macpherson (1978).

14. The focus upon weak conceptions of property rights is one of many features shared by both right-wing and left-wing critics of twentieth-century socialism. See, for example, Wittfogel (1957) and Fehér, Heller and Márkus (1983).

15. For an excellent application of some of Max Gluckman's concepts to the status hierarchy of a Soviet collective farm, see Humphrey 1983.

16. For an interesting argument from a "democratic socialist" theoretical perspective on the need to grant industrial workers *private* property rights in the means of production, see Kernohan (1987).

References

Brus, W. 1975. *Socialist ownership and political systems.* London: Routledge and Kegan Paul.

Burnham, J. 1941. *The managerial revolution.* New York: John Day.

Comisso, E. 1991. "Property rights, liberalism, and the transition from 'actually existing' socialism." *Eastern European Politics and Societies.* 5 (1):162–188.

Engels, F. 1972 [1884]. *The origin of the family, private property and the state.* New York: Pathfinder Press.

Fehér, F., Heller, A., and Márkus, G. 1983. *Dictatorship over needs.* Oxford: Basil Blackwell.

Galbraith, J. K. 1990. "Revolt in our time: The triumph of simplistic ideology." in G. Prins (ed.), *Spring in winter; The 1989 revolutions.* Manchester: Manchester University Press. 1–13.

Gluckman, M. 1943. *Essays in Lozi land and royal property.* Lusaka: Rhodes-Livingstone Paper No. 10.

———. 1965. *The ideas in Barotse jurisprudence.* New Haven: Yale University Press.

Hankiss, E. 1990. *East European alternatives.* Oxford: Clarendon Press.

Hann, C. M. 1980. *Tázlár: A village in Hungary.* Cambridge: Cambridge University Press.

———. 1985. *A village without solidarity: Polish peasants in years of crisis.* New Haven: Yale University Press.

———. (ed.). 1990. *Market economy and civil society in Hungary.* London: Frank Cass.

———. forthcoming. "Market principle, market place and the transition in eastern Europe." in Roy Dilley (ed.), *The market in social anthropological and sociological perspective.* Edinburgh: Edinburgh University Press.

Humphrey, C. 1983. *Karl Marx collective.* Cambridge: Cambridge University Press.

Kernohan, A. 1987. "Democratic socialism and private property." *Studies in Political Economy.* 22:145–166.

Kornai, J. 1990. *The road to a free economy.* New York: W. W. Norton.

Kürti, L. 1990. "Hierarchy and workers power in a Csepel factory." in C. M. Hann (ed.), *Market economy and civil society in Hungary.* London: Frank Cass. 61–84.

Macpherson, C. B. 1973. *Democratic theory: Essays in retrieval.* Oxford: Clarendon Press.

———. (ed.). 1978. *Property: mainstream and critical positions.* Oxford: Basil Blackwell.

Márkus, I. 1980. "Az ismeretlen föszereplö—a szegényparasztság" (The unknown leading actor—the poor peasantry). *Valóság.* 23 (4):13–39.

Marx, K., and Engels, F. 1968. "The Communist manifesto." in K. Marx and F. Engels, *Selected works in one volume.* London: Lawrence and Wishart.

Molnár, F. 1987. "A szövetkezetek sokszinüsége Bács-Kiskun megyében" (The variety of cooperatives in Bács-Kiskun country). in T. Simó (ed.), *Szakszövetkezetek Bács-Kiskun Megyében* (Specialist cooperatives in Bács-Kiskun county). Kecskemét: Kiskunsági Mezögazdasági Szövetkezetek Területi Szövetsége. 17–71.

Newby, H. 1983. "European social theory and the agrarian question: Towards a sociology of agriculture." in G. Summers (ed.), *Technology and social change in rural areas.* Boulder, CO: Westview Press. 109–124.

Nove, A. 1983. *The economics of feasible socialism.* London: Allen and Unwin.

Pavlovits, M. 1990. *A Tázlári "Beke" mg. szakszövetkezet 30 éve* (The "Peace" specialist agricultural cooperative in Tazlar). Tazlar: Béke Szakszövetkezet.

Pryor, F. L. 1991. "When is collectivization reversible?" *Studies in Comparative Communism.* 24 (1):3–24.

Romány, P. 1987. "Elöszó [Foreword]." in T. Simó (ed.), *Szakszövetkezetek Bács-Kiskun Megyében* (Specialist cooperatives in Bács-Kiskun county). Kecskemét: Kiskunsági Mezögazdasági Szövetkezetek Területi Szövetsége. 3–16.

Shanin, T. 1990. *Defining peasants.* Oxford: Basil Blackwell.

Simó, T. 1987, "A szakszövetkezetek es a tarsadalom" (Specialist cooperatives and society) in T. Simó (ed.), *Szakszövetkezetek Bács-Kiskun Megyében* (Specialist cooperatives in Bács-Kiskun county). Kecskemét: Kiskunsági Mezögazdasági Szövetkezetek Teruleti Szövetsége. 72–85.

Stark, D. 1989. "Coexisting organizational forms in Hungary's emerging mixed economy." in V. Nee and D. Stark (eds.), *Remaking the economic institutions of socialism; China and Eastern Europe.* Stanford: Stanford University Press. 137–168.

Swain, N. 1985. *Collective farms which work?* Cambridge: Cambridge University Press.

———. 1987. "Hungarian agriculture in the early 1980's: Retrenchment followed by reform." *Soviet Studies.* 39 (1):24–39.

Szelényi, I. 1988. *Socialist entrepreneurs; embourgeoisement in rural Hungary.* Cambridge: Polity Press.

Wittfogel, K. 1957. *Oriental despotism.* New Haven: Yale University Press.

PART III
Fractured Socialism and the Rise of Nationalism

From the "National Question" to Autogestion and Perestroika: Controversies in Theoretical and Political Approaches to National(ist) Movements

FAHRÜNNISA E. KULLUK

PRELUDE: MARX AND ENGELS ON NATIONALISM

In *The Communist Manifesto* of 1848, Marx and Engels declared the "withering away" of the appeal of nationalist identities and conflicts for the working class as a result of the following processes: (1) The development of the capitalist world market had abolished differences and antagonisms among proletarians in living conditions and perspectives for the future and homogenized their class interests; (2) Because the development of productive forces had transcended the boundaries of the nation-state, communism could be constructed only at the world level. Thus the "national" revolution of a particular proletariat against its "own" bourgeoisie was a step toward world revolution rather than an end in itself.

The arguments of Marx and Engels overlooked the furtherance of the development of the capitalist world market by old and new hierarchies among proletarians at the national and international levels and the politics of the nation-state, the differences among relatively privileged and underprivileged strata of proletarians in immediate class interests, and the possibility of (tactical) alliances between the totality or certain strata of the working class and the "national" bourgeoisie against non-capitalist ruling classes and/or the "foreign" bourgeoisie. For these reasons it failed to foresee and come to terms with the mass participation of proletarians in nationalist movements in capitalist societies since 1848.

The persistent historical reality of proletarian nationalism in capitalist societies led Marx and Engels to change their approach to nationalist identities and conflicts. In both their collective and individual writings, their new approach was dual and contradictory. On one hand, it was based on Engels's differentiation between "historic" and "historyless" nations, whose origins were Hegelian.[1] The nationalism of the former deserved proletarian support: Since they had already developed viable state systems in the past, they would be capable of forming viable new states in the future. The latter had no such tradition of viable state formations and lacked "the ability and energy" to reverse this trend. They would and *should* perish from the stage of history, thus facilitating the revolutionary development of historic nations. Hence their nationalism was counterrevolutionary. Marx and Engels regarded the bigger nations of Western and Central Europe as historic nations while they relegated the southern Slavs, Western European minorities, and some "Third World" nations into the category of historyless nations.

However, Marx and Engels acknowledged that the nationalism of smaller oppressed nations could be progressive both in itself because of its integration of national and class struggle and as a result of its liberating effects on the proletariat of the bigger dominant nations. As long as the smaller oppressed nation does not challenge its subordination, the proletariat of the bigger dominant nation allies with its own bourgeoisie rather than uniting with proletarians of other nations in anticapitalist struggles. This approach is developed in the writings of Marx and Engels on Ireland and Poland.[2]

The later approach of Marx and Engels to nationalism in capitalist society has often been criticized by twentieth-century Marxists. The Austro-Marxist Bauer (1924) argues that the "historyless" central European nations are revolutionary since they also struggle for constitutional rights, independence, and peasant emancipation. Munck (1986) criticizes the Eurocentrism and social Darwinism of Marx and Engels in assigning particular nations to the categories of "historic" and "historyless" nations. Meznarić (1987) concludes that even when historyless nations produce ideologies of self-reduction to a "nonposition" in the history dominated by historic nations, this "labour of the negative" could trigger subsequent efforts for solidarity among historyless nations, which could create an alternative historical "position." Also, when Marx and Engels discussed nationalism without the categories of historic and historyless nations, their approach was subjected to many methodological critiques, of which the economism thesis has been the strongest (Benner 1988).

While Marx and Engels developed a problematic analysis of nationalism in capitalist societies, they produced not even a hint that might be helpful in the analysis of nationalism in postcapitalist societies. Because they imagined Communist society as necessarily egalitarian and harmonious, they did not allow for the possibility that it could develop new forms of inequality and conflict that would lead to the (re)emergence of nationalism.

Twentieth-century Marxism has gone beyond the necessary-but-insufficient task of criticizing Marx and Engels's approach to nationalism in capitalist and real socialist societies. This chapter will present a critical survey of the contribution of twentieth-century Marxism to the analysis of national(ist)[3] movements in contemporary Eastern Europe. I will discuss various positions on the following issues: the concept of the nation, the determinants of national(ist) movements, and their political impacts and potentials.

THE ETERNAL NATION VERSUS PERMANENT NATION FORMATION

Stalin (1955, 32) defines the nation as "a historically constructed stable community of people, which emerged on the basis of common language, territory, economic life and physical nature that reveals itself in a community of culture" and claims that only the availability of all these characteristics at the same time constitutes a nation. This is a static concept of the nation that leaves no theoretical and political space for the analysis of nation formation as a dynamic, permanent process determined by and determining national(ist) movements and their articulation with other social movements. Thus Stalin's concept would not be useful in analyzing actual national formation either in contemporary Eastern Europe or elsewhere. It is politically dangerous because it can be used to deny ethnic groups who do not have (or are not supposed to have) all of the previously mentioned characteristics the right of self-determination in the sense of separation from the oppressor nation or regional self-management within the boundaries of a democratic (centralist) socialist state. Even before the revolution Stalin argued against the self-determination right of the Jews, whom he did not consider a nation. During Stalin's rule and even afterward, his concept of the nation played a key role in the state practice of dividing ethnic identities in the USSR into groups of *plemya* (tribe), *narodnost* (people), and *natsiya* (nation) and in the practice of differentiating between "native," or indigenous, nations and "nonnative" populations within the republics. Millions of Soviet citizens who did not qualify as members of ("native") nations have experienced and still experience discrimination (Tishkov 1989; Skalnik 1990). As long as the real socialist states do not transcend merely condemning the cult of personality and bureaucratic corruption under Stalinism and as long as they do not develop a truly democratic socialist theory and practice, the Stalinist concept of the nation can continue to function as a theoretical foundation of ethnic oppression.

Bauer (1924, 135) defines the nation as "the totality of men and women bound together through a common destiny into a community of character." He stresses that neither "common destiny" nor "community of character" should be understood as static concepts: Nation formation occurs as a result of collective experiences of and suffering under the same destiny in perpetual communication with and mutually affecting each other, rather than as a result of the similarity of destiny per se. Bauer acknowledged the existence of communities other than the nation (e.g., according to social class, occupation, region) and allowed for individual characteristics and differences within the nation, but he regarded the community of the nation as more important than both. However, his own analysis of the nation in class societies contradicts his thesis of the primacy of the nation. He writes that the subordinate classes are no more than the small farmers (*Hintersassen*) of the nation: Their labor and exploitation make possible the development of the national culture, which is the culture of the dominant classes, but they are totally excluded from participating in this culture. Bauer cannot explain why it is that the subordinate classes and the dominant classes share a community of destiny and character even though their material conditions of existence are strikingly different. He also does not consider the kind of nation formation that develops not only against foreign rulers or intruders but against the indigenous dominant classes as well—an ever-spreading process in Eastern Europe. For these reasons, Bauer's version of dynamic nation formation is not a promising point of departure for the analysis of nation formation in contemporary Eastern Europe. Bauer's contribution consists in having argued against static notions of the nation.

A dynamic analysis of nation formation in contemporary Eastern Europe must focus above all on the development of the policies of the real socialist state toward the dominated ethnic groups in its territory, which are not *necessarily* minorities in the demographic sense, and on these policies' effects on the civil society of these groups. These policies have moved in several paths simultaneously:

1. Mostly relative repression. The real socialist state has carried out total repression toward some ethnic groups—in the sense of denying an ethnic group the right of existence in its "native" territory (e.g., the Tartars and the Volga Germans in the USSR) or forbidding an ethnic group the practice of even the most elementary cultural rights, such as the right to use "native" names and language in and outside of its "native" territory (e.g., the Islamic and Turkish-speaking ethnic group

in Bulgaria). But in most cases the ethnic repression of the real socialist state has taken the form of compulsory assimilation of the dominated ethnic groups into the culture of the dominant ethnic group through the policies of, above all, schooling, military service, and mass media.

2. Relative toleration. In order to veil the process of compulsory assimilation and to prevent political resistance to it, the real socialist state has allowed and even fostered partial reproduction of the culture and identity of most of the dominated ethnic groups. It has left the practice of "native" languages and rituals in the private sphere more or less free and has provided means for further exploration of the culture and history of the dominated ethnic groups within the limits of compatibility with the official history and ideology, such as schools, research institutes, cheap books. The real socialist state has also organized relative economic development in the peripheral regions where the dominated ethnic groups live. This process is relative because substantial core-periphery differentials have remained and grave "diseconomies of production" have emerged for the environment and "quality of life" of the dominated ethnic groups. But as an alternative to economic stagnation (and only so far!) it can still be called development. Another aspect of the "relative toleration" path of the real-socialist state is the opportunity of upper social mobility that it grants to those members of the dominated classes who (pretend to) become culturally and/or politically assimilated.[4] These individuals can make careers in the technocracy, arts and sciences, and even the (local) nomenklatura.

3. Employment policies and various social policies that discriminate against those members of the dominated ethnic groups who do not become culturally and/or politically assimilated. The occupational, residential, and other "ghettoes" created by these policies have fostered intragroup communication and solidarity within the dominated ethnic groups.

Hechter's (1975) theory of nation formation is suitable for capturing only the third of the previously outlined real socialist state policies vis-à-vis the dominated ethnic groups. Hechter stresses the positive selection of interclass and intraethnic communication within the periphery by the residential and occupational segregation policies of the core and the subsequent reproduction of substantial identifiable cultural differences between the core and the periphery, such as language (accent), distinctive religious practices, and life-style. Not even the peripheral elites can escape this process. "Phenotypical differences between groups that symbolize differential ethnicity" hinder their cultural assimilation to the core, while the economic (quasi-) stagnation of the "hinterland" of the periphery due to the policies of the core state and core capital limits their opportunities for economic prospects. The prospects of the other option for the upper social mobility of peripheral elites—reformist politics that appeal to the universalistic norms aspired to by many industrial societies—are also contingent and limited.[5] Hechter mentions but underestimates compulsory public education in the English language. He regards it merely as a cause of the decline of Celtic language-speaking rather than as a major component of a broader cultural hegemony strategy of the core state, which triggers, on one hand, cultural assimilation and, on the other hand, new antihegemonic strategies of the peripheral ethnic group.[6]

Nairn's (1981) theory of nation formation addresses only the relative toleration policies of the state toward dominated ethnic groups. According to Nairn, the British have directly organized and indirectly allowed economic development and substantial political and cultural self-determination in Scotland. Britain also gave those members of the Scottish dominant classes who were not satisfied with the role of local patriot the option of integration into positions of power in the international finance world of London and in colonial administration overseas. These policies of the British state have (re)produced a Scottish culture and identity that was compatible with an all-British national identity—a "subnationalism." The capacity of the British state for further relative toleration in the economic sphere has declined with the loss of British hegemony in the world economy. This decline has transformed Scottish subnationalism into a separatist nationalism.

Balibar (1988) argues that the national culture and the identity of the dominant ethnic group as well are organized by the permanent "ethnicization" policies of the state through the institutions of, above all, the school and the family. These policies do not absolutely impose particular symbols of national culture and identity; rather, they offer a set of symbols from which each individual can "freely" select his or her "own" symbols. In my view, the set of symbols in the East European context is characterized by chauvinistic exaltation of those aspects of national history and culture that really or supposedly harmonize with official history and ideology and by tabooing or representing in a distorted manner those aspects that actually or potentially challenge official history and ideology. Members of the dominant ethnic group choose both *from* and *against* this set of symbols. Ralatively autonomous institutions or movements within real socialism (e.g., the church or alternative sects), voices from the underground and outside (secretly available Samizdat, exiles, and Western publications and broadcasts), and a collective memory of national or cross-national solidarities before real socialism (e.g., in the latter case, the ties of Czechs and Hungarians to Central-Western European culture) can provide alternative symbols of national culture and identity. Not allowing for the second option at all and reducing civil society to "ideological apparatuses of the state" constitute the limits of Balibar's analysis of nation formation.

The nation formation of the dominant and dominated ethnic groups is interdependent. When they develop common interests and alliances against the real socialist state, they might appropriate some of each other's symbols of national culture and identity and adapt them to their own. When they compete with each other over the benefits of real socialist or postreal socialist state policies, they might adopt symbols of national culture and identity that intentionally distance themselves from the rival ethnic group(s). Marxism needs to develop systematic theoretical and empirical analyses of both types of interdependency in nation formation.

Substantial nation formation is generally regarded as a *prerequisite* of national(ist) movements. But the case study of Occitany by Touraine (1981) suggests that nation formation might develop primarily *in the course* of a national(ist) movement. Rather than basing itself on a currently used national language, Occitan nationalism is striving to reestablish the Occitan language as the national language. The Occitans are re-creating an Occitan national identity in spite of the big economic and cultural differences within Occitany in the past and at the present—an identity oriented primarily to the future. There are ethnic groups in Eastern Europe whose story of nation formation resembles that of the Occitans (e.g., the Gagavuz in the USSR and Romania). The Gagavuz nationalism is synthesizing the Turkic origins that it is rediscovering, along with the Christianized past and present, as the basis of national culture and identity for the truly independent political unit of the future. Thus the analysis of nation formation by Touraine (1981) has relevance for Eastern Europe as well.

Wallerstein (1979, 1984) has argued that in all countries that remain articulated to the capitalist world economy and the interstate system, each nation formation (which is simultaneously class formation and status group formation) is affected by and strives to affect the social division of labor in the totality of the capitalist world economy and the interstate system. No real socialist state has succeeded in its efforts of withdrawal from the capitalist world economy and/or the interstate system.[7] The postreal socialist state will not even attempt isolationism; on the contrary, it will voluntarily seek increased integration. Thus the global context resumes key importance for nation formation in contemporary Eastern Europe. This is stressed also by Beck (1991) without a Wallersteinian "world-system" perspective.

THE DETERMINANTS OF NATIONAL(IST) MOVEMENTS: GLOBAL AND REAL SOCIALISM–SPECIFIC PERSPECTIVES

Each national(ist) movement expresses grievances and contentions. The processes that (re)produce these grievances and contentions constitute the primary determinants of national(ist) movements. Other processes channel the expression of these grievances and contentions to a national(ist) (i.e., extraclass or nonclass framework) and foster or hinder the success chances of a national(ist) challenge to real socialism. These processes are the secondary determinants of national(ist) movements. Of course "secondary" should not be understood as "minor."

PRIMARY DETERMINANTS

Wallerstein (1979) considers the orientation of production in real socialist countries toward keeping up with capitalist development as the primary determinant of national(ist) movements there. In order to remain at the level of a core industrialized nation in the capitalist world economy, the USSR had to further transform its industry into one with a major export component. As a result of a shortage of unskilled workers in European Russia, unskilled workers were imported from central Asia. Faced with the monopolization of control over presumed class organizations by the middle-income stratum of workers (of largely upper-ethnic origin), the central Asian subproletariat organized to defend its class interests in ethnic organizations.

While Wallerstein regards national(ist) movements in real socialist countries as the class organizational form of underpaid and lower ethnic workers, Touraine and Dubet et al. (1982) assert that the resistance of the better-paid and upper-ethnic workers as well *necessarily* incorporates national(ist) elements for the following reasons:[8]

1. All nonparty workers are economically underprivileged and politically dominated vis-à-vis the managers of the Party-State, who (quasi-)-monopolize power and information and legitimate their power with the discourse of representing and serving working-class interests. In this context civil society struggles for its autonomy from the state and its control over state apparatuses in the name of the nation.

2. The distortion of national history and the limitation of the development of national culture by the educational and cultural policies of the Party-State produce national(ist) reactions.

3. The Party-State in Eastern Europe has a subordinate role vis-à-vis the USSR and the Warsaw Pact. The national(ist) movement reacts and struggles against this subordination, which is economic and, above all, political-military.

All three dimensions are equally important and interdependent. For this reason none of the limits faced by Solidarity—the economic crisis, the hegemony of the Party-State, and the threat of Soviet intervention—have succeeded in steering it into *one* dimensionality.

The alternative for which the national(ist) movement (not only in Poland 1980–1981, but also in Hungary 1956 and Czechoslovakia 1968) contends is autogestion (self-management). There are differences among and within real socialist countries in the interpretation of autogestion. For example, some in Poland stand for a version based on the reestablishment of economic nationality and honest, competent managers, while others insist on the primacy of workers' councils independent even from Solidarity. But common to all conceptions of autogestion are the rejection of cogestion (mere sharing of power with the prevailing power-holders) and the consideration of the liberation of the enterprise as a step toward the liberation of society from the hegemony of the indigenous Party-State and the USSR.[9]

The primary determinants of national(ist) movements in real socialist countries before and after perestroika can be grasped best by synthesizing the *methodologies* of Wallerstein and Touraine et al. by considering both the links to the capitalist world economy and the interstate system and the economic, political, cultural, and military factors internal to the real socialist system. This synthesis would render it possible to avoid both treating real socialism as an island unto itself, which is the problem of a purely Tourainian approach, and *reducing* the internal dynamics of real socialism to the imperatives of the relationships with the capitalist world economy and states, which is the error of a strictly Wallersteinian approach. As far as the *particular* arguments of Wallerstein and Touraine et al. are concerned, certain amplifications and qualifications are needed.

The integration of the USSR into the capitalist world economy was not confined to industry in eastern Russia. Already before perestroika, many Asian regions of the USSR had also been articulated to the capitalist world economy as producers of (new) raw materials and agricultural products (in)directly[10] demanded by the world market. This has called for the transformation of production and social structures in these regions and the creation of new class and ethnic inequalities among and within regions. The grievances and contentions of national(ist) movements in the Asian USSR were related essentially to this transformation. Eastern European industry has not only endeavored to become a successful rival of capitalist industry in the world market but also has complemented capitalist industry as subcontractor—a phenomenon particularly significant in the former German Democratic Republic, Poland, and Hungary. The workers of the Eastern European subcontractor firms were underpaid in comparison with the workers of the Western

European customer firms. Therefore, their economic grievances and contentions were directed *objectively* not only against their economically underprivileged situation vis-à-vis the managers of the Party-State but also *against* their underprivileged location in the *global* hierarchy remuneration and consumption, even when these workers identified subjectively with capitalism rather than with democratic socialist autogestion.

All three allied powers were responsible for the creation of the subordination of the Party-State to the USSR and the Warsaw Pact. They "were convinced equally in having the incontestable right to share world domination among themselves, without even discussing any particularities with the affected parties (and sometimes even continents)" (Heller and Fehér 1982, 15). With this mentality they signed the treaties of Yalta and Potsdam, which assigned Eastern Europe to Soviet hegemony. The United States has always preached "freedom" for Eastern Europe. Yet when the Eastern European nations actually struggled for their national sovereignty, they received either no U.S. support at all (the argument of Heller and Fehér 1982 for Hungary 1956) or U.S. support only as far as they let themselves be exploited for weakening the centrifugal tendencies of the U.S. hegemonic sphere (the more general argument of Konrád 1985, 26). Thus the United States contributed to the continuance of Soviet hegemony over Eastern Europe. In this context, the struggles of Eastern European nations for sovereignty were against not only the Soviet state but also against those advanced capitalist states, especially the United States, that have consented to Soviet hegemony over Eastern Europe. The strictly anti-Soviet ideology of many insurgents and their belief in the availability of U.S. support for their cause did not change this effect (Heller and Fehér 1982, 18). The danger of (nuclear) war was inherent in the system of balance between the United States and the USSR, the NATO and the Warsaw Pact (Konrád 1985). This implies that the struggles of Eastern European nations for sovereignty were also struggles for world peace—even when they were not formally allied with the autonomous peace movements in Eastern Europe.

The relations of the Party-State with the USSR and the Warsaw Pact were not uniform all over Eastern Europe. The spectrum extended from the model of total subordination portrayed by Touraine et al. (valid for the German Democratic Republic, Poland, Bulgaria, and post-1968 Czechoslovakia) to total contestation practiced by Tito's Yugoslavia and Hoxha's Albania. In between there have been two other models. The Romanian state under Ceauşescu questioned certain aspects of Soviet hegemony without withdrawing from the Warsaw Pact and without supporting most of the antihegemonic struggles in other Eastern European countries.[11] The Kádárist Hungarian state pursued pragmatic, diplomatic compromise with Soviet hegemony. In exchange for accepting the principle of Soviet hegemony, it sought to win concessions over the particularities of Soviet hegemony, which might lead to the loosening of the political-military and social framework imposed by Yalta (Konrád 1985). The state's toleration of the development of relatively autonomous civil society was both a prerequisite and a consequence of this compromise strategy.[12]

The differences between Eastern European countries in the relation of the Party-State to the USSR and the Warsaw Pact limited and positively or negatively selected priorities in the grievances and contentions of national(ist) movements. National sovereignty vis-à-vis the USSR and the Warsaw Pact always remained a burning issue in the model of total subordination, while it became marginal in the model of total contestation.[13] In the model of compromise strategy, civil society "self-limited" its struggles against both Soviet hegemony and the power of the Hungarian Party-State—as long as the main foundation of this strategy, the threat of Soviet intervention against "too radical" protest, remained intact. Once Soviet intervention no longer seemed possible (above all because of Soviet preoccupation with ethnic problems and struggles at home), "self-limitation" of civil society gave way to renewed priority of national sovereignty and unlimited nation-formation against the Party-State. The Romanian model was the most complex and contradictory. At first, "the country's national interests, the Romanian people's patriotic aspirations,' their enmity against Soviet imperialism, as well as their traditional attachment to western cultural values, were instrumentalized by the Stalinist regime to win, at a difficult historical juncture, mass support and the intellectuals' political participation (Tismaneanu 1984, 72). This meant common struggle of the Romanian state and civil society for national sovereignty under the limits set by the former. Over time "the gradual distancing from Moscow has resulted in a *paranoid psychology of permanent menace*—a state of *continual mobilization* and the heightening of the regime's repressive-dictatorial features" (Tismaneanu 1984, 77–78). The latter is portrayed by Tismaneanu as the increasing curtailment of civil liberties and rights in general. To this one can add surplus-repression against those dominated ethnic groups who were supposed to conspire with foreign states against Romania—above all, the Hungarians. Ceaușescu's superchauvinistic[14] opening toward the myths of a "Thracian-Dacian" imperialist past was alienating for the dominated ethnic groups. These processes eroded the initial mass and intellectual support for Ceaușescu's regime and prepared the way for

Temesvar in 1989—on one hand, the insurgency of all civil society against the Party-State in the name of the nation and, on the other hand, the specific response of the Hungarians to their experience of surplus-repression.

Neither Wallerstein nor Touraine et al. even mention the role of massive ecological destruction and the consequent deteriorations in the quality of life in generating national(ist) movements in Eastern Europe. Yet both Marxist and non-Marxist analyses of recent ethnic struggles in the USSR stress the ecological grievances and contentions (e.g., Tishkov 1989; Simon 1989). Unfortunately they take ecological destruction as a given instead of explaining why it came into existence.

According to Havemann (1980), ecological crisis is inevitable under real socialism. Neither production nor consumption can be curtailed in order to limit ecological destruction—on one hand, because of the cult of production maximization rooted in the state priority of catching up with and *surpassing* the capitalist West; on the other hand, because of the internal structure of real socialist economic planning, which hinders effective planning of production and consumption. By the latter, Havemann understands especially the lack of freedom of the enterprise in determining the quantity and methods of production and the ultralow subsidized prices for many goods and services, which do not reflect the real costs of production at the base and thereby mislead macroeconomic planners. Havemann's discussion of ecological crisis under real socialism is general. It does not explain if certain regions and ethnic groups are more affected by ecological destruction than others and why. Advanced capitalist firms often "export" those industries or parts of the labor process that are particularly detrimental to the environment to the periphery or assign them to workers of "lower" ethnic origin. It would be interesting to investigate if real socialism has also done so in its "own" periphery. In the case of an affirmative answer, the next question would be about the continuities and changes that this policy has created in the preexisting trends of ethnic discrimination under real socialism.

Both Wallerstein and Touraine et al. write on the preperestroika era. Two facts are obvious about the praxis of perestroika until 1991: the failure in overcoming or substantially modifying the preexisting inequalities of class and ethnicity, and Gorbachev's determination to prevent separatism by all means, including by conventional real socialist military intervention. Did Gorbachev provide an accurate, comprehensive diagnosis of the causes of national(ist) movements and sound solutions at the theoretical level—failing "only" in praxis? Or was the theory of perestroika already in crisis?

The theoretical core of Gorbachev's (1988, 2nd edition) early analysis of the "national question" in the USSR consists of the praise of the Leninist position both in theory and practice and the appeal for its revival and extension through perestroika. He does not address the inherent contradiction between national/regional self-determination and a highly centralized Party-State. He attributes all ills (in ethnic relations and elsewhere) to the deviations from Leninist principles under the "cult of personality" during Stalin's rule, to the "subjective methods" of the Soviet leadership in the Khrushchev era, to the problems created by the change in the early years of the Brezhnev regime, to the persistent inertia, and at a more general level, to "the lack of concern of the bureaucracy with the legitimate problems of the people." He analyzes neither the social processes that enabled Stalin, Khrushchev, and Brezhnev to rise to and remain in power nor the precise links between their leadership styles and the economic, political, and ethnic problems and crises of the USSR. By overconcentrating on the mistakes of particular leaders, he overlooks the *collective* responsibility of the nomenklatura (Yeltzin 1990, 256). In other words, the early Gorbachev analysis of Soviet history is superficial and contains no radical critique.

In his talks, essays, and interviews of 1989–1990, Gorbachev shows *some* signs of a more realistic and critical assessment of the history of ethnic relations in the USSR (Gorbachev 1990, 53–55). He admits the following:

1. The USSR has been in fact a centralized state rather than a federation of republics with equal rights.

2. There are evident problems and contradictions that have been determined through the articulation of the mistakes committed in the regional distribution of productive forces and in cultural and national policies that led to the unequal development of certain regions and to demographic and ecological transformations.

3. Unequal exchange between economic regions has prevailed; resources have been taken away from some regions in order to compensate for sloppiness and laziness in others.

4. There have been "crimes committed against peoples as a whole" that have to be "paid for" now.

Gorbachev attributes the emergence of national(ist) movements to these four aspects of ethnic relations under real socialism to persistent conflicts between nations that have been generated by "religious intolerance" and that predate real socialism, and to the "nationalist anarchy" organized by "centrifugal forces," "opponents of perestroika," and "elements and groups which are enemies of society." He is correct in suggesting that the vestiges of previous ethnic relations and conflicts survive and even become stronger under real socialism. But it is not evident if these conflicts are rooted in "religious intolerance" per se. The last determinant mentioned by Gorbachev sounds like a conspiracy theory.

Gorbachev (1988; 1990) offered the augmentation of the (relative) autonomy of the republics and autonomous regions in the economic, social, cultural, and environmental protection spheres and improvements in the rights of the "nonnative" populations as solutions to the ethnic problems and conflicts in the USSR. His earlier and later understanding of these solutions differed in several aspects. The early Gorbachev sets the continuation in the primacy of "socialist planning" and the leading role of the central Communist Party as limits to self-management in all spheres (Gorbachev 1988; on the basis of analysis of Gorbachev's other texts as well, Dahm 1990).[15] The later Gorbachev regards it necessary to dismantle the "authoritarian-bureaucratic command system." However, he offers an alternative in those cases where the increased autonomy of the enterprise in production and distribution; the development of the market; more "private initiative" through leases, cooperatives, and land-owning peasants; a multiparty system; and an autonomous labor movement coexist with the presidential regime, which *institutionalizes* the superpowers of the president and his narrow circle of top advisers in all spheres of life. Already in its beginnings this regime proved itself as incompatible with the self-determination right of the Baltic nations. Some critics of Gorbachev[16] feared that repression under this regime might extend to degenerate perestroika into a presidential dictatorship à la Pinochet, which would work with free entrepreneurs toward an "economic miracle." Gorbachev's plea for the legal prohibition and pacification of "nationalist, chauvinist and other extremist organizations" which "provoke national conflicts" and "terrorize and intimidate people of other nationalities" suggested the possibility of further and extensive repression. Who belongs to the category to be banned is a matter of definition, and definitions can be manipulated.

Gorbachev's early formula for improving the rights of "nonnative" populations granted them more cultural rights and facilities. Later he abandoned a purely cultural approach and defined the solution as the access of every human being irrespective of his or her nationality to equal rights everywhere in the USSR and in the world, the abolition of all discrimination and restriction based on classification into categories of "natives," "migrants," "emigrants," and so forth. He supported the establishment and protection of equal rights through the constitution and simple laws. But equal rights cannot be achieved only by creating new laws and articles. Fundamental reforms in the totality of the Soviet legal system were needed, as Gorbachev had already realized in 1988. Even more necessary and important was the availability of institutional and autonomous political space to the dominated ethnic groups for safeguarding and extending the legally granted equal rights. A presidential dictatorship (à la Pinochet or otherwise) would have threatened both the independence and the effectiveness of the (reformed) legal system and the political space available to the dominated ethnic groups.

As far as the relations between the USSR and Eastern Europe are concerned, perestroika meant both continuity and change. The continuity has been in the following aspects:

1. Absence of a self-critical Soviet assessment of the history of the relations between the USSR and Eastern Europe.

Gorbachev is silent in both of his books on the role of the German-Soviet Pact of 1939 and Yalta as the foundation of the compulsory incorporation of the Baltic states into the USSR and of the USSR's semi-informal empire over other Eastern European countries. He questions neither the military-political nor the economic functioning of Soviet hegemony in Eastern Europe. The invasion of Hungary and Czechoslovakia remains a taboo theme. Gorbachev (1988) laments the past "deterioration of the friendly relations" with Yugoslavia, People's Republic of China, and Albania, but does not indicate how these "friendly relations" could have been maintained (i.e., whether these contestants should have yielded to Soviet hegemony, whether the USSR should have accepted the legitimacy of their contentions for national sovereignty, or whether a compromise strategy in the Hungarian style would have been the adequate solution). The history of economic relations between the USSR and Eastern Europe is portrayed by Gorbachev (1988) as based on "mutual benefits" and "mutual aid." A future of "increased economic cooperation" is called for.

2. Reluctance to accept the total abolition of the Warsaw Pact (Gorbachev 1990).

The *declared* changes concern the questions of future Soviet military intervention in Eastern Europe and the new mission of the Warsaw Pact. Gorbachev (1990, 100) expresses a position against all intervention in the internal affairs and against the national sovereignty of "allied, friendly, and any other states." He calls for the transformation of the Warsaw Pact from a "military-political" organization into a "political-military" one (1990, 121). The new Warsaw Pact will have the mission of preparing the way into the "totality of Europe" rather than of pursuing military competition and confrontation between the capitalist and real socialist blocs.

Gorbachev's declarations about transforming the relations between the USSR and Eastern Europe were received with skepsis in the Baltic countries. Mavriks Vulfsons, Latvian political scientist and national deputy, regarded Soviet military intervention in the Baltic countries as "the dress rehearsal for Poland, perhaps for Europe" (1990, 139). This scenario was not realized—above all because the USSR ceased to exist. But even if Gorbachev had remained in power, he would have been too preoccupied with and threatened by ethnic and other insurgencies at the home front to dare fighting on several fronts. Furthermore, advanced capitalist countries would have reacted to a Soviet march into Eastern Europe with economic sanctions of a scope and duration that might have been fatal for the already bankrupt Soviet economy. Gorbachev was more likely to pursue a "Young Turk" strategy: giving up the unviable Greater Empire for concentrating on the maintenance of "national unity" in the nucleus of the Empire and then endeavoring to integrate this intact nucleus throughout the "totality of Europe." Yeltsin is now pursuing a narrower version of this strategy: He has also given up direct domination over the periphery of the nucleus of the former Empire—i.e., the Central Asian republics—but he is determined to prevent any ethnic separatism within Russia and to keep Russia in a hegemonic position in relation to other independent republics formed on former Soviet territory.

The end of the USSR is not necessarily the end of the issue of national sovereignty vis-à-vis a superpower in the Eastern European national-(ist) movements of the (near) future. While Heller and Fehér (1990, 281) regard German unification as a process which "could promote the full unification of Europe" and "would discard all dangerous scheming with plans of a new Rapallo," Szelenyi (1992, 236–37) points to the possibility of the hegemony of a united Germany over Eastern Europe:

"If a united Germany were to become an expansionist economic power, then a Central Europe 'Balkanized' into small nation-states may have few countermeasures available to German penetration and may thus simply turn into an equivalent of something like Central America for the United States. One can do worse than to swap the USSR for a democratic Germany as a 'master nation'. But can this region do without a 'master'?"

The Eastern European reaction to German hegemony would not be only in terms of anti-German national(ist) sentiments and movements. It might also take the form of cross-national religious sentiments and movements. The Islamic ethnic groups of Eastern Europe might join the Central Asian ethnic groups in a pan-Islamic fundamentalism.

SECONDARY DETERMINANTS
Theoretical and Actual Political Crises of the Left
The national(ist) movements in Eastern Europe have been positively selected and mediated by the theoretical and actual political crises of

both the official and the dissident Left there. In turn they have forced both types of the Left into reconstruction—with varying degrees of present and prospective success.

The "Marxism-Leninism" of the official Left has been an instrument of domination. Its formulas, above all "the dictatorship of the proletariat under the leadership of its Vanguard Party," "proletarian international-ism," "the free and equal association of socialist nations," and "progres-sive elements in our national heritage," have aimed at denying class and ethnic oppression and presenting an inflated portrait of relative tolera-tion under real socialism. "Marxism-Leninism" as the organic ideology of the nomenklatura has developed as a synthesis of the following processes:

1. Readings of the "classics" in ways that suit the interests of the nomenklatura
2. Tabooing alternative traditions in the Marxist legacy (e.g., Luxem-burg and Trotsky's critiques of Lenin and Stalin, the "national communism" of Sultan Galiev from central Asia, "council com-munism" dismissed even by Lenin as "the infantile disease of communism")
3. New "contributions" from the actual top leaders (e.g., the "Brezh-nev Doctrine" justifying military intervention to Eastern Europe)
4. Distorted readings of national history
5. Condemnation of contemporary critiques of real socialism (includ-ing those by Western Marxists) as anti-Communist, bourgeois, and so forth

National(ist) movements in Eastern Europe are attempts to come to alternative diagnoses and solutions in reaction to the growing gap be-tween the preachings of the official Left and its practices in class and ethnic relations. Official Marxism-Leninism has lost its credibility and viability in the eyes of the dominated classes and ethnic groups even as a framework of struggling for *future* rights as appeals to values of the powerful. Achieving rights through autonomous national(ist) mobiliza-tion has become preferable to trying to convince the nomenklatura of the necessity of overcoming actual class and ethnic oppression because of its incompatibility with the "real essence" of Marxism-Leninism.

The official Left responded to its theoretical and actual political crises in a variety of ways. In Albania and post-Ceauşescu Romania, it tried to save face without substantial self-transformation. This meant in Albania the introduction of limited political and economic reforms from above simultaneous with the retirement of the too obviously Stalinist elements of Marxism-Leninism. In Romania it meant making Ceauşescu alone the scapegoat and representing the "new Communists," supposedly previous intra-Party dissidents, as *the* guarantee of "national unity" in the post-Ceauşescu era. The Soviet response was the promise of major social transformations and self-transformation of the Party-State through perestroika, the inclusion of some top dissidents on the list of candidates to the People's Councils as a "politics of symbols" (Staniszkis 1990, 83), and the rehabilitation of *some* taboo figures from the Marxist legacy (e.g., Bukharin and Trotsky, but not Sultan Galiev). The official Left in Hungary opted for its "social democratization" combined with the multiparty system and parliamentary democracy (Staniszkis 1990).

The Albanian and Romanian responses did not convince anyone, since it was obvious that they were minimal concessions intended as a life jacket for the submerging power of the Party-State. The Soviet response did attract both mass and intellectual support at the beginning. But the praxis of perestroika not only failed in even partially solving the economic, political, and ethnic crises of the USSR, it also better revealed the theoretical limitations of perestroika—insufficiently radical diagnoses and self-contradictory solutions. This led both the masses and the (top) dissidents either to total disillusionment with perestroika and (further) autonomous organization and mobilization or to support for "radical reformer" Yeltsin. Rehabilitated Trotskyism within or outside the party did not have much prospect for success: The Soviet nations were reluctant to replace one kind of "proletarian internationalism" with another. In Hungary, the "social-democratized" official Left lost in the "politics of competition" (Bruszt and Stark 1992).

Tismaneanu (1988) discusses the following dimensions of the crisis of the dissident Left in Eastern Europe:

1. Many Left dissidents have confined themselves to abstract and linguistically difficult philosophical exegeses on "real" Marxism rather than addressing the concrete problems of their societies at the present.
2. Other Left dissidents, who have pursued neo-Marxist politics in both theory and praxis from the late 1960s to the early 1980s, have begun to regard Marxism as an obstacle to their further quest for "truth." This has led them to abandon Marxism completely or partially in the latter 1980s.

The first dimension is no uniquely Eastern European phenomenon; Anderson (1976) has pointed out the same tendency among Western Marxists as well. Both in the East and the West, such specialists in "Glass Bead Games" (Hermann Hesse's term) have contributed significantly to the disillusionment of the dominated classes and ethnic groups with Marxism. They respond to their crisis mostly by mere product differentiation, which also remains alienating.

Partial departure from Marxism in the analysis of concrete social and political problems is not only a *sign* of the crisis of the dissident Left, it can also constitute a step toward the *overcoming* of this crisis. No system of thinking can produce by itself all concepts necessary for understanding all dynamics of a complex and contradictory world. The insistence to cook in its own juice only would deprive Marxism of opportunities for analytical self-improvement.

The most important way for the dissident Left to overcome the crisis is by developing organic ties with all types of mass organizations and movements—class-based ones, ethnic-based ones, and new social movements. These ties should be based on mutual exchange and learning and on openness both to solidarity and conflict rather than on the development of a new ethos of interventionism and vanguardism.

Communication with Other National(ist) Movements

National(ist) movements often draw on the legacy of past national(ist) movements for self-legitimation and in the choice of their organizational and mobilizational forms. Michnik (1985, 85–105) describes the collective memory of the struggle for Polish national sovereignty that was waged by Jósef Pilsudski, the prominent ideologist of the Polish Socialist party and later chief of state, against both tzarist Russia and the USSR as a process of educating future generations of Poles into independence. Pilsudski has often symbolized the critical position against the conformist, intellectually and morally lazy, and reactionary elements within Polish society as well as the vision of new political and social forms that would make it possible for many nations to live together in peace and equality in a common territory. Touraine et al. (1982, 42–59, 97–103) discuss the continuity and the radicalization of the theory and praxis of autogestion from the Titoist rupture to Hungary 1956, Czechoslovakia 1968, and Poland 1980–1981.

The chain reaction effect of contemporary Eastern European national-(ist) movements on each other is well known. These movements might have been encouraged also by the Afghan resistance against the Soviet invasion, which demonstrated the inability of the Soviet state even in its stronger days to win a victory against a small nation determined to fight to the end for its national sovereignty.

Economic (In)viability of Political Separatism

Nairn (1981, 56) argues that the emergence of new economic resources (e.g., the discovery of oil and multinational investments in Scotland) might increase both the frustration of the dominated ethnic group with the preexisting nation-state and its hopes for the economic viability of political separation. Gorbachev (1990, 55–58) regarded the economic integration of the ethnic groups/regions aspiring to political separatism from the preexisting nation-state as *the* factor that would render political separatism economically unviable for *both* sides. He portrayed the economic integration of the Soviet republics as "not just a sum of productive capacities but a unitary economic organism."

What were the implications of these theses for the politically separatist Eastern European nations? Vulfsons's (1991) arguments suggest that political separatism might become economically viable not only when new economic resources are *given*; it might become the *prerequisite* for the *creation* of such resources. Hence the expectations of a dominated ethnic group for the creation of new economic resources after political independence might already suffice to increase its frustration with the preexisting nation-state. Vulfsons accepted the dependency of Latvia on the USSR for raw materials but remarked that Latvia possesses potentials more important than raw materials: "an intellectual potential, which with western aid could rapidly get in the world-economy, and the possibility of using Latvian ports as a bridge between the EEC and the USSR." He also allowed for other forms of economic cooperation between the independent Latvia and the USSR in industry and agriculture—provided the prices and terms of delivery could be negotiated freely. In other words, contrary to Gorbachev's (1990) argument, political separatists in the Baltic region did not plan to cut off all economic ties with the USSR and thereby ruin the Soviet economy. What they opposed was the unilateral imposition of the terms of trade by the USSR.

However, political separatism is not an economic panacea. The independent Baltic states would benefit from better terms of trade with the former USSR and from the opportunities offered by Western aid and investment. But these benefits might be (partially) offset by the disadvantages of greater integration to the world economy—more vulnerability to the fluctuations in demand, the burden of foreign aid repayment, and the huge profit repatriation of multinational corporations.

THE POLITICAL IMPACTS/POTENTIALS OF NATIONAL(IST) MOVEMENTS

Early twentieth-century Marxists assess the political impacts and potentials of national(ist) movements according to the following criteria:

1. Ideology ("reactionary," "bourgeois-democratic," "self-determination") in the Marxist-Leninist sense
2. Relations with and effects on the labor movement (obstacle or ally)
3. The organizational form anticipated for the period after the achievement of political independence (bourgeois nation-state or socialist).

On the basis of these criteria, Rosa Luxemburg (1987) regards national(ist) movements *in general*[17] as reactionary alternatives and as obstacles to internationalist class struggle. For Lenin (1974) and Stalin, those national(ist) movements that have a socialist ideology, that are led by the vanguard party of the proletariat and strive for regional, multiethnic self-administration within the boundaries of a centralized socialist state, are progressive. For Bauer, progressive nationalist movements are those that strive to establish culturally autonomous associations of nations that will be linked to each other at the economic level through international trade and at the political level through a federal and democratic world-state.

The Eastern European experiences of real socialism as well as the theoretical reflections relevant to these experiences have shown the inadequacy of these criteria for the assessment of the political impacts and potentials of national(ist) movements. National(ist) movements contribute to the transformation of the power relations of real socialism regardless of whether their ideology and anticipated organizational forms are "progressive": "Nationalism has an objectively necessary role to play in the destruction of the holy alliance of 'party apparatuses,' in as much as it shows that these have not settled the national question in any productive way" (Bahro 1977, 396); "The increasing nationalism—and this means concretely 'anti-Sovietism'—in Eastern European countries has a progressive function, *in so far* as it aims itself *against the chains set by the Soviet apparatus on the internal social development of these countries*" (Bahro 1977, 402).

Arato (1990, 26–27) also points out the social transformations realized in Poland, Hungary, Czechoslovakia, and the German Democratic Republic through the revolt of civil society against the party-state, even when the party-state was not equipped with "progressive" ideology and/or organizational forms:

The essential institutional patterns of these regimes, which I define by the primacy of prerogative power linked to paternalistic shortage economics, bureaucratic bargaining and clientelism and cultural heteronomy, have already been shaken beyond any possibility of reconstruction. Equally important, the outlines of the new, consisting of parliamentary, multi-party rule of law states, interest group pluralism, market economies and emancipated publics, have been already laid down. . . . In this context we can no longer speak of reform, even radical reform, which would imply changing some or more institutional patterns in order to preserve the identity of others deemed more essential.

Nairn and Wallerstein assess the progressiveness of national(ist) movements in terms of their relations to the class and/or extraclass inequalities in the world economy and the international states system. National(ist) movements struggle against these inequalities even when they have a nonclass or anticlass and "backward-looking" ideology. In fact it is the organizational and interactional structure of the world economy and the international states system, rather than "false consciousness," that makes it not only possible, but even *necessary*, for interclass and intraclass struggles to be articulated in nationalist terms.[18] Furthermore, national(ist) movements without "progressive" ideologies and/or organizational forms also can succeed in directly challenging or indirectly weakening economic, political, cultural, and military hegemony in the world economy and the international states system.

However, those nationalist movements that (would) take the organizational forms advocated by Lenin and Stalin or Bauer are not necessarily progressive. This is or would not be the consequence merely of the distortion of Leninist-Stalinist or Bauerist principles by corrupt bureaucrats. These organizational forms have more fundamental problems. The compatibility of *real* regional self-administration with a centralized nation-state is highly questionable. Even in federal nation-states, regional self-administration is often limited (even nullified) by the financial controls and manipulations of the central state. In Stalin's centralized socialist state, ethnic groups did not even have the right of autonomous organization and mobilization for struggling against the political and financial controls and manipulations of the center. Even as members of the class-based Vanguard Party, oppressed ethnic groups have to obey the majority. The first problem raised by Bauer's principle of culturally autonomous organization is that several nations that have been in conflict with each other (for example, Turks, Kurds, Armenians) might claim the same territory exclusively. How can one prevent the cultural autonomy of one nation in a territory from developing into exclusion or oppression of the other nations there? The controls on immigration and emigration, which have been advocated by Bauer for maintaining the homogeneity of culturally autonomous nations, can hinder the development of national culture itself (since mutual interactions of national cultures are integral to this development) and foster ethnocentrism. An "imperialism of trade" (Arghiri 1972) can develop also within the exchange of goods and services among culturally autonomous nations and can create new forms of class and/or ethnic inequality on an international level. Finally, the development of *multiple* ethnic identities as a result of demographic, migratory economic, and cultural processes in contemporary societies presents a major challenge to both the Leninist-Stalinist and the Bauerist organizational forms. This process implies that the right of self-determination cannot be confined to the territory and/or ethnic group that one is born into or ascribed to by state policies. It must become legitimate to contend for this right in *several* settings *simultaneously*.

National(ist) movements whose ideologies and/or organizational forms are progressive in a new Leftist sense can also have a "shadowy" side. Touraine et al. (1982, 231) describe this aspect of Solidarity as follows:

> Worker consciousness is a claim of workers' rights, but also a populist defense of the small against the big and the starved consumers against monopolizers; national consciousness is affirmation of a national identity, but can also become aggressive nationalism; the democratic will itself, almost always associated to the defense of liberties, can become a call to the people, to the base against all leaders and the demand of a quasi-military discipline for saving the threatened nation.

This "shadowy" side is not only a theoretical possibility. Touraine et al. (1982, 232–233) report actual cases of anti-Semitism among the militants of Solidarity.[19]

Under these circumstances, it is obvious that the political impacts and potentials of national(ist) movements cannot be determined once and for all according to the ideology and/or organizational form they have adopted at a particular point in time. They should be assessed and reviewed continuously according to the *effects* they create over time on (1) the global structures and relations of real socialism, world economy, and international states-system; (2) class and ethnic relations in the new nation-states (to be) established by national(ist) movements (i.e., whether and how far the forms of class and ethnic oppression in the old nation-state are transformed, whether new forms of class and ethnic oppression arise, and which remedies are developed for the latter).

The future effects of national(ist) movements will be determined by the internal contradictions, crises, and conflicts of the preexisting and future hegemonic forces and, even more important, by the ability of national(ist) movements to maintain and extend self-critical grass-roots mobilization and to enter into tactical and strategic alliances (but not symbiosis) with other antisystemic social movements. According to Touraine (1981), these obstacles and limits lie, above all, in the contradictory composition of nationalist–regionalist movements: The more they emphasize their characteristic as a classical "national liberation movement," the less they have to offer as a broader emancipatory "new social movement"; the more they strive to be a "new social movement" above all, the less they can be effective in struggling against ethnic or regional oppression specifically. Arato (1990) argues that neither unregulated liberal markets nor welfare state interventionism can offer the viable alternative of socioeconomic reconstruction in the postreal socialist Eastern Europe; both would instead produce disorganizing, demobilizing effects on the civil society formed in the course of struggle against real socialism. Wallerstein (1989) considers solidarity among antisystemic movements in different zones of the world economy as limited by the fact that antisystemic movements in one zone can realize their demands often at the cost of the social base of antisystemic movements in other zones. But I agree fully with Wallerstein (1989, 176) when he points out that the obstacles and limits faced by antisystemic movements and their lack of a totally coherent alternative strategy are an occasion for intensive intellectual and political work rather than a reason for discouragement.

Notes

1. For a detailed discussion of "historic" and "historyless" nations, see Munck (1986, 9–15).
2. See above all Marx and Engels (1972).
3. Certain social movements in contemporary Eastern Europe express the economic, cultural, and political grievances and contentions of particular ethnic groups without a specifically nationalist ideology and political program. These social movements, which sound closer to the labor movement or to new social movements, can be called national movements. Those ethnic struggles whose ideology and political program is closer to a national liberation movement can be called nationalist movements. The struggles of a particular ethnic group might contain national and nationalist fractions. This differentiation is based on Touraine et al. (1982).
4. As long as the members of the dominated ethnic groups accept political assimilation, their maintenance of cultural identity might even be acceptable to the real socialist state as "proof" of its success in managing the "national question." Thus many "folkloristic" writers, artists, etc., from the dominated ethnic groups could reach privileged social positions in the USSR.
5. The success of reformist politics of peripheral elites depends on factors such as the relative numbers of core and periphery groups, the indispensability of the periphery's role in the national economy, and the kinds of policies adopted by the central government.
6. Hechter discusses how the periphery might maintain some of its *preexisting* cultural characteristics (e.g., religion) in resistance to the cultural hegemonic strategies of the core.
7. Wallerstein points out that all real socialist states (with the exception of Kampuchea under Pol Pot) have not even attempted withdrawal from the international state system. Right from the beginning of their existence they have sought acceptance and power in the international state system.

8. Touraine et al. portray the nationalist fraction in Poland as the minority.
9. For similar analyses of struggles for autogestion in Eastern Europe, see Donath (1982) and Konrád (1985, 119–140).
10. On one hand, these raw materials and agricultural products are sold directly to the world market; on the other hand, they serve as inputs for the export industries in European Russia.
11. Ceauşescu openly declared himself against the Soviet invasion of Czechoslovakia and implied sympathies with Albania. But he was no fan of the other Eastern European struggles against Soviet hegemony. Solidarity in Poland was for him particularly counterrevolutionary and therefore deserved Soviet military intervention.
12. Vajda (1988, 356–358) also confirms the relative autonomy of civil society in Kádárist Hungary, while Heller and Fehér (1982, 179) regard it as both nonexistent and impossible. The thesis of Konrád and Vajda is a better approximation to the reality in Kádárist Hungary.
13. It became relevant only when the threat of Soviet intervention became reactualized—for example, right after Tito's death in Yugoslavia.
14. The typical chauvinism in the ethnicization and cultural assimilation programs of the real socialist state toward the dominant and dominated ethnic groups, respectively, is *völkisch-heroisch*. Ceauşescu also practiced this kind of chauvinism but identified additionally with the glamour of the imperial past. In this sense he was superchauvinistic.
15. This does not mean that Gorbachev intended to leave "socialist planning" and the central Communist party exactly as they had been before his rule. He advocated flexibility within the former and relative democratization of the latter.
16. These critics are Janis Jurkans (minister of foreign affairs in Latvia), Mark Sacharow (national deputy from Moscow), Leonid Gossmann (psychologist and member of the Moscow Tribune, a forum of democratic movements), and the magazine *Nowoje Wremja* (*Der Spiegel*, 28 January 1991, 137, and *Die Tageszeitung*, 30 January 1991, 10). I disagree with these critics when they say that Gorbachev's *intentions* were to establish a Pinochet-style regime as the *first choice*. But if Gorbachev had remained in power and had kept failing in peaceful solutions to the economic, political, and ethnic crises in the USSR, he would definitely have preferred the "Pinochetist" alternative to the "separatist" one. He might have preferred the "Pinochetist" alternative also to the neo-Stalinist one: The former would have attracted much more aid and investment from advanced capitalist countries for the transformation of the bankrupt Soviet economy.
17. But Luxembourg did regard the national(ist) movements in Turkey as progressive (Munck 1986, 56).
18. See Nairn (1981, 353) and Wallerstein (1979, 193–201 and 1984, 123–131).
19. But Touraine et al. (1982, 233) report that this kind of "nationalism" is a minority tendency among the militants of Solidarity; the majority "continues to be moved by positive projects."

References

Anderson, P. 1976. *Considerations on Western Marxism*. London: New Left Books.

Arato, A. 1990. "Revolution, civil society and democracy." *Praxis International* 10(1–2):24–38.

Arghiri, E. 1972. *Unequal exchange: A Study of the imperialism of trade*. New York: Monthly Review Press.

Bahro, R. 1977. *Die Alternative: Zur Kritik des real existierenden Sozialismus*. Köln/ Frankfurt am Main: EVA.

Balibar, E. 1988. "La forme nation: Histoire et idéologie." in *Race, nation, classe: Les identités ambigues*, ed. I. Wallerstein. Paris: Éditions de la Découverte. pp. 117–143.

Bauer, O. 1924. *Die Nationalitätenfrage und die Sozial-demokratie*. Vienna: Verlag der Wiener Volksbuchhadlung.

Beck, S. 1991. "The phantom limb." Unpublished paper.

Benner, E. L. 1988. "Marx and Engels on nationalism and national identity: A reappraisal." *Millennium: Journal of International Studies* 17(1):1–23.

Bruszt, L. and Stark, D. 1992. "Remaking the political field in Hungary: From the politics of confrontation to the politics of competition." *Eastern Europe in revolution*, ed. I. Banac. Ithaca: Cornell University Press. pp. 13–55.

Dahm, H. 1990. "What restoring Leninism means." *Studies in Soviet Thought* 39:55–76.

Donath, F. 1982. "1956 and self-management." *Telos* (53):160–163.

Gorbachev, M. 1988. *Perestroika. Die zweite Russische Revolution. Eine neue Politik für Europa und die Welt*. Munich: Droemer Knauer.

———. 1990. *Meine Vision. Die Perestroika in den neunziger Jahren. So geht es weiter*. Rosenheim: Horizonte.

Havemann, R. 1980. *Morgen. Die Industriegesellschaft am Scheideweg. Kritik und reale Utopie*. Munich: Piper.

Hechter, M. 1975. *Internal colonialism: The Celtic fringe in British national development, 1536–1966*. Berkeley: University of California Press.

Heller, A. and Fehér, F. 1982. *Ungarn '56*. Hamburg: VSA.

———. 1990. *From Yalta to Glasnost: The dismantling of Stalin's Empire*. Oxford: Basil Blackwell.

Konrád, G. 1985. *Antipolitik. Mitteleuropäische Meditationen*. Frankfurt am Main: Suhrkamp.

Lenin, V. I. 1974. *Über die nationale und die koloniale Frage*. West Berlin: Neue Einheit.

Luxemburg, R. 1987. *Politische Schriften*. Frankfurt am Main: Athenäum.

Marx, K., and Engels, F. 1972. *Ireland and the Irish question: A collection of writings by Karl Marx and Friedrich Engels*. New York: International.

Meznarić, S. 1987. "A neo-Marxist approach to the sociology of nationalism: Doomed nations and doomed schemes." *Praxis International* 7(1):79–89.

Michnik, A. 1985. *Polnischer Frieden. Aufsätze zur Konzeption des Widerstands*. Berlin: Rotbuch.

Munck, R. 1986. *The difficult dialogue: Marxism and nationalism*. London: Zed.

Nairn, T. 1981. *The break-up of nationalism: Crisis and neo-nationalism*. London: Verso.

Simon, G. 1989. "Perestrojka und die nationale Frage in der Sowjet Union." *Beiträge zur Konfliktforschung* 19:69–84.

Skalnik, P. 1990. "Soviet ethnografiia and the national(ities) question." *Cahiers du Monde Russe et Soviétique* 31(2–3):183–192.

Stalin, J. 1955. *Der Marxismus und die nationale und koloniale Frage*. Berlin: Dietz.

Staniszkis, J. 1990. "Patterns of change in Eastern Europe." *East European Politics and Societies* 4:77–97.

Szelenyi, I. 1992. "Social and political landscape, Central Europe, Fall 1990." *Eastern Europe in revolution*, ed. I. Banac. Ithaca: Cornell University Press. pp. 225–241.

Tishkov, V. 1989. "Glasnost and the nationalities within the Soviet Union." *Third World Quarterly* 11(4):191–207.

Tismaneanu, V. 1984. "The ambiguity of Romanian national communism." *Telos* 60:65–79.

———. 1988. *The crisis of Marxist ideology in Eastern Europe: The poverty of utopia*. London: Routledge.

Touraine, A. 1981. *Le pays contre l'état. Luttes occitanes*. Paris: Éditions du Seuil.

Touraine, A., Dubet, F., Wieviorka, M., and Strzelecki, J. 1982. *Solidarité: Analyse d'un mouvement social. Pologne, 1980–1981*. Paris: Fayard.

Vajda, M. 1988. "East-central European perspectives." in *Civil society and the state: New European perspectives*, ed. J. Keane. London: Verso. pp. 333–360.

Vulfsons, M. 1991. "Jetzt haben es die Letten satt." *Der Spiegel* 45(5):138–141.

Wallerstein, I. 1979. *The capitalist world-economy*. Cambridge: Cambridge University Press.

———. 1984. *The politics of the world-economy: The states, the movements, and the civilizations*. Cambridge: Cambridge University Press.

———. 1989. "Révolution dans le système mondial." *Les Temps Modernes* (514–515):154–176.

Yeltsin, B. 1990. *Aufzeichnungen eines Unbequemen*. Munich: Droemer Knauer.

Yugoslavia and the Rise of *Volkgeist*

DEJAN TRICKOVIC

The rising of the infamous iron curtain marks the end not only of a specific political and military order in Europe but also of those structures of thinking, weltanschauungen, that flourished in the symbols on the Berlin Wall and reveal the conflict between socialism and capitalism, East and West, democracy and totalitarianism, freedom and oppression. For four decades, people on opposite sides of the divide knew exactly who their enemies were, who they were supposed to fear and hate, and what sacred values they needed to safeguard at any cost. Underlying rules shaped not only the official "proestablishment" ideologies but, implicitly, dissidence as well. Capitalism's recalcitrant children, Brigatte Rosse and the Rote Armee Fraktion (RAF), for example, found a source of their inspiration in Lenin's ideas and in Moscow's remarkable accomplishments, such as, for example, the supposed abolishment of unemployment and exploitation. Their not-so-radical but equally dissident counterparts in Poland or Czechoslovakia were motivated by the human rights record in the West or, at a somewhat more practical level, by the obvious advantages of an Opel or BMW over a Trabant or Skoda. This crisscross pattern of political and ideological allegiances was the mirror reflection of a larger sociocultural arrangement in which East and West were *juxtaposed* as two halves of *one and the same sociocultural whole*. After four decades of cold warfare, the adversaries were, in reality, caught in a (dialectical?) network of interdependence: In socialist countries, capitalism was one of the axiological pillars of discourse, an incarnation of evil, and the home of exploitation, alienation, and oppression of human by human. Conversely, in the West socialism and communism were depicted as dark prisons in which hundreds of millions became hostages of a totalitarian ideology. Within their respective contexts, all these concepts were imbued with the same dual purpose: They were effective as invariably pejorative definitions of the principal political and military rival *and* they also set a negative standard against which "we" and "our traditional values" (even if we did not really know what they were) would always appear in an unmistakably positive light.

With the advent of Eastern Europe's "peaceful" revolution, this entire structure's *causa sufficiens* had dissolved and its collapse became imminent. For the first time since the late 1940s, socialist and capitalist Europeans found themselves in a world conspicuously devoid of that traditional adversary of mythic proportions and appetites. It was a world that had in effect rendered obsolete, meaningless even, all those ideologies and self-identities that embodied the simplified Manichean scheme of the "negative other." As a result, some serious adjustments of *worldviews* and identities—from political, national, and cultural all the way down to personal—have become inevitable on both sides of the old "curtain."

While it did play a major role in post–World War II Europe, the iron curtain did not affect equally all of the countries of the old continent. There were neutral states that, like Sweden or Austria, did their best to maintain a healthy distance from all the entanglements of bloc politics. Furthermore, one country was the only European member of the Non-aligned Countries Movement. This country's love for experiments and precedents earned it "semicapitalist" status in the Soviet bloc, while the average Westerner never changed his or her opinion of it as a Communist and totalitarian state with a few cosmetic improvements only. Yugoslavia's legacy includes "epochal" innovations such as "socialism with a human face," "ethnic harmony through brotherhood and unity," "ideal synthesis of East and West," and "socialism with passports." For forty years this country thrived in the interstice of the wall that divided Europe. Now that the wall has been torn down and new coordinates of thought and practice are emerging in Europe, what consequences will it have for Yugoslavia?

Since the spring of 1990 and the first electoral victories of the national parties, in Slovenia and Croatia, the land of south Slavs has become a regular visitor to the front pages of newspapers across the world. With the Soviet Union this region usurped the space that had been traditionally reserved for Lebanon and topics such as civil strife or parallel governments. The fall of the "evil empire," in a curious way, added fuel to the flames of crisis that had already been burning for a decade and that now threatened to reduce to ashes the last remaining symbols and institutions of Yugoslavia. Prima facie, Yugoslav drama is manifested through the recrudescent surfacing of ethnic rivalries and, as of July 1991, open armed conflicts between the representatives of the two key nations of Croatia and Serbia. The origins, motives, and stakes behind the apparent chaos are, however, very complex, and their elucidation requires a joint effort of a multidisciplinary team of preferably cool-headed experts. This is something for our reader to keep in mind before judging the merits and shortcomings of this text. Through three relatively independent sections, the specific objective of this discussion is to illuminate the Serbo-Croat problem in Yugoslavia and its place in the context of real events as seen from the specific theoretical perspective of "discourse" and "discursive formation." The first part looks at the direct implications of the rising of the curtain; this is followed by a historical survey of the origins of the Serbo-Croat dispute, while the third and final section presents a summary of the developments in 1989–1990.

Before going any further, I ought to further clarify the theoretical perspective employed here and the specific issues we will concern ourselves with. This "theory," in fact, is no more than a set of concerns and propositions common to a very broad and heterogeneous intellectual lineage whose origins can be traced, roughly, to the opus of Friedrich Nietzsche. Despite many obvious and, in some instances, insurmountable theoretical and conceptual differences, there seems to be one crucial thesis that is universally endorsed by all the authors who constitute this post-Nietzschean tradition, known also as "the linguistic turn" in Western philosophy. It lies at the core of that one narrow domain where, for instance, Gadamer's "linguistic constitution of the world" complements Heidegger's "language as the house of being"; or where ("late") Ludwig Wittgenstein's "language-game" can be used interchangeably with Michel Foucault's "discursive formation" or "episteme," to mention a few examples. The juncture point of all these concepts and projects is the idea that language is a sui generis entity that is no longer viewed as a means or tool at the disposal of some subject. Quite the contrary, language comes in first now, as the *only reality* that can be taken for granted, while the aspiring subject of language—be it "us," "the mind," "absolute idea," "transcendental ego," "God," or who-knows-what—becomes a philosophical, in fact metaphysical, problem.

It is, then, language that we are concerned with—language viewed as an event, a social event, that is. Instrumental to language are (1) the *rules and regulations* for its use and (2) a set of *elementary truths* or axioms that are taken to be self-evident and that are not questioned within a given (sociohistoric) context. These elements are not prescribed by some linguistic authority but acquire their form and meaning through concrete social practice. The meaning of a word is in its *use*, a conclusion Wittgenstein lucidly came to and Clifford Geertz (1973) later borrowed. In other words, society and language are the two sides of one and the same coin, which I will call, following Michel Foucault (1970) (but not subscribing to all of his theoretical innovations), "discursive formation." Throughout the text, I will use this syntagma interchangeably with "culture," finding justification for it in the fact that a language's rules and axioms also determine the structure of reality and the limits of sense and meaning-fulness in a concrete society. These are a society's fundamental beliefs, norms, values, and so on—the usual components of culture that we find in most sociology and anthropology textbooks.[1]

In principle, discursive formation can be broken down into sections distinguished by their dominant themes and particular combinations of axioms, rules, and possibilities for meaningful action. I shall call these "regions of discourse," or *topoi* (sing. topos—Greek for "place"). It is important not to confuse *topos* with "topic," which is the *subject* of conversation or writing, an abstract concept or idea, that is. A *topos* refers to an active area of culture and includes both its "topic" (rationale, motive) and corresponding institutions and practices.[2]

If one wished to take a look at a classic example of research into the problematic of *topoi*, I think that Michel Foucault's (1970) *The Order of Things* (*Les mots et les choses*) would be the right choice. Both its short-comings and its accomplishments are illustrative of the inherent com-plexity as well as the enormous potential of this field. In this volume, Foucault examines the historical development in the West[3] of the so-called modern *episteme* (or discursive formation), which was made possible by the previous emergence of a particular topos—and a whole new way of "looking at things" that was born with it. In Foucault's view, the concept of man was at the heart of this topos; not just "any man," of course, but "the historical a priori which, since the nineteenth century has served as an almost self-evident ground for our thought" (1970, 344)!

This text, too, represents an inquiry into a certain topos, named here *Volkgeist*. The latter word translates literally as "the people's (nation's) spirit" and comes to us from the intellectual workshops of German philosophers and poets from around the turn of eighteenth century.[4] In our presentation, *Volkgeist* denotes a domain in a discursive formation (or culture) that is centered around the axiomatically posited concept of nation. This concept is both metaphysical and ahistorical—the sup-posed "self" of a people that has been present throughout the history in its pristine form. The fact that a nation has always been an "imagined community" (Anderson 1983) takes nothing away from its active pres-ence throughout history; in fact, its amorphous and vague structure always made it ideal raw material in the hands of scores of manipulative national leaders and ideologues. *Volkgeist*, it should be clear, is much more than nationalism as ideology or nation as myth. In addition to these, *Volkgeist* includes an infinite set of issues, ideas, questions, doubts, as well as actions in which these are materialized as ideals, rational proofs, reasons, objective viewpoints, topics for discussion, and so on. In present Yugoslavia, *Volkgeist* has become the dominant topos of social discourse, comparable in significance and practical implications to Foucault's "man" in the epoch of modernity. The concerns with "who we are" or "have been," where "we are going," who "they" are in relation to "us," and so on, have become the universal discursive form in all of Yugoslavia's six republics. These issues are actively shaping people's interests, concerns, visions about the future, and also their options in their selection of allies and enemies. In its role of a factor that determines the limits of sense and meaningfulness, *Volkgeist* has in effect rendered all alternative topoi, especially the ones based on directly opposing premises, meaningless or simply wrong for the time being.[5]

A few words on the methodological framework. There are, essentially, two kinds of data that have gone into the making of this text: historical and ethnographic. The latter are based on my own observations during two six-month visits to Yugoslavia, in 1989 and 1990. The chief reason for my travels, admittedly, was the fieldwork I planned to undertake as part of my doctoral dissertation project.[6] However, the astounding pace and depth of political, social, and cultural transformations that occurred in this same period with the abrupt unfolding of Yugoslavia's crisis of identity and an exponential rise in tensions between the emerging nation-states, opened up a whole new problematic that was impossible to ignore. Ergo, in no time at all, I found myself involved in a parallel project that absorbed practically all my free time between interviews and archival research. As the emergence of the new topoi was most visible in the newly established national media (vs. the waning Yugoslav TV, radio, and press), I decided to focus my attention on a comparative analysis of the media in Serbia and Croatia. At the time of my research, these were totally politicized (and by 1989 still were, for the most part) and were key instruments in the promulgation of the policies of national homogenization.[7] The contours of the emerging single-nation cultures, which began to replace the pluralist culture of Yugoslavia, were most visible in the daily and weekly publications, now characterized by an exceptionally high degree of consonance and an unprecedented uniformity of both style and substance (within their respective national boundaries, of course). A record of these changes, observed through comparative analyses of daily and weekly publications, makes up the empirical basis for the final part of this discussion. I should also mention that during my stay in Yugoslavia I actively initiated numerous conversations on these matters with people of different national, socioeconomic, and educational backgrounds. Although my fieldwork took place between Titovo Uzice and Beograd (both in Serbia), I did manage to visit Zagreb on two occasions. Personally, I was eager to see whether any of my old friends were succumbing to the challenges of *Volkgeist* and also, I wanted to feel the pulse of the ordinary citizen who was the target of the media propaganda. I was both delighted and relieved to find my friends on their usual tracks and even joking about the bellicose atmosphere in Zagreb. But, already some of my friends' friends were in a different mood altogether, as were all the people whom I got to speak with in town. Just like in Beograd, but under a different flag, I was impressed by the consonance between the views of average citizens and the themes concocted and disseminated by the powerful government and media trusts. Needless to mention, however, these findings remain subjective perceptions only (albeit by a social scientist) or hypotheses at best, the strength of which has yet to be tested in a systematic study of comparable population samples from the two republics.

YUGOSLAVIA, THE WALL, THE CURTAIN

Symbols are most anthropologists' soft spot. Some can spend half their lifetime unraveling the hidden meanings in a single ritual; others look at everything through the glasses of symbolic analysis and parallel realities. Succumbing to the same professional lure, I have anchored this part of my presentation in the symbolism of one particular event: the majestic concert under the Brandenburg Gate that marked the end of the Berlin Wall.

The Berlin Wall had been a vivid symbol of our divisions, hatreds, enmities, and of that eternal bond between human ignorance and the will to power. It was to no one's surprise, then, that its coming down was also pregnant with so many symbols, only of a different kind. This time, there were symbols of hope, goodwill, and cooperation; there was a festive air of joy and celebration. Perhaps the concert was too pathetic, too kitschy, too corny, but why not, in the end? Why not have the greatest Jewish composer since Mahler conduct a mighty orchestra of Bavarians, Saxons, and Prussians—*alles zusamen*, for the first time since 1945—in the performance of the most spirit-elevating and triumphant of all symphonies ever written! In the East, millions joined the chorus in the singing of "Ode to Joy" because the decades of *The Captive Mind, The Gulag Archipelago*, and the days that saw *Darkness at Noon* were being buried in the graveyard of history.[8] The West rejoiced because here was the final proof that they had been right all along but were just too considerate to follow all their MacArthurs and McCarthys to the very end.

Squeezed between the East and the West, between the two worlds celebrating the beginning of an end to their imposed divisions, was a country that had been, paradoxically, the *beneficiary* of the cold war and much of what the Berlin Wall had stood for. Yugoslavia's break with the Soviet Union in 1948 had enabled this country to play the role of an in-between power whose skillful chief navigator, Josip Broz Tito, learned quickly how to use such a situation to the best of his personal goals and the goals of his autocratic rule. Although Yugoslavia remained socialist-Communist, after 1948 it became living proof that socialism was feasible outside the tutorship of the USSR.[9] This was good enough reason for the capitalist West to promote Yugoslavia into an important and privileged economic partner. In the ensuing years, Yugoslavs were the beneficiaries of many favorable financial agreements with the Western banks and, in spite of the structural deficiencies of their system as such, attained a standard of living other East Europeans could only dream of. Between the years 1953 and 1965, Yugoslavia's GNP grew at an annual rate of 8.3 percent, which was one of the highest in the world.[10] Even the bitterest among Tito's enemies had to admit that, economically at least, the country was not doing bad at all. The death of Stalin in 1953, paradoxically, presented Yugoslavia with a new challenge from the Soviets. Namely, now that Stalin, and allegedly Stalinism, were dead and Khrushchev had made a public confession that the Soviet (i.e., Stalin's) policy toward Yugoslavia had been wrong, all the preconditions for Yugoslavia's coming back to the merry family of *realsozialismus* were formally fulfilled. Using much subtler methods this time, the Soviets pressed Yugoslavia for closer ties that were "in the very nature of socialism as a world movement." But the profits of the in-between position were too great to be relinquished for ideological reasons. Tito found a solution in masterminding a whole new ideology to fit his practical needs, a solution compatible with socialism on the domestic plane but irreconcilable in principle with membership in *any* political or military bloc. In September 1961, Beograd was the birthplace of the Movement of Nonaligned Countries—de facto a new bloc comprising countries that were de jure against bloc politics! In the 1960s and 1970s the names of Tito and Yugoslavia acquired an almost mythic stature throughout the third world. The more palpable effect of this development was economic expansion; now Yugoslav construction companies were building roads in Zambia; dams in Uganda and Ghana; entire urban sections of Kuwait City, Baghdad, and Algiers; and hospitals in Libya, Tanzania, and Pakistan. Politically, this further solidified Yugoslavia's position in the West, for now Yugoslavia was looked upon as an important mediator in matters related to the underdeveloped countries.

The nonaligned were also a massive voting block in the international organizations, the UN most importantly, and Yugoslavia's influence in the movement could not be underestimated.

That, in brief, is the historical content of the proposition that in Tito's Yugoslavia the iron curtain, indirectly, turned out to be an important factor of economic growth and also a source of the government's ideological legitimation in the sphere of foreign policy. What, then, did the iron curtain's disappearance mean for the Yugoslavs in 1990? One decade after the death of Tito, on the eve of the historic concert that symbolically marked the rising of that same curtain, the Yugoslavs' feelings were mixed at best. On one side, they watched with unhidden joy the resolutely brisk movements of Bernstein's baton, symbolically marking the tempo for a countdown to the beginning of a new Europe— a Europe that would be built on tolerance, cooperation, and constructive thinking. Given the somber reality of the Yugoslav situation, however, given Yugoslavia's painful search for a rationale ever since Tito had died, these were the more abstract of the moment's considerations. Down on the earth, where practical concerns outweighed noble ideals, the southern Slavs—Croats, Macedonians, Muslims, Serbs, and Slovenes as well as their non-Slavic "roommates," most notably Albanians and Hungarians—were already caught in the webs of a real-life drama whose script was becoming strikingly similar to the course of events that preceded the civil wars of 1941–1945. The fragmentation of the country along ethnic lines and the federal government's inability to resolve a single issue of importance were ominous signs of the days ahead. Until the "peaceful revolution" there were still hopes that Yugoslavia's international position would miraculously provide a stimulus through some new financial arrangement, a new credit, rebalancing of debts (over 20 million dollars by now!), anything. But now, with General Electric starting to build plants in Hungary (of all places!), Ford negotiating with Skoda, and FIAT investing heavily in the Soviet auto industry, that last straw of hope was gone. Yugoslavia's unique ability to cash in on the latent war between the two blocs in Europe had come to an end. The country's strategic importance as a buffer zone between NATO and the armies of the Warsaw Treaty, or as a useful reminder in the eyes of the West of "dissident communism," had dissolved into thin air. This was the final blow to the country's already disastrous economic situation and the annual inflation rate of over 1,000 percent (yes, thousand). This was the last nail in the coffin, putting a definite end to all hopes that the "second Yugoslavia"—that post–World War II creation that managed to unite the ideological projects of socialism, self-management, and nonalignment with an autocratic system and one-party rule—might still be saved. It was also the final call for Yugoslavia's nation-republics to begin to run for *their own* lives and abandon the sinking ship as quickly as possible. Each of the separate national dwarf-states was now in a hurry to declare independence and build its own army; each began to search relentlessly for new allies outside Yugoslavia, expecting—somewhat naively or out of sheer despair, perhaps—that it would be the only one to win the hearts and dollars of the rich West while the rest of Yugoslavia would be consigned to the endless agony of economic poverty and civil war.

The Berlin Wall was not the main cause of Yugoslavia's drama but it definitely accelerated the centrifugal processes in the country. Watching their TV sets and listening to Beethoven's Ninth as Europe was burying the Berlin Wall, Yugoslav viewers felt sadly miscast that night. Quite possibly, some perceived the broadcast of "Ode to Joy" as a provocation or even as an insult; Mozart's or Verdi's "Requiem" would have been much more appropriate.

YUGOSLAVIA AND THE *VOLKGEIST*

Where are the origins of Yugoslavia's contemporary *Volkgeist* drama? It might scare off the prospective scholars on Yugoslavia to learn that in order to grasp the meaning of ethnic disputes in this country and the Serbo-Croat question, in particular, one has to travel far back in history, to the time of Emperor Constantine and the dedication of Constantinople—"the new Rome"—as capital of the Eastern empire, on May 11, A.D. 330. This division of the great empire, which was primarily administrative, in reality had planted the seeds of a later bitter political and military rivalry between Constantinople and Rome, between Byzantium and the Roman Empire. In the eleventh century, the competition was extended into the religious sphere; the result was the outbreak of the first major schism in Christianity between Catholic Christians in the West and Orthodox Christians in the East. The internal polarization of Christ's church opened a permanent source of tension in Europe, sort of a general "discursive framework of conflict" that would remain a cultural and political factor to be reckoned with until this very day. In the Balkans, the borderline between Catholic and Orthodox Christianity became the border between the Croats and the Serbs, respectively. It was also here that religion would be elevated to the status of the principal determinant of national identity: While these two ethnic groups spoke the same language (with insignificant dialect differences) and represented two branches of one and the same ethnic tree—the (southern) Slavs—there was never any doubt that a Serb could *only* be of Orthodox denomination and a Croat of Catholic.[11] Throughout the centuries of foreign

rule—until almost the beginning of the twentieth century—the significance of the religious difference between Serbs and Croats had been
minimized and overshadowed by the reality of other political confrontations (Austria vs. Turkey, most notably). It was only after the last of the
Italians, Hungarians, and Austrians had kissed Croatia good-bye and
the Turks were nowhere in sight in Serbia, after these two nations had
been finally *left to themselves and their own fortunes*, that is, that their
similarities and differences came to play a much more prominent role.

Despite its sketchy and drastically digested form, this historical introduction should serve its purpose in the context of this presentation: to
elucidate the "pre-Yugoslav" origins of Yugoslavia's *Volkgeist* problems.
Our examination of their lineage until 1918, the year Yugoslavia was
officially born, also has important theoretical implications. Namely,
since the Serbo-Croat question, as a reflection of the larger dispute
between Catholicism and Orthodoxy, had been in existence since long
before Yugoslavia, it is not quite correct to say that already at her birth,
in 1918, Yugoslavia had the Serbo-Croat problem. The truth of the
matter is that at the time of her conception, Yugoslavia was *part of* the
dispute between Eastern and Western Christianity, which was reflected
in the Serbo-Croat question, among others. Generations of people who
were, as of 1918, born and raised as citizens of Yugoslavia were de facto
born into an already prepared cultural setting in which the issue of
religious schism and its offspring in the form of national rivalry were
among the most important constitutive elements. This individual, or
personal, aspect is of crucial importance here because it emphasizes the
active historical role of what is an ideological or dogmatic dispute or, to
rephrase Marx, it stresses the fact that every Yugoslav Serb or Croat
was, already at birth, a potential "material weapon" of either one of the
two confronting ideologies. Both the so-called first Yugoslavia of 1918–
1941 and its heir, the second, or Tito's Yugoslavia of 1945–1990 represent but two relatively brief chapters in a voluminous magnum opus
that has been in the writing for centuries. One important theoretical
implication of this historical predicament is that the key events and
processes in Yugoslavia's history cannot be understood properly so long
as one remains *inside* the Yugoslav frame of reference. It is in direct
response to this prerequisite that the discourse paradigm has been
employed. It transcends the Yugoslav framework in two ways. Historically,
it elucidates the continuity and the significance of the "pre-Yugoslav"
origins to the issues that have been perceived, more narrowly, as
"Yugoslav." Thematically, however, our theoretical approach enables
us to focus our attention on the key *themes* or ideological concerns that
have often been the invisible force behind the historical events on the

surface. One such force—and also our main concern in this discourse—
has been the self-perpetuating structural conflict between two opposed
camps as, de facto, two partners in the historical unfoldings of one and
the same Volkgeist principle.

What was the role of Serbian and Croat *Volkgeist* in the formation of
Yugoslavia, or how was it possible for Yugoslavia to become united in
the first place? *Volkgeist* as the domain in which both Serbian and
Croatian national interests were articulated was, unquestionably, a factor of paramount significance in the unification of southern Slavs under
one flag. But, what is of crucial importance here is that during the
decisive months of 1918 both in Serbia and Croatia it was articulated
along lines *other* than the East-West Christianity conflict. Given the
rather extraordinary political circumstances in Europe at the closing of
the First World War, at least two other projects came to play a more
influential role in the formulation of national policies in Serbia and
Croatia in 1918. One was the anti-Hapsburg sentiment,[12] as the reflection of another "discourse of conflict" with some history in these
lands—namely the Slav-German rivalry—and also as a consequence of
the nineteenth century's national awakening in Europe. Until the war's
breakout in 1914, national selfhood in Croatia was asserted—quite
logically—against the immediate oppressor and foreign ruler who was,
in this case, Austria and the Habsburgs. In Serbia, which had been
independent since the mid-nineteenth century, Austria was uniformly
disliked for being a direct obstacle to unification with Serbs from "across
the river Drina," in Bosnia and Croatia, that is. Another ideology of
major influence in this period was the Yugoslav movement, a southern
offspring of pan-Slavism that had gained momentum during the
nineteenth century and was particularly popular among students and
liberal intellectuals.[13] Reflecting different sociopolitical contexts and individual national problems among Serbia, Croatia, and Slovenia,
"Yugoslavism" encompassed a very broad spectrum of political projects, some of which were even incompatible with one another. In its
most general form, which was acceptable to all, it included plans for an
ideal state that would be the safe home for all southern Slavs (those
already mentioned plus Bulgarians) and whose military might would be
a powerful deterrent against their traditional enemies: Germans,
Hungarians, Turks, and Italians, for a start.

What was so extraordinary about the political situation in Europe in
1918, and why were the topoi that embodied these ideologies politically
more effective than the East-West discourse of conflict? As a consequence of the First World War, Europe's political order had been radically transformed between 1914 and 1918.[14] Most important, where once a

mighty central European empire had stood, there were now free nations: Slovenes, Croats, Czechs, Slovaks, and others; Austria-Hungary had been buried in the graveyard of history. Despite heavy personnel losses, Serbia emerged triumphant and was already assuming the role of a southern Slav Piedmont. Serbia's crucial contribution to the victory over Austria had earned it respect and even the status of liberator among its southern Slav brothers and sisters who were, for the first time in their history, free to choose their state and flag. To both Croats and Slovenes, who were faced with the general problem of underdeveloped state mechanisms, the Serbian offer in the form of a proposal for a federation of three equal nations appeared at the time as the most plausible and least complicated of all options. If not satisfied, they reasoned, they could always leave the kingdom to form their own independent states.

On December 1, 1918, the Kingdom of Serbs, Croats, and Slovenes, unquestionably a child of World War I, was created. This was the same war, in fact, that broke out when a young Serb from Bosnia shot and killed Francis Ferdinand, Austria's heir to the throne. If only we had the opportunity to positively ascertain *Yugoslav motives* behind Gavrilo Princip's terrorist act of June 28, 1914, we could conclude, somewhat poetically, that the *idea of Yugoslavia* gave birth to the war and the war gave birth to Yugoslavia. But Princip and his underground organization Mlada Bosna (Young Bosnia) could have been, just as well, the extended hand of *Serbia's national expansionism only*. During the war, the two projects had one common strategy, and it wasn't really important to determine which set of motives was guiding the Serbian commander in chief. In peace, however, this evolved into the crucial question that loomed over the first Yugoslavia. The two possible answers have always reflected two conflicting approaches to the idea of any Yugoslavia. In the western parts, the more radical clerical Catholic elements did not feel comfortable with the idea of a state in which their denomination would be a minority, nor did they consider the replacement of an Austrian monarch by a Serb to be a sign of improvement. They a priori condemned the Yugoslav idea, favoring instead an independent and ethnically and religiously "purified" Croatia. Those Croats who were farther away from the influence of the church were also more tolerant toward Yugoslavia although, for the most part, they too found it difficult to accept "royal constitutionalism" and the Serbian (Orthodox) dynasty as the a priori determinants of that state. In Serbia, Yugoslavism as the primary ideological frame of reference was never officially abandoned. Whether, *in reality*, Serbs represented the country's privileged caste remains a question that has not been settled to this day.

After only ten years, Yugoslavia was in an agony typical of bad marriages that cannot find a way to divorce. Among Croats, the idea of their own independent state had become something of a national obsessive neurosis; the Serbs' pathological obsession was to prevent the Croats' obsession from ever becoming reality. The problem was not that Serbs were not willing to "let Croats go" but that they could never settle the issue of borders. Throughout Bosnia and much of Croatia, these two ethnic groups were so intermixed that it was technically impossible to draw a single line of division without leaving at least half a million people of either group in another's national state. *Volkgeist*, which was now firmly anchored in the East-West conflict, came to dominate Yugoslavia's reality as a powerful catalyst of disintegrative ideologies and practices. Here are some of its major "accomplishments" until the breakout of World War II: Because of the growing separatist tensions and the deadlock that the parliament had found itself in over a number of crucial issues, on January 6, 1929, King Alexander I unilaterally dissolved Parliament and suspended the constitution. This was the beginning of a period of royal dictatorship that would last until the king's premature death in 1934. While on an official visit to France, in Marseilles, Alexander fell the victim of the assassination plot that was jointly planned and executed by the members of VMRO, a nationalist organization of ethnic Macedonians, and the Croatian extremists, Ustashe. This was only the most prominent of many examples where two or more different national groups joined forces against the one common enemy and the supposed boss of Yugoslavia—Serbia. Upon the death of Alexander, Yugoslavia's monarch ruler became Prince Paul (Pavle), who was to be the regent until Alexander's son, Peter II, turned eighteen and was old enough to be crowned king. The period between 1934 and 1941 was marked by further Serb-Croat disputes and constant government crises. By now Serbs were stereotypically perceiving Croats as traitors who betrayed the Yugoslav dream and even killed their king. To Croats, the Yugoslav dream was more of a nightmare in which they were reduced to the status of second-class citizens in a Serb-dominated state. To prevent further interethnic complications, the government of Dragiša Cvetkovic (a Serb) and Vlatko Macek (a Croat) came forth in 1939 with a plan for the self-governing province (*banovina*) of Croatia, which also included a considerable Serb population. This was considered a major success for Macek and his HSS-Croatian Peasant party, which had been the main vehicle for the articulation of Croatian political interests. The Serbs had ambivalent feelings about this innovation. On the one hand, they saw in it another step toward definite disintegration of federal Yugoslavia and its turning into a "parafederation" or confederation of semi-independent national states that would pose an immediate threat to the well-being of those Serbs across the Drina River. On the other hand, the plan was a compromise that had the potential, at least, to satisfy Croatian national pretensions in the long run and hence bring lasting peace to the country.

Unfortunately, world events were becoming less and less conducive toward a final consolidation of Yugoslavia's domestic disputes. The emergence of new polarizations and alliances in Europe had its repercussions for Yugoslavia, where various political groups were stepping up their preparations for another major war and the expected redrawing of the borders. Caving in to the growing pressures from Italy and Germany, the Yugoslav prime minister and minister of exterior affairs signed on March 25 in Vienna the protocol of adherence to the Tripartite Pact. Only two days later, however, Yugoslavia had its first coup d'état in which a group of officers led by Colonel Dušan Simovic toppled the Cvetkovic-Macek government and annulled the protocol with the Axis. Prince Paul was forced to leave the country and young Peter became the new monarch. The coup too showed Yugoslavia's ethnic divisions: In Serbia, the officers enjoyed exceptionally wide popular support and the entire event was marked by huge demonstrations of exuberant people united behind the memorable slogans *Bolje grob nego rob* (Better grave than a slave) and *Bolje rat nego pakt* (Better war than a pact)! England and France extolled the Serbs' brave decision to uphold Yugoslavia's national dignity rather than succumb to the Nazi threats. In Croatia, the mood was dull and the heads of the Catholic church were deeply concerned over the possible consequences of such an uncivilized, "typically Byzantine" breach of international treaty. Indeed, only two weeks later, Yugoslavs had the unwelcome opportunity to examine the actual costs of their bravery and to experience the ominous prophecy of their own slogans.[15] Without warning or official declaration of war, on April 6, 1941, the capital of Yugoslavia and Serbia, Beograd, was half-obliterated by the bombs from German planes. The message was loud and clear: Yugoslavia was to get both a grave and the misery of slavery in one package.

Not all of Yugoslavia, however. Hitler knew too well that anti-German and anti-Axis feelings were spread mostly amongst Serbs, while Croats were mainly preoccupied with their own problems within Yugoslavia. Germans astutely concentrated their attacks on Beograd and Serbia while openly encouraging, on the other side, Croatia's secession and the installation of a pro-Axis regime there. On April 10, the Independent State of Croatia (Nezavisna Drzava Hrvatska, NDH) was declared, led by the profascist Ustashe. Their leaders had returned from political emigration in Hungary and Italy and, standing on the shoulders of the duce and the führer, assumed the role of Croatia's saviors. Italy, for its own pragmatic reasons, of course, had provided a safe haven for the exiled Ustashe and its leader, Ante Pavelich. The material proof that this was a well-calculated policy came promptly at the declaration of Croatia's independence. Mussolini, who knew exactly what form of compensation would reward Italy for its "unselfish support of the Croatian national cause," swiftly annexed Dalmatia and all but four of the Adriatic islands. An independent Croatia without Dalmatia, without practically more than a third of its legitimate territory and population, was a severe blow to the grand plans of Ustashe and Croatian national pride in general. Still, whatever his personal feelings were at the time, Pavelich had no other viable alternative but to continue to obey the rules of his mighty allies. He would be offered in turn the territory of Bosnia with its predominantly Muslim population. This was gladly accepted, and Croatian propaganda miraculously converted Muslims into "the flower of the Croatian nation."

Following the Yugoslav army's surrender on April 20, the rest of Yugoslavia was quickly sectioned into occupation zones that were then handed as presents to the more faithful partners in the Axis alliance. Italy took Montenegro while the scavenging appetites of Bulgaria, Hungary, and Romania were quenched with fairly large pieces of Serbian and, unofficially, Macedonian territory. What was left of Serbia was administered by a puppet government headed by General Milan Nedic and whose political prerogatives were strictly limited to providing the necessary transmission mechanism between the real authority—reich, that is—and the Serbian people.

The partitioning of the country's territory was only the prologue to the Yugoslav tragedy, meaning not the tragedy of some abstract state or political system but the physical, mental, and emotional devastation brought upon the people by the chaos of *Volkgeist* turned into civil warfare, a Hobbesian *bellum omnium contra omnes* in its rawest form. At the beginning of World War II in Yugoslavia there was a concentration of armies and soldiers, leaders and prophets, doctrines and ideologies that was without historic precedent in these lands and that could hardly be compared with any other country in the world. After June 20, 1941 and Germany's surprising attack on the Soviet Union, the situation became even more complicated. Until that day, Yugoslav Communists, respectful of the Comintern's policies and the explicit orders of comrade Stalin himself, had been lying low so as not to provoke any reaction on the part of the "Soviet ally." The only resistance in the entire territory of Yugoslavia came from the so-called Chetniks, a Serbian nationalist and proroyalist guerilla organization led by Colonel Draža Mihailovic and a group of some 300 ex-officers of the Yugoslav army who had not surrendered to the Germans.[16] After June 20, practically overnight, the Communists were undergoing a collective metamorphosis out of which they would emerge as the country's most fervent freedom fighters. Add this "emotional factor" to the facts that all party members had had some prewar experience at underground, covert, and occasionally terrorist operations, that they had been trained to be disciplined and never to question their superiors and, finally, that the Communist party had at its disposal scoreless prewar networks and connections, and the total comes out in the form of a powerful, extremely well-organized, and strategically mature guerilla army—Tito's Partisans. Hence, less than three months after the beginning of the war, just on the territory of Serbia there were Mihailovic's Chetniks, Tito's Partisans, Nedic's Poljska Straza (Field Guards), and also the Fascist and pro-German Zbor, led by the most prominent prewar ideologue of the corporate state, a lawyer from Smederevo by the name of Dimitrije Ljotic. In addition, in the southern province of Kosovo with its majority ethnic Albanian population, one encountered formations of Albanian Balists who were collaborating with the Germans and whose ultimate aim was to unite Kosovo with Albania. In the Independent State of Croatia, besides the fanatic Ustashe there were also Domobrani (Home Guardians, roughly). Both were legal armies of the young state, and the differences between them were analogous to those that distinguish the elite and more privileged SS from the regular army of *Wehrmacht*, respectively. Their opponents in the regions between mainland Croatia and coastal Dalmatia were Dalmatian Chetniks and also Partisans. Both were recruiting the majority of their soldiers among the local Serbian population who had practically no alternative in the face of brutal ethnic persecutions and the policy of Aryanization of Croatia spearheaded by the Ustashe. In the Bosnian parts of the Croatian state one encountered the same constellation of armies and uniforms with the addition of exclusively Muslim divisions. These were sponsored and organized by the Ustashe, who knew that the centuries-old tradition of hostility between Islam and Orthodoxy would produce some of the most dedicated soldiers against any proroyalist and pro-Serbian resistance.[17] In Slovenia, which was under Germany's occupation, there were pro-German Belogardejci (White Guards) and also an indigenous resistance movement— Osvobodilna Fronta (The Liberation Front)—which later joined Tito's Partisans to form the Yugoslav National Army.

The concentration of so many armies on a relatively small territory could produce only one result—the bloodbath that would become the most conspicuous characteristic of the Second World War in Yugoslavia.

When it was finally over, when all the statistics were calculated, Yugoslavia ranked third on the list of countries with the heaviest casualties, surpassed only by the USSR and Poland. What the simple black-on-white figures could not explain, however, were the why's and how's of the astoundingly large number of casualties for such a small country. The dilemma that we are still left with is essentially this one: Either the destruction of Yugoslavia was one of the primary Axis objectives *or* the largest number of Yugoslavs were killed by other Yugoslavs for reasons that yet need to be historically, politically, sociologically, and even psycho(patho)logically elucidated.

The fact that this very question was something of a taboo in postwar Yugoslavia is a vivid illustration of the Titoist approach to the perennial problem of *Volkgeist*. Do not forget that the party that in 1945 assumed control over Yugoslavia's development in peace was that same underground party of 1941 and nucleus out of which grew the most powerful and efficient resistance in the whole country. The intrinsic qualities that had been indispensable to its prewar underground operations and had served so well its military objectives in the war(s) of 1941–1945 (e.g., internal discipline, unquestioning obedience, dogmatic acceptance of one truth and one leader) remained its structural and operational tenets in the post-1945 period as well. Mutatis mutandis, with the Communist Party of Yugoslavia (CPY) as the chief of all of Yugoslavia, what used to be the party's structural principles only now became the foundation of social discourse in general. In lieu of the expected transformation of CPY through demilitarization, dedogmatization, and modernization, the party remained essentially unchanged after the war, while the entire Yugoslav society was transformed to emulate the static, rigid, and in many ways archaic structure of CPY. In the ensuing decades, the undisputed authority and personality cult that characterized Tito's leadership in CPY were expanded to include *all* Yugoslavs; the standards of "ideological purity" were introduced into *all* state enterprises; the party's numerous adversaries (the list of whom was virtually endless) had become the personal enemies of every Yugoslav citizen, and so on, ad nauseam.

The same rigid and dogmatic approach was used in the party's "solution" to the ethnic issues. A drastic and quite primitive epistemological break was implemented whereby all inquiries into who was killing whom during the war or any other issue that could potentially arouse nationalist and chauvinist sentiments was brushed aside as nonexistent. The problems that in reality nourished *Volkgeist* sentiments were thus never resolved; nor were the conflicting interpretations of events from the past ever confronted in a tolerant and scholarly atmosphere. The sheer power of force was used to propagate an idyllic picture of a multiethnic society living in perfect harmony; Brotherhood and Unity became the slogan of the day and also a symbol of two parallel realities, the officially permitted one and another, behind the decor, where people lived with their real feelings of frustration and vengeance. Such an arrangement was directly contingent on the survival of the power system that sustained it and that, in Yugoslavia's case, was centered around the living authority of none other than J. B. Tito. With his personal charisma and authority removed from the picture, it was inevitable that the whole system would begin to collapse and that the problems (real or imagined, all the same) that had been forcibly suppressed over forty years would begin to surface again. The Croatian nationalist uprising of 1971, whose leaders were some of the top officials in the Croatian Communist party, gave Tito a firsthand sense of his waning authority and the problems that could no longer be kept under the carpet. Although he managed to suppress the rebellion, many of the Croatian demands were de facto taken into consideration when the third postwar constitution was drafted in 1974. It opened the way toward a gradual *confederalization* of Yugoslavia, which, as the events after Tito's death in 1980 have poignantly shown, was the first precondition for the disintegration of Yugoslavia. In this final decade, the rule of Tito's regime was becoming more and more reminiscent of the techniques used by the British colonial administrators in Africa. Instead of being involved in a further expansion of the Yugoslav project, the country came to exist as the common name for six relatively independent and politically autonomous states, each one weak enough to be manipulated and controlled from one center that was J. B. Tito.

With the death of Tito and the dissolution of the country's only power center, the centrifugal forces could not be controlled anymore. In April 1981, Albanians in the autonomous province of Kosovo took to the streets demanding the status of a republic. Over the next five years the Yugoslav government and the collective presidency were trying to settle this problem, but with no apparent success. Still shunning any rhetoric that would be a sign of acknowledgment of nationalism as a political factor, the dwarf keepers of Tito's legacy called Albanian demonstrations counterrevolutionary. When it finally became clear that the Kosovo challenge was too big a problem for Yugoslav federal authorities who were victims of Titoist taboos and who refused to see the reality behind the Kosovo drama, that is, that Albanian demands were directed against Serbia and Serbs, Serbia woke up as a nation. In 1987, the new Serbian leader became Slobodan Milosevic, a Communist, but more important, a fervent Serbian nationalist who showed that Serbia alone could handle the Kosovo problem without having to wait for the impotent Yugoslav government to fulfill its empty promises. This, in effect, unleashed a whole series of national paranoias: First Slovenes and then Croats became concerned for their own well-being and worried by the prospects for Milosevic's coup d'état on the level of Yugoslavia and his stepping into Tito's shoes. In both these republics there was a rise in anti-Serbian and also anti-Yugoslav sentiment. In a revival of prewar language and style of propaganda, Yugoslavia was once again being increasingly represented as Serboslavia. In the background of the war of words were real fears that the Yugoslav National Army, with its 70 percent Serbian cadre, could strike a deal with Milosevic and turn the prosperous western republics into a war zone. Building their campaigns on such fears, the nationalist parties carried the first democratic elections in Slovenia and Croatia in 1990. This, however, only elevated the *Volkgeist* drama to a new level. In Croatia, the local Serbian population decided not to wait, like they did in 1941, for some new Ustashe to begin to exterminate them systematically but took to arms and even proclaimed the independence and sovereignty of Krajina, that part of Croatian territory in which they constituted the majority. The *circulus vitiosus* of sovereignty was not without its comic aspects as the village of Kijevo—a Croat island in a predominantly Serbian-populated Krajima—proclaimed *its* independence from Krajina's authority. Finally, a Serb butcher living in Kijevo proclaimed *his* independence and sovereignty by raising the Serbian flag on the roof of his store. He did not recognize Kijevo's sovereignty, Kijevo did not recognize Krajina's, Krajina did not recognize Croatia's, and Croatia did not recognize Yugoslavia's!

THE SERBO-CROAT QUESTION 1989–1990

By the end of 1989, the only significant Yugoslav institutions left in the country were the eight-member presidency and the government—both equally ineffective in resolving the interethnic tensions—and the Yugoslav National Army. In all the six republics, the elections were won by nationalist parties (in Serbia and Montenegro by the ex-Communists; in Slovenia, Croatia, Bosnia, and Macedonia by the newly formed rightist-nationalist parties), with the so-called Yugoslav parties suffering heavy losses everywhere.[18]

In a number of important ways, Serbia and Croatia were becoming very much like one another, with rather superficial and symbolic differences remaining. Both republics now had strong, autocratic presidents, whose one common talent was to make hair-raising public statements as if they were saying hello. For example, Franjo Tudjman was quoted as saying that he was thankful to God that his wife was neither Serbian nor

Jewish. Milosevic, in talking to the Serbian commune presidents, said that the Serbs maybe did not know diplomacy but when it came to brawls—that was their specialty. And he added, in the same lingo of an experienced Serbian hero from restaurant and bar brawls, "I hope that the Croats are not that crazy to think that they can fight us!"[19]

Another common development was the more tolerant attitude toward the local quislings from World War II who were no longer denounced for their nationalism but only for being too radical in their methods and strategies. In Croatia there was more talk about the Partisans' atrocities against the Ustashe and Domobrani. In Zagreb they changed the name of the Victims of Fascism Square into the Square of Croatian Rulers. In Serbia, the once-tabooed Chetnik insignia were prominently displayed by kids of sixteen and seventeen years of age. Soccer matches between Beograd and Zagreb or Split clubs were a test of nerves for the police and the players. In May 1990, the Dinamo (Zagreb)–Red Star (Beograd) match never even started because of the bloody confrontation just minutes before the scheduled kickoff. In the fall in Split, in the middle of the match between the local Hajduk and Beograd's Partisan team, hundreds of local fans poured onto the field and, in the climax of their orgy, raised a burning Yugoslav flag on the official flagpole.

And the media? They never stopped their iron pumping, nor was there a single attempt on either side to bring some sense and order into the impending chaos. The standard stereotype on both sides was the presentation of "us" as the victims and "them" as the aggressors and criminals. Whatever crime one of "us" was charged with, there was always a reason behind it: "Our 'boys' were provoked by their hooligans" or "we must have guns to protect our own lives." The very choice of words and language in general was also a function of the same policy. One day, the Beograd daily *Politika* printed a thick-lettered headline on its front page: Croatian Special Police are Tossing Serbian Children. Of course, there were always photographs of mourning mothers, children whose father had just been killed by bandits. Reporting on the same incident in which a Croat and a Serb were killed, Zagreb papers printed only the photos of the Croat boy's grief-stricken family. Of course, we all knew whom the Beograd papers were going to show. More and more, the media were openly calling each other Ustashe and Chetniks, reviving the same scary *Volkgeist* of 1941–1945.

Here I will summarize only some of the main themes that constituted the *Volkgeist* topoi in Serbian and Croatian media during 1989 and 1990. The block quotations are in fact my own reconstructions of the most representative views that were associated with the newly awakened *Volkgeist*. The form in which this national spirit speaks is the first person plural, as that all encompassing "We" and the focal point of the unbroken tradition of nationhood since time immemorial.

1. Serbian pride. Supposedly, Milosevic let the Serbs speak freely and with pride about their national and religious identity.

> During Tito's reign, anything with the "Serbian" prefix was considered "bad" and we had to hide our national feelings. All that has changed now and we ought to give Milosevic the credit for bringing us back into life!

2. Kosovo. This troubled province became the focus of Serbian revival. In 1389, Kosovo was the venue of the most tragic event in the history of Serbia—the fateful (lost) battle against the Turks, which was the prelude to the five centuries of Turkish occupation and Serbian slavery. The myth of Kosovo had been preserved in national poetry and was an important factor in the preservation of national spirit throughout this period. Now, six centuries later, the Serbs were fighting another battle on Kosovo. Again, the foes were the "infidels" (Albanians are mostly Muslims) and the Serbs were, in their own eyes, the guardians of the Christian world. The claims of the Albanians were seen as wholly unjustified because, although they did represent the majority in the province, no country in the world would willingly amputate a piece of its territory simply because of the demands of the local population.

> Kosovo is the soul of Serbia and we shall never give it away!

3. Tito, the Comintern and the Vatican. In the Serbian media, a most unusual anti-Serbian alliance was given prominent exposure. Its central objective was, allegedly, to dismember Yugoslavia and prevent the formation of a powerful Balkan state in which the Serbs—traditionally a "proud and freedom-loving people"—would be the most populous ethnic group. Tito, who was a Croat, was only an extended hand of this policy that was jointly created by the Vatican and the Comintern. It is no secret that at one point the disintegration of Yugoslavia indeed was the strategy of the Comintern (probably because Stalin feared that a strong federation in the Balkans could be an obstacle to the realization of the Soviet policies there), as it is also true that the official Vatican was never particularly fond of Yugoslavia as a state in which Catholics were the minority and the "schismatic Orthodox" the majority. But, it is quite absurd to claim that these two organizations, who have been each other's archenemies for so long, were united and that Tito was working for both of them.

4. Serbia, the winner in war and the loser in peace. Supposedly, the Serbs have always fought just wars, they always came out as victors and

even sacrificed one-third of their male population in World War I so that all their southern Slav brothers could live a free life in a common new state. But, when the first opportunity arrived, their "brothers" and "sisters" turned against them (e.g., the assassination of King Alexander, the creation of the Independent State of Croatia, etc.).

In the Second World War, it was again the Serbs who made up the vast majority of the partisan army, again their sacrifices were the largest and yet, after the war, it was only Serbia that was divided into the so-called autonomous provinces. Why was Croatia spared this segmentation and, especially, why were the Serbian-populated territories within Croatia not given the status of an autonomous province? Obviously, because Yugoslavia was run by Tito, a Croat, and Kardelj, a Slovene, who were deeply anti-Serbian before anything else. Further proof of this is the Constitution of 1974, drafted mainly by Edvard Kardelj, which elevated the autonomous provinces of Kosovo and Vojvodina to the status of political units with direct representation in the federation, bypassing the institutions and legislatures of the republic of Serbia of which they were an integral part.

5. The Croats.

Having sided with the Albanians in the Kosovo conflict, the Croats showed once again that they could not be trusted as allies. History is repeating itself over and again and we Serbs seem to learn little from it. How long will it take before we realize that the only thing on the Croats' minds is treason? How could we ever forgive and forget the atrocities of the Croatian Ustashe during the war? The Jews have made the whole world feel responsible for the holocaust while we Serbs have forgotten the 700,000 martyrs who died in the Jasenovac concentration camp only! And all this for some stupid and unrealistic policy of Brotherhood and Unity! How naive we have been!

There were indeed atrocities committed by the Ustashe during the war and even the German command in Croatia was appalled by the level of their brutality. Without the slightest desire to discuss this difficult problem in extenso, here is a short passage from neither Serbian nor Croatian sources, but the *Encyclopedia of Holocaust*: "The Ustasha regime in Croatia, and particularly this drive in the summer of 1941 to exterminate and dispossess the Serbs, was one of the most horrendous episodes of World War II. The murder methods applied by the Ustasha were extraordinarily primitive and sadistic: thousands were hurled from mountaintops, others were beaten to death or had their throats cut, entire villages were burned down, women raped, people sent on death marches in the middle of winter, and still others starved to death. . . . Many Catholic priests, mainly of the lower rank, took an active part in the murder operations. . . . A bishops' conference that met in Zagreb in November 1941 was not even prepared to denounce the forced conversion of Serbs that had taken place in the summer of 1941, let alone condemn the persecution and murder of Serbs and Jews" (Gutman 1990, 323–328). Despite the proven record of Ustashe atrocities, one question that remains is How much sense does it make to define a priori a whole nation as genocidal? The Serbian media were clearly imputing that "Ustashe-ism" was synonymous with being Croat.

6. Yugoslavia.

Serbs were always prepared to put their Serbian identity second to the interests of Yugoslavia. However, it was now clear to the Serbs that unity with those who had never wished them well was not only complicated but mindless. It was time for us to rid ourselves of the Yugoslav dream and start to mind our own business. Why should our soldiers die for the freedom of others? Why should we be the guardians of their safety and well-being? What a mistake we made when we laid the foundations for the Kingdom of the Slovenes, Croats and Serbs! We would have been spared all the ensuing disappointment and anguish had we formed a greater Serbia in 1918, composed of only of those territories where Serbs were the majority. Indeed, that was one of the options which we were given at the peace conference in Versailles, but our love for our Slav brothers was more powerful than our narrow national interests. How foolish and miscalculated!

7. The "misunderstood" Serbs.

We Serbs are a tragic people, like the Jews. The world has never really understood our readiness to sacrifice for the other, our willingness to go to wars so that our brothers and sisters would see the light of freedom. Today, the world does not understand the problem of Kosovo either and gives their support to the Albanians. But, still, we are not going to go around convincing the more powerful countries of our national and historic rights. We have nothing to prove to none, because our motives have always been pure and just!

8. "Serbs are not going to be Europe's slaves." Milosevic said in one of his speeches that "we are not going to go to Europe as slaves, but as equal partners." He was making reference to the Slovenes and, to a lesser extent, the Croats, who were sending their delegations all over Western Europe, trying to obtain support from the countries of the European parliament for their plans for independence.

The Croatian *rinascimento* begins in spring 1990 with the election victory of the Croatian Democratic Union (HDZ) and its leader, Dr. Franjo

Tudjman (the president of Croatia as of 1990). The emergence of Croatian *Volkgeist*, which paralleled the change in government, in many ways resembled that in Serbia. For example; Croatian views might be expressed as follows:

1. Croatian Pride.

In Yugoslavia, it was forbidden to say that you were a Croat. Our national songs were forbidden, our flags were locked in the communist closets, our name had all but disappeared completely. Now, thanks to Dr. Tudjman and the HDZ party, we are alive again. Alive and proud of our heritage and our national being.

2. One thousand years of culture.

One of the most conspicuous elements of our national pride is our 1,000-year-old culture. We are the most civilized part of the Balkans and an integral part of the heritage of the western Roman Empire. The Roman emperors built their fortifications and resorts in Dalmatia; the Austrians always respected our autonomy, cultural and political. The "East" of Yugoslavia (Serbs, Montenegrins, Macedonians) has not even been touched by this tradition. They still have a long way to go before they acquire the most elementary forms of culture in the proper sense of that term.

3. The Serbs.

The Serbs, of course, are essentially barbarians.[20] While our tradition stems from the Holy Roman Church and Western civilization, the Serbs were part of the half-civilized Byzantium and later, of the Ottoman Empire. They have no respect for laws or institutions of state. Union with them means historical regression for us. The election of Milosevic has further proven that Serbs are also inherently Bolshevik, the last truly Communist nation in Europe, and that they will not progress toward civilization because they do not have the basic prerequisites for it. They should remain part of the Eastern Orthodox world, the capital of which is Moscow.

Curiously enough, just as the Serbian media were identifying Croats *en bloc* with Ustashe and fascism in general, so were the Croats launching a propaganda campaign in which they tried to represent the Serbs as genetically predestined to be dogmatic Communists.

4. The Independent State of Croatia (NDH).

Yes, the Ustashe did commit atrocities against the Serbs, Jews, and Gypsies in the Second World War, but that was only a reaction against the ruthless exploitation of our lands and peoples by the Serbs during the so-called first Yugoslavia. Furthermore, the number of Serbian casualties is being blown out of proportion. They claim that in Jasenovac alone they lost 700,000 people. This is absurd! We allow for 30,000–40,000 at the most.

Again, as an illustration only, here is another "third party view" on the issue of Serbian exploitation of their Slav brethren. Reminiscing about the Paris Peace Conference, where Serbia appeared in the role of the south Slav Piedmont, Stephen Count Bethlen, Hungarian premier from 1921–1931, said, in 1933, that "Croats and Slovenes . . . were never asked what their desire was but were allotted . . . to the Serbs [on the basis of] their southern Slav origin; [this was] a procedure in which nobody even thought of safeguarding in any form the national individuality and character of these peoples. . . . In consequence, their conditions in the . . . Kingdom of Yugoslavia have become absolutely intolerable because they are considered not even as minorities. They belong to a special category of nations which we might most properly call the oppressed majority" (Langsam 1951, 45, emphasis added). Still, one may ask, is this sufficient reason for the policy of genocide?

5. Yugoslavia.

We do not believe in any Yugoslavia anymore. In fact, looking in retrospect we now see that the name itself has always been used as a disguise for greater Serbia. The only Yugoslavia that still might be acceptable to us Croats is a very loose confederation in which Croatia would have all the prerogatives of an independent state. We want to exercise full control over our national product, our domestic and foreign policies, and our defense. Moreover, we will no longer support the federal funds for the so-called underdeveloped regions in Yugoslavia (Bosnia, Kosovo, Montenegro, Macedonia).

6. Europe.

Europe is really where we belong, particularly "Central Europe," which needs to be revitalized as a loose union of nations who were once the constituent provinces of the Austro-Hungarian empire. Our culture has nothing in common with Serbs, Montenegrins, or the Macedonians, while, on the other hand, it shares a common tradition with Austria, northern Italy, Bavaria, and Slovenia. Catholicism has been the torch that has kept our cultural and national awareness alive. We Croats are quite likely among the most devout Catholics in the entire world.

7. Krajina.

The Serbs living in Krajina are a bunch of troublemaking barbarians. They will never get their political autonomy, while their demands for secession and becoming a part of Serbia are utterly preposterous. Also, despite all their provocations, we are not going to let ourselves be drawn into a major military conflict, like the Serbian government did in the case of Kosovo Albanians. We are going to let them carry on with their primitive methods of rebellion and terrorism, until the whole world understands that it is the two concepts of culture that are confronted here: one, a barbarian and Byzantine, and another, European and civilized.

The main purpose of our inquiry has been not to prove or disprove a specific hypothesis or theoretical proposition but to *describe* an actual cultural situation seen from a particular angle; that is, its intent has been more ethno*graphic* than socio- or anthropo-*logical* ("graphe" vs. "logia," writing vs. reasoning). There are, therefore, no particular conclusions or lessons for the future to be drawn from it. Still, two points need some additional clarification. First, the rather detailed outline of the perspective used in my descriptive endeavor and the ensuing analysis of Yugoslavia's disintegrative processes as seen through the lens of discursive formation, topoi, and *Volkgeist* might have created an impression that this author does not find other approaches and models of inquiry of much use. If this has indeed been the case, then I owe an apology to those readers who have been misled by my writing. This despite the fact that a careful reading of the first part of the text shows that such a conclusion cannot be warranted. The discourse approach has its advantages as well as shortcomings, pretty much like any other theoretical model, from Spencer's evolutionism and Marx's conflict paradigm to Geertz's "interpretive" and Tyler's "postmodern" anthropology, or even Richard Schweder's "confusionism."[21] If we have learned anything from a century and a half of social scientific research, it is that the world of Anthropos is of such vast proportions that it a priori belies any single theory's ambition to capture its meaning, historical telos, or empirical structure.

The one rather obvious area where the discourse paradigm has been found wanting is that of power and its subjects (as well as casualties). This has been, in my opinion, the most vital problem with all attempts to employ in concrete sociohistoric research the philosophical idea of a "subjectless" social reality. Again, the texts of Michel Foucault, in which he is struggling so hard to tailor the concept of power so that it fits the existing theoretical frame, are a stark illustration of the problem at hand.[22] This study of Yugoslav nationalism(s) has implicitly opened many important questions about power, which it has stopped short of articulating, not to mention trying to answer. With the exception of Tito, no other key participant was given prominent exposure; even Tito's own role was explained more in discursive terms, as the locus of Tito-*ism*, which was the name for the discursive formation of postwar Yugoslavia. Is our position so farfetched as to claim that King Alexander's dictatorship was the work of some topos and that the fact that he paid with his own "real" life for his equally "real" arrogance is irrelevant to our investigation? Are we that blind not to have seen that the estimates and projections of *real power*—both "ours" and "theirs"—as measured by the number and quality of men with arms, military equipment, foreign allies, etc., have become the most active area of politics in all of the six republics since the 1990 elections? Are we claiming that war games along the Zagreb-Beograd trajectory can be fully understood without elucidating the personalities and active roles of the new Balkan czars: Slobodan Milosevic in Serbia and Franjo Tudjman in Croatia?

All these questions can be answered with an unambiguous no. The discourse approach, as corroborated here, does not address the power/subject issue in Yugoslavia because it simply is not equipped to deal effectively with such questions and *not* because it underestimates their significance. As ethnographers, however, we have no reason to bind ourselves to one theory only. In principle, we should be able to employ *in a complementary fashion* different views and models of inquiry wherever such strategies can yield the best results. That, in sum, is the position of this author. The who's who of Yugoslavia's nationalism, the "real people" who were instrumental in the revival of *Volkgeist* and the mechanisms of power that were employed in that process are all legitimate concerns that, however, were not included in this discussion.

It is hoped that this perspective has advanced our understanding of Yugoslavia and its current crisis by enabling us to look into the key determinants of the actual cultural setting that all of the aforementioned "real people" have had to take into account, no matter how historically original or individual they and their projects might have been. We have seen some of the cultural a prioris—the discursive topoi, that is—that distinguish Yugoslavia from other cultural settings. We have seen a contemporary revival of the topos of *Volkgeist*, which has been a potent cultural determinant in these lands over almost ten centuries! Finally, it should be understood that Yugoslavia, too, can be looked at as a particular topos, one that emphasizes international cooperation, tolerance, and even a willingness to modify one's own aspirations so that they do not present a threat to others. As such, it is a topos that also has a long history in these lands and is no more or less legitimate than *Volkgeist*. The tragedy of the Yugoslav idea during Tito's reign was that it was instituted from above, with the power of the army and police ensuring its survival. This was a perversion of the true Yugoslav discourse as a discourse of tolerance and understanding between Eastern and Western Christianity, two worlds that were artificially divided at one point in history. Like in some cheap psychoanalytic novel, the dissolution of the power mechanisms through which Yugoslavia was artificially sustained and the death of its progenitor left a void quickly filled by the *Volkgeist* topos—that same topos that had been forcibly suppressed by these factors. Nevertheless, in contrast to 1941 when foreign powers played a crucial role in bringing the "first" Yugoslavia to its brutal end, the current processes of integration in Europe will work in the long run, it is hoped, in favor of the discursive topoi that emphasize cooperation and desire for mutual understanding. It is my belief that the initial spirit that inspired the Yugoslav movement will therefore continue to thrive, even if there is no Yugoslavia as such. *Volkgeist* will not disappear altogether, but clearly its role will become more and more counterproductive in the broader context of a united Europe in the aftermath of its iron curtain. For Yugoslavia and Yugoslavs, the only *real* question is, how many lives will be lost in vain until that moment finally arrives?

POST SCRIPTUM

This text had been brought to completion in May 1991, that is, before the Serbo-Croat conflict escalated into the bloodiest civil war on Europe's soil since the end of World War II. From the factographic point of view, therefore, it appears incredibly outdated and pristine. In terms of its contents and the idea of *Volkgeist*, however, I have not seen any reason to revise what has been said. Unfortunately.

Notes

1. With the works of Sapir and Whorff, anthropology had already made its early and quite original entry into this problematic. The particular significance of the "Sapir-Whorff hypothesis" lies in the fact that it was the result of extensive ethnographic research rather than "philosophical contemplation." More recently, there has been a revival of interest among anthropologists for the implementation of discursive models in the study of culture (cf. Clifford and Marcus 1986; Geertz 1973).
2. Another word that has become popular with anthropologists lately and that seems to bear some semblance in meaning-content is "trope." Its use, however, establishes an important difference from topos: namely, "tropes" are the stylistic/conceptual patterns in ethnographic writing while topos belongs to the realm of discursive formation (or culture) that is the subject matter of that writing. See, for example, Stephen Tyler and Mary Louise Pratt's essays in *Writing Culture* (Clifford and Marcus 1986).
3. One of the more important criticisms of Foucault's work points to the gap between his theoretical objectives and the empirical data, particularly striking when one tries to assess the geographical and cultural applicability of his

results. Especially the critics of his works on madness and clinical medicine have shown, in extenso, that the bulk of his evidence pertains to France only while it is his ambition to diagnose the transformations in "Western attitudes" or "Occidental discourse" at large (See, for example, Doerner 1981; Rothman 1971; or Midelfort 1980).

4. Of course, the importance of the political and social backdrop against which Fichte, Schleirmacher, Herder, and Hegel wrote their texts must not be overlooked. Two "social facts," in my opinion, deserve special mention: (1) this was the time of the unification of Germany, and (2) the philosophers in Germany were always a highly respected caste who were expected, in return for their prestige perhaps, to actively contribute to the political debates of the time.

5. Here is a selection of useful sources on nationalism in Yugoslavia: Banac (1984), Beard and Radin (1929), Burg (1977), Cviic (1990), Dyker (1979), Fisher (1968), Hondius (1968), Rusinow (1988), Shoup (1968), Vukadinovic (1988).

6. The dissertation's title is *Revolution and Stigma: The personal narratives about the Yugoslav revolution and the construction of the "bourgeoisie."* Based on personal narratives (oral histories) and the analysis of relevant archival documents, I examine how the "bourgeoisie" in a small town in postrevolutionary Yugoslavia learned to cope with the imposed stigma of the "enemy of the people and progress in general." From another perspective, the dissertation is a study in *meaning as use* of a particular word: "bourgeoisie."

7. The most recent wave of unrest in Serbia, the Belgrade demonstrations from March 9 to 15 in which two people were killed and seventy-five wounded, began as a protest against the political manipulations of the media.

8. [Editor's note] *The Uncaptive Mind* is a monthly journal on Eastern European affairs published in English. *The Gulag Archipelago* (Solzhenitsyn 1985) and *Darkness at Noon* (Koestler 1940) gave graphic literary descriptions of life under state socialism.

9. More on the Yugoslav-Soviet dispute can be found in Banac (1988), Bass and Marbury (1957), Farrell (1956), Johnson (1972), Ulam (1952), and Vucinich (1982). The correspondence between the Cominform and the Central Committee of the CPY was already published in November of 1948 by The Royal Institute of International Affairs in London (1948).

10. Lampe et al. (1990, 76). This publication is also a detailed summary of Yugoslav-American economic relations after World War II. Other useful sources on this topic are Baldwin (1966), Larson (1979), Markovich (1975), Sukijasovic (1968), and Vasic (1963).

11. On linguistic variations between Serbs and Croats see (exceptionally illuminating) Birnbaum (1980).

12. The rural population (80%–90% of the total population) in Croatia and Serbia alike never distinguished Austrians from Germans. This is reflected in their usage of one and the same (slightly pejorative) name for either one: "Švabo" (lit., "roach").

13. On Pan-Slavism and the Yugoslav (southern Slav) movement see Fodor (1937), Kohn (1953; 1962), MacKenzie (1967), Mijatovic (1973), Stavrianos (1950), Vucinich (1954), Young (1915).

14. Serbian objectives and the role of other southern Slavs in World War I are well documented in D. Djordjevic (1980).

15. Hoptner (1962) is a thoroughly documented and quite illuminating study

of the events that preceded and the tragic consequences of the coup of March 27.

16. The whole Chetnik episode remains a hotly contested issue in Yugoslavia. For a well-documented and unbiased historical analysis see Roberts (1973).

17. The role of Muslims in Yugoslavia's *Volkgeist* dramas is a topic in itself, with yet another long history. As Serbia in the nineteenth century gradually won its independence from Ottoman rule, the position of local Muslims changed from privileged elite to oppressed minority. The champions of Serbian nationalism around the turn of the century were successful in the creation of a Muslim stereotype whereby these people were depicted as the descendants of the Serbs who, centuries earlier, had converted to Islam and had in fact betrayed their national and religious identity. The Muslims became something of a stain on an otherwise perfect Christian-Orthodox-Serbian body. It goes without saying that this ideology was sure to produce strong anti-Serb sentiment among Muslims, at first silent but, when the first opportunity came, quite loud and brutal. It also explains, in part, the pragmatic background to the sudden outbursts of love for Muslims on the part of Ustashe and other Croatian nationalists in 1941.

18. By "Yugoslav parties" I am referring primarily to the Reformists, who were founded by the country's prime minister, Ante Markovic, and also by the UJDI (Association for the Yugoslav Democratic Initiative), a broad-based organization that seemed at one point to be a viable alternative to the disintegrative nationalist policies.

19. See the Jugoslav journal *Vreme* no. 25, (April 15, 1991) p. 66.

20. In a lucid and thoroughly informed presentation at the AAA Annual Meeting in New Orleans in 1990, Robert Hayden of the University of Pittsburgh made a parallel between Edward Said's (1979) "orientalism" and the more recent neo-orientalist looking glass through which Serbs were depicted in Croatian media. The presentation was a short version of a forthcoming publication with M. Bakic as the coauthor (Hayden and Bakic 1990).

21. Schweder gave an elaborate presentation of the "confusionist paradigm" in his distinguished lecture at the Central States Anthropological Society's Annual Meeting (Notre Dame University, March 1988).

22. This new concept of power is the central subject matter of *Power/Knowledge* (1980) although it is present implicitly throughout Foucault's opus. It has been criticized by many authors and from various theoretical and philosophical platforms. Taylor (1984) is still my favorite, unsurpassed for its succinctness and clarity of argumentation.

References

Anderson, B. 1983. *Imagined communities: Reflections on the origin and spread of nationalism.* London: Verso.

Baldwin, D. A. 1966. *Economic development and American foreign policy 1943–1962.* Chicago: University of Chicago Press.

Banac, I. 1984. *The national question in Yugoslavia.* Ithaca: Cornell University Press.

———. 1988. *With Stalin, against Tito.* Ithaca: Cornell University Press.

Bass, R., and Marbury, E. (eds.). 1957. *The Soviet-Yugoslav controversy, 1949–1958: A documentary record.* New York: Prospect Books.

Beard, C., and Radin, G. 1929. *The Balkan pivot: Yugoslavia.* New York: Macmillan.

Birnbaum, H. 1980. "Language, ethnicity, and nationalism: On the linguistic foundations of a unified Yugoslavia." in *The creation of Yugoslavia, 1914–1918,* ed. D. Djordjevic. 157–182. Santa Barbara: American Bibliographic Center—Clio Press.

Burg, S. L. 1977. "Ethnic conflict and the federalization of socialist Yugoslavia: The Serbo-Croat conflict." *Publius* 7(4): 14–25.

Clifford, J., and Marcus, G. E. 1986. *Writing culture: The poetics and politics of ethnography.* Berkeley: University of California Press.

Cviic, C. 1990. "The background and implications of the domestic scene in Yugoslavia." in *Problems of Balkan security,* ed. P. S. Shoup. 89–119. Washington, DC: Wilson Center Press.

Djordjevic, D. 1980. *The creation of Yugoslavia, 1914–1918.* Santa Barbara: American Bibliographic Center—Clio Press.

Doerner, K. 1981. *Madmen and the bourgeoisie: A social history of madness and insanity.* Oxford: Blackwell.

Dyker, D. A. 1979. "Yugoslavia: Unity out of diversity." in *Political culture and political change in Communist states,* eds. A. Brown and J. Grey. 66–82. New York: Holmes and Meier.

Farrell, R. B. 1956. *Yugoslavia and the Soviet Union 1948–1956.* Hamden, CT: Shoestring Press.

Fisher, J. C. 1968. *Yugoslavia: A multinational state.* San Francisco: Chandler.

Fodor, M. W. 1937. *Plot and counterplot in central Europe.* Boston: Houghton Mifflin.

Foucault, M. 1970. *The order of things.* (French ed. *Les mots et les choses*). New York: Random House.

———. 1980. *Power/knowledge: Selected interviews and other writings, 1927–1977,* ed. C. Gordon. New York: Pantheon.

Geertz, C. 1973. *The interpretation of culture: Selected essays.* New York: Basic Books.

Gutman, I., (ed. in chief). 1990. *Encyclopedia of the holocaust,* vol. 1, New York: Macmillan.

Hayden, R., and Bakic, M. 1990. "Orientalism in the Yugoslav national question." Paper presented at the annual meetings of the American Anthropological Association of New Orleans.

Hondius, F. W. 1968. *The Yugoslav community of nations.* The Hague: Mouton.

Hoptner, J. B. 1962. *Yugoslavia in crisis 1934–1941.* New York: Columbia University Press.

Johnson, A. R. 1972. *The transformation of Communist ideology: The Yugoslav case, 1945–1953*. Cambridge: MIT Press.

Koestler, A. 1940. *Darkness at noon*. London: Cape.

Kohn, H. 1953. *Pan-slavism: Its history and ideology*. Notre Dame: University of Notre Dame Press.

———. 1962. *The age of nationalism*. New York: Harper & Row.

Lampe, J. R., Prickett, Russell O., and Adamovic, Ljubisa S. 1990. *Yugoslav-American economic relations since World War II*. Durham and London: Duke University Press.

Langsam, W. C. 1951. *Documents and readings in the history of Europe since 1918*. Chicago and Philadelphia: J. B. Lippincott.

Larson, D. L. 1979. *United States foreign policy toward Yugoslavia 1943–1963*. Washington, DC: University Press of America.

MacKenzie, D. 1967. *The Serbs and Russian pan-Slavism*. Ithaca: Cornell University Press.

Markovich, S. C. 1975. "American foreign aid and Yugoslav international policies." *East European Quarterly* 9(2): 185–193.

Mijatovic, E. 1973. "Panslavism: its rise and decline." *The Fortnightly Review* 20: 94–112.

Roberts, W. A. 1973. *Tito, Mihailovic and the allies, 1941–1945*. New Brunswick: Rutgers University Press.

Rothman, D. 1971. *The discovery of the asylum*. Boston: Little, Brown.

Royal Institute of International Affairs. 1948. *The Soviet-Yugoslav dispute: Text of the published correspondence*. London and New York: The Royal Institute of International Affairs.

Rusinow, D. I. (ed.). 1988. *Yugoslavia: A fractured federalism*, Washington, DC: Wilson Center Press.

Said, E. 1978. *Orientalism*. New York: Pantheon.

Shoup, P. 1968. *Communism and the Yugoslav national question*. New York: Columbia University Press.

Solzhenitsyn, I. 1985. *The gulag archipelago*. London: Collins Harvill.

Stavrianos, L. S. 1950. *The Balkans since 1453*. New York: Holt, Rinehart and Winston.

Sukijasovic, N. 1968. *Foreign investments in Yugoslavia*. New York: Oceania.

Taylor, C. 1984. "Foucault on freedom and truth." *Political Theory* 12(2): 152–183.

Ulam, A. B. 1952. *Titoism and the Cominform*. Cambridge: Harvard University Press.

Vucinich, W. S. 1954. *Serbia between East and West: The events of 1903–1908*. Stanford: Stanford University Press.

———. 1982. "At the brink of war and peace: The Tito-Stalin split in historical perspective." *East European Monographs*. New York: Columbia University Press.

Young, G. 1915. *Nationalism and the war in the Near East*. Oxford: Oxford University Press.

Interethnic Relations in the Soviet Union during the First Years of "Restructuring"

ANATOLY M. KHAZANOV

It has already been pointed out by many scholars that the supranational Soviet state met many sociological criteria of an empire.[1] Thus, it was populated by many different ethnic groups that did not join the state voluntarily, having all been conquered in the past or incorporated into the state by force. Further, these groups are still forcefully kept together, even though force is far from being the only factor. Last but not least, the Soviet empire, like any other, had one dominating nation: the Russians. Thus, many regularities in other empires may also be applicable to the former Soviet Union.

The October revolution was not only a social revolution; it was accompanied as well by national revolutions of several ethnic groups of the former Russian Empire. One of the reasons the Bolsheviks won the civil war was that at that time they made many concessions to the non-Russian ethnic groups, temporarily managing to attract the sympathy of some, or entered into coalitions with several national movements. The multiethnic character of the former Soviet Union and unstable relations between Russians and non-Russians made and still make a great impact upon every aspect of life in the Commonwealth of Independent States. It is impossible to understand the Soviet Union without taking into consideration the so-called national question. Together with many other Soviet problems, the national question was inherited by the Gorbachev leadership from its predecessors. By the mid-1980s, the country's ethnic situation had the following features:

THE ETHNIC SITUATION IN THE USSR FROM THE 1960s TO THE MID-1980s

There are three main tendencies that may be considered as characteristic features of the ethnic processes under way in the USSR during its last decades.

182

The first tendency was the process of social and cultural unification of all Soviet ethnic groups on the basis of Russian or, to put it more exactly, Soviet Russian culture. There are a number of objective reasons for this tendency. After all, all the Soviet peoples historically had to coexist with each other and with the Russians for considerable periods of time, first under the tsars, and later under the Soviets. Under the circumstances, it was inevitable that some common cultural elements would develop and that most of them would be borrowed from Russian culture.

However, one must take into account the deliberate policy of the Soviet government, which favored the unification of its peoples, not because of the well-known Marxist dogma but rather out of the pragmatic necessity to rule and impose its will on such a vast and diverse country as the USSR.

Since the Russians were the largest and most powerful nation in the USSR, and were considered the traditional stronghold of the Russian and Soviet governments, the primary aim was the creation of a common Soviet Russian–based social culture and the linguistic Russification of all the Soviet non-Russian ethnic groups. In other words, the aim was to turn the Soviet Union from a supranational into a quasi-state.

The official interpretation of the ethnic situation in the USSR was that ethnic and national processes under socialism were essentially different from those in capitalist countries. In the Soviet Union a new historical, social, and international supraethnical unity—the Soviet people— emerged as a result of dialectical processes of simultaneous flourishing (*rastsvet'*) and convergence, or rapprochement (*sblizhenie*), of different ethnicities.[2] This new unity was to be bilingual, with an increasing use of the Russian language.

It should be noted that the Soviet leadership achieved a certain amount of success in its ethnic policy. According to the 1979 census, 62.2 percent of the entire non-Russian population of the country was fluent in Russian; 16.3 million non-Russians considered Russian as their mother tongue (Isupov 1980, 23; Guboglo 1984, 65–66). First higher education, and subsequently secondary, primary, and even preschool education, were consistently converted to the Russian language in the union republics, and particularly in the autonomous republics. The active influence of the non-Russian languages was increasingly restricted, more often than not through purely administrative measures.

In some publications, the neglect of non-Russian languages was even praised as an achievement. Thus, the authors of *Present-day Ethnic Processes in the U.S.S.R.*, published in English translation, noted with satisfaction that in many autonomous republics and regions of the Russian Soviet Federative Socialist Republic (RSFSR) all children of the indigenous ethnic groups were taught in Russian (Bromley 1982). In another book published in 1987, the leading Soviet anthropologists Yu. V. Bromlei, I. S. Gurvich, and V. I. Kozlov complained that a fluent knowledge of Russian was more characteristic of the peoples of the autonomous republics than of the peoples of the fifteen union republics and expressed a hope that new measures undertaken by the party and the government would "improve" the situation (Bromlei 1987, 146).

There was yet another factor that contributed to the intensive acculturation of different Soviet ethnicities: the internal migration of the Soviet population, often deliberately channeled by the government. Sixty million people (about one-fifth of the whole population of the USSR) lived outside their ethnic republics and autonomous areas (Isupov 1980, 98–99). About one-sixth of all Soviet families were made up of spouses belonging to different ethnicities (Bruk 1986, 146).[3]

Moreover, most of the non-Russian administrative formations have developed a complex and mixed ethnic composition with a large Russian component. In the early 1980s 17.4 percent of Russians were living outside Russia proper. However, while the Russians had their schools and other educational and cultural institutions all over the country, the non-Russian ethnic groups had native-language schools, not to mention other institutions, on the territory of their ethnic republics and autonomous areas (and in some cases, not even there). As a result, the non-Russians were particularly prone to acculturation.

It is no wonder that many ethnic groups were particularly anxious about the continuing influx of Russian settlers into their territories. "Russians go home" is by no means a new slogan. Between the 1970s and the early 1980s this slogan was constantly used during ethnic demonstrations and disturbances in the Baltic republics, Central Asia, and some other areas.

The second tendency was the process of internal consolidation of the major non-Russian ethnic groups in the USSR, or, in other terms, the obliteration of tribalism and of other local divisions.

These processes were directly influenced by two factors. The first was the trend favoring unification rather than differentiation through modern ways of life, politically controlled education, mass media, and information. The second factor was the deliberate policy of local authorities in ethnic republics to assimilate or suppress ethnic minorities (except the Russians) in their territories.

The central leadership in Moscow did nothing to prevent the second factor, with rare exceptions made in cases when the situation became explosive (as, for example, in Abkhaziia in the 1970s). As a result, the Azerbaidjanian authorities practiced for many years the policy of forced assimilation of all Moslem ethnic groups on their territory, particularly the Iranian-speaking Tats and Talyches. The same policy was conducted with respect to the Georgian minority on the territory of Azerbaidjan (Ingeloitsy), while the Armenians, through the use of open and concealed discriminatory measures, were forced to leave this republic.

The Georgian government followed the same line toward some Iberian (Mingrelians, Swans, Adzartzy) and even non-Iberian (Ossets, Abkhaz) ethnic minorities. The Uzbek government strove to assimilate the Tadzhiks residing on the territory of Uzbekistan, while the Tadzhik government conducted a parallel policy in relation to the Iranian-speaking (i.e., "mountain Tadzhiks") minorities. It would be easy to provide many more examples of this kind.

Nevertheless, the success of this policy should not be exaggerated. Not only the numerous ethnic minorities in the non-Russian Soviet republics but also the more pure forms of tribalism and local particularism displayed a considerable amount of vitality. This was felt in many parts of the Soviet Union where ethnic self-consciousness in some respects maintained its hierarchical nature. People saw themselves as belonging to a separate ethnicity when it was placed in opposition to other ethnicities, but in intraethnic relations considerable importance was attached to one's tribal or local belonging. In Central Asia, it became common practice for a newly appointed first secretary of the republican Communist party to reserve leading or privileged positions for members of his tribe or local subdivision.

One may conclude that processes of consolidation within many ethnic groups in the Soviet Union were at times fairly contradictory and far from complete. This has been apparent even from some Soviet publications of the past few years. As one Soviet scholar admitted:

> For decades our literature maintained that all the U.S.S.R.'s peoples have fully consolidated into socialist nations and nationalities. Any mention of persisting cultural differences between separate parts of ethnoses was deemed inappropriate. The noting of vestiges of tribal divisions among certain previously backward peoples was regarded as completely impermissible. Even respectable ethnographic monographs said nothing about the ethnographic groups that exist within virtually every sizable or widely dispersed people. (Natsionalnye protsessy V SSSR, 1987, 72)

The third tendency was growing nationalism among many non-Russian ethnic groups and their opposition to Russian dominance and to the policy of Russification. Soviet colonialism revealed the same regularities as that of the capitalist countries. Colonialism involves the development of colonies and the creation of nontraditional elites. This development, in its turn, leads to a growth in nationalism.

Some exceptions like the Jewish or Crimean Tatar movements notwithstanding, it was virtually impossible to discuss organized national movements in the former Soviet Union until in its last few years. All forms of opposition, including the nationalistic kind, had been severely suppressed. The label of nationalist was a direct ticket to the Gulag, and a majority of political prisoners in the Soviet Union in the post-Stalin period were people accused of nationalism. At best, organized national opposition consisted of small and short-lived underground groups that, although attracting respect and sympathy, were not, for obvious reasons, sufficiently numerous and influential. Most of the open ethnic unrest in the Soviet Union in the 1970s and the early 1980s was of a more or less spontaneous nature. Although these groups demonstrated a deep-rooted and powerful antagonism, they were sparked by particular localized events only.

However, the basic definition of the word *dissent* is "disagreement" or "rejection." Therefore, although the objectives of the Soviet system were Russification and the creation of a single Soviet nation, ethnic dissent was extensively and intrinsically vital to the maintenance of ethnic identity and its specific interests, even in cases where those interests were not officially prohibited by Soviet legislation. First, because the survival and particularly the development of different ethnic groups and their cultures were incompatible with the aims of the regime; and second, because the expression of ethnic differences, particularly the emphasis on these differences, resisted ultimate Soviet goals.

This passive and covert resistance was rather widespread, involving different strata of Soviet society and taking different forms in different areas: for example, the refusal to speak Russian in public, opposition to intermarriage with Russians, insistence on bilingual or native language education, and sympathy toward all kinds of political and ethnic movements and events outside the Soviet Union that were not welcomed by the Soviet government.

INCONSISTENCIES IN SOVIET ETHNIC POLITICAL PRACTICE

There were some very significant inconsistencies in Soviet ethnic policy that were directed toward the acculturation of the non-Russian ethnic groups of the Soviet Union and their linguistic Russification. However, their complete assimilation was by no means the immediate intention and purpose of the Soviet leadership. Moreover, it was almost impossible for individuals, and even more so for entire ethnic groups, to change their ethnic identification, particularly to become identified with the Russians.

The whole administrative concept of ethnicity in the Soviet Union differed from the Western concept. It was neither based on citizenship or religion nor left to the individual's free choice. In Soviet practice, it was decided by ascription. In fact, the Soviet administrative practice of ascribing ethnicity was based on blood affiliation, and in many cases on fixed ethnic divisions through heredity. Individuals could not change their ethnicity through legal action if and when they wished; it was prescribed to them, they were required always to belong to the ethnicity of their parents. Only if one was the offspring of a mixed marriage did one have the right to a limited choice: one could choose either the father's or the mother's ethnicity.

Ethnic identification was an extremely important issue in the Soviet Union. It was registered on birth certificates and identity papers (internal passports), which every Soviet citizen, starting from the age of sixteen, was required to have in his or her possession. Ethnic identification had to be declared and was taken into consideration in all important events in the life of an individual: for example, in trying to enter the university, in looking for a job, in requesting promotion, or in emigrating from the Soviet Union. As Tishkov, the director of the Institute of Ethnography of the Academy of Sciences of the USSR, admitted, a rigid system of fixed ethnic identification based on the ethnic origin of an individual often served as a pretext for discrimination or privileges (Tishkov 1989, 54).

Thus, a very significant contradiction existed in Soviet ethnic policy. On the one hand, policy promoted Russification; on the other, it set up a very serious obstacle against this very Russification ever taking place. It denied those individuals and ethnic groups who would have liked to become Russian this opportunity. A great number of people in the Soviet Union, particularly among dispersed ethnic groups or those residing outside their ethnic formations, would like to have been registered as Russians, either to make their lives easier or because they were already Russified. However, they found it impossible to do so by any legal action.

This inconsistency in Soviet ethnic policy was noticed by the Soviet authorities themselves. Before the 1977 constitution was adopted, ethnic policy was discussed in the press and at various public meetings. Some people suggested making ethnicity a matter of voluntary choice or removing the "nationality" clause from identity documents. These suggestions were published by Soviet newspapers.

However, everything remained unchanged, and, in my opinion, for several different reasons. On the one hand, any changes in the existing practice of ethnic identification would hardly have been welcomed by Russian chauvinists. Chauvinism was deeply rooted not only in the minds of ordinary Russians but also among the party and government officials of Russian ethnicity, and even the Russian intelligentsia. The fear of competition for prominent positions and the desire to have an easily identifiable scapegoat—like the Jews—might have served as additional factors. On the other hand, there was also the danger that some ethnic groups, considering such a change as another step in the policy of Russification, might have resisted it.

There was yet another important factor, perhaps the most crucial one, that prevented any changes in ethnic identification in the Soviet Union. Soviet ethnic policy had several goals. The most important one was always the maintenance of the existing sociopolitical order in the country. Obviously, Soviet leaders perceived the practice of ascribed ethnicities as the best possible way of achieving this aim. On the one hand, this practice guaranteed the support of the Russians since it made them the dominating ethnic group. On the other hand, leaders had to secure the support of certain strata of non-Russian ethnic groups by reserving for them preferential treatment and a percentage of privileged positions and high-level jobs in their own republics and autonomous formations.

However, the very impossibility of crossing ethnic borders sometimes only inspired nationalistic feelings. A Zionist movement in the Soviet Union in the late 1960s and in the early 1970s was to a large extent initiated by some very acculturated secular Jewish intelligentsia as a reaction against discrimination and an anti-Semitic atmosphere in the country.

It can be concluded that Soviet ethnic policy in the USSR's last few decades was actually marked by certain contradictions in the choice and application of the appropriate measures needed to facilitate its practical realization. Growing competition for a limited number of privileged positions between Russians and non-Russians made a Soviet version of affirmative action unattractive to both sides. To the former it seemed like an encroachment upon their rights and privileges; to the latter it was simply not sufficient. The ever-increasing dominance of the Russian language (in politics, the party and administrative apparatus, the army, science, education, etc.) constantly raised the required level of knowledge of the language, and this alone placed the non-Russian ethnic groups at a disadvantage. To give only one example, in most of the union republics, not to speak of the autonomous republics, all official correspondence was conducted in Russian, and people had to speak Russian at all official meetings and gatherings.

At the same time one might doubt the political effectiveness of a policy of linguistic Russification. Examples from many modern countries, including the former Soviet Union, illustrate that linguistic assimilation alone, far from easing the ethnic tension, often only results in its aggravation. On many occasions, I heard members of the non-Russian intelligentsia make the following claim: "Even if somewhere toward the twenty-first century we are forced to forget our native language and switch to Russian, our children and grandchildren will have even better reasons for writing in Russian anti-Russian slogans."

THE ETHNIC SITUATION UNDER THE GORBACHEV REGIME: GENERAL CONSIDERATIONS

The policy of glasnost did not solve any ethnic problems in the Soviet Union. It only exposed them by uncovering the existing ethnic tensions and frictions. In other words, it made it obvious that the crisis in the Soviet Union was not only of a purely economic order, it was also a crisis in ethnic relations.

First, we witnessed numerous open protests against the policy of Russification, as well as demands for more rights and more autonomy for non-Russian ethnic groups, or even demands for the recognition of their right to secede from the Soviet Union. Even in 1985 demands for secession led to imprisonment; in 1986 and in 1987 they were considered as extremist and unrealistic; but in November 1988 the legislature of Estonia proclaimed the republic's sovereignty, and in May 1989 the legislature of Lithuania declared that the republic wanted to reestablish its independence. National movements and manifestations expressed in different forms embraced most of the non-Russian areas of the former USSR, from the Baltic republics to Yakutia in eastern Siberia, and from the Caucasus to Ukraine, including even such republics considered "quiet" in the not-so-recent past, as Belorussia and Moldavia. Such small ethnic groups as the Gagauz (140,000) and the Bulgarians (80,000) strove for cultural concessions from the Soviet authorities. Even the Selkups, an ethnic group in Siberia that numbers hardly more than 700, demanded education in their own language and territorial autonomy.

Although some of the later ethnic manifestations, like those before, were more or less spontaneous, others were rather well organized and promoted by various nationalistic organizations and movements that enjoyed wide support from different strata of their ethnicities and operated with relative freedom of action.

Not only have different nationalist dissident groups become much more active and demanding than ever before, but those that in the recent past preferred to keep a low profile have dared to openly express opinions that I would define as a loyal opposition. There are many intellectuals and even officials among them who are well adapted to the Soviet way of life. One of the issues that has been troubling them the most is linguistic Russification.

Many of these people participated in a movement that can be described as the Soviet Greens. However, ethnic issues were very important in their actions, which usually protested the damage caused to the natural environment of their ethnic territories by industrial projects undertaken in the so-called interests of the union. (This movement was particularly strong in Armenia, Georgia, Ukraine, and Estonia; it also has been gaining momentum in Azerbaidjan, Uzbekistan, Turkmenia, Moldavia, and Lithuania.)

It is remarkable that many national movements also included specific economic demands. In the opinion of many non-Russians, economic development in their areas served the interests of the Russian center, or of the Russian migrants to their areas, at the expense of the indigenous population. Thus, a very popular demand in the Baltic republics was to change priorities in economic development and to stop further industrial construction whose requirements could not be satisfied by the local labor resources. These requirements often served as a pretext for the continuing in-migration of Russians.

Second, the strained relations that had existed in the past between different ethnic groups of the Soviet Union were revealed more openly. Groups made territorial claims and demanded elevated status or reconsideration of the borders between different ethnic formations; not only between Armenia and Azerbaidjan, but, for example, between Georgia and Azerbaidjan, Tadzhikistan and Uzbekistan, between several northern Caucasian ethnic groups, between the Volga Tatars and the Bashkirs, and so on. Until the events in Armenia, the Moscow leadership was rather tolerant of this kind of friction providing the Russians were not involved directly in these disputes and were not the immediate target. It seems that the old imperial principle *divide et impera* still served as a useful tool in Soviet ethnic policy.

Third, the Russian right-wing, antiliberal, xenophobic, and nationalist movement was gathering more and more force. The existence and activities of a grass-roots organization called Pamiat', with its patently anti-Semitic, anti-Western, and chauvinistic program, was remarkable in itself. Notwithstanding the mild criticism offered in some of the Soviet newspapers, not a finger was raised against this organization, and no restrictions were imposed on its activities. Its influence and membership increased, and its leaders boasted that their organization had become the second largest organization in the country after the Communist party. The organization even dared to attack those Politburo members, like Alexander Yakovlev, who were considered its opponents. Such attacks on top-level dignitaries were unprecedented in the Soviet Union.

Not only the Jews but many other ethnic groups took this organization very seriously. Quite obviously, Pamiat' enjoyed the tacit support of some groups within the ruling Russian elite, and the more-or-less open support of many Russian intellectuals, who complained that the Russians were economically underprivileged in the Soviet Union and were suffering from the affirmative action program. At the same time, it would be completely wrong to think that the entire Russian nationalist movement was inspired by the opponents of the restructuring policy. Many participants of this movement claimed—and there is no reason to doubt their sincerity—that they supported restructuring because it legalized their activities for the first time in Soviet history.

The idea of replacing a discredited Communist ideology with the ideology of Russian messianism (or totalitarian nationalism, with which some groups even wish to combine Orthodox Christianity) received in the Soviet Union a wider circulation than might be expected, even penetrating into certain groups within the privileged and ruling Russian elites.

RECENT TRENDS IN SOVIET ETHNIC POLICY (1985–1989)

It is quite obvious that even in 1989 the Soviet leadership did not have any consistent policy on the national question. It tried different approaches, and all of them failed. By 1989 Soviet ethnic policy under Gorbachev went through three stages:

1. The continuation of Brezhnev's previous policy
2. A policy that secured further privileges for the Russians at the expense of non-Russian ethnic groups of the USSR
3. The stage of certain oscillations in formulating and implementing the ethnic policy, which possibly even reflects some disagreement on this issue among the leadership

Originally, the Gorbachev leadership simply followed the policy of the previous leadership, with its distinct emphasis on linguistic Russification. However, in 1986 it became apparent that this policy was being supplemented with another, that of emphatic reliance on the Russian element in the non-Russian republics and autonomous formations of the

Soviet Union, as well as further restrictions on the non-Russian elites in respect to their rights, privileges, and even numbers. These new tendencies manifested themselves most clearly in Central Asia and the Caucasus, and in their implementation the Soviet leadership was apparently guided by the following considerations:

First, concern over growing nationalism, which met, to say the least, virtually no opposition from the local non-Russian authorities, was often tacitly encouraged and occasionally was viewed by the Soviet leadership as an obstacle even to the external political goals of the Soviet Union. The invasion of Afghanistan, unpopular among all the Soviet ethnic groups, especially those of Central Asia, led to a whole series of antiwar rallies and widespread evasion of military service (Kuzio 1987, 112–113).

Second, there was concern over the dangerous effect that the growing influence of Islam could have on nationalism of the Moslem peoples of the USSR. Regardless of the policy conducted by the Soviet Union with regard to the Moslem states, inside the country Islam was subjected to persecution. By 1986, there were only 751 officially registered Moslem congregations left in the USSR (compared to 6,794 Russian Orthodox, 1,099 Catholic, 2,976 Baptist, and 843 Pentacostal congregations.)[4] The official Moslem clergy were no less servile than their Russian Orthodox counterparts, placed totally under government control and having little authority among the population. At the same time, the Soviets admitted that the level of religious observance in the Moslem areas of the USSR, rather than declining, was rising noticeably, as was the activity and influence of self-proclaimed, unregistered clergymen and of the Sufi orders. The Soviet leadership became increasingly uneasy about the growth of Islamic fundamentalism and even about the immediate effect of the Islamic revolution in Iran on the growth of nationalism among the Moslem ethnic groups of the USSR. Indeed, from the early 1980s, tapes with recorded speeches of Khomeini were widely circulated throughout Central Asia, Azerbaidjan, and the northern Caucasus, while Khomeini's portraits could even be found in the homes of the Europeanized local intelligentsia. The local leadership showed its inability to effectively resist Islam and often had no desire to do so. It became apparent that many leaders, especially from the lowest ranks, succeeded in combining ostentatious devotion to Communist ideals with the observance of many rules of Islam in their private lives.

Third, the anticorruption campaign and the beginning of the perestroika campaign revealed the total corruption, incompetence, and ineffectiveness of the local non-Russian elites in Central Asia and the Caucasus, which sometimes exceeded even the normal Soviet standards.

All in all, it is obvious that the central leadership in Moscow came to the conclusion that some preferences in such areas as education and job promotion, which the non-Russian ethnic groups had been granted in their own ethnic formations in order to give them a stake in the perpetuation of the political system, did not prevent the growth of their nationalistic sentiments.

In other words, the Soviets faced the same "colonial ingratitude" that other colonial powers have faced in the recent past. Moreover, just like in the other colonial empires, the new nationalism came mostly from new and educated strata that in functional respects may be considered as the equivalent of the middle class in other empires; this nationalism is also to a large extent a product of these empires, of modernization processes, and of a sheer necessity for colonial rule.

The urbanization that took place in many ethnic areas of the Soviet Union, and the influx of indigenous populations to the cities where the Russians constituted a majority of the population, in many cases only increased competition and aggravated national relations. This was not characteristic of the Soviet Union only. As Smith (1979, 185) pointed out:

> Modernization is not only uneven; it involves group competition for scarce urban facilities. Hence, it not only throws together hitherto relatively isolated ethnic groups, but it also sets them against each other. Their economic and cultural roles are no longer complementary, but competitive; they duplicate each other's activities well in excess of given levels of need.

Possibilities for securing the support of certain strata of non-Russian ethnic groups by reserving for them a percentage of high-level jobs and other preferential treatment in their ethnic areas became more limited because non-Russians migrating to the cities definitely preferred white-collar and intellectual professions to industrial labor.

Another shift in Soviet ethnic policy might be seen in the changing attitude toward elites in the non-Russian republics of the USSR. From the very beginning of the Soviet regime, relations between the central Russian-dominated elite in Moscow and local ethnic elites were always strained. The latter, though purged more frequently and more severely than any other ruling or privileged group of the Soviet society, nevertheless repeatedly tended toward regionalism and nationalism. However, the general tendency in the changing balance of power was always the same: an increase in central power and a corresponding decrease in the autonomy of the local ethnic elites. Central authorities were always wary lest the ethnic elites reverse Stalin's demand. Instead of being "national in form and socialist in content," they might become "socialist in form and national, even nationalistic, in content." Often the latter formulation was closer to the truth. The solution was found by depriving ethnic elites of any real autonomy, either political or economic, and by excluding them from any real participation in serious decision-making, even on the local level.

It is true that from time to time strong leaders emerged in ethnic republics, like Shelest in Ukraine, Rashidov in Uzbekistan, or Kunaev in Kazakhstan. But their strength depended primarily on their influence in the center and on their personal allegiance to the most powerful figures in the Moscow hierarchy. In their case, the individual power of officeholders was stronger than the power of office. It is hardly accidental that all three of them were accused of nationalistic deviations, Rashidov posthumously. The only task that the state-imposed and state-maintained ethnic elites were entrusted with was the implementation of policies dictated by Moscow. They had to supervise the daily affairs in their ethnic formations and facilitate the policy of Russification.[5] Moreover, this had to be done under the increasing supervision of Russians introduced into their midst. Expanding the compulsory use of Russian in administration and in all channels of mass communications was considered the minimal demonstration of loyalty. A Kirghiz writer, C. Aitmatov (1986, 4), complained that this situation had brought to life a specific type of demagogue who almost made it his prestigious profession to praise the Russian language and to demean his native tongue. Ordinary Bashkirs and Tatars noticed with bitterness that their authorities were afraid to speak even once on television and radio in their own languages because they cared for their positions and had to be obsequious toward the Russian chauvinists (Koroteeva and Mosesova 1988, 8).

Nevertheless, in 1986 and in the first half of 1987, the central authorities in Moscow demonstrated numerous signs of their dissatisfaction with non-Russian elites and increasingly tended to replace them with Russians. Because of their ambiguous position, these elites failed to meet all Moscow's demands. Their loyalty to the Soviet regime and their vested interest in the continuation of the system turned out to be inadequate. Still, these elites realized that the policy they were ordered to follow inevitably eroded the foundation of their own support and influence. If they identified completely their own interests with the interests of the ruling elites of the dominating nation, and if they sincerely promoted Russification, they would become dispensable. If they maintained their non-Russian identity, they would be suspect.

I have had many occasions to talk to members of these ethnic elites in different parts of the Soviet Union. When they demonstrated to me their allegiance to the official line, they always praised the elder brother of all

Soviet peoples—the Great Russian people. However, if and when the same people became more frank with me, their complaints were always the same: "We are loyal Communists. Why are we not trusted, why are we not permitted to carry on our affairs? Why do the Moscow authorities fail to understand that the policy of Russification is dangerous not only to our ethnicities but to the future of the entire Soviet Union?"

The non-Russian elites in the Soviet Union were at a double disadvantage compared to the Russian elite. First, the central avenues of upward mobility were extremely limited to them even under the condition of their assimilation into the Russian elite. The elite had no intention of sharing their power and privileges with the others.

After the dismissal of Aliev on October 21, 1987, and until the last party congress there was only one non-Slavic member in the then-ruling Politburo—Shevardnadze. In the 1980s, and particularly during the last few years of the Soviet Union's existence, the number of non-Slavs dropped sharply in the ruling Politburo, in the Central Committee of the Communist party, in the Council of Ministers, the military command, and all other central bodies of power.[6]

Even in their own ethnic formations, the non-Russian elites experienced a growing competition from the local Russians and from those who were imposed on them by Moscow. As a result, the careers of lesser officials became increasingly stymied. During the anticorruption and other campaigns initiated over the last years, hundreds, if not thousands, of non-Russians were dismissed from their privileged positions and replaced by Russians.

These new tendencies reached their culminating point with the replacement of Kazakh Kunaev with the Russian Kolbin as first secretary of the Communist party of Kazakhstan, and with the campaign against nationalism, which followed a wave of unrest in Alma-Ata in December 1986 (Kuzio 1988, 79–100).

The situation in Kazakhstan deteriorated for many years. After the bloody collectivization and sedentarization of the Kazakhs in the 1930s that cost about two million lives, the Kazakhs became a minority in their own territory. The virgin lands campaign brought another wave of migrants from the European part of the USSR. By 1962, the proportion of Kazakhs in Kazakhstan dropped to 29 percent. However, later the situation began to change. Birthrates of the Kazakhs increased more than did those of the Russians, and by 1989 the Kazakhs already constituted about 40 percent of the population and had a very good chance of again becoming a majority in their country not later than at the beginning of the twenty-first century (Khazanov, in press).

In the 1970s and in the beginning of the 1980s many Kazakhs moved from rural areas to the cities, where the Russians were occupying the dominating positions. This migration increased competition for positions in administration, intellectual fields, and even in white-collar professions. Since a perfect knowledge of Russian served as one criterion of selection for these positions, many Kazakhs opposed a policy of Russification and a subsequent limitation of the social functions of their own language. Some Russians began to leave Kazakhstan; many more complained that they would leave if the situation did not change. During the first half of the 1980s, ethnic tensions and frictions in Kazakhstan were growing, and the dismissal of Kunaev was at any rate partially connected with his "nationalistic deviations." It is well known that Kunaev to some extent favored the Kazakhs in Kazakhstan at the expense of the Russians and that during his twenty-four-year incumbency he moved natives into many key positions. Whenever possible he tried to promote the Kazakhs and to reserve for them important positions in the party and government hierarchy. He even encouraged and protected some Kazakh cultural and educational activities, actions that were considered nationalistic given the conditions existing at the time. Thus, a famous Kazakh poet, Olzhas Suleimenov, who many times was severely criticized by Moscow for his so-called nationalism and even pan-Turkism, not only managed to continue to publish his works but even to occupy prominent positions in the cultural establishment of Kazakhstan because of Kunaev's personal protection.

Immediately after the Alma-Ata riots of December 17 and 18, 1986, the Soviet press launched an unprecedented campaign not only against the Kazakh nationalism but practically against the Kazakh culture, language, and the nation itself.[7] Arguments used in this campaign were remarkable by themselves. Some Kazakh newspapers were accused of devoting most of their articles to the Kazakhs while ignoring the Russians living in the republic. The Kazakh literary magazine was scolded for publishing Kazakh authors only instead of translating authors writing in other languages. In 1986 several Kazakh newspapers published letters from many parents who insisted that their children be allowed education in the Kazakh language, at any rate in kindergartens. Their demand was supported by a poet who claimed that it was a duty of all Kazakhs to preserve and develop their own language. The parents were accused of propaganda promoting "national segregation," and the poet of "national egoism." One journal was criticized for publication of articles on the history of Kazakh clans and tribes. The critic explained that the past of a nation was a proper subject for an international education but not for national aspirations. The same journal was also blamed for the publication of data on the growth of the Kazakh population in Kazakhstan. Thus, the future of the nation became an even more dangerous subject than the nation's past.

Soon after the events in Kazakhstan in February 1987, a very remarkable paper was published in *Pravda* by the late academician Bromlei, at that time the director of the Institute of Ethnography of the Soviet Academy of Sciences. Bromlei claimed that trans-Caucasian and Central Asian republics had acquired inequitable economic privileges and that in many ethnic formations of the Soviet Union non-Russians had easier access to higher education than did Russians.[8] He insisted that all these and other similar practices and privileges should be eliminated (Bromlei 1987c).

In the Soviet Union, Bromlei was not only considered an expert on ethnic problems, he was notorious for his ability to sense the slightest shifts in Soviet policies. In 1987, this was not too difficult, since Gorbachev himself already had come out against "the mechanical distribution of places and posts according to nationalist criteria" (Gorbachev 1987, 4). It became apparent that a new trend in Soviet ethnic policy was the order of the day, and in following numerous publications and in practical measures, the aim of the forthcoming change in direction was declared quite frankly: to curtail affirmative action policy in the non-Russian areas of the Soviet Union and to end the alleged practice of infringement upon the rights of nonindigenous ethnic groups. This euphemism supported the Russians in the non-Russian republics of the USSR. New measures were aimed at eliminating discontent among the Russian settlers and migrants, who often complained that they were underprivileged and deprived of better positions.

The Russian population in non-Russian areas of the USSR was one of the main strongholds of the Soviet regime. The Soviet government always encouraged migration there, even at the risk of depopulating some parts of Russia itself. Among the many reasons for this practice, there was the desire to create reliable and loyal elements in border areas and to facilitate the policy of Russification. After all, border areas had always been important to continental empires and were often repopulated with loyal elements. This policy was pursued by the Roman, Ottoman, and by many Chinese and Russian governments. Soviet policy was simply a continuation of the old practice.

The very conditions of their migration and livelihood in non-Russian parts of the USSR made these Russian settlers the most conservative, chauvinistic, and at the same time the most loyal and pro-Soviet elements of Soviet society in general. During more than twenty-five years of fieldwork in different parts of the Soviet Union, I had the opportunity to meet with and to talk to many of them. Very often I had the impression of talking with French or British colonists of the nineteenth or the twentieth century somewhere in Africa or Asia. They had a typical white-man's-burden attitude; their values and superstitions, though sometimes more concealed, were nevertheless essentially the same.

The Soviet leadership also hoped that the changes it was going to introduce in ethnic policy would help to prevent the tendency toward the out-migration of the Russian population from non-Russian republics and autonomous areas back to Russia proper. Beginning in the seventies this tendency, which for the past ten years has spread to almost every area (with the exception of the Baltic, which remained attractive to Russians due to its higher standard of living), became increasingly alarming to Moscow.

Soviet economists claimed that Central Asia and other ethnic areas were overpopulated. Nevertheless, all attempts to relocate some of their indigenous populations to the Urals, Siberia, and even to European Russia, where there was a shortage of labor power, failed completely. Notwithstanding the demands made by some local leaders, Moscow remained reluctant to invest more money in overpopulated ethnic areas to create additional jobs there. Thus, all requests to develop a textile industry in Uzbekistan failed to get a positive response. The implementation of the Siberian project to divert water from western Siberia to Central Asia was stopped in 1986 (Micklin 1987). Notwithstanding its dubious economic effectiveness and its potential danger from an ecological point of view, this project was considered in Central Asia as a solution to many local problems, and its formal termination disappointed high expectations. Under all these circumstances, it would have been natural to not oppose the out-migration of the Russian population. However, political and strategic considerations again prevailed over economic ones.

Such was the situation in the first half of 1987. However, starting from the second half of the same year, the Soviet leadership began to realize that simply following the previous course in ethnic policy given the new conditions would bring overwhelming complications to the system in general and to the policy of perestroika in particular. Gorbachev himself admitted this quite frankly when he stated that the success of restructuring would depend to a decisive extent on how national relations problems were handled and solved (Gorbachev 1989).

The growing discontent and even unrest in many non-Russian republics and autonomous areas of the USSR, specifically the events in Kazakhstan, Armenia, and especially the Baltic demonstrated the possibility of a dangerous alliance between different social segments of society in ethnic areas, including even the local elites. In Nagorny Karabakh, the party and government leadership, despite explicit orders from Moscow, openly supported demands of the local population, a case unprecedented in the history of the USSR since the 1930s. In the Baltic republics the local party elites supported, though sometimes reluctantly, many demands of the nationalist movements, thus demonstrating that given a proper situation, even a split of the Soviet Communist party along national lines was in principle not impossible.

Apparently, the central leadership began to realize the necessity for a more flexible policy where the national issue was concerned. At any rate, for the first time it openly admitted that the problem, far from being solved, was still very much alive in the Soviet Union, and that it represented a certain obstacle to the implementation of the restructuring policy. At the same time, it was obvious that no consistent program had yet been worked out in regard to this issue. It is revealing that the date of the special plenary session of the Communist Party Central Committee on the national question was postponed several times. It is no less revealing that Moscow was clearly trying to put off a decision on many acute problems.

By 1989, one could see only partial and limited modifications in Soviet national policy. Thus, certain concessions were made with respect to cultural development and education in national languages. This was particularly desired by the non-Russians, including the party elites, in the Baltic, Transcaucasia, Ukraine, Kirghizia, Kazakhstan, and a number of other republics who insisted on more schools and publications in their native languages and further that the local Russian population should study and make use of indigenous languages.

It was not improbable that the replacement of non-Russian personnel by Russians in the union republics would be stopped, or would be conducted in a more veiled fashion. By that time, the central authorities preferred to appoint ethnic Russians to such areas as Karabakh, where they could play the role of unbiased arbitrators in local interethnic conflicts. In other instances (Azerbaidjan, Armenia, Uzbekistan), they preferred to appoint to the leading positions Russified members of indigenous ethnic groups, who had worked for many years in other places, and therefore had no links to the ordinary population and the local elites.

One could expect that some concessions in creating and developing educational and cultural institutions would be made to the ethnic minorities and to the non-Russians living outside their ethnic areas. A special commission for preservation and development of cultures of small ethnic groups was established by 1989 as a public organization, under the auspices of the Soviet Cultural Foundation. Gorbachev (1989) himself made a remarkable statement: "We cannot permit even the smallest people to be lost; we cannot permit nihilism with regard to the culture, traditions, and history of peoples, be they big or small."

One might wonder about the underlying reasons for this sudden concern for the ethnic minorities. It might have been connected with a desire to counterbalance a growing nationalism of locally dominant non-Russian ethnic groups in the union republics and to encourage migratory patterns of non-Russians in directions desirable to the Soviet leadership. At the same time it was necessary to boost the morale of the Russians living in the non-Russian areas of the Soviet Union who had become very anxious about recent developments, to reassure them of the continuing support of the central authorities, and to prevent their out-migration. Remarkably enough, the efforts of the Baltic republics to elevate the status of their native languages met with opposition from the Russian population there and with a negative campaign in the central Soviet press. The Russians constitute about one-half of 60 million people who live outside their ethnic formations, or lack such formations at all. However, for the reasons that I have discussed previously, if this group of Russians were awarded the same status as non-Russian minorities, these Russians would again be placed in a privileged position. Be that as it may, the whole issue of ethnic minorities hardly went beyond promises and discussions in the press.

The same is true with respect to the constituent republics. Apart from some concessions in linguistic and cultural matters, the central leadership was very reluctant to give them more economic, and particularly political, rights. Although the general political framework of restructuring should have allowed for a certain decentralization and granting of somewhat wider rights to the non-Russian republics, they were still excluded from participation in the process of making important political decisions. A solution of the key problem—a balance of power between separate republics and the center—would have been difficult even for a genuine federal political system. In the Soviet Union it took on particularly painful forms. The possibility of further conflicts was demonstrated by a constitutional crisis over the Nagornyi Karabakh issue, and also in relations between Estonia and Lithuania, on the one hand, and the central government, on the other.

In 1989 it looked as though the Gorbachev leadership did not know how to deal with these problems and preferred to delay any serious decisions in this field. In January 1989 the Central Committee of the Soviet Communist Party promised a considerable expansion of the rights of the republics and a strengthening of their sovereignty but simultaneously called for "a strong center and strong republics" (Tsentralnyi 1989, 1). How it was going to solve this contradiction remained unclear. Moreover, in an attempt to solve the old problems in interethnic relations by half-measures and palliatives, the Soviet leadership only created new ones, a situation not uncommon to crises of this type.

SOME CONCLUSIONS AND PROGNOSES

The ethnic situation in the USSR as of 1989 proved again that in spite of numerous declarations and incantations to the contrary made by Soviet politicians, ideologists, and scholars for decades, ethnic problems in the Communist and non-Communist countries were similar (Khazanov 1990). Up to 1989, the Soviet Union had failed to solve its national question.

If Ernest Gellner (1983) was right in his assertion that nationalism is a concomitant product of modernization, then one could expect that ethnic conflicts in the Soviet Union were inevitable as more ethnic groups there became modernized or took steps on the path of modernization.[9] The Soviet leadership empirically understood this danger quite well; hence its drive for homogeneity and linguistic unification of the country.[10] However, in the USSR this effort inevitably meant an encouragement of one kind of nationalism—Russian—at the expense of the others.

By 1989, it was possible to predict that any solution to the national problem within the existing Soviet political system would be impossible. One did not have to be a prophet to predict that ethnic contradictions and tensions in the Soviet Union would only increase in the near future. The Soviet system had effectively eliminated the possibility of any large-scale collective action, except ethnic ones, and for this reason alone national movements constituted the most dangerous internal problem in the Soviet Union, more dangerous than all other, purely political dissident movements, or even economic difficulties. It was quite possible that in the future ethnic conflicts would bring about changes which at present are impossible to foresee.

ADDENDA: MAY 1991

This article was written in the spring of 1989 and was submitted for publication in the summer of the same year. Though most prognoses that I have made above turned out to be true, the ethnic situation in the Soviet Union during the last two years continued to deteriorate while some trends in its development became more conspicuous.

Only in early 1989 did Gorbachev recognize the gravity of the "nationality" question in the country with the announcement that the success of perestroika would depend on the improvement of interethnic relations.

However, for many months afterwards he was still only making vague promises to change the structure of the USSR and to grant more rights to republics. The long awaited Plenum on the nationality question, which took place in September 1989, did not bring any positive results. By the end of 1989, the positions of the sides were clearly defined: the Moscow center versus the national movements—and even the Moscow center versus many constituent republics.

At present, the centrifugal forces in this country are gathering strength as the non-Russian ethnic groups demand independence, sovereignty, or more autonomy. It looks like Moscow may no longer be able to control these movements, even with the use of force.

There are two alternatives to force: the peaceful disintegration of the Soviet empire or its transformation into a confederation of commonwealths. These alternatives will not eliminate all of the ethnic conflicts in the country between Russians and non-Russian ethnic groups (and among many of the latter). The causes of these conflicts which will remain active are the following:

1. Ethnic competition in economic, political and linguistic spheres. Ethnic competition exists in almost all multiethnic states. Many of the Soviet republics will remain multiethnic even if they achieve independence. Economic difficulties will only make the situation worse. If this happens, the fight for control over natural resources, industrial enterprises, etc. could intensify, as well as the attempt to gain a higher political status for ethnic groups and to reserve certain advantages for them, including privileged, prestigious, and highly paid jobs and professions.

The fight for the wider use of native languages in education, culture, and administrative practice is also connected not only with the growth of ethnic consciousness and the wish to prevent acculturation, but also with more mundane reasons—to place members of one's ethnic group in more advantageous positions. As a result, many ethnic groups will continue to try to achieve more independence and to raise the status of their national-political formations. Such a desire has already been expressed by the Poles, Kumyks, Lezgins, Balkars, Karachay, Nogai, Ingush, and others. In many cases, this can also threaten the existing national-political structure and offend the interests of other ethnic groups. The territorial integrity of Moldavia and Georgia are now threatened, as well as that of Kabardino-Balkaria, Karachaevo-Cherkessia, and even Dagestan. In the future other republics and autonomous areas could also be threatened.

2. Territorial disputes and conflicts. At present, not only the Armenians and Azerbaidjanians are involved in a territorial conflict but also the Russians, Ukrainians, Belorussians, Lithuanians, Estonians, Molda-

vians, Gagauz, Georgians, Osetians, Avars, Chechen, Ingush, Balkars, Karachay, Kabardinians, Shapsugs, Kalmyks, Buryats, Uzbeks, Tadzhiks, Kazakhs, Kirgiz, and several other ethnic groups. If the USSR weakens further, the number of these conflicts will grow.

3. The problem of persons and groups living outside their national-political formations. At present, in the Soviet Union there are about 60 million residing outside of their national areas—about 25 million of them are Russians. Events of the last several years have shown that their situation and relations with the predominant ethnic groups in the corresponding republics and autonomous formations are often the source of conflict. If the Soviet Union is broken up or transformed into a confederation, the number of such conflicts and their seriousness can increase.

4. The problem of dispersed and exiled ethnic groups. This problem takes into consideration such ethnic groups as the Jews, Germans, Greeks, Crimean Tatars, Meskhetian Turks, Kurds, and several others. Their situation in the circumstances of growing interethnic conflicts could get even worse because they are often put in the role of the scapegoat. The first three groups have the alternative to emigrate, but the other groups have nowhere to emigrate. At the same time, as the example of the Meskhetian Turks shows, their return to their homeland will almost certainly meet with opposition from nationalistic forces in the corresponding regions of the country.

5. The problem of recent ethnic refugees. There are already about 600,000 refugees in the USSR, and in the circumstances of interethnic conflicts, their number will surely grow. The number will become even more impressive if the number of involuntary migrants is added to the number of refugees. Migrants are those forced to abandon their homes due to unstable circumstances, pressure from other ethnic groups, or a lowered ethnic status. So far, only a comparatively small number of Russians have left the Baltic republics and Moldavia, but their out-migration from Azerbaidjan and Central Asia has increased significantly. Yeltsin has stated several times that Russians living outside of Russia will have to be granted not only the right but the possibility of returning to Russia. However, in the conditions of the economic crisis, it is not so easy to do this. In addition, the influx into Russia of a large number of refugees and involuntary migrants could also further complicate the political situation. Representatives of the liberal-democratic camp say that such people are usually reactionary and view the reformers as traitors. Already the current leadership of Russia is accused of betraying the Russians living in national republics.

All in all, it will be impossible to solve the nationality problem in the near future whatever form of political development the country takes.

Moreover, this development itself will be largely defined by the character of the interethnic relations in the country. Even empires must fall apart with time. In this regard, the Soviet Union is an anachronism because for more than seventy years it was a direct successor of the Russian empire. However, even Communism turned out to be powerless against nationalism.

What is going on now in the USSR in the sphere of interethnic relations in many respects resembles corresponding developments in several third world countries. The majority of Western democratic countries have already passed through this stage. The Soviet Union has skipped the twentieth century. The process of creating national states and even the simple formation of modern nations on its territory remain incomplete. Now it must pay the price for this as well.

If the political development of the country will happen along the lines of political and economic pluralism, then it will be possible to avoid some of the interethnic conflicts and to alleviate others, or at least to give them more or less civilized forms. However, it will be impossible for the USSR to avoid interethnic conflicts entirely.

Notes

1. This imperial quality of the Soviet state has already been noticed by many scholars. See, for example, Allworth (1971), d'Encausse (1979), Conquest (1986), and many others.
2. The Soviet literature, which propagandized and gave a detailed exposé of this concept, is so enormous and monotonous that there is neither the possibility nor the necessity to provide even a selective bibliography here. Of the works by anthropologists see, for example, Bromlei (1975; 1987b, 97–163) and Drobizheva (1981). Bromlei (1987a) gives an extensive bibliography on the question.
3. However, the number of marriages between members of different ethnicities declined sharply in several Soviet republics. In addition, interethnic marriages often resulted in a significant number of divorces (Bohr and Kocaoglu 1989).
4. This information was revealed by the chairman of the Council for Religious Affairs, K. Kharchev, in his interview to the Soviet journal *Nauka i Religiia*, No. 11 (1987), 21–23.
5. Mark Beissiger (1988, 71–85) described this situation in the Ukrainian context.
6. A Novosibirsk scholar, A. I. Prigozhin (1988, 10), pointed out that "the leadership is drawn from the Russians. They predominate among the heads of the main agencies of power, in the Academy of Sciences, in the Central Committee [of the Communist party], in the All-Union Central Trade Union Council, and so on. In addition, Russian leaders also hold a special position in the national republics."
7. Of the numerous publications of this type see particularly *Pravda*, February 11, 1987.

8. However, Bromlei did not mention that living standards in central Asia were still much lower than in European parts of the USSR (cf. McAuley 1986, 165).
9. I am not sure that he is right completely but I am ready to admit that serious differences exist between ancient and medieval nationalism and its modern counterpart. Unfortunately, Gellner's (1983) brilliant book on nations and nationalism avoided the question of the effect of modernization on ethnic conflict in the Soviet Union.
10. From time to time even more far-reaching goals were put on the agenda, as reflected in the slogan "to embark on the merging of nations" (Khruschev in 1960; Andropov in 1982). Gorbachev (1989) boasted that he himself had prevented one of these attempts, which he characterized as a "dangerous formulation."

References

Aitmatov, C. 1986. "Tsena zhizn." *Literaturnaia Gazeta*, August 13:4.

Allworth, E. (ed.). 1971. *Soviet nationality problems*. New York: Columbia University Press.

Beissiger, M. 1988. "Ethnicity, the personal weapon, and neo-imperial integration: Ukrainian and RSFSR provincial party officials compared." *Studies in Comparative Communism* 21(1):71–85.

Bohr, A., and Kocaoglu, T. 1989. "Central Asian notebook." *Report on the USSR* 1(6):21–24.

Bromlei, Y. V. (ed.). 1987a. *Etnicheskie protsessy v sovremennom mire*. Moscow: Nauka.

———. 1987b. *Etnosotsialnye protsessy: teoriia, istoriia, sovremennost'*. Moscow: Nauka.

———. 1987c. "Natsional'nye protsessy v SSSR: Dostizheniia i problemy." *Pravda*, February 13:2–3.

———. (ed.). 1975. *Sovremennye etnicheskie protsessy v SSSR*. Moscow: Nauka.

Bromley, J. V. (ed.). 1982. Present-day ethnic processes in the U.S.S.R. Moscow: Progress.

Bruk, S. I. 1986. *Naselenie mira: etnodemograficheskii spravochnik*. Moscow: Nauka.

Conquest, R. (ed.). 1986. *The last empire: Nationality and the Soviet future*. Stanford: Hoover Institution Press.

d'Encausse, H. C. 1979. *Decline of an Empire: The Soviet socialist republics in revolt*. New York: Newsweek Books.

Drobizheva, L. M. 1981. *Dukhovnaia obshchnost' narodov SSSR: Istoriko-sotsiologicheskii ocherk mezhnatsional'nykh otnoshenii*. Moscow: Mysl'.

Gellner, E. 1983. *Nations and nationalism*. Ithaca, NY: Cornell University Press.

Gorbachev, M. S. 1987. "O perestroke i kadrovoi politike partii." *Pravda*, January 28:1–5.

————. 1989. "Narashchivat' itelektual'nyi potentsial perestroiki." *Pravda*, January 8:1–4.

Guboglo, M. N. 1984. *Sovremennye etnoiazykovye protsessy v SSSR*. Moscow: Nauka.

Isupov, A. A. (ed.). 1980. *Naselenie SSSR: Po dannym vsesoiuznoi perepisi naseleniia 1979 goda*. Moscow: Politizdat.

Kharchev, K. M. 1987. "Garantii svobody." *Nauka i Religiia* 11:21–23.

Khazanov, A. M. 1990. "The ethnic situation in the Soviet Union as reflected in Soviet anthropology." *Cahiers du Monde Russe et Soviétique* 31 (2–3):213–222.

————. *Ethnic Stratification in Kazakhstan* (in press).

Koroteeva, V. V., and Mosesova, M. N. 1988. "Problemy natsional'nykh iazykov i ikh otrazhenie v obshchestvennom soznanii." *Sovetskaia Etnografiia* (5):4–14.

Kuzio, T. 1987. "Opposition in the USSR to the occupation of Afghanistan." *Central Asian Survey* 6(1):99–118.

————. 1988. "Nationalist riots in Kazakhstan." *Central Asian Survey* 7(4):79–100.

McAuley, A. 1986. "Economic development and political nationalism in Uzbekistan." *Central Asian Survey* 5(3–4):161–182.

Micklin, P. P. 1987. "The fate of 'sibaral': Soviet water politics in the Gorbachev era." *Central Asian Survey* 8(2):67–88.

Natsionalnye protsessy V SSSR-Resultaty tendentsii i problemy. Round-table discussion. Istoriia SSSR, NG, 1987, 50–78.

Prigozhin, A. I. 1988. "Demokratiia est' konflikt" *Vek XX i Mir* 12:8–17.

Smith, A. D. S. 1979. *Nationalism in the twentieth century*. New York: New York University Press.

Tishkov, V. 1989. "Narody i gosudarstvo." *Kommunist* (1):49–59.

Tsentralnyi Komitet KPSS. 1989. "K partii, sovetskomy narodu." *Pravda*, January 13:1.

From *The* People to *One* People: The Social Bases of the East German "Revolution" and Its Preemption by the West German State

WILLIAM GRAF, WILLIAM HANSEN,
AND BRIGITTE SCHULZ

It is not too soon to begin systematically to attempt to explain the course of the 1989 East German "revolutions"—the extraordinarily concentrated and eventful period bounded by the Leipzig mass demonstrations commencing on October 7, and the succession of events from the opening of the intra-German border on November 9 until the end of the year. The period began with a popular democratic movement aimed at domestic renewal (*wir sind das Volk*) and ended with a strong nationalist revival (*wir sind ein Volk*) that ideologically rationalized the 1990 reunification of Germany.

Already this period of transition and adaptation is undergoing revisions for purposes of incorporation into the respective mythologies of the Left and the Right. On the right, the *Anschluss* of the East German state and society into the Federal Republic is generally styled as the logical and desirable outcome of a "socialist" system lacking any moral, functional, or political raison d'être, and as an unqualified triumph for capitalism. On the left there is a growing sense that the democratic stage of the "revolution" represented a long overdue but nevertheless auspicious attempt at overcoming, *from within*, the pathologies of bureaucratized, paternalistic socialism and at creating an indigenous form of democratic socialism; only the intervention of West German capital foiled the transformation and, on the strength of superior economic power, "hijacked" the revolution. In this latter view, there were indeed certain "socialist achievements" worth preserving, and left to its own devices, a reformed GDR could have found its way toward some variant of the "third way" between capitalism and state socialism, combining the best features of both.

These embryonic myths, each with its own selective core of reality, are perhaps more telling about the respective interests of their propagators than about the phenomena they attempt to interpret. In this chapter, we examine the social bases of the East German "revolutions" within the peculiar socioeconomic context in which they evolved.

THE SOCIOECONOMIC AND IDEOLOGICAL CONTEXT OF CLASS FORMATION IN THE GDR

The origins of the German Democratic Republic, it should be recalled, lay in the exigencies of Soviet policy in the East-West confrontation. In their zone of occupation the Soviets ceded large areas of the former Reich to Poland and the USSR, thus burdening the GDR with a huge antinationalist legitimacy deficit from the outset. They then imposed a new and unpopular elite on the area under their control. Despite their later claims, these men (and a few women) were not the leaders of a victorious working-class party embarking with revolutionary élan on the construction of socialism. Rather, they were for the most part functionaries who, like Walter Ulbricht and Wilhelm Pieck, had lived in exile in Moscow for the duration of the Third Reich. Some, Erich Honecker being one, had spent long years in Nazi prisons. Unlike many cadres who had perished in the anti-Nazi struggle, these new rulers were hardly visionary revolutionaries. Rather they were experienced survivors of the murderous internecine party wars that had characterized Stalin's Moscow. Their fundamental outlook was that of the small-minded, authoritarian bureaucrat with an unwillingness to deviate from established patterns and a deep-seated fear and resentment of those who did. These men were the advance cohort of a stratum that proliferated and came to dominate East German society culturally as well as politically and economically; what the first Permanent Representative of West Germany to the GDR, Günther Gaus, later so aptly described as *Kleinbürgertum*—people with neither taste nor vision (Gaus 1983). The at least partly coerced union of the Communist and Social Democratic parties to form the SED (Socialist Unit Party) in 1946 (see, e.g., Kaden 1964) simply reinforced this tendency and led to an exodus of independently minded members from that party.

In order to counter this growing legitimacy deficit, the SED from the outset attempted to appropriate for itself the "progressive" currents in German history, ranging from Thomas Münzer (the Protestant reformer and insurgent leader during the sixteenth-century peasant war) up to the anti-Nazi resistance. At the same time, the FRG was depicted as the current manifestation and repository of all that was reactionary in the German past, from Martin Luther, who had supported the princes in the Peasant War, through Bismarck's Prussian authoritarianism to Hitler's Third Reich.[1]

In particular, the East German regime sought to identify itself with the then popular anti-Fascist movement, a democratic and socialist current that enjoyed substantial mass support throughout postwar Germany and that contained a preponderance of Social Democrats and Communists operating largely outside the purview of centralized authority.[2] Although the anti-Fascism of the GDR initially appeared credible as a *moral value* in the light of the Left's important sacrifices for and contributions to the struggle against Hitler, it was quickly converted to a *functional ideological concept* by an SED bent on instrumentalizing it to vindicate unpopular government policies and eliminate political opponents. Thus the moral invocation of anti-Fascism in the struggle for democratic socialism was debased into the dichotomy, Whoever is not for us must be against us and is therefore a Fascist. Any critique, any opposition toward the SED was, ipso facto, motivated by Fascist intent (see Grunenberg 1990, 176). Of course the transformation of anti-Fascist ideology in this way could only be accomplished by suppressing the elements of a democratic political culture and permanently damaging the emergent civil society—a project that could be realized all the more readily in a historically authoritarian post-Fascist society.

Perhaps even more crucial than this legitimacy deficit was the economic deficit with which the GDR was simultaneously encumbered. In accordance with the Yalta and Potsdam accords, the Soviet Union extracted maximum reparations from its part of Germany even while the United States, after levying token initial reparations until 1974, poured at least $16 billion into the economy of "Trizonia," then the Federal Republic. According to estimates by Arno Peters (1990, 13–16), by 1953 the GDR, with a population of 49,763,000 paid DM 99,138,888,882 (1953) values to the Soviet Union, whereas the FRG paid some $2,161,060,000 to Britain, France, and the United States. In terms of late 1980 values, every inhabitant of the GDR paid DM 16,124, or 127 times the amount paid by each West German, namely DM 126. In this sense the GDR in fact bore the reparations burden for all Germany. This, together with the corresponding absence of investment capital needed to restart production and rebuild infrastructures, ensured that the GDR's level of economic development would lag behind that of the FRG for at least a generation.

Thus, even while the FRG was building its economic miracle upon the Korean War boom, the SED pursued a policy of Bolshevizing the relatively underdeveloped part of Germany under its sway. At its 1952 Party Congress the SED decided to embark on the "construction of socialism." This entailed a policy of emphasizing investment in heavy industry at the expense of the consumer and the beginnings of widespread nationalizations of enterprises of all sizes. This period also witnessed the beginnings of agricultural collectivization. The working class was neither consulted nor did it consent to this policy.

Nineteen fifty-three was a watershed period in the history of the GDR. In June spontaneous large-scale strikes broke out among the industrial working class in most of the big cities. The immediate cause of the unrest was the arbitrary imposition of increased work quotas by the state with the near-total compliance of the trade unions. However, tension had been building for months, particularly among urban workers. The monthly emigration rate to West Berlin had increased by over 100 percent during the first part of 1953. By the end of the year nearly 2 percent of the total population had left. Workers showed increasing resentment toward the growing dictatorial character of the state. Any semblance of independence on the part of the official trade union had long since been eliminated as the FDGB (Free German Trade Union) absorbed the old independent workers' commissions and brought them under SED control. The economy was afflicted by rising prices, a decline in living standards, a sudden drop in food supplies, and a worsening of the supply of already scarce consumer goods. The workers struck.

The strikes, accompanied by demonstrations, demands for free trade unions, free elections, and the ousting of Ulbricht, were violently crushed by the state with the help of the Red Army. Significantly, of all the demands made by the workers for substantial changes in GDR society none were for the return of capitalism and the reprivatization of national enterprises. Thirty-six years later, the next time large sectors of the East German working class took to the streets in open opposition to the regime, this was no longer to be the case.

The situation of June 1953 was "normalized," however, when the SED, at the insistence of the Soviet government, embarked on the so-called New Course, which, among other things, made a number of concessions to popular desires for consumer goods. The economic situation gradually stabilized and the country achieved substantial growth rates and an increasing standard of living. Even emigration leveled off through the rest of the 1950s, although it never ceased to be significant: at least 150,000 people per year. Moreover, the emigrants tended to be those the GDR could least afford to lose—younger (particularly skilled) workers and younger members of the technical intelligentsia. From 1949 to 1961 more than 2.6 million people fled the GDR—over 10 percent of the population (Minnerup 1982, 10). The more who left, the more who sent back glowing reports to their friends and families in the East. Thus, by 1960, emigration began to increase rapidly and, in so doing, imposed an increasing strain on the GDR economy—what the SED state labeled with some (but only some) truth as "economic sabotage."

In the late 1950s the SED decided to accelerate what it called its programs of "socialization." The agriculture sector was almost completely collectivized, and much of the small craft and retail sector was brought under state control. This gave a further spur to emigration, and the labor shortage in the GDR was exacerbated to the point of becoming critical. Finally, rampant rumors in the months before August 1961 that the border would be closed instigated a virtual stampede to get out before it was too late. On August 13, 1961, soldiers closed off the border to West Berlin and began construction of what would become the "anti-Fascist Protective Wall" to insulate the "Workers' and Farmers' State" from fascism. This protection was quickly extended the length of the German-German border and featured razor-topped fences, automatic firing mechanisms, land mines, guard dogs, and much else.

THE CRYSTALLIZATION OF SOCIAL STRATA UNDER PRUSSIAN SOCIALISM

By adding the suppression of freedom of movement and freedom of choice to a long list of lost civil liberties, the SED elite not only put paid to prospects for the development of a legitimizing civil society in the GDR, it also (and paradoxically) created a measure of stability and hence predictability within which to pursue policies of economic growth and consumer-needs satisfaction. This situation permitted a kind of modus vivendi to develop between the increasingly isolated party elite and the population. The party would attend to economic development; this it formalized in the 1963 New Economic System, which promised greater economic decentralization, more rational application of technology, and promotion by merit. In return, the people would refrain from political protest and opposition and would at least passively support the regime's policies. Thus, the one channel for popular dissent after the erection of the Berlin Wall was to retreat into what Guenther Gaus called the "niche society" (*Nischengesellschaft*), that is, an "internal emigration" in which the mass of the people refrained from any involvement in public life.[3] The spirit of this internal emigration was captured by the notion that the people had been *entmündigt*, or rendered into political minors existing in a *vormundschaftlicher* (tutelary) state.[4] Those with actual citizenship rights—the power to make choices and have their opinions heard—were only those at the upper echelons of the party-state, always popularly referred to as "they" or "them."

Resistance, consequently, largely took the form of sullen noncooperation. Virtually the entire society embarked upon what might be called a permanent "go slow": a vast common conspiracy to do absolutely nothing if that were possible and only the absolute minimum when forced. This phenomenon, of course, explains the constant exhortations from the SED and other institutional structures to what was referred to as "socialist emulation," mass initiatives, patriotism, and greater intensity of work; as if voluntarism and slogans alone could motivate an unwilling population.

It is in this context of polarization and alienation, of the destruction of civil society coupled with a more "democratic" sphere of social services and increasing consumerism, that one can examine the emergence of two distinct social strata—whether conceptualization in terms of Meillassoux's social corps or Bahro's more conventional social classes[5]—in East Germany, namely the workers and the intelligentsia.

After 1953 the working class as a whole ceased any active, concerted opposition to the state, a behavioral pattern that was to be largely maintained until the "revolutions" of 1989. From the point of view of these "proletarians" active opposition was practically impossible. Attempts at independent organization had either been absorbed into the official structures or had been suppressed. Even many working-class bars were closed as they had traditionally been points at which workers would gather to discuss their mutual problems. The state sought, and largely managed, to eliminate all venues where people could gather to talk. Social clubs, independent organizations of all types, workers' cabarets—all were closed and banned.

It is not that workers, particularly young workers, refrained from other expressions of antisystem activity during the twenty-eight years between the erection of the Berlin Wall and the uprising that began in the summer of 1989. Young workers were always present in the vague and largely unfocused countercultural movements that periodically circulated throughout East German society, most often the consequences of Western influence. In the amorphous movement of the late 1960s and early 1970s that resulted in relatively free access to Western rock music, which had been previously forbidden by the regime, young workers became a prominent pressure group. Similarly, some were involved in the Protestant church and the church-connected activities of the late 1970s and 1980s that together with other dissident groups produced the Independent Peace Movement. But it was evident that, in the Workers' and Farmers' State, the working class had been reduced to a sullen, suppressed, and *entmündigt* majority whose support for the regime depended more and more on its concrete outputs: social services and economic growth.

The role of the intelligentsia was, by contrast, much more nuanced and hence complex. Even arriving at a definition of this heterogenous stratum is rather problematic: One study (cited in Dennis 1988, 51) provides sixty different definitions of this concept. One widely used criterion, both in government publications and in popular usage, was that it meant anyone with a postsecondary education from either a university or one of the myriad of technical and other colleges. This invites a further division of this stratum into three categories, all of which, naturally, had significant overlaps: (1) the party and government apparatus itself, namely those directly involved in administration and policy-making; (2) the specialized technocratic groups that managed production and distribution, including those in the professions (Bahro (1978, 20), following Lenin, prefers to call these people "specialists"); (3) that group that might be called the "traditional" intelligentsia, encompassing academics and scholars in higher education, writers, artists, musicians, and others involved in official and unofficial cultural production. In general one could say of the intelligentsia that, as a whole, it was more supine toward the SED state than was the working class. As a social category the intelligentsia almost uniformly supported the state.

In the immediate aftermath of the defeat of the Nazis a significant purge of the existing Fascist-tainted intelligentsia was carried out. In the East— despite some prominent exceptions—it was much more far-reaching than in the Western zones. The SED began a massive campaign to recruit from the working class and train an entirely new intellectual cohort. By the mid-1960s 80 percent of those with higher education had done their training in the post-Nazi period (Dennis 1988, 51). Thus, combined with leftist intellectuals returning from exile, the GDR's intelligentsia was largely home grown and, significantly, from working-class origins.

However, as Bahro has pointed out, one's present position within a hierarchical and antagonistic social formation is much more a determinant of one's politics than one's origins. Workers who became intellectuals in "actually existing socialist" societies no longer were proletarians in terms of life-style and career prospects. Because the division of labor was not essentially changed in those societies, these former workers become the "movement's officers": "After the victory, they confront their class comrades as functionaries in the ruling apparatus" (Bahro 1978, 194).

By the mid-1950s the East German intelligentsia had largely been co-opted by the regime. Those who refused to cooperate were silenced or made to emigrate. During the workers' uprising of 1953 the intelligentsia mostly sat on their hands or explicitly supported the state's crackdown. It was academics who helped develop the later official story that right-wing thugs from the West and local counterrevolutionary groups had caused the trouble and that class-conscious workers, supporting the regime, had engaged the enemy in fierce combat to save socialism.

However, it was also from the various sectors of the intelligentsia that came most of the articulate, semi-organized opposition that sporadically surfaced within the GDR from the crushing of the workers' opposition in 1953 to the opening of the Berlin Wall in 1989. The best-known of these was the circle that formed around the figure of Wolfgang Harich. The so-called Harich group suggested that the wholesale application of Soviet-style socialism to East Germany might be inappropriate and advocated an end to ultracentralism, the adoption of a more gradual approach to the socialization of the economy, and the development of a democratic socialist politics both within the SED and in society as a whole. The Soviet smashing of the Hungarian uprising in October 1956 set the stage for a conservative counterattack. Harich was arrested the following month and in March 1957 sentenced to ten years in prison for instigating an "antiparty" group. Even mild reformists were purged from the Politburo and Central Committee, and orthodoxy reigned supreme.

For some members of the intelligentsia, the building of the Berlin Wall represented a chance to achieve stability and staunch the outward migration. With stability, it was felt, the conservative, orthodox leadership of the Ulbricht clique might be successfully challenged and more scope might be credited for democratic socialism to develop. One academic, a longtime member of the SED and a committed socialist, remembered the early 1960s from the hindsight of nearly thirty years:

> Many of us thought the building of the Wall would be temporary— only for a few years. It would allow us to stabilize politically and economically from which we could build a genuinely democratic socialist society. We all had great hopes then.—When Czechoslovakia was invaded that put an end to all our illusions.[6]

The thaw that briefly accompanied the New Economic System of the mid-1960s fostered a measure of decentralization in the economic sphere as individual factories were given greater autonomy from the ministries than they had enjoyed theretofore. Greater emphasis was placed on the use of high technology, and skills and competence rather than simple political reliability became relatively more important. Greater publishing leeway was allowed writers like Christa Wolf, Stefan Heym, and others.

It was during this period that Robert Havemann, a professor of chemistry in East Berlin, became a locus for intellectual and political dissent that continued to his death in the early 1980s. A longtime Communist who had been imprisoned by the Nazis, Havemann argued that the rigid, Stalinoid political and economic order was antithetical to socialism and impeded its progress. His criticisms, however, attacked the very basis of the apparat's source of power and privilege. Using the Marxist classics to demand democratic freedoms and human emancipation was more than the nomenklatura was willing to tolerate. Havemann lost his academic post and was expelled from the Academy of Sciences. A few years later Havemann supported the Prague Spring and was instrumental in the protests that surrounded the GDR's participation in the invasion of Prague. Many of the "unofficial" intellectuals who became active a decade later in the independent peace movement were deeply affected by the antiwar and countercultural wave associated with the "New Left" in the West and by the failure of the Prague Spring.

One of those deeply disillusioned by the events in Czechoslovakia was Rudolph Bahro. Whatever one may think of his "alternative," his well-known critique (1978) of the internal contradictions of the system was powerful and compelling. The response of the apparat was immediate and ferocious. In the tradition of Lenin and the Bolsheviks he was accused of being an agent of imperialism and silenced.

The link tying Harich, Havemann, and Bahro together was that they engaged in a form of "socialist apostasy," as had Kautsky so many years earlier. As within the medieval church they had to be cast out so as not to contaminate the masses, whose commitment to authorized doctrine was always suspect by the party leadership anyway. Bourgeois opposition was understandable and, in a perverse way, even desirable. Criticism from the Left using Marxian categories was intolerable as it undermined the entire moral and theoretical structure used to legitimize the nomenklatura's rule, a legitimacy needed in order to exist as a ruling class. As Bahro (1978, 239) insightfully noted, "The Marxism which they have betrayed and spoiled is still the currency in which they conduct their usury."

Of the three, only Havemann had any sort of a following and that was confined to a relatively small group of intellectuals. Harich represented a reform impulse within the party and Bahro, although an SED member, was a middle-level labor functionary in a factory. Havemann continued to exercise an influence in the dissident community for two decades after his first expression of opposition, but Bahro and Harich were virtually unknown outside their immediate environs and only became familiar to the wider GDR public after they had been silenced and their plight was exposed in the West. What they did represent, however, were attempts by intellectuals within the Marxist context to stimulate discussion and political movement that would lead to a revivication of socialist political life and the development of socialism as a democratic and emancipatory system. As sources of internal reform they failed. The forces of conservative reaction were always too strong. Any threat to their hegemony was crushed. However, these critics were influential precursors of a movement that was eventually to succeed, albeit outside the Marxian context.

In 1976, the year before Bahro published *The Alternative*, for which he was arrested, imprisoned, and expelled, the dissident balladeer, Wolf Biermann, was deprived of his citizenship and prevented from returning from a concert in West Germany. The "Biermann Affair" elicited widespread opposition from both within and without the GDR. A large number of the cultural intelligentsia, most of whom had so far not directly defied the regime, signed a statement criticizing the decision. Many observers have cited it as the final incident in a long series that convinced them that the system itself was incapable of internal transformation; it would have to be overturned.[7]

It was indicative of the fragmented nature of the East German intelligentsia that as late as the March 16, 1990, elections, 26 percent of them voted for the Partei des Demokratischen Sozialismus (PDS), 24 percent for the Allianz, and 23 percent for the Social Democratic Party (SDP). It was also an indication of the extent of worker alienation in the SED state that 59 percent of that stratum voted for the Allianz (Oldenburg 1990, 3).

CONJUNCTURAL FACTORS

As generally happens in state-socialist economies, the onset of the GDR's final economic crisis appears to have coincided with the transition of its economy from its postwar extensive phase (retarded, of course, by the reparations and exactions of the Soviet occupying power as referred to previously) into the intensive phase required by the evolving international division of labor.[8] For the GDR this crisis developed during the 1970s but became particularly severe in the early to mid-1980s. Faltering production allowed incomes to rise much more rapidly than the supply of consumer goods and services. As costs and prices consequently escalated, the purchasing power of the GDR mark dropped, causing exports to decline. Investments were then not forthcoming, so that by 1985 their level was considerably lower than in 1977.[9]

Meanwhile, existing plants and machinery became ever more outmoded and decrepit, while infrastructures decayed. A longtime adviser to West German business operating in East Europe, Axel Boje, provided one of the more incisive summaries of the malaise of East German industry, showing, for example, that in the coming four years it would require investments of DM 450 billion in equipment, machines, and plants (or about DM 150,000 for every person employed in the branch) as well as at least DM 60 billion annually for their maintenance and repair, spare parts, and financial servicing. More than 85 percent of GDR plants and factories, he found, corresponded to 1965, or earlier, levels attained in the West. Further, investments of DM 100 billion were needed in the sphere of raw-materials production, semi-manufactures and components, DM 60 billion for housing, DM 103 billion for infrastructures, and DM 260 billion for interest repayment, public services such as the health system, agriculture, etc. (*FAZ*, December 12, 1989, 3).

The GDR, thus incapable of entering into the intensive phase of growth, could not develop the sophisticated modern technology required for further economic progress. In 1986, for instance, there were 4,500 advanced industrial robots in the whole country—considerably fewer than in any one of several large West German corporations. Or in 1990 the estimated 170,000 personal computers in the GDR compared with the yearly output of 1.2 million of one American company, Apple (Dennis 1988, 65–66). The technology gap between East and West Germany was commonly estimated at a decade and more.

The country's inability to incorporate modern technology was bound up with its increasing centralization—the latter mainly a function of its political legitimacy deficit. Even while some other East European economies—notably Hungary—were decentralizing and opening during the 1970s and 1980s, the GDR was implementing even more severe state controls in the illusion that these could maintain social stability. Thus, centralized, top-down state planning became dysfunctional in an international political economy that increasingly required flexibility, responsiveness, and, above all, popular inputs. Not surprisingly, the competitiveness of East German products dropped in the world market and the country's share of world trade was in decline, especially trade with the West. Productivity by 1989 was some 40 percent of that in the West—though still some 50 percent higher than in the Soviet Union.[10] Also by 1989 the national budget deficit was about DM 17 billion, and zero growth was predicted for 1990 (Stinglwagner 1990, 239–240). In fact, in the first quarter of 1990 industrial production was not even up to the level of 1985 and it was projected to drop 4 to 5 percent for the whole year (*Die Zeit*, February 9, 1990, 3).

Naturally this economic privation was increasingly manifest in the daily existence and consciousness of the GDR population. Chronic shortages of consumer goods, deteriorating public services, crumbling infrastructures, outdated equipment, and a nearly destroyed environment were its obvious symptoms.

Nor could the economic crisis be deflected, as to some extent in the past, by trade relations with the USSR. Although the SED state had once profited from the low prices of oil, gasoline, and raw materials sold to it by the Soviet Union, the terms of trade were reversed in the 1970s and 1980s. For instance, East German exports to the USSR had to be tripled during the 1970s to pay for rising energy prices (Krisch 1985, 110) while in the early and mid-1980s the Soviets doubled the price of their oil exports so that the GDR was paying twice as much for its oil products as was the FRG in the world market (Childs 1985, 110). In this way the Soviet Union exacted an increasing share of GDR exports and paid less for them. This made it more and more difficult for East Germany to repay its debts to Western banks, in turn lowering its international credit rating and hence its access to further loans. The gap was only partly filled by special credits from the FRG, but then at the internationally humiliating cost of allowing certain categories of GDR citizens to migrate to the West.

However, absolute economic decline does not have the same explanatory force for East Germany as it does for the remaining peoples' democracies. It must be recalled that right up to the end, GDR citizens enjoyed living standards higher than anywhere else in the noncapitalist world. In fact, growth rates consistently achieved the stated goal of 4 percent per annum right up to autumn 1989 (Goldberg 1990, 449). But in *relative* terms, of course, the East Germans' reference point had always been the FRG, whose way of life they had come to know (in a selective manner) through television and radio. When the regime's implicit promise to raise living standards and leave personal niches untouched was shattered by growing controls and repression, opposition developed rapidly.

WIR SIND DAS VOLK

During the late 1980s, popular pressures for liberalization and decentralization grew in proportion to the relative decline of the GDR's economy and its consequent inability to fulfill not only the rising expectations of its population but even their (expanding) basic human needs. As these developments unfolded, the social bases and ideological bent of the opposition in East Germany were transformed.[11] If until the mid-1970s the limited opposition that did exist came almost completely from within a dissident Marxist intelligentsia, both academics and apparatchiki, the groups that began to emerge in the late 1970s and early 1980s had several defining characteristics that separated them from their pre-decessors. First, they originated overwhelmingly from the generation that had grown up under state socialism. They had known neither fascism nor war nor the privations of postwar reconstruction. Most of them had only the vaguest memories of a life before the enclosed world behind the Wall. In terms of social category the distinction between worker and intelligentsia became increasingly blurred. Young workers were certainly a significant component. Advanced secondary school students completing their university-entrance qualifications were large-ly absent from these new groups for fear of jeopardizing their chances for university admission. Similarly, university students refrained from involvement for fear of hurting their future career opportunities. Many of the new activists, as workers, were simultaneously part of an alterna-tive, countercultural intelligentsia: theologians, musicians, artists, writ-ers, filmmakers, and others who had been able to carve out a precar-ious niche on the fringes of GDR society.

These younger people had absorbed, albeit selectively and partially, many of the attitudes associated with the socialist idea—peace, fairness, equality, women's rights, freedom, ecological concerns, third world solidarity, even a rejection of most features of Western capitalism—even if it was a socialism they had never experienced. They did not, however, situate their no less fundamental critique of "actually existing socialism" within the Marxist paradigm. Their access to and familiarity with the debates that had been raging within Western Marxism since the late 1950s were very limited. Furthermore, in their experience, Marxism (most of the time interchangeable with the words *socialism* and *commu-nism*) was a set of slogans and policy applications embedded in dictatorial rule and cant, which they had come to despise. Marx and the ideas of Marxism were not so much wrong as they were irrelevant, as was continuing to debate endlessly the degree to which the SED and the entire socialist bloc had strayed from the Marxian ideal.

If any broad ideological direction could be said to have characterized these groups, it would be something, even to those nonbelievers among them, akin to a vague Christian socialism or secular humanism. This general outlook of the new opposition, still more of an amorphous concept than a clear ideological perspective, is what came to be known during the fall of 1989 as the Third Way. Although these were the people who were to become the core of the mass opposition to the regime and to play a central role in its collapse, their program for where they wanted to take East German society in the wake of the SED's fall never struck deep roots among the masses. This is evident in the extreme marginalization that was to be their fate in the aftermath of the Wall's opening and eventual German unification. They were viewed as heroic but disorganized and chaotic, lacking a clear program and direction.

The factors leading to the emergence of this new opposition, which gradually came to be referred to by the umbrella term "independent peace movement," were varied. Some of them had origins internal to the GDR and some came from the outside. It was their symbiotic interaction that gave rise to the movement. One important factor was the growing self-confidence of this youthful generation and its willingness simply to show open disdain for the authorities. In part this self-confidence was the fruit of the collective experiences of opposition to the invasion of Czechoslovakia and the expulsion of Wolf Biermann along with other struggles, largely in the cultural sphere, for some sort of independent space. In part the self-confidence was made possible by the changing role of the Protestant church and the space that provided for an articulation of dissent. A third element was the relative restraint the regime was forced to show toward internal opposition as the price of international acceptance in the wake of Willy Brandt's *Ostpolitik* and the ensuing Helsinki Final Act creating the Conference on Security and Cooperation in Europe.

From the end of the war until the mid-1960s the Protestant church had been actively hostile to the atheist SED and socialism. By the late 1960s this began to change as East German Protestants separated from the pan-German church organization, to which they had hitherto belonged, and formed a separate organization. From this grew the concept of a "church within socialism" as distinguished from one that opposed it. By the late 1970s a modus vivendi had been reached between the church and the SED. What this meant was that the church agreed not to oppose directly the SED's right to rule in exchange for a great deal of latitude and independence in conducting its own affairs. This latitude allowed the emerging dissident groups some space, under the church's protective umbrella, for discussion, debate, and activities separate from the party-state as long as they were not in direct opposition to it. As Christian Weber, an East German activist, has suggested, "The SED needed the Church. It functioned as a pressure valve that had the advantage of keeping opposition within controllable channels."[12] As the dissident groups became more and more active into the mid-1980s, tensions naturally arose. The boundary between independent activities and direct opposition was not a well defined one and the church authorities had to walk a narrow line in ensuring that its rank-and-file activists did not overstep those bounds. From the SED's point of view such an overstepping had already occurred in too many instances. Still, the state was unwilling to or constrained from cracking down completely, which meant that the boundaries of what was tolerated were constantly being tested and stretched.

In West Germany the Green party had become the point at which opposition to the arms race, ecological concerns, feminism, a broad variety of other social issues, along with anti-imperialism and third world solidarity, merged into a broad-based political movement. In East Germany there had always been an "official" peace movement, but this was disdained as a mere mouthpiece for the SED and Warsaw Pact military policies. In part via Western radio and television, in part through personal contacts (contacts West German Greens throughout the 1980s created and maintained with their Eastern counterparts), and in part through the GDR's own media, which constantly trumpeted the extent of West German opposition to NATO armament policies, the ideas and influences of the West German peace movement in general and the Greens in particular came to have a significant impact on the rise of the "unofficial" peace movement.

The East German oppositional groups thus shared a number of salient characteristics: They sought constitutionalism and liberal reforms, they had long-term ecological concerns, and they advocated nonviolent methods and greater public participation in decision-making. They all assumed the continued existence of two German states. Their organizational bases, under the umbrella of the church, were the peace, environmental, human rights, women's, and internationalist groupings.[13] At the same time, although they generally envisioned some form of democratic socialism, they failed to spell out the substance of that socialism and, indeed, paid very little heed to the needs and prospects of the workers, from whom they were largely estranged. Karl Wilhelm Fricke (1990, 268–269) imputes a certain *vormärzlichen Geist* (pre-1848 spirit) to the GDR opposition of the late 1980s. By this he means a liberal, intellectual movement that looked rather more "upward" to the authorities than "downward" to the people for the realization of its aims:

> In late twentieth century Europe such a resort to revolutions of one and a half centuries ago might seem amazing. It would not be incorrect, though somewhat precipitate, if one were to see in it primarily the expression of the interests of a class of urban intellectuals that views its own development as hindered less by material suppression than by authoritarian political oppression.

The essentially liberal and system-immanent nature of the opposition that had developed within the SED state largely explains the cry *Wir sind das Volk!* For this first "indigenous revolution" was primarily *political* and aimed at delegitimizing the increasingly unresponsive and ossifying *political elite*. The popular claim to "be" the people, it must be recalled, did not originate only in the Leipzig mass demonstrations following the violent suppression on October 7, 1989, of the popular protest that attended the fortieth-anniversary celebrations of the GDR and Gorbachev's ambiguous indication that the time had come for a leadership renewal in the GDR. Rather *Wir sind das Volk* was also, and perhaps primarily, a reaction to the *Wir wollen raus* syndrome of the refugee and out-migration wave of *Westwanderer* that had grown throughout the summer of 1989. The occupation of Western embassies in Budapest and Prague, the opening of the Hungarian border to East German refugees, and the international publicity that accompanied all this were an important incentive to the domestic GDR opposition. This opposition expressly rejected migration as a solution and countered it with *Wir bleiben hier* and *Freie Wahlen jetzt*.

It must further be recalled that whereas the out-migrators represented in particular the disaffected working class, especially skilled workers, as well as technicians, professionals, and artisans—and therefore a vast majority of mainstream society—the *wir sind das Volk* grouping was constituted essentially of marginal and nonconformist associations: pacifists opposed to war and cold war, dissatisfied and alienated youth, Christians with a social commitment, dissident Marxists and various "postmaterial" groups such as women's liberation movements, gay-rights groups, the ecologists of Left and Right, and many others. Until the peculiar conjuncture of the late 1980s, such groups had not seen themselves as an opposition but rather as a corrective. In the course of pre-October developments they consolidated themselves into rather spontaneous party formations such as New Forum (NF), the Social Democratic Party (SDP), Party of Democratic Breakthrough (DA), the Green Party, United Left, and Democracy Now.[14]

In that situation, these groups quickly became the focus and reference point for the mass demonstrations that characterized the first stage of the "revolution." Where the early Leipzig demonstrations had only attracted 5,000 (September 25) and 20,000 (October 2) persons, they grew rapidly after the fortieth anniversary celebration to 70,000 (October 9), 120,000 (October 16), and to consistently over 300,000 in late November and throughout December (figures from contemporary press accounts). At the same time, this spontaneous form of protest, involving strict nonviolence, human chains, burning peace candles, and collective solidarity, spread to all the major centers of the GDR: Dresden, Erfurt, Gera, Rostock, Zwickau, Schwering, Magdeburg, and elsewhere. By November 4 some one-half million people demonstrated in this manner on the Alexanderplatz in East Berlin. The democratic-participatory "revolution" was able to compel first the Honecker government to resign (October 17), then the Krenz-Stoph regime to step down (November 7), thus bringing to "power" the Modrow interregnum whose main task was to prepare for free elections. Most importantly, the "revolution" brought about the dismantling of the German-German border on November 9.

WIR SIND EIN VOLK: FROM THE THIRD WAY TO THE FAST WAY

Paradoxically, however, many of those same qualities that enabled the oppositional movement to overcome the SED regime prevented it from consolidating as a political power force. The movement's emphasis on grass-roots democracy and the single-issue orientation of so many of its subgroups precluded any central organization. More reactive than offensive in style and more culturally than politically oriented (see Knabe 1990), the movement—unlike the antiregime movements in Hungary and Poland—did not have an infrastructure of power, a government-in-waiting. Its leaders and activists originating in a relatively narrow stratum, it remained largely unaware of the material demands of the rest of society, particularly of the workers. The resultant combination of *power vacuum* and *unmet material expectations* created strong pressures with which the democratic coalition was ill-prepared to cope.

Moreover, peaceful mass demonstration is in itself not conducive to the formation of a concerted, power-oriented opposition—a historical lesson which the "1968ers" of the West German extraparliamentary opposition (APO) had also experienced. The political opponent could not be defeated in open confrontation (violent or otherwise) because it successively retreated from the arena in which such a confrontation might have been enacted. The consequent absence of a polarizing power struggle reinforced the fragmented, spontaneous nature of the oppositional groups and furthered the illusion that the "revolution," and hence the postrevolutionary order, did not need organization or direction but would evolve, as it were, from out of the solidarity and goodwill engendered by the conjuncture of forces.

As already suggested, material and political motives were closely interlinked in the behavior of the mobilized East German masses in the autumn of 1989—even if the indigenous oppositional groups did not entirely perceive this duality. Indeed, the strong material component in the uprising was in large part a reflection of the SED state's failure to develop a socialist historical project. Rather it had, in many respects, depoliticized the people and had preconditioned them to exist in a kind of alienated and alienating consumer socialism that was largely captured in the official slogan Ich leiste was, ich leiste mir was (I work, I buy).

The rather precipitate dismantling of the German-German border on November 9 thus both marked the political success of the mass opposition movement and constituted the preconditions for its transformation. For an *external* opposition to the GDR had always existed in the form of the FRG with its anti-Communist raison d'être (see Graf 1984), its intrusive television and radio programming, and its very prosperity. But with the fall of the Wall, these outside forces were free to enter the East German political vacuum with money, well-established organizations, techniques of persuasion and propaganda, and large numbers of experts and administrators.

The open border suddenly made the decades-old fantasy world of Western television a reality. Now it may well be true, as Erich Kuby (1990, 14) has written, that the opening of the Wall did not instantly make the GDR population into a nation of beggars; in fact they were relatively well off by international comparison. But their perception—fostered by the West German media and politicians—of being supplicants of course made them more amenable to being taken over by the West Germans. In the consumer-socialist and patriarchal state that the GDR had become, the desire for material improvement was closely linked to the need for greater disunity and expression of self-worth. Indeed, it was bound up with popular concepts of fundamental justice:

> They experienced a humiliating West-East gap in living conditions, more drastic and direct than could be depicted on TV and in the mail order catalogues. They realized they were Germans, but only second class Germans. The new national experience and the sense of social humiliation combined in their heads and hearts into a strong feeling of injustice. GDR citizens, who for a long time had not experienced deep social tensions, articulated their discontent at a post-war situation that had so blatantly discriminated against them. The demand "we are one people" here had a much deeper . . . motive (Roesler 1991, 12).

In this context the permeable boundary—failing any prior "structural adjustments" to the GDR economy—produced a sense of extreme insecurity on the part of the popular classes. To the decline in living standards was now added a fear of large-scale job losses (1) in the cities, owing to the possible collapse of uncompetitive state-owned plants or the privatization of large sectors of the economy and (2) in agriculture, as cheaper EEC imports became more widely available. Further shortages were created as GDR citizens, fearing a disadvantageous currency changeover, bought up stores of durable consumer goods such as televisions, freezers, refrigerators, and the like. West Germans, for their part, contributed to the situation by crossing the now open border to drink and dine cheaply in GDR pubs and restaurants and buy up the state-subsidized goods such as sausages, meat, fish, butter, and cheese— probably for a total of at least DM 4 billion in 1990 (*Die Zeit*, February 9, 1990, 25).

The East Germans' apprehension and fears could be alleviated and channeled into an identification with the West Germans. There had always been a strand of opposition in the GDR for whom the advocacy of reunification represented a form of anti-SED activity: The 1949 and 1968 East German constitutions had espoused the goal of ultimate reunification. But the 1974 constitution—promulgated in the face of strong delegitimization tendencies arising from West Germany's successful *Ostpolitik*—dropped all such references, while at about the same time all allusions to national unity, notably the phrase *Deutschland, einig Vaterland*, were excised from the GDR's national anthem. Thus, to favor reunification (or even rapprochement) by invoking unity and solidarity became a form of opposition to the policies of the SED leadership. But the desire for unity not only expressed political opposition to bureaucratization and dictatorship as well as yearnings for better standards of living and material security, it also created, or re-created, strong feelings of *nationalism*. Regardless of regime form or economic system, Hungary remains Hungary or Poland, Poland. But for the GDR the removal of the SED state was at the same time a renunciation of any separate identity. For the self-image of the GDR had hitherto been based on its (imposed, state-) "socialism" as embodied in the SED. The abandonment of this "socialism" was simultaneously a declaration for a specifically German identity. This being so, many believed that the GDR, as an appendage of the FRG, could enter into the world capitalist economy without the very real risks of marginalization and peripheralization to which the other former Peoples' Democracies were subject. It is this desire to escape the worst consequences of the imminent economic collapse of state socialism by transferring much of the onus for recovery onto the West Germans that may explain the rapidity with which *Wir sind das Volk* was replaced not only with *Wir sind ein Volk* but also *Nie wieder Sozialismus*, DM-jetzt, *Keine Experimente mehr*, and so forth.

Such feelings were reinforced by ongoing revelations of corruption at the very highest levels of the party and state (including the indictment of Erich Honecker himself), of secret-service infiltration into all "niches" of East German life (up to 25 percent of East Germans may well have served the Stasi in one or more capacities), and of the true extent of the economic problems facing the GDR. This awareness enhanced the growing "identity deficit" among the East Germans. Shocked at learning that their socialist identity was ephemeral and an instrument to legitimate elite rule, many GDR citizens attempted to compensate for their lost identity by recalling that they, like their West German counterparts, were all Germans after all.

It might therefore be said that, in terms of the dominant political and economic interests in the FRG and the disorganized and fragmented nature of the indigenous opposition, the outcome of the East German popular uprising was too important to be left to the East Germans themselves. The original opposition groups, whose grass-roots agitation over the years had developed a critical popular consciousness, thus making the "revolution" possible in the first place, were, in retrospect, doomed the moment the border was dismantled and the East German state renounced its separate "socialist" identity. Once Chancellor Kohl submitted his November 1989 ten-point plan for reunification—without consulting his NATO or EEC allies—the setting of the East German political agenda went over to the West, with each of the political parties there rushing to shore up its Eastern counterpart. These parties were relatively minor groupings who, after some forty years of active collaboration with the SED in the governing National Front, suddenly discovered their "independent voice," which they expounded in newspapers and journals for which start-up funds and expertise were suddenly abundantly available. This pressured GDR president Hans Modrow to advance the date set for the elections, which allowed the East German parties some two months to prepare for the first open elections in more than a half-century. Canadian observer John Gray (*Globe and Mail*, March 20, 1990) described the outcome in this way:

> The pros from the West took over. They brought bananas and Cocacola and computers and vast sums of money and stars like Mr. Kohl and former chancellor Willy Brandt and Foreign Minister Hans-Dietrich Genscher. More than that, they wrote the political programs and determined the style and priorities of the campaign. It became a West German election.

Not surprisingly, parties backed directly by the FRG took about 75 percent of the vote.

Encouraged and supported by the Christliche Demokratische Union (CDU)-West and reflecting its priorities, the Allianz für Deutschland (a fusion of the CDU-East, Deutsche Sozial-Union and Demokratischer Aufbruch) placed immediate unification on the basis of an expanded market economy at the core of its platform—indeed, made it its platform—and fought the election campaign under the motto Freiheit und Wohlstand—nie wieder Sozialismus. The Alliance's total adaptation to the CDU line and hence to the FRG's socioeconomic order resonates in its postelection policies: To facilitate currency union on July 2, 1990 the Volkskammer agreed to adopt intact all existing West German laws respecting private property, banking, finance, commerce, competition, bankruptcy, and taxation. In anticipation of political union the five former provinces on GDR territory were restored from the SED administrative districts and were simply made into new *Länder*. Traditional "socialist" rights to housing, employment, and education were scrapped entirely.

CONCLUSIONS

The first free election in the GDR produced a government whose mandate was to carry out a "revolution" from above and from without because the "revolution" from below and within did not take place. In this chapter we have sought to demonstrate that the "missing" revolution was primarily a function of the mass social bases of both the SED and the indigenous opposition. In both cases the failure was primarily a failure to enlist the working classes, the SED by suppressing them and buying them off, the emergent opposition by ignoring them and by somewhat arrogantly purporting to act on their behalf.

The former block parties and the ruling West German parties were thus able to capture mass loyalties and effectively integrate them into the dominant historical project of the "post-Fascist" society, namely the restoration of the pre-1933 class structure. In the Western partial state this had been accomplished by the late 1940s. In the East the project had to wait out a forty-year hiatus; but its completion there has been immensely facilitated by a population that has been deprived and *emtmündigt*, disciplined and debased.

The *ein Volk* syndrome justifies both the surrender of a separate "socialist" identity and the incorporation of the GDR—via Article 23 of the Basic Law—into a *Gross-Bundesrepublik*. As an essentially apolitical assertion of an ethnic, cultural and/or linguistic identity, it celebrates and enforces homogeneity. Where *das* Volk antedates the state and in a sense creates it, *ein* Volk follows state formation and makes it an instrument of ethnic or communal life, thus enforcing and imposing homogeneity and, by extension, conformity. Not only resident foreigners and "guest workers" but also citizens of different ethnic and/or national origins are more readily relegated to the role of outsiders and potentially disruptive elements. The growth of greater German nationalism has been accompanied by manifestations of anti-Semitism, racial persecution, xenophobia, and the like.

From the perspective of the ruling classes in All-Germany, the emergence of these ersatz enemies is highly functional. The *das Volk* project was, in its ultimate effect, not merely a protest against the SED nomenklatura and its agents; it was a direct offensive against elitist rule in all its forms. *Ein Volk* affirms an identity between leaders and the led; it simply rules out the distinction between rulers and ruled, between "above" and "below." Instead, the differences between one's own people and other peoples are emphasized. In this way the political dimension of class conflict is submerged under the call for national solidarity and cohesion.

Historians may one day conclude that the transition from *das Volk* to *ein Volk* was in many ways a new version of the *Einheit* versus *Freiheit* process that characterized the formation of the Second Reich. Then as now, *Freiheit* included a popular movement for democratic reform and a struggle against a centralized authoritarian structure. *Einheit*, on the other hand, involved the abandonment of the political struggle against nondemocratic authority and the consequent search for personal freedom in the extrapolitical realm. Although Helmut Kohl is not Otto von Bismarck and free elections are not a policy of blood and iron, the reunification process, particularly in the development of its social bases, has still not run its course.

Notes

1. This theme runs through most East German historiography and was particularly prevalent in the 1950s and 1960s. A more recent example of this good-evil dichotomy in English is Heitzer 1981.
2. See, e.g., Graf 1976, 21–27; Dennis 1988b, 12–16; Naimark 1989, 5–12.
3. Gaus (1983: 156–233). What Gaus was referring to here was the tendency of most East Germans to go about their daily tasks with as little effort as possible and then disappear with a few friends and/or family into their various niches, niches that cut them off from the rest of society. In one of its best-known forms this meant spending nearly all of one's nonworking time watching West German programs on television.
4. The term *entmündigt* is most suggestive in German and connotes disempowerment, lack of self-determination, and the inability to exercise one's rights independently of a superior person or institution. Rolf Henrich's *Der vomundschaftliche Staat* (The Tutelary State) is the title of one of the best East German attempts to analyze the interaction between the people and the elite prior to the events of autumn 1989 (Reinbeck: ro-ro-ro, 1989).
5. See, respectively, supra., ch. 1 and Bahro 1978. Whether these formations were more ancillary strata as suggested by Meillassoux or a distinct new class controlling rather than owning the means of production is an analytical problem of considerable intrinsic interest, but it need not be resolved here.
6. Comment by Bernd Wolf in March 1990. Hansen and Schulz have had

numerous discussions with Wolf, formerly an economist at the Hochschule für Ökonomie, since 1983.

7. Interviews with many GDR citizens during eight months in 1983–1984 and on numerous shorter research visits prior to the opening of the Wall in 1989 and two lengthy stays during 1990 found many referring again and again to the "Biermann Affair" as the point at which they lost any hope that change could come short of an antisystemic confrontation.

8. This section relies heavily on William Graf and Alfried Schulte-Bockholt, "The Transformation of the GDR and the Future of the (West) German State: Towards a Gross-Bundes-republik," paper presented to sixty-second Annual Canadian Political Science Meeting, May 27–29, 1990, Victoria, B.C.

9. For an analysis of these trends, based mainly on GDR sources, see Stingl-wagner 1990, 237–241.

10. On this, see *Stern*, March 8, 1990, 201; and Martin McCauley 1988, 480.

11. The following discussion of the emergent dissident movement in the late 1970s and early 1980s comes, in large part, from hundreds of interviews and conversations with alternative academics, SED members, members of the Protestant church, and GDR citizens in general from 1983 to 1990, during which time the authors collectively spent about twenty-four months in the GDR. Further interviews with East Germans have taken place in West Germany and the United States since the Wall was opened in November 1989.

12. Interview with Christian Weber, January 1991; here see his "The Independent Peace Movement and Its Impact on the Peaceful Revolution of 1989," unpublished paper, October 1990. Weber, a theology student in East Berlin, was an activist during the events of late 1989 as a member of the alternative group Initiative for Peace and Human Rights. He was one of their representatives to the so-called Round Table that shared power with the SED from late October 1989 until after the elections of March 1990.

13. In 1989 a lengthy State Security (Stasi) report enumerated some 160 such groups, of which 150 were said to be associated with the churches. They included 35 peace groups, 39 ecology associations, 23 mixed peace-environmental groups, 7 women's associations, 10 human rights, and 39 "World Groups." See Fricke 1990, 256–257.

14. "Wo in Deutschland Volk ist, ist auch ein Feind nicht weit;" Baier 1990, 40.

References

Bahro, R. 1978. *The alternative in Eastern Europe*. London: Verso.

Baier, L. 1990. "Des Volkes Feind, Zur Wiederaufstehenung des antiintellektualismus." *Freibeuter* 43: 38–41.

Childs, D. 1985. *The GDR: Moscow's German ally*, London: Allen & Unwin.

Dennis, M. 1988a. "Economic and social challenges of the 1980s: The GDR approaches the 1990s." *East central Europe*, vol. 14–15: 49–80.

———. 1988b. *The German Democratic Republic*. London: Pinter Publishers.

Fricke, K. M. 1990. "Die Wende zur Einheit." *Politische Studien* 311 (41, May–June): 265–274.

Gaus, G. 1983. *Wo Deutschland liegt: Eine Ortsbestimmung*. Hamburg: Hoffman und Campe.

Goldberg, J. 1990. "Die Wirtschaft der DDR—eine Ortsbestimmung." *Blätter für Deutsche und Internationale Politik* 5 (May): 444–450.

Graf, W. 1976. *The German left since 1945*. Cambridge, U.K.: Oleander Press.

———. 1984. "Anticommunism in the Federal Republic of Germany." in *The Socialist Register 1984*, London: Merlin, pp. 164–213.

Grunenberg, A. 1990. "'Ich finde mich überhaupt nicht mehr zurecht': Thesen zur Krise in der DDR-Gesellschaft," in *DDR—Ein Staat vergeht*, ed. T. Blanke and R. Erd. Frankfurt: Fischer. pp. 171–182.

Heitzer, H. 1981. *GDR: An historical outline*. Dresden: Verlag Zeit im Bild.

Kaden, A. 1964. *Einheit oder Freiheit: Die Wiedergründung der SPD 1945/46*. Hanover: Dietz.

Knabe, H. 1990. "Politische Opposition in der DDR." *Aus Politik und Zeitgeschichte* B 1–2 (January 5), pp. 21–32.

Krisch, H. 1985. *The German Democratic Republic*. Boulder: Westview Press.

Kuby, E. 1990. *Der Preis der Einheit*. Hamburg: Konkret Literatur–Verlag.

McCauley, M. 1988. "Soviet-GDR relations: The GDR approaches the 1990s." *East central Europe*, 14–15. pp. 461–482.

Minnerup, G. 1982. "East Germany's frozen revolution." *New Left Review*, 132: 5–32.

Naimark, N. 1989. "Forty years after: The origins of the GDR." *German Politics and Society* 17 (summer): pp. 1–12.

Oldenburg, F. 1990. "Die DDR im Übergang: Von der Volksrevolution im Herbst 1989 zur Bildung der Grossen Koalition im April 1990." *Aktuelle Analysen* 29 (April 23): pp. 12–15.

Peters, A. 1990. "Reparations-Ausgleichs-Plan." *Blätter für Deutsche und Internationale Politik* 1 (January): 13–18.

Roesler, J. 1991. "The transformation of the East German economy: The vision of the German parties and governments—and the reality." in *The internationalization of the German political economy: Evolution of a hegemonic project*, ed. William Graf. London: Macmillan (forthcoming: here quoted from manuscript).

Schüddekopf, C. (ed.). 1990. *Wir sind das Volk! Flugschriften, Aufrufe und Texte einer Deutschen Revolution*, Reinbeck: ro-ro-ro.

Stinglwagner, W. 1990. "Schwere Zeiten für die DDR-Wirtschaft." *Deutsche Archiv* 2 (February): 237–241.

PART IV
The Transition: Identities, Ideologies, and New Utopias

The Struggle for Space and the Development of Civil Society in Romania, June 1990

SAM BECK

John Galtung, in his *Structural Theory of Revolutions*, concluded that "In conflict one not only acts but interacts, and in so doing one not only lives but lives socially [his emphasis]" (1974, 67). I understand this to mean that conflict does not silence discourse among participants; it redefines it. In conflict over power and economic resources people use symbols to challenge hegemonic codes, which help them determine social interaction and resist domination. According to Alberto Melucci, "The mere existence of a symbolic challenge is in itself a method of unmasking the dominant codes, a different way of perceiving and naming the world" (1988, 248). The challenge inherent in conflict, then, reveals the nature of power relations.

The Communist regimes of East European societies discouraged and criminalized public opposition. Under such conditions, challenges to power were virtually impossible, causing the fusion of civil society and the state. The workers' victory in the class struggle was supposed to bring about a harmonious relationship between the state and society. Where harmony was not reached, the blame fell on external sources of trouble or internal enemies of the state. In Hungary and Czechoslovakia in the 1950s and 1960s, for example, civil society confronted the state; the state sought to totally annihilate civil society. The state, of course, did not succeed because power and control is never total. According to John Keane, "Civil society tends to swell rapidly from below. It feeds upon whatever gains it can wrench from the state, which normally lapses into confusion and paralysis" (1988, 35). Society is ready to take advantage of openings left by the state. While the weakened Communist states of East Europe have succumbed to popular revolts in relative peace and nonviolence, violence remains a possibility in post-Communist states. In the reformation of the state, control over violence has remained concentrated in the state; such concentration may once again become the catalyst for repression. This tendency is much closer to the surface of everyday life in Romania (and the Balkans) than among its Central European neighbors.

In an earlier paper, "What Brought Romanians to Revolt" (1991, 59–71), I discussed some preliminary thoughts. What I failed to emphasize there is that civil society is the antithesis of (but integrally linked to) the state, even a repressive, violent, totalitarian state. The idea that civil society and the state are dialectically linked is as crucial in understanding the development of emergent post-Ceausescuite or post-Communist societies and states as it was in understanding the nature of second and colored (black or grey) economies and societies within "actually existing socialism." That is to say, civil society is as much a product of the state as the state is of civil society. This should not be understood in structural terms, as in a dual opposition model or a complementarity of public/ private or civil society/state, but in terms of a process imbedded in historical changes. Gail Kligman made a similar observation in regard to the events after December 22, 1989. She said,

> It is one thing to overthrow a dictatorship; it is another to participate in the establishment of a democratic public sphere and of civil society. They are more exemplary of the inherited legacy of the Ceauşescu years, in which public behavior was thoroughly ritualized, than they are progressive steps on the road to democratic practice (1990, 411).

That is to say, public behavior as "ritual" in the post-Ceauşescu period, according to Kligman, is a legacy of Ceausescuism; it is being reproduced. This means that public behavior has not been transformed to meet the challenges of democratic social and political interaction.

In attempting to understand the violence of the Romanian revolution, in contrast to the "velvet" revolutions of Central European societies,[1] it is crucial to focus on the idea that under Ceausescuite conditions, any opposition was defined as *external* to the system. Hence a foreign enemy by virtue of its very being was an enemy of the state, and hence state violence against an enemy was righteous. The reproduction of this notion in the context of the post-Ceausescuite period is a potential both as an inherited element of how state formation is being determined by the country's leadership and as an aspect of wielding and manipulating power and control over the organs of state and the public. Dealing with external or internal enemies of the state is a state prerogative, although mob violence may at times carry out justice on its own initiative with or without support of the state.[2]

This chapter documents one particular conjuncture of the social movement and the violence that took place in University Square in the heart of Bucharest in 1990. I outline (1) the conditions and contexts of the conflict between the Romanian state as it was represented in June by the Iliescu government and the demonstrators, made up of students, workers, and the intelligentsia; (2) the formation and meaning of a public space; and (3) the growth of democratic discourse among ordinary people. Since the revolution of December 1989, a narrative of opposition and dissent was generated among demonstrators. This included the invention of new symbols imbedded in violence and the redefinition of urban space as elements of resistance against the totalizing tendencies of the post-Ceausescuite regime and alternately the validation of the public's proactive participation (as opposed to involvement merely as passive, compliant spectators) in the political arenas of the state.

Through their presence in University Square, the Bucharest demonstrators sought to exercise rights of freedom of speech which the government was attempting to deny them. In requesting, among other things, the creation of an independent television station so that demonstrators could debate government leaders on issues regarding the revolution, elections, and policies, they wanted to open a dialogue through which a silenced citizenry could be better informed. The demonstrators sought to "interact" and "live socially" with the government in a manner that would generate new social institutions, provide a public voice for the voiceless and silenced, and render power explicit. The discourse that would, according to demonstrators, be aired on national television and radio, would generate democracy by virtue of choices the listening public could make. The attempt to bring the new government into participation with the opposition as it was constituted in University Square was an effort to acknowledge and legitimize initiatives of the public qua civil society. According to demonstrators, it was Iliescu's rejection of public access to a proposed meeting between demonstrators and Iliescu that prevented such a meeting from taking place.[3]

The demonstrators, but also an increasing number of Romanian citizens across the country, were learning about civil disobedience. These acts of disobedience have become a learning context for the nation. In that public discussions about national policies were not customary under Ceaușescu, the conversations in the square were consciously conceived by demonstrators as a step leading toward democratic behavior. The inability of the demonstrators to dialogue with Iliescu left them to carry on "the discourse of the streets"—a discourse in which clarity regarding the opponents or partners in the conversation was never reached, even months after the event. What is clear is that University Square became a crucial feature in the struggle between demonstrators and the government.

In witnessing and participating in the events of June 13 and 14 in the streets, when demonstrators were ejected from their space and stormed the television station and when miners reclaimed the city for the government, I came to understand that space not as a passive arena, a context in which social interaction occurs, but as a social construct that is used to generate discourse that redefines social interaction. By creating a new discourse, one in opposition to that of the state, confrontations over urban terrain made power relations visible and recognizable. In such instances, according to Melluci, "power can be confronted . . . because it [state power] is forced to take differences into account" (1988, 250).

While democratic discourse and narratives are important, the learning of political behavior includes experience. However, experience, just like theorizing, is not alone sufficient to bring about action. Paulo Freire (1970) has suggested that one requirement for the participation of individuals in society as political beings is the opportunity for structured reflection on the power structures and relations that envelope the individual in society. This is so because the experience of permanent submission under Ceauşescu created the general acceptance of what is. If this is to change, people must have opportunities to critically reflect on the possibilities of change and have a hand in directing change. The demonstrators in the square understood the importance of providing people with opportunities to acquire political literacy through dialogue.[4]

In contrast to the new discourse is the old discourse, which was dominated by the silencing of public exchanges to the point that even in the privacy of one's own home, windows and doors were shut and the radio or television volume was turned up to prevent eavesdropping. The old discourse was one of disguise, one in which slogans served to shield the individual from the regime. Some have referred to this mode of interaction as "ritualized behavior" (Kligman 1990, 411). However, this type of ritualization is based on veiling the significant—under Ceauşescu even the everyday lived—aspects of life. To escape the "silencing" of the past and its potential in the present, new standards of discourse and behavior had to be invented and applied in public arenas and spaces. These standards were created out of the physical and spiritual forces that were released from or generated out of the acts of resistance and the battle against tyranny. The reenactment of resistance and struggle after December 22 became a public display of new behavior, an act of popular disorder that was neither sharp nor linear, nor one that could be claimed, led, or controlled by any one particular group. Here "ritualized" could be used to refer to that complex set of symbols that came to represent a particular social act, the Romanian Revolution of 1989–1990. The control over definable, physical spaces was important. It was a concrete presence of opposition. It enabled the mingling, separation, and rejection of diverse voices. Control over the space meant power to control a terrain, even if that power was only a power of resistance.

UNIVERSITY SQUARE

I arrived in Bucharest on June 6, 1990. The protest encampment at University Square was located in the very center of the city in front of the Romanian National Theater, the Inter-Continental Hotel, and the University, and had been in place for weeks. Canvas pup tents housed a ragtag community of hunger strikers and demonstrators. People milled about and gathered to discuss the issues of the day. Disagreements animated the crowd that assembled to take part in public discussions. Public address systems were used by common people to give voice to their individual and political identities. People announced news regarding opposition events in other parts of the country; pronounced their opposition to neocommunism, communism, Ceauşescu, and Iliescu; said prayers; sang songs; and organized others for the activities of opposition. All of this was carried out in a public space and through public debate.

Open disagreement regarding politics, even after the December revolution, was not comfortably accepted among Romanians. It flew in the face of collectivism, which had been demanded by the Ceausescuites as an aspect of good citizenship and national loyalty. While people in the square spoke about privatizing democracy, the idea of collectivism was not renounced by the Iliescu government. Neither did the majority of Romanians wish to totally reject the paternalistic system of the past in order to turn to the individualism implied by the turn toward capitalism.

Inherent in the television coverage of University Square was the portrayal of the demonstrators as riffraff and anarchical members of Romanian society who had no rights to claim legitimacy over the revolution. They were a mob, not the rightful inheritors of civil order. While diversity defined the interaction of postrevolutionary events, the discourse was dichotomous—"us" and "them." The participants in the demonstration saw themselves as serving the interests and the benefit of society, desiring liberty from tyranny. For the moment of the demonstration, people felt solidarity with each other and against those who wished to perpetuate prerevolutionary conditions. This is not to say that people acted with one mind and one thought; quite the reverse. Demonstrators had divergent views, for example, regarding the extent and the speed of privatization and marketization. They were in the square as *independenti*.

Participation in the square represented opposition to the newly elected government and the state. Their presence was a political act of resistance. The demonstrators voiced their opposition to Ceausescuism and the continuity of his ideology and to the "new" dogma as embodied in Iliescu. Demonstrators referred to the new dogma as "neocommunism," what they understood to be the continuity of Ceausescuite politics. University Square was a crucial space in which students and the others who dared faced off the army on December 22 and then in January, too. University Square became a space in which demonstrators resisted the authorities. The square became a sacred space because, as one person put it, it was "the very place in which in December 1989 the Revolution marked the most important first success. And [here] are present the souls of the Revolution's heroes, indicated by the many crosses."

UNIVERSITY SQUARE AS METAPHOR AND AS PHYSICAL OBSTACLE

The people in the square represented one part of the social cleavage created by Ion Iliescu's political victory. This cleavage was reflected in the built environment in the center of Bucharest where a major thoroughfare was blocked by symbolic barricades of rope that enclosed most of University Square and that the demonstrators called a neo-Communist free zone. Taxi drivers cursed at the barricades and the people who maintained them, as did the people who wished to use the space as was normal.

Romanians were divided by their attitudes about their new economic and political situation. On one side (the majority) were those who unconditionally supported the Iliescu regime, knowing full well who buttered their bread. On the other side were those who were absolutely opposed to it, who knew this government did not represent democracy. Yet there was a third group that suspended judgment, not automatically supporting the government but also not accepting the opposition as a democratic alternative. They were either attempting to be careful not to commit themselves out of concern that they might make a mistake or were waiting to make up their minds, to see what happened before joining one side or the other.

According to Octavian Paler, honorary editor of *Romania Libera* (an opposition newspaper targeted by the miners and whose office was destroyed by them on June 14), the social divisions were much broader and more complex. In an article published in *Romania Libera* on May 29 (republished in *Uncaptive Minds*), he focused on the successes of the National Salvation Front. "The bureaucratic apparatus of this totalitarian state," he wrote, "remains virtually untouched—only its overlords have changed" (1990, 11). After this change, a series of psychological blows were delivered to the Romanian body politic, workers were pitted against intellectuals, miners against the people of Bucharest, the old against the young, Romanians at home against Romanians abroad. Before the elections on May 20, 1990, the opposition's main target was the nomenklatura. They sought to end Iliescu's participation in the elections as well as that of other old Communists like Brucan, Bîrladeanu, and Martian. After the elections the opposition sought to end the monopoly of the single television station and wanted to terminate the "Communist methods of governing," among other demands.

The Inter-Continental Hotel also was an icon used by the demonstrators to portray the government. In part because it towered over the square, the demonstrators claimed that agents of the government were watching their activities and the participation of the populace, filming and photographing everything. In June the hotel also housed one of the offices of Prime Minister Petru Roman. Officials walked in and out of the building all the time. The idea of constantly being violated as objects of observation, which the looming structure represented to the demonstrators in the square, had particular importance for them as a symbol of continuity with the Ceausescuite government. On June 13, demonstrators sought refuge in the hotel after being attacked by uniformed and club-wielding men but were turned away. For the demonstrators University Square was a metaphor in the struggle for democracy.[5]

This was a "free zone," an area of transition and an arena in which alternative and independent viewpoints could be proclaimed in public. It was, in fact, called "the first neo-Communist free zone," implying that other zones would follow. University Square also was called Golania, the land of the *golans* (hooligans), the term used by Ion Iliescu to refer to the University Square demonstrators.[6]

VIOLENCE

Crises within domestic polities often bring about a struggle between authorized groups, mandated by a state's monopoly of violence, and those unauthorized to use violence. The perimeters of tolerance regarding the use of authorized violence and the intensity of resistance against the state are tested in such times. In Romania, violence defined the transition from the Ceauşescu to the post-Ceauşescu period. Violence was real but it also became symbolic, a right of passage of a society in transition, a ritual cleansing that marked the passage from one stage of development to another.

The symbolic feature of the deaths, after the successes of the revolutionary events in the afternoon of December 22, 1989, while used by the

Iliescu regime to legitimize its role in this transition, was understood by the opposition as a masquerade. Opposition members claimed the December revolution as their own and that what followed was a theft of their heroic efforts. The Iliescu regime, according to the opposition, claimed continuity with the popular revolution, masking its manipulation and ultimately its co-opting of the revolution in the elections.

Christine Gailey recently pointed out that "state formation as a process is actively shaped and limited by the resistance civil authorities encounter as they attempt to determine or extend their control over the culture and production of subject peoples" (1987, 36). In Romania the Communist party and the economy it was able to sustain created a kind of social contract between the state and its people, an agreement that neither Iliescu nor the majority of the people wanted to change, even in this period of transition. A popular saying from the Ceausescuite period aptly encapsulated the nature of the agreement between the people and the state. People used to say, "We pretend to work and they pretend to pay us." However, since December 22, a small opposition was able to challenge the transitional government and raised a question that remains unanswered: What happens when civil authority is viewed as illegitimate?

On June 12, negotiations between Iliescu and the representatives of the University Square demonstrators were broken off by Iliescu. On June 13 massive confrontations took place over the refusal of the demonstrators to leave University Square, which they controlled. At four o'clock in the morning, the central authorities ejected them, beat and arrested many of them, and retook possession of this public space. The struggle over the square was punctuated by violence, which both demonstrators and the state claimed as the heroic continuity of revolutionary struggle. The demonstrators knew they could expose Iliescu as antidemocratic by sustaining their efforts in the square and waiting for the government's reactions.

> At least 6 people (some say more) were killed when ten thousand miners (some say fifteen thousand), who were invited into Bucuresti by the Iliescu government, took over the contested terrain used by the demonstrators. On June 14 and 15 hundreds of people were wounded as the miners assumed control over the center of the city and beat people into submission. Thousands of people were intimidated into silence. (Hunt 1990)

I was shocked by the brutality displayed against the demonstrators and the ambiguity with which people dealt with the situation. Vintila Mihailescu properly captured the sentiments of the populace:

The capital of the country was ravaged by fire and sword, a part of the population breathing with relief and the other part shocked with horror. In Magheru Boulevard—a main thoroughfare of Bucharest—four miners were carrying a young man by his arms and legs. His head had been crushed and he was nothing but a blood-stained shape. A hysterical mob—including a government worker—accompanied him shouting, 'This one insulted the miners!' While they were passing, people shouted, "Very well, serves him right, now we can calm down." Somebody, horrified, asked aloud more to himself, "How is it possible to applaud when a man is killed?" He was immediately seized and beaten. Frightened, the others ran away.

A venerable physician caught in the confusion of the June fighting, woke up in a hospital ward near two miners. After the first shock he asked them how they had gotten there. "We didn't want to beat who they told us to beat and then . . ." (Hunt 1990)

Near the Inn of Manuc [in the central city of Bucharest] I saw with my own eyes a child of about seven who had been seized by the miners and held against a cement pillar. They asked him, "Which hand did you throw the stone with?" The child held his hand against the pillar and said, "This one." A man hit the child's hand with an iron bar 10 to 15 centimeters long with so much force that the bar penetrated the flesh. (1990, 13–14)

Normally, the rulers of states have exclusive rights over the use of domestic physical violence. This monopoly is critical in its link to the pacification of the populace. Norbert Elias referred to this as "the balance between the two functions of the monopoly of violence" (1988, 179), what he also referred to as the "civilizational process." The acceptance of this process, according to Elias, brings about an adjustment of the personality structures of individuals. "They develop a certain reluctance or even a deep loathing or disgust towards the use of physical violence" (1988, 180). It is this condition, I believe, that in great part held Romanians imprisoned in a web of coercion, pacification, and duplicity in the Ceausescuite period. As a result, when public violence did occur in the context of political divisions within the government itself, it unleashed civil violence. The violence in June had two faces, repressive and liberatory. Both were simultaneously present and interconnected.

While reflecting on the control of violence by states in the domestic sphere, Elias pointed out the lack of such control internationally. The absence of power in the international sphere is related to the unequal relations among states, which is regulated as much by levels of fear as by economic relations. Success in the domestic sphere, according to Elias, may transform "feelings of weakness . . . into feelings of unlimited strength and its inferiority complex into an unparalleled self-esteem" (1988, 183). Romania's inferiority in the international sphere gave rise to heightened levels of self-esteem. By manipulating nationalism and Romanian ethnocentrism, the government simultaneously brought about a relative acceptance of increasing violence monopolized by agents of the state.

The workings of the Securitate and its ability to be violent or threaten violence was accepted within the ethos of working people in part because, much like all other social relations, interaction with the Securitate could bring about privileges, benefits, access to scarce resources, favors, and other of life's possibilities in short supply. Violence against Romanian citizens most often took the form of coercion that forced people to compromise their values and thus submit themselves to the authority of the state. Physical violence occurred infrequently, but often enough to confirm people's worst fears about state control.

While the Ceausescuite system was severe, paradoxically, people gained access to resources and influence by establishing and using kin, friend, neighbor, and occupational networks to gain access to the "second economy." Vintila Mihailescu put this in a dramatically clear way:

> Local networks of people brought together by bartering, with everybody paying and receiving one kind of tribute or another, were spontaneously created all over the country. These networks were necessary for survival. In this way the Romanian civil society changed its structure and behavior with the Power residing no longer only "beside" it but "inside" it as well. Almost every Romanian thus became a kind of Dr. Jekyll and Mr. Hyde, victim and victimizer of his fellow Romanian, giving and receiving the tribute necessary for his survival. (1990, 4)

In an economy of scarcity, the means for acquiring goods, resources, and services were almost always tied to whom you knew. As a result, almost every family was somehow implicated by this regime, tolerating the behavior of the Communist party and regime-aligned members. With almost four million Communist party members and twenty-two million inhabitants, it is most likely that at least one member of every household was in the Communist Party, was a member of the Securitate, or was an informer.

The totalizing social nature of these circumstances and its reproductive force in part explains the overwhelming victory during the 1990 elections of the National Salvation Front with Ion Iliescu at its helm. People understood the rules of social interaction, which they helped establish as an accommodation to or self-defense against oppression. People feared the loss of their jobs, particularly if rapid privatization schemes were enacted. In the context of potentially rapid transformations, people, particularly those who lived in rural and provincial settings, were not willing to give up their jobs and the networks they had constructed; they were situated within a reciprocating clientage system of social interaction. The National Salvation Front and Ion Iliescu promised a slow transition at best and a maintenance of Romania's political economy at worst.[7]

MEMORIAL TO THE DECEMBER REVOLUTION

For the demonstrators, the experience of participation in the December revolution was intensely personal. The exhilaration and release felt by people as a result of Ceaușescu's fall sustained their desire to reproduce the feeling they referred to as *libertate* (freedom). The physical organization of University Square included a substantial area in which the December revolution and the symbols of its martyrs were enshrined by wooden crosses and makeshift memorials that dotted other contested areas as well. Passersby lit candles to God and left flowers for the victims. Poetry written on pieces of paper was tacked up on crosses to commemorate the struggle against tyranny or for a victim who had fallen in battle. University Square was invested with the meaning of independence, and the struggle for it. One demonstrator claimed that "all the people here were on the front lines" during the December revolution. This gave the participants an elevated status in that they had risked their lives to liberate society from tyranny. In no uncertain terms this put them in competition with the National Salvation Front, which claimed this status for itself. Both the demonstrators and the Iliescu regime claimed that they represented the continuation of the revolution. In defending the square, the demonstrators generated the discourse of opposition and created an alliance of *independenti*, independent people. The *independenti* were those who were willing to risk not being identified with the newly elected government, yet not willing to identify themselves with any other parties.

The government had no formal institutions with which to deal with this social movement represented by the demonstrators in the square. Nor, it seems, were such institutions desired. Hence, its response was in keeping with the style and manner customary of the past regime— confrontational and violent. The lack of institutionalized means to resolve crises of this sort was aggravated by the absence of effective opposition parties. The two larger so-called historical parties, the National Liberal party and the National Peasant party, were discredited because their leaders had lived ten years (Campeanu) and thirty years (Ratiu) in enforced exile. They were accused of not being in touch with Romanian realities or needs, probably rightly so.

MORAL LIFE

The demonstrators held together through their ritualized presence in the square and in their common struggle against the government, which attempted to manipulate the movement's leadership and constituents through private and secret negotiations, surveillance, and other means of coercion. The government exploited divisions among the different groups that made up the "organized" elements of the demonstration. The demonstrators believed that their strength was a straightforward matter of holding true to the moral principles of the movement that toppled Ceauşescu. The demonstrators in the square thought of themselves as creating a new principled mode of social life. The government did not understand the demonstrations to be a matter of principle but one of opposition, opposition to it. This was not simply a matter of protest but one of counterrevolution.

The use of fear, intimidation, and manipulation as a government tactic supported the "continuity with Communism" thesis developed by the demonstrators. The manipulation of demonstrating groups by the government through secret negotiations served to divide the movement. The leader of the university students, Marian Munteanu, for example, was said to have made a pact with Iliescu that led him to support the reduction of the University Square demonstration to one day each week, rather than the full-scale demonstration that was in force. The apparent absence of support led to the construction of a speaker's tower opposite that of the "balcony" that was controlled by Munteanu and the street-level speaker's area below the balcony. On June 14, Munteanu was severely beaten by the miners, hospitalized, and then arrested, indicating that perhaps things were not as they seemed.

For those involved in the demonstration, the struggle became an act of heroism from the perspective of the past weeks and months, starting with the Timisoara uprising. Crucial to this heroism was violence, facing it, surviving it, and facing it again in standing up for moral goals and against the corruptions of those in power and those who supported those in power.

During the six months after the anti-Ceauşescu revolt, the more or less democratic elections were held, the anti-neo-Communist demonstrations were held, and the violent suppression of this opposition had been carried out. To the demonstrators, the government made itself appear corrupt and corrupting. As a result even after the elections, which Western observers judged to be fair, those who remained in opposition saw themselves as representing a moral force. Every action against the opposition illustrated to the demonstrators the government's complicity and moral laxity. The longer a visible and spatially defined resistance to the government took place, the more pronounced was the discourse of opposition and the easier it was for a "tradition" of opposition and dissent to establish itself.

Among the demonstrators, the revolution of December 22 and each following event associated with its continuity invoked the moral forces at work in the struggle against evil. Each account of encounters with government violence against the demonstrators was replete with examples of moral stamina and sacrifice in the name of the Romanian people. Each confrontation was an event that helped the creation of the discourse of opposition.

The movement generated its own narrative of history, creating out of discrete events a cast of heroes, villains, and martyrs. The narrative transformed the sequence of separate events into a coherent whole. When recounted it was to convince others of its truth, justice, and mission. The narrative became particularly effective when stories were able to symbolize events with which people could identify by having participated in the experiences described and interpreted in the narrative.

CONCLUSIONS

The history and traditions thus created were formulated in particular physical spaces, which took on a distinct political character when events were recounted. Success in maintaining a physical presence on the square in part defined the limits of the state.[8] In its day-to-day use this space was constantly redefined, mostly as a result of the unfolding activities to which the landscape was put. University Square first became an assembly point, then a recruitment space, and then a space for mobilizing people into action. Now and again it was used as a battlefield. These different meanings and uses created the central antagonisms with the Iliescu regime and its adherents. That is why the surfaces occupied by the hunger strikers and stained by their blood had to be cleansed, washed away. The historical precedence the demonstrators had attempted to set had to be removed.

That Gypsy street sweepers cleaned up after the police and removed the encampment and its occupants was ironic, reproducing stereotypes of Gypsy behavior embedded in the history of non-Gypsy people.[9] Gypsies used hand-held hoes to neatly and systematically hack up the earth that had been hard packed by the occupants of the tents. According to some witnesses who saw the police invasion of the square earlier in the day, hoses were used to wash away the traces of blood that were spilled when the demonstrators' resistance was quelled and the demonstrators were taken away.

The occupation of the space by the demonstrators was a political action that not only symbolized resistance to the authorities but also the capture of terrain from normal use. It was symbolic in that the historical events represented the struggle against repression in general and the accumulated actions that have taken place in the square since December 22. The closing off of University Square inconvenienced anyone attempting to drive through it. The occupation and the activities there also challenged normality. On the whole, how normality was challenged and defined was in the hands of those who had the strongest commitment to the narrative and the traditions of opposition they had created.

The day of June 13, after the barriers on the streets had been removed and the demonstrators had regrouped, police buses and trucks were strategically parked and torched to return the square to the demonstrators. This process and its unfolding remain unclear. The confusion is indicative of the events. Was it agents of the Securitate, the FNS, or provocateurs of the "Right," represented by elements of the historical parties, who caused the violence and burning? Accusations are made from all sides. Pavel Campeanu expressed this well:

> The horrifying destruction of the television station, of the Interior Ministry, of the police headquarters of the Liberal National Party (LNP) and of the National Peasant Party (NPP). While the television station presented the former with legitimate indignation, it showed the complete devastation of the parties' headquarters without the slightest sign of regret, creating the impression that there is unacceptable destruction and excusable, if not desirable, destruction. We [the Group for Social Dialogue[10]] are against any destruction, and we consider it invariably damaging, humiliating, and reprehensible (1990, 730).

According to official explanations, the reprehensible acts of June 13 were the work of a Fascist coup.

The use of violence by the police in the early morning of June 13 escalated the response by the demonstrators. The demonstrators were not one unitary force. They were an amalgam of individuals and groups of people whose loyalties to each other under these circumstances were quite fluid. It was not possible for me to perceive a formal organization out of the masses of people who assembled and in clusters moved down the boulevard over which they had taken control and down which they moved to reach the television station buildings. By removing the demonstrators in the manner they did in the early morning of June 13, the authorities had defined the nature of the subsequent discourse and actions. The demonstrators organized a march to the television station and then attempted to enter it and gain control over the broadcasting studios. Attempts to sack the Interior Ministry and the police station also caused some fire damage. Reports that arms were looted from these buildings circulated among demonstrators.

The landscape was given a moral meaning and as a result by entering its space people entered another world, a moral terrain whose rules of behavior differed from those on the other side of the barricades. It was a space representing a superior morality to what the National Salvation Front could offer. It was an implicit distinction between civility and nurturing *and* ruthlessness; honesty, integrity, and truth *and* repression, pragmatism, and fraud. Life within the space was deemed authentic. Here people practiced debate; discussion was permitted; diverging views could be presented; even outrageous pronouncements could be made. In this space, people gave up their other lives to live simply. A poignant illustration of this was the hunger strikers who sacrificed even food for the good of society—for a better, more just society. The discussions that took place in clustered groupings in the square were sincere and, for the most part, a search for "truth." Any appearance of violence or the threat of violence was smothered, with offenders ushered to the sidelines by individuals who implemented the code of nonviolence in the neo-Communist free zone.

This was a space in which people refused to be made superfluous, where they refused to be marginalized and made irrelevant, as the denunciation by Ion Iliescu implied when he called the demonstrators *golani*. In the past, the government had been able to silence the population through nonphysical means of intimidation and through acts of selective violence. In University Square, government violence raised the specter of the past in the present, providing the demonstrators with the sense of justice to go on. Rather than marginalizing the demonstrators, the government emboldened and legitimized them, heightening in intensity the political confrontations between the government and the opposition and making visible the difference between the two.

In conclusion, from the vantage point of the streets, what the Romanian revolution and the events in the month of June 1990 make clear is that meanings of social events and their relationships both shape and are shaped by practice and by the involvement of people and groups of people in action. In order to understand the complexity of the situation, it is important not to dichotomize, separate, or ignore cultural meanings in favor of the material basis of social relations, or vice versa. Neither analytic element should have a necessary conceptual advantage because both are elements of a single process. However, that is not to say that priority does not exist for either one at any given point in time and situation at the local level, but that is something that has to be determined in practice and history.

APPENDIX I: ORAL HISTORY

INTRODUCTION

I arrived in Bucharest on June 6, 1990, stayed in the city for two days and then made my way to the village in Transylvania where I had carried out two years of anthropological fieldwork to learn from the peasant-workers there how they had experienced the ten years since I had been there. I stayed in the village until June 12 and returned to Bucharest to witness the police attempt to eject the demonstrators from University Square. Hunger strikers and some of their supporters had camped out on the front lawn of the National Theater and the Bucharest Inter-Continental Hotel, opposite the university. Every day thousands of people would gather and debate, "learning how to be democratic," according to some of the people who spoke there and encouraged the discussions. It appeared to me to be a large teach-in. People clustered to argue and discuss the issues of the day. People were not used to speaking so openly, and for many the ability to speak made them deliriously happy. They returned to the square to test themselves and their ideas again and again.

I had never seen anything like this in Romania and was saddened by harassment experienced by those who opposed the government in the square. On the morning of June 13, the police came into the square and with brutal force ejected the campers, cleaning up the barricades that had marked the "Neo-Communist free zone," which the self-defined "independent" movement had successfully held as a zone of opposition and resistance. The demonstrators closed off traffic in the middle of the city.

In the afternoon those in opposition gathered again in the square and once again took control over the space. The buses, trucks, and cars used by the police were hijacked, looted, and torched. Black smoke billowed out over the city center as heavy rain fell on the scene. Tires and gas tanks exploded—rolling across boulevards and neighborhoods at a distance, bringing fear to those who supposed that war had broken loose. People who had been beaten with truncheons appeared stripped to the waist to give proof of the brutality of the authorities. Long red welts gave evidence of the objects that must have been used in clubbing the demonstrators. One young man had his entire face bandaged and through tears that rolled down his bandages explained how they had come at him in the morning. I saw a man in his late fifties reach out to stroke the young man's hair to comfort him. He said, "You are our heroes. We will remember your deeds." People were shaken by the signs of this brutality.

As the afternoon wore on, speakers with megaphones arrived and organized groups of 100 and 200 demonstrators who marched down Magheru Boulevard to eventually collect in front of the television station. By the time I arrived at the television station, thousands of people had collected on the street and on the front lawns of the buildings and had forced themselves into the area in front of the entrance. The police and the military lined the building in the front. Tanks and armored vehicles stood ready. However, even as the television station building was forced open and people entered, the armed personnel next to them stood aside. I saw an officer wave his unit even further back from the people who had assembled.

This was a frightening situation. Periodically, quite unexpectedly, I could see groups of men chase another man, often hitting him with clubs or branches from trees that lined the boulevard. Even when such a person was unlucky enough to fall down to the ground, the blows would not stop. People hit him and kicked him until they were certain he could not move. If the victim was fortunate, an unexpected volunteer would step in front of the club- and fist-wielding crowd and usher the victim to safety.

At times the crowd would move; people would walk rapidly or run in one direction or another. Usually a fight brought people to imagine greater danger, such as police or security police action. In fact, a truck-load of people in civilian clothing armed with clubs did attempt to beat back some people, but they were chased away. The surges of the crowd were horrifying in that they caused people to panic in an already tense situation. A mass of people rushed in one direction and then another to escape real or imagined threats.

As the day turned to dusk, I saw some children who could not have been beyond their mid-teens jump onto the roof of the suspended passageway that connected two of the buildings that made up the television station offices. Some of the children were dark-skinned, and I believed them to be Gypsies. They walked on the roof and suddenly I saw them inside the passageway, gesticulating wildly to the crowd to join them. People pressed toward the entrance, but most people stayed outside, looking on the scene that was unfolding.

In the meantime, between surges of the crowd, some of the vehicles that had been hijacked from the police were being driven back and forth between the television station and University Square. The drivers and occupants of the vehicles were youths, in their teens and perhaps in their twenties. They had broken out all the windows of buses, trucks, and cars. A few held flags while balancing themselves on the roofs of the vehicles. They seemed excited, shouting various anti-Communist and anti-Iliescu slogans.

More people entered the television station. Three people stepped out on a ledge on the third floor and then later I saw a flag being pushed out on the eleventh floor of the building. By 9:30 in the evening, people started to throw stones and other objects against the windows of the television station, breaking the glass with audible thuds. Fire hoses appeared at one end of one of the buildings and forced demonstrators to retreat. But they returned. It was a hot and muggy evening. Many people occupied positions across the street from the television station in buildings that had been abandoned after the December revolution. Only some buildings were shot up, burned out, and now in the process of being rebuilt. It was here that people picked up debris and scaffolding as potential weapons. I fled the scene as the level of danger escalated.

I watched the rest of the rebellion as it was broadcast on television. It seemed to me that the demonstrators were struggling with building personnel over entry into the television station. Apparently, some of the office workers in the television station did not escape the wrath of the rebels. One man wearing bandages on his head and arms and showing a stab wound on his side was televised for everyone to see. The damage done to offices and the exterior of the building was also broadcast, leaving the viewer with the impression that the rebels had gone on a rampage of destruction. The entire day's events had been videotaped through the use of helicopters and some ground crews.

Later the accusation by government officials was that the rebellion was organized to topple the newly elected regime and represented an attack from the political right, that it was the political right that had manipulated the demonstrators' sentiments of liberty and free speech. The accusation by demonstrators was that the government had pro-vocateurs within the ranks of the rebels and was responsible for all the violence. Others speculated about the divisions within the NSF leadership and understood the lack of response by the military and the police as an internal struggle for power.

On the morning of June 14, I returned to the television station. The buildings were a shambles, windows had been smashed on most of the lower floors. The military now was at the fence close to the street, as much as fifty meters from the building where they had been the night before. Now, however, instead of the demonstrators massing at the entrance of the television station, it was miners from the Jiu valley and workers from Bucharest factories who shouted slogans. They were well disciplined and marched in a regimented fashion, leaving the television station as they assembled there and then marched to University Square. I walked the entire distance alongside them, listening to them chant pro-Iliescu slogans.

When I reached the area near the University Square, I was held up every two or three meters by miners requesting my identity papers. The miners had taken over the street, controlled vehicular and pedestrian traffic. The miners held a variety of weapons that included some of their hand-held mining tools such as pick axes. However, what struck me most were the new wooden axe handles that many of them held or waved above their heads. These were one-meter lengths of shaped wood. Others either had one-meter lengths of cables with a diameter of up to three centimeters or plaited wires shaped into truncheons with a neat loop to fit a miner's hand.

As the miners walked in their groups down the boulevard, periodically I saw one or two men break ranks to confront a person on the sidewalk. They were always joined by a few more miners who broke rank, and at times I could see them raise their weapons to bring them down on their victims. This occurred so rapidly that it was difficult to fully comprehend. However, when miners chased down one young man who fell against some steps at a one-meter distance from me and was beaten with axe handles, I was confronted with the horror of this event. The men who were doing the beating were remorselessly forcing their weapons down on him with all their might, anywhere they could reach him. The victim attempted to protect his head and his face. When he stopped moving, the miners continued to beat him and kick him. Suddenly a crowd of miners circled around the body and moments later a black car drove up, the body was forced into it, and the young man—or what was left of him—was driven off.

The miners had taken over the city center. Some of them drove around in large open trucks. Others made themselves as comfortable as they could, receiving bread and mineral water by the truckful. Civilians, too, nonminers, came up to the trucks to obtain water and food, something that made me wonder about how all of this was organized and who was taking responsibility for what was going on. I did not want to believe that the government was directly responsible for this, but all evidence pointed to this fact. Similarly, I did not want to believe that among the miners were agents of the former Securitate, who were said to be responsible for the most violent acts.

Especially violent attacks were made against Gypsies, whose position in Romania has become particularly threatened in recent times. The dramatic rise of xenophobia and racism can only be understood in relationship to the five-or-six-hundred-year-long history of Gypsies in Romania. The Roma, or Gypsies (locally referred to as *Ţigani*), are viewed at times as an ethnic group and at times as the lowest possible class. When viewed as a class, they are perceived as a pariah group without a culture of their own and hence a sense of separate historical development and linguistic origin is denied to them. When viewed as an ethnic group, they are frequently perceived as biologically and culturally inferior, a group whose inherent capacity for civilization was never developed. In either case, Gypsies are relegated to the category of people least desirable, but also feared for their strange language and customs. Those Gypsies who accept the dominant Romanian culture are no longer considered *Ţigani* and their desire to identify with their heritage and culture is seen as proof of their inherent retrograde character. According to some, Gypsies were especially active during the December revolution and voted for the most part for Iliescu and the National Salvation Front. The miners wanted to remove and silence the Gypsies as much as they wanted to remove and silence the demonstrators.

INTERVIEWS WITH DEMONSTRATORS AT UNIVERSITY SQUARE

The following is a compendium of interviews obtained on June 5, 1990, from demonstrators and participants of the opposition in University Square. I edited the interviews into one narrative in order to provide the material with coherence and one voice.

WHO WERE THE TERRORISTS?

Terrorists did not exist. People were fighting each other, but they weren't terrorists who were attempting to return Ceauşescu. They were people who were fighting among themselves. There were two forces, among whom one was able to gain power, and those were the exact people who won, the friends of Iliescu. It was they who in the end were victorious. They had for the most part the *Securitate* working with them.

WAS IT A TYPE OF COUP?

No, it was trickery perpetrated against the people. We were tricked into thinking that those of us who participated in the revolution of December 22 had been responsible for toppling Ceauşescu. In reality this is not what happened. Do you think that the *Securitate* had nothing better to do than to shoot at people? No, once they saw that the military lost its leadership (General Milea had committed suicide), they sat and waited to see what would happen. And what they waited for did indeed happen.

Those of us who were there [at the television station] would follow just about anyone who arrived there and that's what happened. What did we know about running a government? I left. They won because there wasn't anyone who stood up against them.

The fighting that took place after the twenty-second of December was to misdirect our attention in order for them to direct their attention in forming a government.

The people who entered the television station were those of the [National Salvation] Front party. People saw what they did on television. [They appeared as the heroes of the revolution.] If it wasn't the terrorists who did the shooting and killing, who was it? For them [the people], it is difficult to imagine someone else—for others to have been involved. Who would it have been?

Yes, in reality it was—some fired at the people and at the army. But that it was thousands of terrorists—to reverse the revolution. No, it couldn't have been. Perhaps it was all a spontaneous lie. Perhaps it was that.

Those whom you see here [on University Square on June 6, 1990] were all on the streets on December twenty-first and twenty-second and the next days. For a people of twenty-two million there exists one million protestors. One out of twenty-five should be out on the street—to fight while twenty-four are relegated to look on. In Bucharest there are only two and one-half million people. So twenty-five thousand are likely to go out into the streets to fight. In practice there were perhaps fifty thousand who went out every day. It is the same people who are going to go out into the streets. The people don't change; it's the same people going every day. So, it is the same people who are here, the ones that saw the reality and are the same dissatisfied people, the same who are not satisfied with the "truth" as spoken. People were defamed who should not have been defamed.

All the wrongs collect themselves, they collect and create a reaction. A person should have the freedom to have a reaction, the ability to protest. What the people want here is a means for public opinion information that is not controlled by the government. A private television station would assure objectivity. People would work for objective information and for their own salaries. And in the tone of presentation. It doesn't have to be a voice of opposition [to the government]. It would be an aberration to acquire a television station for Ratiu, for example. No one here wants the PNT [National Peasant Party] to have a television station. This might not be democracy, some say, if PNT has a television station and others don't. Well, why don't the other parties have one too? If they have enough money and spirit, why shouldn't they have one, if they have their own newspapers and journals? How can this be an antidemocratic action? Some say this would open up the doors. The doors to what, I ask?

We don't want this here on University Square. We want an independent TV station. We don't necessarily want that the station belongs to an individual or some party—only that it be independent.

Many people do not understand why we continue this manifestation. After having given so many days and nights, your heart will not allow you to renounce your commitments and to capitulate. It's not a question of an absurd inertia. It is simply a respect for the action and commitment of people.

However, the moral force has been lost. From the groups that participated in the early manifestations, some could continue every Thursday. As a result we lost lots of members. At the start we had a lot more people and now we are decreasing in numbers every night. The energy doesn't exist anymore.

To tell you the truth, those of us who are here, we do not doubt that we are right about what we are doing. We have no doubt. To say *jos communismuliu* [down with communism] is still a frightening thing in this land. We don't believe in the government that was legitimated [through the election].

This manifestation doesn't have the force that it once did. They [the government] don't even come to the dialogue. They probably know (and they are right) that we will get bored [tired] and will go home [from the manifestation]. I go home all the time. I take my exams. But when I have a few free hours, I come here. I come because when I don't come for a few days, I get a telephone call at home and am asked, "Hey you, why haven't you come?" Did something happen to you? Did you have some problems? Were you interrogated by the police? Were you beat up? There were a lot who were beaten up by the police. As people would leave the Communist free zone and would go down one of these streets, they were beaten up by five or six people.

WHEN? IN MAY?

Before and after. There were brief interrogations by the police. People were called to the police station for verification. Some were visited at home. They wanted to remind people that the possibility existed for them to be called by the police. This was a subtle method of discouragement. However, no one here would be or could be discouraged by these methods or others. No one is afraid or will hide the fact that they are participants of the manifestation at the University. They would walk down to the Miliţia [sic!], the police station, they remained the Miliţia, and present their identity cards and claim that they were dissidents at University Square. No one is afraid to do this. In any case, we all have been photographed and we have been asked our names. We are on so many lists. It is very clear who is participating here. They must have identified over 500 thousand people in this square. Not one of them came only one time.

The groups that are represented here are the following: Alianţa Poporuliu, Asociaţia 16–21 Decembrie, Asociaţia 21 Decembrie, Liga Studenţilor al Politehnica, Liga Studenţilor al Universitate, Asociatia Studenţilor Arhitect. In general the student associations were not present on the first day (i.e., in the first days of the rebellion). They joined in the second and third days—in the first week.

The first group, at the base of the movement, was Alianţa Poporuliu. They coordinated the manifestation.

The leader of Alianţa Popuruliu was Dinca Dumitru (most likely a Romanian of Romany [Gypsy] origin), who had the idea of staying overnight—to carry out a watch. It was not planned; it just happened as a result of some old person who was hit over the head and people decided to remain overnight as a patrol [to protect people]. It was decided that the only alternative left to us was to remain here to fight against the passivity of the government and their silence, a lack of information from them, until they carry out a dialogue [public dialogue] with us; one they have not carried out until now.

On the days of December twenty-first and twenty-second in the front lines there were children of nine and ten years old; those who most likely didn't know why they were there, but still were very courageous. Some of them remained with a flag in their hands when they were being shot at. Probably they didn't know what they were doing. They still had courage.

WERE THERE ALSO GYPSIES AMONG THE DEAD?

Yes, of course! In proportion to the masses of the manifestation, they were there in much larger numbers than they are in proportion to the country as a whole. So, they were much more active than the Romanians. This is explainable. People collected after work and people without work collected. Among Gypsies there are large numbers without work. No one came out of curiosity. There was an extraordinary unity against Ceauşescu. This was our point held in common. We all contested him.

There are some Gypsies who come now. Their being here and with us is seen outside as somehow characterizing the demonstration as people with poor qualities. The quality of the people doesn't matter. What matters is what they want.

We need to respect the wishes of people. They want to replace Ceauşescu with someone who is better. Why should they want to replace him with someone worse [i.e., Iliescu]? That just doesn't make sense! That's what I don't understand about the Romanian people. How can you condemn people who want to have leaders who are better than Ceauşescu? They come to this manifestation to find something good, not bad. We don't want anything bad. If we had 10 percent out of the Romanian population who would contest the present situation [the election of the Iliescu government], this would be sufficient to bring about change. The rest of the people would then be happy for the change. And this is the paradox and what is sick about society. A person is asking for something and then contest the validity of his claim. This is fantastic!

It is very difficult for Iliescu. There are lots of people who say this man is great! With high intelligence. I don't believe he is that great—I think he is an ordinary person. For such an ordinary person, it is very difficult to go down the road of betterment of the social structure, the political structure, and our lives. People feel lied to and feel that aggressiveness has been applied to them; they have been offended. People who feel this way, under these conditions hold this inside and I suspect will allow this to manifest itself somehow, sometime.

A man who lives with the fear that he will be overturned [speaking about Iliescu], he will need around him a cadre of people, informants, with whom we have been saturated. We are saturated up to our ears with informants. He would need to keep a type of people who helped him in "unclean" operations in this period of provisional government. Of course these people have family [kin] and friends and they, too, have family and other work colleagues and other colleagues. And this will lay on top of him, like layers of sickness. This is a sickness of our people that will hold onto him and not let him go.

Among those he has held onto, this faction of the Securitate has friends who were not in this faction, who know the truth. These two groups then will have to tolerate each other. Look, and that is how these respective groups stay in their functions and so it goes on. It is not difficult to guess that this chain will continue. Whether or not Iliescu wants this. He has no choice. The average person feels that he needs to be compensated for what he has done, how he voted, and how he fought, whom he has supported. And at the same time, he is not patient to see the return of the past, the return to the filth where we have ended up.

We want to abandon the promotion of the ideology of collectivism. The workers sympathize with Iliescu. They are waiting to see what will happen. One variant of the future is that we will have to endure a similar person at the head of state as in the past until we can't take it anymore. The problems are very difficult. One of the questions is how many Communists will remain after the election. We still don't know. We only have some suspicious. We are not ready, like some people who say Let's leave Iliescu alone for two years to see what the NSF will do. You are not going to invite an ex-convict into your house for two years to see how much he is going to steal, are you?

From the very start, we stated that we won't accept him. Not even for two years. We are afraid that they will organize and start all over again with the single-party system. So, it may not be only two years. We can discern what is happening. The methods used by the NSF to win the elections showed us. It would not have been embarrassing for the NSF to have won with a strong opposition. It would have been good for them had the NSF won with 45 percent. It would have been very good. That they won with 67 percent is very bad for them. I am sorry about it. Now we know what is going on. It is the same situation [as before]. It is laughable to have the total opposition with 20 percent of the vote in the parliament. It's like puppies that are tied around the neck and fastened onto the fence.

So You Are Not Terribly Optimistic?

We are not a pessimistic people. Hope exists. We don't believe that the NSF will have a Communist platform. No. They want to change—bring a total change—the NSF will want to have a people left of center. Why we are pessimistic is that they gained power through illegal means and we can't let them continue this way with a person like that as head.

They created a game of the dead in reality. How could the terrorists be so incompetent not to have killed more people than they actually did? And yet they killed enough. In any variant of the story they look bad and do not emerge with a clean face. I won't talk about the other things that have appeared, the *bijnicari* [illegal entrepreneurs] that have flowered. I won't talk about the inflation that will be born. The fact that Romanians don't consider the law (i.e., that they are doing illegal things), this didn't occur from what is going on in the University Square "because there people don't respect the law," as is written in their newspapers. No. This happened long before. The only law that the Romanians paid attention to is to obtain baksheesh or steal material from work. This is an attempt to undermine the state, the state of Ceausescuites. This was the only major illegality that people carried out. As people saw that today is a law and tomorrow there isn't one and that you can play around with the law, now people are doing things as they think. It's very difficult to get people to own up to responsibilities.

In the electoral campaign we had lots of deaths. It's one thing where in a state it is legal to carry arms and at a football match two get into an argument and one draws a pistol and kills the other. It is another thing when two are on a single team, where people are very nervous and where people are not armed and one takes a hold of an axe or a knife and one kills the other in this fashion. For this kind of aggression there is a need to bring perpetrators to take responsibility for such a crime. Those responsible for this should be brought to trial, even if it is their leaders, and this is exactly what happened. They have a moral responsibility to own up to what was done even if they weren't the ones who held the axe or the knife.

We do not consider this or admit to this state of immorality. We do not own up to it. It has nothing to do with our resistance to the state, the authority of the state, or that we contest the law. We just do not believe that this man was elected in a democratic manner through a secret vote!

SO, WHAT WILL HAPPEN NOW? YOU WILL STAY HERE FOR
ONE WEEK MORE, TWO . . . PERHAPS ANOTHER MONTH.
WHAT WILL HAPPEN THEN?

Those of us who have sufficient force continue without thinking about what will happen. Those who believe in what they think and for the ideas that started it all will continue. They have no other choice but to respond to this situation. Those who abandoned their own thinking and do not have sufficient force within them to have the goal to make a permanent demonstration here, they will come every Thursday and every twenty-first of December of every month [times that were reserved by some of the less radical groups to display their opposition to the government]. Those are the largest number of the large manifestations, actually, at the University Square. None of them come here to wait and see how it is going to end. I don't come here to wait to see how it is all going to end. It is going to end somehow. We do not see a final end. We don't know how it is going to end—there is no end in sight. What we hope for is that there will be a dialogue, a dialogue where we will succeed to pay back, to be in a dialogue where we can accuse, to see how they respond to our accusations—with seriousness or not. They will not be able to get around our accusations, and they will have to respond [in a public forum broadcast on television]. We do not want to offend or shock the population through what we do, but to raise this information, these issues, to the level of the nation [state].

HOW WILL THIS OCCUR?
HOW DO YOU THINK THIS WILL OCCUR?

At one point, the government accepted this discussion [that this discussion would take place], but they had certain conditions: with doors closed, all closed off, and with a stenographer. That is to say, the government would be prepared to go into a room with the representatives of the demonstrators of the University Square. There they would discuss, perhaps play a hand of "skeptic"—it would not matter what happens. People would hold onto what they said and wanted. They would be able to do what they wished. No one would know what really happened—the truth. We don't want to do this. We want to have the presence of the radio and television and independent people, and independent people of the press who would assist in this dialogue. But they didn't accept this form of dialogue. They don't want to accept the popularity of this dialogue. They refused this modality of this dialogue with the press, television, and radio. Only on the basis of a stenographer. You see, under these conditions, those who represent the participants of the manifestation didn't think this would make any sense, to have a dialogue with closed doors. If a dialogue takes place, then it has to take place within the framework I outlined so that people could participate in it. A person could turn on the TV and see the dialogue take place, a dialogue that would take place with patience so that all the problems (issues) could be discussed. Each day needs to be discussed with summaries and responses from all the parties. Each day a new problem arose and so needs to be discussed, each day new situations had to be faced. This has to be illuminated.

NOW SUMMER IS APPROACHING AND
THE STUDENTS WILL GO HOME

Yes, the students from the provinces will go home, but don't forget that the students from Bucharest have to complete their terms, so the number of students will be the same. The fact is that it isn't the students who represent the majority of people here. In any given day there are a lot of students here. This is true. But for the most part, here are workers. Here are simple people. This just happened. No one planned it.

COULD YOU CREATE A CHRONOLOGY OF THE EVENTS OF THE REVOLUTION
THAT TOOK PLACE, BUT IN RELATIONSHIP TO YOU AND YOUR OWN LIFE?
WHAT HAPPENED TO YOU AND HOW DID YOU THINK ABOUT THE EVENTS?
WHERE DID YOU GO FROM THE TIME BEFORE TIMISOARA AND AFTER?

Yes. We were prepared! I think a lot of (very many) people were prepared for the start of the revolution.

HOW DO YOU MEAN PREPARED?

In the first place with the internal situation, which was insupportable. There was a burning here in this country as we heard what was going on in East Europe from our own broadcasts and I won't even mention the foreign broadcasts from Voice of America and Radio Free Europe, which all are listening to even now. They presented daily reports. This incited us. The international political context in which we were involved, the processes of democratization that started in the countries around us couldn't bring us to any other situation except to get our population to the point that we now know about.

For us the movement in Timisoara did not catch us by surprise. It was a release for us, a breath of fresh air in an environment that we couldn't take any more. On the thirteenth of December my greeting to friends was "Jos Ceauşescu" [Down with Ceauşescu]. I felt that he only had a few days left and I was convinced that he would not experience the new year. We waited for the important evenings—the evening of Christmas, the evening of December thirtieth. Something had to happen. Something that would bring us all out into the street—so that we could see each other, meet each other, to sing, so that we would feel a tie among us all, to feel a force, to enter the street at that moment so that all activities would cease and a general strike would start. I did not imagine the protest under the form that it took place. I imagined a passive protest. Being in the street, without shouting, not doing anything to be in the face of these people [the leaders], in the face of an economy that had stopped, in a country that does not produce anything, to decide what to do since not even they would be eating. So the events in Timisoara occurred precisely when we had a need for them. I personally did not leave the radio. I was listening to Radio Free Europe when it started to transmit from seven p.m. until four a.m. Until four in the morning I would listen to the radio.

WERE YOU AT HOME?

What?! I didn't go to school again. I wasn't even interested in school, the fact is that vacation had started. Immediately vacation was announced. The eighteenth was the last day of school. The students from the provinces were effectively gone. They represented a danger in Bucharest. There were too many of them and they were sent home and in the last few days they were given cold food at lunchtime so that they would go to the cantina in the evening and so that they would leave after lunch.

I waited for things to start in Bucharest. I went out into the street at lunchtime, in the morning, at night. I felt the tension in the air. I could feel the tension from the people who were in the street. It was impossible to get fifty people together, perhaps you could get ten around you. I am not exaggerating! There were an extraordinarily large number of patrols. Every hundred meters, there were two Miliţia [police] and two

Patriotic Guards with machine guns on their backs. Similarly, the Miliția had machine guns on their backs. Two Miliţias and two Patriotic Guards. Always two and two and they would patrol the larger streets. The smaller streets they didn't bother with—but neither did groups form there. You couldn't anyway. No organizations were formed by us [before the revolution] because the Securitate was so strong and pervasive. You wouldn't risk getting caught by one of them because it would be like getting caught by the devil. There were never groups of more than ten to twenty people who knew one another. We were all waiting for something that would unite us, bring us together. Such a day was offered to us by Ceaușescu on the day of December twenty-first. On the day of the twenty-first, I listened to Radio Free Europe, just like I had done before. I listened until four a.m. in the morning. I cried over the sequence of the shooting that took place in Timişoara. You felt like your heart would break. Your hair would stand on end. It was a fantastic moment.

When I found out that people were gathering at the Piața Regala— that's what I call it—in front of the CC [Central Committee] for that meeting and people were not shouting and not whistling, I knew that the manifestation was starting. No contesting current had formulated itself, as yet. I couldn't believe it. So I got myself dressed and thought to myself, I am going to go over there and if I am the first to shout *Jos Ceaușescu* it doesn't matter. In any case, I was convinced that others would shout it, too. It was impossible to think that it wouldn't happen. I didn't have any doubts but that was how it would be, how great that would be. So as I walked to the center—it is about fifteen minutes from my house—the manifestation, in fact, had already started. Later, I saw the interruption of the live broadcast on TV, with the whistling with women's laughter, and so on. Torn posters and banners, his picture torn and thrown down on the ground.

WERE YOU ALONE?

Yes, I left alone, but I got into a maxi taxi and accidentally I met with three of my colleagues from the Polytechnic University who had the same intentions of getting to the manifestation and so we arrived as a group at the manifestation. Initially I was with the group from the Romana. I stayed there until about three o'clock, until the fire fighters doused us with water and the police arrived with protective gear, brought in to capture the demonstrators. When I saw that the number of the Miliția was increasing and were coming with the same intention, I understood that something would happen and I ran away by going behind the buildings and came here to the university. There were many more people here and they [the Miliția] couldn't do anything about it.

Perhaps twenty thousand people collected at that time in a fantastic atmosphere. We shouted with great force. I made myself hoarse. For six days I couldn't make a sound. My throat was paralyzed. We all shouted with all the force we had in our lungs. We all shouted—I don't remember what we shouted. The entire world knows what we were shouting then. In any case, at this time we were not shouting Down with Communism. I admit this with honesty, we did not shout *jos communismu!* because of a strategy that we all felt was proper. We didn't want those around Ceauşescu to unite themselves around the Central Committee and to make themselves of one mind. We shouted *jos Ceauşescu* to disassociate him from them. But in the morning when we took the Central Committee, the first thing we did, those who were there first, was to shatter the inscription *Sa Traiasca Partidul Comunist Roman* [Long Live the Communist Party]. It was smashed by their feet. Our attitude toward the Communists was clear. There is material evidence as to our sentiments against the party and the character of the revolution. Because it was said they shouted or did not shout—this does not represent evidence. The fact is that the placards were broken immediately and this demonstrates the anti-Communist character of the revolution. There were about ten who broke it with their feet and the entire square applauded them. By the twenty-first I stayed until I felt too tired to stay on my feet. There was an accident here [in University Square] where a truck ran into the crowd. I think that the driver lost control over the vehicle because the truck hit soldiers as well. I felt that something would happen, and I told those who were in front of me to retreat toward the university so that we wouldn't be the ones to suffer the consequences. Those in front of me were convinced that they would not be shot at. They felt that the soldiers wouldn't have the courage to shoot at a population of two million people because they would make "cabbage" [mincemeat] out of them. I didn't believe this. I retreated; in five minutes they started to shoot. They were shooting and I ran here and there. A group would gather and we would shout. Trucks came shooting water. There was an atmosphere of chaos. I went home to eat and to drink some water. I had not rested—I didn't even have a glass of water to drink. My girlfriend and my mother forbade me to return. They knew they were shooting. They locked the door.

WHAT DID YOU THINK ABOUT THE ARMY AT THIS TIME?

I knew that those soldiers of the army just like those of the Securitate who were simply banal people who were taken to complete their tours of duty. Even if they shot, they did not shoot for the pleasure of shooting. They followed orders. No one among the soldiers shot with a clean conscience. I know that the cadre of the Securitate did it even with pleasure. I refer to the officers with a high rank; people who were loyal to Ceauşescu, who knew who it was that had helped them as orphans. I had known such people for a long time. Those were the people I was afraid of, who would shoot—and this they did, too. On the twenty-second I couldn't leave for home. I left before dinner. I was at work at about five thirty in the morning at the university. It was very hard and full of emotions until the army allowed us to get on top of the tanks. That's when we knew we would win. That is when a part of the army was with us, we were overcome with a fantastic courage. The assault we were able to carry out on the transports in the last zone near the CC was much more intense and firm. Resistance declined much more rapidly than when fighting took place with the tanks. Information about General Milea's death reached us. I was among the first to enter the CC when the doors were broken down. I stayed until they started to talk on the microphone. I was surprised because I had awaited a discussion that was much more to the point and with an object in mind. People were deliriously happy about Ceauşescu's fall, that Ceauşescu had escaped with a helicopter. We were free. They said nothing concrete. I found it tasteless and I lost my enthusiasm. What happened there? People fought over the microphone to talk to the twenty to twenty-two million people who were listening. I felt a need to leave, and that's what I did. With very great difficulty, I succeeded in pushing my way through the crowd, which was so extraordinarily tight. So I went home. I was sure that hard fighting would break out. Ceauşescu had not been captured yet. In fact, fighting had already broken out. Others, behind the scene began to assert their interests. These were manipulating the army to create theater in the street.

Notes

I am grateful to the Soviet and East European Studies Program of Cornell University and the New York State College of Human Ecology for funding research that led to this paper. I am equally grateful to Marianne A. Cocchini for recommending David Apter's book on development (1987) and helping to make this essay clearer and more concise. David Kideckel made extensive remarks on an earlier version. I am grateful for his insights. An earlier version of this paper, but without the oral account, appeared in *Socialism and Democracy* (1991).

1. I make this distinction because the events in Romania and the manner in which a Communist leadership took over the reins of the state and has attempted to manage the shift in political economy from above is more like the political shift that was experienced in Southeastern Europe (the Balkans)

than the changes in Central Europe. I do not believe that the normal journalistic explanation of "Balkan traditions" or the "absence of democratic traditions" is adequate to describe or explain the events and processes in the Balkans. In fact such a formulation of the problem disguises the forces that are generating autocratic rule. In order to understand what is happening, we must seek the answers in the intersection of the social relations of Romanian life with the political economic forces that tie the country to the global context in which the events are situated.

2. The internal enemy played itself out in relationship to Romania's Gypsy population, whose social place within the Romanian state is more often than not seen as dubious if not downright hostile (see Beck 1989). During the Ceausescuite period and after the events of December 22, Gypsies have experienced what they are referring to as "pogroms" against them. They refer to the organized attempts to drive them out of their communities and other violent actions aimed at them as a pariah population (Avem Amentz, Romale 1990; Mihalache 1990; Radu 1990). Between January and October of 1990, the Democratic Romani Union of Romania documented a total of fourteen Romani settlements all over the country that have suffered violent attacks against their inhabitants.

3. It was not a secret. The demonstrators, if given the chance, would have grilled him on live television. Furthermore, no one has found an explanation for how and why Iliescu and the members of his group who made up the transition team found themselves in what turned out to be the most strategic building during the days of the revolution, the television station.

4. It is no accident that the intellectuals in the opposition banded together as members of the Group for Social Dialogue. Dialogue serves the interests of democratization.

5. The violence associated with Ceauşescu and that which was being ascribed to Iliescu was a reminder of this continuity, as was the violence perpetrated on the site. For the demonstrators with whom I spoke, the events of December 22 were more important than the demise of Ceauşescu, than the spontaneous rebellion of Timisoara on December 16 and 17. However, Timisoara was not discounted and figured in the accounting of events that led to independent political expression. The resistance to Ceauşescu in Bucharest was the decisive action that brought about his failed escape. The narrative that many of the participants referred to always recounted the bloody details: "People died," they said.

6. With a healthy dose of sarcasm and irony, the demonstrators accepted this epitaph hurled at them by Iliescu as a badge of honor. The demonstrators quickly fashioned signs that they wore on their clothing or around their neck that said, "I am a *golan*."

7. See Vintila Mihailescu's (1990) discussion of all the fears of Romanian citizens in this period of transition.

8. Not the state in its reified form but the state as it is defined, perceived, and experienced by the actions of leaders and those who implement their decisions.

9. It is not an uncommon element of Romany (Gypsy) history that they were often chosen for the most onerous tasks. In Romania's medieval period in Romania, Romanies (Gypsies) cleaned up the dead animals in settlements where they resided or acted as the hangmen of a town or city. That they cleaned up after the spilling of blood, then, is not surprising and reinforces

their dubious role in Romanian society, supporting the predisposition of Romanians to despise (and fear) the Gypsies.
10. According to Pavel Campeanu, "The reason for the Group's existence is the replacement of violence, as a negation of the very human substance, with dialogue, as a substance of democracy" (1990, 729).

References

Apter, D. 1987. *Rethinking development: Modernization, dependency, and postmodern politics*. Beverly Hills: Sage.

Avem Amentza, R. 1990. *Publicatie a romilor din Romania*. No. 2.

Beck, S. 1989. "The origins of gypsy slavery in Romania." *Dialectical Anthropology* 14:53–61.

———. 1991. "What Brought Romanians to Revolt." *Critique of Anthropology* 11(1):59–71.

———. 1991. "Toward a Civil Society: The Struggle over University Square in Bucharest, Romania, June 1990." *Socialism and Democracy* 13:135–154.

Campeanu, P. 1990. "The comfort of despair." *Social Research* 57(3):719–732.

Elias, N. 1988. "Violence and civilization." in *Civil society and the state: New European perspectives*, ed. J. Keane. 177–198. London: Verso Press.

Freire, P. 1970. *The pedagogy of the oppressed*. New York: Seabury Press.

Gailey, W. C. 1987. "Culture wars: Resistance to state formation." in *Power relations and state formation*, eds. T. C. Patterson and W. C. Gailey. Washington, DC: Archeology Section, American Anthropology Association. 35–56.

Galtung, J. 1974. *Structural theory of revolutions*. Rotterdam, Netherlands: University Press.

Hunt, K. 1990. "Letter from Bucharest". *The New Yorker* 66(July 23):74–82.

Keane, J. 1988. "Despotism and Democracy." in *Civil society and the state: New European perspectives*, ed. J. Keane. 35–71. London: Verso.

Kligman, G. 1990. "Reclaiming the public: A reflection on recreating civil society in Romania." *East European Politics and Societies* 4(3):393–439.

Melucci, A. 1988. "Social movements and the democratization of everyday life." in *Civil society and the state*, ed. J. Keane. 245–260. London: Verso.

Mihailescu, V. 1990. "The politics of 'scapegoat' in Romania." Conference of the Anthropology of Politics in Post-Communist Europe, Zaborow, Poland, September 29–October 4.

Mihalche, A. 1990. "Agresiune sau raspuns la agresiune" (Aggression or a response to aggression). *Romania Libera* (October 30):3a.

Paler, O. 1990. "The Romanian elections: A dangerous victory." *Uncaptive Minds* 3(3):11–12.

Radu, D. 1990. "Pogromul din comuna Mihail Kogalniceanu" (The pogrom of Mihail Kogalniceanu). *Opinia Studenteasca* (No. 7):1.

The Wingless Eros of Socialism: Nationalism and Sexuality in Hungary

LASZLO KÜRTI

Jeffrey Weeks, in his seminal work *Sexuality and its Discontents*, suggests that "there is . . . no simple relationship between 'sex' and 'society' . . . the mediating elements are words and attitudes, ideas and social relations" (1985, 4). If we are to analyze the intersections among gender, sexuality, and state ideology, we will, I suggest, benefit from a closer examination of the powerful popular nationalistic ideology, parading in the mantle of democracy, that binds men to be providers and women to remain reproducers. As anthropologists have shown, sexual and local identities fluctuate in accordance with changes in the international scene while remaining attached to dominant paradigms of cultural knowledge, nationalism, and state interests (Lamphere 1986, 127–129; Moore 1988, 183–185; Strathern 1988, 317–319). It is curious that notions of sexuality, love, and gender appear to have coalesced to form a cultural paradigm in the imaginings of Hungarian society during the 1950s, owing no doubt to what Benedict Anderson calls *official* nationalism (1983, 144). By the time state socialism had been delegitimized, it was replaced by *popular* nationalism, but with the strikingly similar separation of traditional sex roles; moreover, the redomestication of women and the redivision of labor were refitted to the "needs" of the new nation-state. The creation of a new utopia, that is to say, a modern European and democratic Hungarian society, is concomitant with a new ideology based on the biological imperatives of sex that espouses the "natural" and "traditional" place of women in the home, the family, and in their reproductive role as mothers (Rogers 1980, 12–15).

Alexandra Kollontai's essays on sexuality in Communist society written in the 1920s invite contemporary reflection on the application of her ideas to working men and women in Hungary, long considered the most progressive nation of the former Communist East bloc. In retrospect, forty years of socialism and the world of workers provide a dynamic social laboratory for assessing the validity of Kollontai's vision of the transformation of eros, sexual relations, and gender roles. My

266

anthropological fieldwork in Hungary during the 1980s convinced me that the convergences and disparities between Kollontai's vision and contemporary Hungarian sexual politics are striking. For at the heart of today's realities lies a contradiction: On the one hand, pronatalism encourages biological and cultural reproduction of Hungarians, while on the other, the emergence of a democratic, civil society and a liberal conception of gender roles advocates freedom from the pressure to reproduce.[1]

The complexity of these issues is perplexing for anthropologists, accustomed as we are to isolating cultural notions of gender, ethnicity, and national movements. In attempting to reconcile these notions, recent scholarship has rekindled contemporary interest in gender, ethnic, and national identities, interrogating Western models from cross-cultural perspectives (Inglis 1989; Jayawardena 1986; Kapferer 1988; Kikumura 1986; Mosse 1988).[2] Such endeavors have shifted the scope of inquiry from previously dominant epistemic paradigms of sexuality and race to a more holistic, integrative investigation of the ways in which nationality defines and/or manipulates relations of sexuality and gender relations and consciousness. In this chapter I analyze the convergence of nationality and sexuality by focusing on notions of love and gender identity in contemporary Hungary. I begin with an overview of Kollontai's views, proceeding to interpret them first in light of the working-class eros of the 1950s and second, that of the 1980s. Next, I consider the implications of these findings for anthropologists studying the intersections of nationalist ideologies and gender relations.[3]

HISTORICAL BACKGROUND

In comparison with small-scale tribal societies or multinational capitalist states, the nation-states of the East bloc, the former "existing socialisms," were unique social experiments, first conceived and later founded through revolutionary movements and a tyrannical, central control of both economy and society in the shadow of the Soviet Big Brother. Both in their embryonic theoretical stages and as implemented social policy, East European versions of socialism—the "moribund utopias" of the Czech writer Milan Simecka (1984, 170)—aimed to erase social differentiation and to eliminate remnants of the bourgeois past. As socialists, Soviet bloc nations were thus to be classless, stateless, homogeneous in ethnic composition, and to guarantee equal status for all by eliminating private property, socializing the means of production, and providing a fair and equitable system of redistribution (Wilczynski 1982, 2–3).

The realization of this model was to have been achieved through the creation of an internationally conscious proletariat, a class of workers united in its unrelenting construction of socialism. This "fetishism of the working class" (Berki 1975, 110), reached its apex in the Soviet Union in the 1920s and 1930s.[4] According to Pavel Campeanu, the new working class was called upon to fulfill three preponderant roles: revolutionary vanguard, agent of management and ownership, and productive force (1988, 53–54). The proletariat, then, was to be led by the Communist party, a trained elite guard whose mission it was to serve as well as guide the people.[5]

Just as other utopias reject the morality of an existing order, so too did the Communist utopia envision its foundations as resting not on the former bourgeois system of production and cultural values but rather on the new pillars of Communist society. Antagonistic relationships between the sexes were seen as a remnant of the bourgeois, capitalist past; the state sought to replace them with harmonious, balanced contact among the working masses. Emphasizing differences between "bourgeois" and "Communist" love and sexuality, and caught up in the revolutionary spirit following the civil war in the Soviet Union, Kollontai characterized bourgeois gender and family relations as at once individualistic, isolated, and promiscuous. In a seminal essay, "Make Way for Winged Eros," she criticizes bourgeois morality for its narrow definition of love:

> Love is permissible only when it is within marriage. Love outside legal marriage is considered immoral. Such ideas were often dictated, of course, by economic considerations, by the desire to prevent the distribution of capital among illegitimate children. The entire morality of the bourgeoisie was directed towards the concentration of capital. (1977, 284)

Kollontai elaborates on this phenomenon by discussing the difference between the bourgeois "wingless eros,"the unadorned sexual drive, and a more desirable "winged eros." The former, based as it is only on "unhealthy carnality," she contends, serves only the interest of the ruling classes in capitalist society. "Winged eros" is absent in this society in which emotional ties and biological drives are separated, leading men to desiring ("lusting for") other women and fostering prostitution as well as perversion (1977, 286).

In the utopian "new world" of her dream, on the contrary, men and women would enjoy a camaraderie based on love and work, channeling desire into communal activity rather than "excessive" conduct outside of marriage. In this society love is defined not narrowly in the sexual sense but as "an emotion that unites and is consequently of an organizing character. . . . [It] can and must play [a role], not in strengthening family-marriage ties, but in the development of collective solidarity" (1977, 285).

The Communist "winged eros" of Kollontai was to have liberated both men and women from the traditional bonds of gender roles and sexual identities, transforming selfish economic exchange into comradely, collective love. Moreover, such eros should "facilitate the triumph of the ideal of love-comradeship" (1977, 288), a basis that prompts the proletariat to seek attachment not only among lovers, friends, and relatives but, equally important, among workers of the collective in general. Thus tamed, the Communist eros of her future would satisfy individual needs while serving the common good. "Wingless eros" should be controlled, for it is excessive and results in physical and mental exhaustion, which reduces both individual and collective energy for labor, energy that should be utilized for building the future Communist state.

In Kollontai's utopian proletarian state, the new working-class morality recognizes love as both a psychological and social force, a new eros uniting humans both in production and reproduction. In order for this life force to succeed, it must acquire new inner qualities "necessary to the builders of a new culture—sensitivity, responsiveness and the desire to help others" (Kollontai 1977, 289). In the development of proletarian love-comradeship these qualities should, however, conform to three basic ideological principles: (1) to end masculine egoism and the suppression of female personality, equality in relationships must be achieved; (2) to abandon the principle of property in sexual relationships and recognize the couple's individuality; and (3) to maintain a "comradely sensitivity" and the ability to listen to and understand one another, a requirement demanded only of the woman in bourgeois society.

The ultimate goal is thus to overcome individualism by subordinating the personal and subjective eros to the "more powerful emotion of love-duty to the collective" in order to enhance cohesion and happiness among the people. At the same time, the "winged eros" should provide a new socialist identity for both men and women.

THE MAKING OF COLLECTIVE LOVE

After World War II, to assure production and the payment of reparations—Hungary was required to pay $300 million compensation on account of its wartime alliance with Germany—state intervention in all aspects of industry was introduced, and state control was fully established throughout the economy by 1948. The weight of this burden motivated the radical reforms enacted by the new Communist leadership of Hungary. As a result of Stalinist policies of rapid central-ized planning, industrial centers such as Csepel, Sztálinváros, Diósgyör, Tatabánya, and others became small replicas of the emerging socialist state, as greater numbers of young men and women flocked to heavy industry from the countryside. Because of their former "red" heritage and their speedy recovery after the war, these cities were hailed as models for socialist reconstruction. Targeted for special state support, they received primary status in industrial relations and boasted a work force earning well above the national average.

Their unique status quo during the Rákosi era from 1948 to 1956 helped bring into being the new socialist man and woman, the "socialist person" so eagerly sought by the Stalinist state.[6] As in other Soviet bloc societies, the presocialist sense of national identity was muted or repressed, only to be replaced by a contemporary "socialist proletarian consciousness" and "proletarian internationalism." In the vanguard of this newly invented tradition were the Stakhanovites, young men and women, mostly of poor blue-collar or peasant backgrounds, laboring to produce dramatically *beyond* established quotas. These "model workers" were fashioned after Soviet patterns of the 1930s, not without the influence of the American scientific work-management of Taylorism (Shlapentokh 1988).

The creation of these new workers paralleled the new Communist party ideology that eschewed "love" and "camaraderie" for the greater good of "internationalism" and the Soviet Union. A popular joke of the time tells of a teacher who announces to her pupils that the class in sex education will not be discussing sex between men and women, the heterosexual relationship, because students know all about that. Nor, she says, will the class discuss sex between people of the same gender, a homosexual relationship, because students know about that too. In-stead, the class will take up a different form of sex: the great love between Hungary and the Soviet Union.

This Stalinist nation-state was legitimized as a "workers' state" whose leaders acquired mythical proportions. Both Hungarian party chief Matyas Rákosi and Stalin were idolized as "fathers," inspiring numer-ous novels, poems, films, songs, and posters describing their heroic deeds for the "socialist patria."[7] According to one slogan: *Rákosi a legjobb apa, szereti is minden fia* (Rákosi is the best father to all his country's sons). A common joke during the height of Rákosi's reign targeted the succession of conjugal systems: First there was matriarchy, then patriarchy took its place, and in Communist society both are replaced by the Communist secretary.[8]

This ideological transformation can be read anthropologically as the

Stakhanovite masculinization of Hungarian culture, which rejuvenated industrial production and fostered the implementation of social policies. The educational system was restructured, and vocational training received the lion's share of state support, thereby encouraging young men and women to seek industrial occupations and to move to centrally planned "new towns." Propagandistic slogans, repeated elsewhere in Eastern Europe, proclaimed: *Tied az ország, magadnak épited*, "This country is yours, you are building it for yourselves," or *Elöre a szocialista haza épitéséért*, "Forward for the construction of our socialist homeland." In contrast to the model workers, peasants were considered antirevolutionary, retrograde, and nationalistic, suffering forced collectivization, resettlement, and second-class status. The formation of a new working class, then, overlapped and crosscut that of national identity.[9]

Equally extraordinary were the measures taken to curtail women's rights, sexual practices, and family life, and the general subordination of women to men concomitant with the solidification of a masculine gender model. Foucault's observation that the modern state attempts to regulate a specific sexual discourse (1980, 33–34) is applicable to socialist states as well, where constraints were placed on fecundity and reproductive behavior. Young males and females were viewed as essentially masculinized workers, an image reinforced by the blue overalls so visible in the media of the 1950s, and aided by the ungendered Hungarian language.[10] Their individualistic desires and sexual pleasures—the "bourgeois wingless eros" of Kollontai —were thought to require taming. The newly conjured citizen of the socialist state was to replace the selfish, egotistic, bourgeois personality. Women were to bear children for Rákosi's "homeland"; *Asszonynak szulni kotelesseg, lanynak dicsoseg*—"For a married woman to bear a child is obligation, for a girl, it is honor"—according to still another slogan. Such mothers were identified as progressive and socialist, receiving maternity leaves, supplementary consumer goods, and "multiple-child bonuses." Abortion was outlawed, childless families were forced to pay a surtax, and contraception was available only in extreme circumstances in the progression toward a Communist utopia. At the same time, women were encouraged to be educated—often only at the Marxist-Leninist High School of the Communist party—and to take an active role in politics. A national women's party was created (following the earlier Soviet pattern of the *zhenotdel*) to address the needs of all women in Hungary. Known as the Hungarian Women's National Council (MNOT), this organization played a supportive role but eventually became overbureaucratized and politicized, lacking any real lasting social impact or efficacy.

These ideological and economic incentives and pressures were extremely successful: To date there have been only three years during which Hungary achieved a population boom—1952, 1953, 1954—when children (like myself) were called "Ratko kids" after the Stalinist minister of health, Anna Ratkó. The demographic changes during the early 1950s are instructive indices of Stalinist redefinitions of gender roles and the ways in which these patriarchal tendencies simultaneously undermined and elevated the status of women. It may be argued that the Rákosi regime and the Communist party had embarked upon a monstrous course of irrationality in its quest for target plans and quotas in industrial production. The perverse connection between the "number crunching" strategies deployed both for factory production and the womb served the state's utopian goal: the creation of a Communist nation-state of Hungary.

We must not fail to note, however, that, in addition to these benefits and monetary incentives, the reasons for the success of state ideology were manifold and complex. They include, among others, the traumatic experiences of Hungarian young men and women growing up in a war-torn country with enormous losses both in lives and material goods; and the presence of state terror, in particular after the show trials of 1948, which launched a massive campaign not only against rich kulaks, bourgeois sympathizers, and former intellectuals but, equally important, against all those identified as class enemies. Rural, blue-collar, and white-collar youth, for example, were thought by the party to be dangerous on account of both their inclination toward Western values and goods and their ambiguously defined symbolic status: the working class of the future.

The effectiveness of Stalinist state ideology in creating a concomitant social practice was based on three additional criteria: first, the presence of Big Brother (the Soviet Union and Stalin himself) forcing millions to submit; second, a new atmosphere following the death of Stalin in which citizens began to question state leaders and state policies; and third, the lack of significant opposition to the state—which came, ultimately, in the guise of the Hungarian revolution of 1956—to facilitate the creation of an alternative platform and develop an antistate political discourse. Thus, the question of the reasons for the success of the Rakosi regime's policies among Hungarian women and men must be answered in light of the social realities of the Stalinist period between 1948 and 1956.[11]

THE MAKING OF INDIVIDUAL LOVE

It should be recalled that the immense changes brought to Soviet society in the 1920s with regard to women's rights, divorce, and the "new morality" had almost entirely disappeared in less than ten years (Reich 1970; Farnsworth 1980). In Hungary, too, Stalinism and the winged eros were not to endure, although certain ideas survived their makers. After the suppressed revolution of 1956, the reorganization of industrial relations went hand in hand with Hungary's delayed reentry into the international capitalist world market (Berend 1965). As a result, following the failed New Economic Mechanism of 1968, large industrial enterprises were dissolved into independent factories and the tightly centralized political structure was gradually abandoned in favor of a more flexible "socialist market-oriented economy" (Berend and Ranki 1985).[12] By the late 1970s and early 1980s, a crisis was emerging. On the one hand, Hungarian society was slowly liberalized and westernized, while on the other, for the first time in the socialist era, industrial complexes lacked state funding, blue-collar jobs were devalued, and unemployment rose. The once enormous industrial labor force had disappeared within a few years. A massive flight of blue-collar workers from heavy industry into the service economy and information technology took place, a trend that was to become the rule throughout Hungary.

In the wake of this industrial reorganization—a period that coincided with the "intensive period of socialist economy" characterized by chronic labor shortage (Kornai 1982, 109)—a new cultural attitude became apparent toward work, the state, and sexuality, emphasizing security in the labor market and within the family. Both at home and in the workplace, men identified so closely with the second economy that being a breadwinner was tantamount to holding an additional job. "You gotta work fourteen hours to keep your family alive," lamented a mechanic among those I interviewed. With the new technology, skilled male workers became a desirable commodity, and competition in the labor market marked a new beginning. As men became more competitive, taking well-paying jobs in addition to those in the second economy, young women, especially those with little or no occupational flexibility, were marginalized. Their pauperization meant not only decreasing opportunities for well-paying jobs, but in the symbolic realm, they were relegated to a second-class status. This new feminine stereotyping was rationalized in popular humor by a rather cynical joke defining a "modern woman" as carrying shopping bags under her right arm and a crying baby under her left, her drunken husband staggering behind her as she gazes forward to the next five-year plan.

By the mid-1980s, under the sway of the liberalized economy, shifts were extended and skilled workers, technicians, and young workers with vocational diplomas were drawn further into the flourishing second economy. The newly acquired and updated Western machinery—primarily computerized machine tools and information technology—became the fetishized objects of this technological revolution. In turn, both emerged as quintessential masculine properties. The dirtied, smoke-filled, noisy shop floors; pinup posters decorating the machines; and the sexual language of working gestures only hint at the misogyny of industrial life that the British sociologist Paul Willis (1981) has called "shop-floor masculinity."[13] Whereas for youth these jobs were not sufficient—"not snazzy enough," as they put it—the male bias associated with them survived into the new era.

In this atomized and constantly fluctuating male-ruled labor force, men remained hesitant to work with women in blue-collar jobs, relegating them either to janitorial or semiskilled tasks such as crane operation. They spoke of *férfi munka* (manly work) as heavy/hard (*nehéz* in Hungarian means both), important, and "true" labor, whereas woman's work was seen by males primarily as "soft," marginal, and confined to "lighter" administrative areas. At the same time, women's reproductive roles were facilitated by the more relaxed state ideology: Although abortion committees remained in place—a remnant of the Ratkó era—the 1973 decision of the Council of Ministers identified ten legal social and health reasons required of a woman requesting abortion. As one of my informants glibly stated, "to get an abortion is as easy as getting an ice-cream cone." Furthermore, after 1974 sexual education became a part of elementary school curricula; by the late 1970s, women were allowed to take leave for up to three years to raise a child. By the late 1980s, there were no more abortion committees and paid maternity leaves (GYED and GYES in Hungarian) rose from 141,000 in 1970 to 241,000 in 1989, resulting not in more births—as the state planners had wished—but rather in fewer (KSH 1990, 24). These policies did, however, limit women's equal participation in the labor force and, subsequently, their progress in the managerial and industrial hierarchy.

The reemergence of these values and the restructuring of social relations were coterminous with popular sentiment desiring national security and the reassessment of a new, non-Communist Hungarian national identity. In the wake of liberalized Hungarian-Soviet relations and the resurgence of antagonism between Hungary and Romania over the fate of Hungarian minorities living there, a new Hungarianness was consolidated by the elite opposition. In everyday parlance, gender and national identities were fused into a heterogenous yet interconnected discourse quite unlike that of the Stakhanovites. Love, friendship, sexuality, and nationality acquired new meanings. As distinct from the early 1950s, among blue-collar working youth, love and friendship became two distinct entities. Love, whether parental or peer, was hailed as a private matter. "You love your parents, your children and spouse," commented a worker. Few youthful workers expressed "love" for the state or the Hungarian Socialist Workers' Party (MSZMP), the Communist party or its youth guard, both of which faced serious decreases in membership by the late 1980s; and no love was lost between them and the neighboring East European states, especially Romania.

For the new technologically oriented male working class, modernity meant strength, speed, individual careers, and opposition to state and Communist party ideology; at the same time, values and ideas connected to the old system became outdated as well as unnecessary. As the Ratko kids matured and the opposition slowly acquired strength through its gatherings, rallies, and *samizdat* publications, sharp distinctions between love-sexuality and friendship-camaraderie were also created. Kollontai's original vision of the winged eros among youth "in relation to all members of the collective" has clearly *not* been realized in Hungary. On the contrary, individualism, open material advancement, and personal gratification in the real as well as the symbolic realms have been identified as the ideal qualities of progress; or, in the case of males, true manliness. As the resurrected hero, Imre Nagy, received his state burial on June 16, 1989, Hungarian youth were given public reassurance of their socialization into a different nonsocialist, national ideology based on a new masculine role model and sexual symbolism: that of the father, the fighter, the martyr. Through this symbolic inversion—from János Kádár, the impotent, dying Communist leader to Imre Nagy, the potent, resurrected national hero—the emerging proponents of nationalistic ideology achieved what forty years of Communist indoctrination could not: They regained the allegiance of Hungary's youth by overthrowing the government in a peaceful revolution. Indeed, the "velvet revolution" of Vaclav Havel was played out in Hungary as a Greek tragedy. In this revolution, the wife of Imre Nagy, often caricatured as the "nation's widow," the heroes of the 1956 revolution, and the dispossessed as well as repressed masses were resurrected. Their reunion was achieved through their paternal culture hero Nagy, who led them symbolically in their struggle to overthrow the Communist regime and to create a new Republic of Hungary.[14]

With this ritual resurrection, heterosexual images, codes, and behavior were transfigured into a dominant mode of discourse, just as they were in Hungary's presocialist past. Women, married or single, were offered yet another model for continuing to live under the constraints of prevailing male-dominated sexual politics. By the end of 1989, Budapest, under the spell of democratic renewal and technological advancement, boasted over a thousand joint East-West ventures as well as sex shops, sex clinics, and the first legally operating brothels in Eastern Europe.[15]

The concepts of the Communist Homo politicus and "free souls"—articulated desires of the early feminist theorists—are now at an even greater remove from present-day morality than before World War II. Awakened by these profound alterations, turning toward Western styles of popular culture, working youth have found themselves trapped between nationalist drives and dreams promulgated by the Western media cultures by which they measure themselves.

Most Hungarian critics of the socialist system have agreed that problems of youth, the family, gender inequality, and pronatalist policy are attributable to shortcomings in the socialist system. Or, as Milan Simečka has argued, in socialism "there is an eternal tension between the utopian promises of the past and the caricatured present" (1984, 170). The problems were obvious: repression of political dissent; a tightly centralized planning system resulting in what János Kornai calls "shortage economy"; failure of a balanced redistribution of goods and resources; and the creation of what the Hungarian sociologist Elemér Hankiss has termed "second society" and "second consciousness" (1990).[16]

The search for theoretical solutions to the conflicts that disrupted family life, forced ethnic Hungarians to flee from neighboring Romania, and created sexually repressed workaholics was in vogue and strongly encouraged by emerging oppositional factions after 1988. Though the search was atomized and fragmented since its inception—clear dividing lines can be discerned, for example, between the stands of the Free Democrats (SZDSZ) and the Young Democrats (FIDESZ) and the Democratic Forum (MDF)—such assumptions nevertheless suggested a reconfiguration of the pairing of nationalism and sexuality. Nationalism and its cultural variants of populism (in Hungarian *népi mozgalom*) fed early attempts of "democratization" and "liberalization" on the part of center-right oppositional movements. This ideological position has been especially noticeable in the program of the Hungarian Democratic Forum.[17]

Since the beginning of 1988, when the Kádár government was replaced with the more liberal Grosz government, protagonists of the opposition movement rejected communism as a foreign political, economic, and ideological tyranny over their nation-state. The Communist party-state was also singled out for its "debasement" of women by placing them at odds with their traditional roles, thus jeopardizing their reproductive function. We have only to recall recently published statements of the Hungarian Democratic Forum (MDF), once one of the most powerful oppositional groups in the vanguard of the Hungarian opposition and a clear winner of the March 1990 elections. In its first legal congress, in 1989, the following amendment was unanimously passed by the membership:

It is most desirable that upon regional elections local organizers of the MDF take into consideration that women, who comprise the majority of society, receive their respective positions in our movement; and, further, that in social policies women—especially mothers who ensure the nation's future—will be granted support and help. (Hungarian Democratic Forum 1989, 51)

An article by Gyula Fekete, Hungary's foremost neopopulist writer (and a former member of the Presidential Council of the ruling Democratic Forum who in 1990 became president of the Hungarian People's party) cries out against the dangers of "mother-killer feminism." He says:

The way I see it, feminism is regressive, anti-evolutionary, and reactionary; mainly because women are forcing upon themselves the norms of masculinity and by doing so are losing their real identity as "women" thus relegating themselves to secondary activities . . . Society should place only as much burden on woman's shoulders as she can easily manage along with her loving and responsible vocation as a mother. (Fekete 1989, 60)

That the Democratic Forum's male chauvinistic agenda struck an extremely responsive chord is clear from subsequent vehement debates in the media concerning women's rights and abortion.

By the beginning of 1990, the Democratic Forum had increased its nationalistic propaganda against women's reproductive rights, arguing that 90,000 abortions in Hungary in the previous year was too high for a country with a decreasing birthrate. While it is true that the number of live births decreased steadily from 151,819 in 1970 to 120,566 in 1989 (KSH 1990, 18), the number of abortions was halved after the 1970s and grew only insignificantly in the late 1980s. The numbers are especially revealing: In 1970, 192,300 abortions were performed, or 7.2 per hundred women. These figures are 80,900, or 3.1, for 1980, and 90,000, or 3.5, for 1989, respectively (see KSH 1990, 20). However, nationalistic propaganda unleashed an enormous energy of patriarchal norms, and other attacks on women followed in rapid succession. In a shocking statement issued by the society Pacem in Utero, influential political, religious, and intellectual *males* signed a five-point declaration, a manifesto exhibiting the kind of extreme conservatism familiar in the United States and in the West where the New Right has gained a political footing.[18] Entitled "Consensus in the Defense of Life," it argues that (1) life begins at conception; (2) abortion is not a solution; (3) prevention is the best way to avoid unwanted pregnancies; (4) instead of abortion, family planning should be encouraged; and (5) the unborn life has legal rights (Sandor 1990, 9). Noteworthy is the fact that with the exception of one small group, Equal Chance, there was no substantial countervailing force voicing its opposition to such developments.[19] Moreover, the pro-choice movement received another serious blow with the appointment of the new minister of welfare of the Christian Democratic People's party, the only party adamantly and explicitly opposed to abortion even before the national elections on March 25, 1990.

The results of the election and the dispossession of women from the political arena provide yet another example of the asymmetrical realignment of gender relations in contemporary "democratic" Hungary. Out of a dozen major contending parties, only the Hungarian Social Democratic party listed a female candidate. Its platform and agenda was equally as reform-minded as those of the more numerous Alliance of Free Democrats, Democratic Forum, or the Smallholders. However, from the start of the election campaign, the Social Democrats and their female leader, Anna Petrasovits, became a target of constant ridicule in the media and in popular parlance. As the only female leader of a party in the political arena, she faced not only inexperience and remnants of the centrally controlled system but, more seriously, bigotry, male bias, and outright sexism. Not surprisingly, the Social Democrats sustained dramatic failure and were unable to secure the minimum number of votes for seats in the new parliament.[20] Consequently, as of 1990 the number of women in the new parliament was well below 9 percent (their actual number is twenty-five), and there were no signs on the horizon that women's participation would be substantially enhanced given the prevailing cultural notions of femininity, masculinity, and the ubiquitous misogyny of the current political climate.[21]

The emergence of multiparty politics, a conservative ideology combined with Western technological assistance, a drive toward Western-style democracy, and a pluralism in religious tolerance has left the Hungarian political scene more vulnerable to the mobilization of conservative power. Simultaneously, social discourse and a gradual redefinition of sexuality and gender roles have suggested a powerful emblem around which this new type of nationalist politics may well coalesce.

In Hungary, where the nationalistic agenda of the government and its ruling party, the Democratic Forum, is still of fundamental moment, defense of the family and traditional gender asymmetry have effectively united the particularist concerns of political factions into a viable religious platform. The repoliticized churches and religious parties seemed to be enacting the assumption that "all of the world's major religions serve as arbiters of moral systems, an important aspect of which is usually sexuality" (Ross and Rapp 1983, 62). Both Catholic and Protestant denominations have been vitally important in the articulation of the new moral agenda and the reformulation of sexual practices. Thus, mobilization in the defense of family and morality and an increase in population growth have become primary emotive rallying points, especially in the party programs of the MDF and the center-of-right parties, the Smallholders and the Christian Democrats.[22] The conservative religious practices and behavior concerning the family, kinship, and marriage that Jack Goody sees in Eurasia continuing throughout history (1990, 465–466), I see as true as well for post-Communist Hungarian and other East-Central European societies. The questions of pro-choice and pro-life that were but a small point of contention in 1988 had by spring 1990, when the new Antall government took office, become an open legal debate in Hungary. The unprecedented—at least since the forced reproduction policies of the Rákosi regime—opening of these issues rekindled a new spirit that cannot fail to hold serious repercussions for the future "democratic utopia" of women's rights, reproductive behavior, and cultural notions of love and sexuality.

Implicit in this new reactionary, or in Peter Alter's terminology "integral," nationalist ideology (1989, 37–38) is the notion that in the future, all current evils will be eliminated once women have fulfilled their primary function, that of motherhood. In this view, it is maintained that eventually a "democratic society" will enable men and women to emerge as partners in both work and love relations. Through the creation of a multiparty system and popular elections and through the elimination of Communist party rule, broken families, spouse-battering, unequal gender status, and problems of youth will be erased once democracy wins over existing socialism. The victory over communism is thus in a sense also a victory over woman; "democracy" in this case comes to represent the abolition of all previous rights and privileges of women in relation to their own bodies, to their unfettered participation in the labor force, to their own lives.

CONCLUSION

In an influential article on the nature of the utopian world, Barbara Goodwin writes:

> The position of women is surprisingly unaffected by economic and social egalitarianisms. . . . Nearly all utopians from Plato onwards recognize implicitly or explicitly that sexuality is a public, not a private, matter, a revelation which leads either to puritanism (which is usually synonymous with severe restrictions on women viewed, as in

the most primitive cultures, as the source of evils which promiscuous sex unleashes) or to curious forms of liberality. (1984, 78–80)

As a committed Marxist and as an ideologue, Alexandra Kollontai maintained that "As the cultural and economic base of humanity changes, so will love be transformed" (1977, 291). While there is little disagreement among researchers that state socialism transformed relations of production, bringing some advances along gender lines in East and Central Europe (Gray 1990; Dolling 1989), it is also recognized that state control of economy and central planning—characteristics of the socialist utopia—created unforeseen difficulties for working men and women, old and young alike. Among the gravest was the problem of working-class and gender identities. Iván Szelényi, a Hungarian sociologist and a staunch critic of the system, argues that "In state socialist societies . . . the worker is deprived not only of the products of his labor, but also of his social identity" (1985, 61). While I agree with Szelényi that the state and the "new class," the apparatchik of the Communist party oligarchy, foisted a specific social identity upon the masses, it nevertheless must be acknowledged that social identity is a complex conglomerate of identities not affected equally and simultaneously by state ideology (Denitch 1990, 49). As I have suggested, gender bias, a generation gap, and traditional patriarchal ideas survived despite Stalinist policies and by the mid-1980s were revitalized and repoliticized during a period of acute socioeconomic and political crisis, offering an irresistible weapon to Hungarian men and women in their battle against state ideology (Bohlen 1990, E1–2).

The discourse of young workers suggests a profound paradox in sexual identity and nationalist objectives: Conceived as a proletarian nation-state, Hungarian Stalinist ideology of the 1950s required citizens—the apotheosis of whom were to be found among the Stakhanovites—devoted to building a new world for men and women. Willing or not, millions labored under the spell of the state myth to build a better society with their work and their bodies. However, after the collapse of the New Economic Mechanism of 1968, as Hungary has gradually become more westernized, the Stakhanovite free souls and Kollontai's socialist "winged eros" became footnotes to history. By the mid-1980s, Hungarian workers, like their counterparts elsewhere in East-Central Europe, were eagerly engaging in various forms of a legalized second economy, a development that modified their relations to production as well as their daily concerns with regard to reproduction. This transformation, rather than clipping the "wings of bourgeois culture," has regrafted them more firmly still.

By the time the short-lived Grosz government had been delegitimized in 1989, Hungarians, together with Poles, Czechs and Slovaks, Serbs, Croats and Slovenians, were on the move to rejoin Western Europe and shed their despised Stalinist and state-socialist heritage (Ash 1990; Djilas 1989). However, in this "springtime of the nations," with its drive toward westernization and technological supremacy over other East European states as well as the Soviet Union, a dominant nationalistic agenda has been created that appropriates a male-centered world view and a post-Communist eros not unlike those of the more "modern" democratic United States.[23] If the current freely elected conservative Hungarian, Romanian, Croatian, and Polish governments have their way, the eastern half of the New European Home will be built of a myriad of creches and kitchens. For in their unbridled search for *Mitteleuropa*, these East-Central European administrations have rapidly shifted from hardline to software, and their versions of democracy are coupling with the wingless eros of nationalism.

Notes

This paper was elaborated from earlier talks delivered at the "Conference On Nationalisms and Sexualities," Harvard University, June 16–18, 1989, and the panel Nationalism and the Future of Minorities: Eastern and Western Europe toward 1992, Seventh International Conference of Europeanists, Washington, DC March 23–25, 1990. I thank Catherine Portuges, Mary Russo, William Leap, Brett Williams, and the two anonymous reviewers of *Anthropological Quarterly* for reading and commenting on earlier versions of the manuscript. As always I wish to express my affection to my mother Magda Hajdrik for her support during the difficult years when I was a student and a worker, and for the unlimited love she offered throughout my life. She, too, played her part as a worker in building Hungary in the time of Stalinism and, subsequently, Kadarism.

1. Some of the issues concerning women in existing state-socialist societies were analyzed earlier by Volgyes and Volgyes (1977); Scott (1974); and Denitch (1974).
2. For a useful recent survey of gender relations in Eastern Europe, see the special issue of *East European Quarterly* vol. 13, no. 4, Winter 1990, "Gender Contradictions/Gender Transformations: Cases from Eastern Europe."
3. I will not analyze here issues of traditional gender roles and sexual identities in Hungarian peasant societies. I believe, however, that the differences between rural and urban and local and national identities as they relate to gender issues are important and deserve more scholarly debate. For sexuality and gender in peasant society see Morvay (1956), Fel and Hofer (1968) and in general H. Sas (1984).
4. One of the most thorough as well as sympathetic accounts of Soviet

nationalism based on firsthand observation of the Soviet Union in 1931 is that of Kohn (1966).

5. I cannot here fully describe or do justice to the diversity of opinions concerning the role of the Communist party in the early days of the Communist movement in the Soviet Union. That task has been done in several excellent works (Campeanu 1988; Kolakowski 1978). However, it is worth pointing out that this issue marks one of the first gender-based distinctions and arguments in the history of the Communist movement. It was Rosa Luxemburg who opposed V.I.U. Lenin, arguing that the party, and especially its main organ, the Central Committee, should not hold all power over the proletariat, rejecting as well the necessity of the dictatorship of the proletariat (Luxemburg 1970, 68–72).

6. For the creation of the new Soviet man and woman, see the useful overviews by Attwood (1986) and Heller (1988).

7. For a discussion on the personality cult (*kult lichnosti*) and the continuation of the male (God-like) rulers of both the Russian (tsar) and Soviet (Stalin) motherland, see Berki (1975, 110–111). In the summer of 1990, an exhibit was opened in Budapest, "Sta-lin, Rá-ko-si," which was the hit of the season.

8. Fulop-Miller (1935, 365), an ardent observer of cultural practices in the new Soviet society, has observed: "In the new Russian children's clinics, mother's milk centers have been established, as important nuclei for the collectivization of mankind. In these institutions, the mothers do not put their own infants to the breast, but milk themselves into bottles, from which this depersonalized milk is fed to the children." The author illustrates this practice with a caption that reads: "Collectivization of breasts in a Moscow nursery."

9. For an excellent recent study on Stalinism and its legacy, see Tucker (1990).

10. While Hungarian language does not possess gender, the speakers are obviously endowed with gender identities; for an insightful description of language choice and gender in a Hungarian-German multilingual peasant community, see Gal (1978). In Hungarian, the term *ember* means both "man" and "human," with the former connotation being more prevalent and recent. However, etymologically the term is composed of *em*, originallly meaning female, and *er*, referring to male and masculine properties. Thus, I would hypothetically argue that the original meaning of *ember* was "fe + male", i.e., "human," and only with the adoption of medieval Christian ideology and masculinity was the usage limited to the masculine noun.

11. Here I also find parallels between Stalinism and nazism in providing an ideology for the masses to be especially telling. The question succinctly expressed by Richard J. Evans in his *Comrades and Sisters: Feminism, Socialism and Pacifism in Europe*, of why German women voted for the Nazis in 1932 can be answered simply: because their *men* also voted for the Nazi party (for more detail see Evans 1987, 183–184).

12. I am unable here to specify the results of the second economic reform following the failed 1968 New Economic Mechanism when a new socioeconomic policy and concomitant educational structure was put into effect. These changes are well documented in Berend and Ranki (1985).

13. For a more detailed anthropological discussion in English of industrial organization and working-class life in Hungary, see my studies (Kurti 1990b; 1990c).

14. Elsewhere, I have dealt with the symbolic themes of Nagy's funeral and its fundamental role in creating a symbolic platform for the open admission by the Communist state and its leadership of their mistake and guilt concerning the 1956 revolution and, in so doing, providing a possibility for the oppositional forces to claim victory over the state before the world (Kurti 1990c).

15. See, for example, the pages of *Magyarorszag* (1989/52, p. 32) and *168 Ora* (1989, December 12, 1/32, pp. 26–28) for the description of these newly created sex shops and brothels hailed as the emerging spirit of business ventures.

16. Elie Kedourie has aptly noted that the centralized control of the Communist party only "serves to disguise the tyranny of one group over the other" (1966, 127).

17. On the resurgence of a nationalistic program and its wellspring of Transylvanism in the mid-1980s, see Kurti (1990a).

18. These five men represent the three most conservative forces yet to emerge in Hungarian politics: the Foetus Defense League (*Magzatvedo Tarsasag*, founded in November 1988), the Association of Christian Intellectuals, and the Red Cross of the Semmelweiss Medical School in Budapest.

19. Feminism, as one of the anonymous readers similarly observed, does not yet seem to be an issue in Hungary. It is only recently that questions have been raised concerning a radical and separate feminine consciousness, and signs are on the horizon that *because* of contemporary conservative developments, an independently organized, grass-roots women's movement may develop in the near future (see Mohas 1990; Mork 1990). One enormous obstacle is societal (heterosexual male?) bias concerning any organized women's movement, for such activity is seen as a remnant of the Communist past. Therefore, women willing to publicize their collective "feminist" agenda face the label "Communist" and are ostracized for their "outdated views" or "privileged positions" inherited from the party-state. The women's movement in Hungary was an important, if small, factor in the interwar tapestry of political culture; see Cornelius (1990) and Zsuppan (1990).

20. Another historic event should be noted here. The Social Democratic party (SZDP) also attempted to unite under a resurrected hero: socialist Anna Kethly, who died in Western exile. The SZDP made efforts to repatriate Kethly's remains and provide her with a stately—if not state—funeral. However, the SZDP sustained catastrophic losses at the ballot boxes and consequently the funeral was not realized until early November 1990 when it became only a minor media event outside of mainstream politics. Despite the efforts by some factions of the SZDP, however, Anna Petrasovits was reelected as president of the SZDP.

21. In a revealing interview, three elected parliamentary congresswomen were asked about their opinions concerning the possibility of participating in Hungarian politics. Only one mentioned "feminine sensitivity" to everyday problems such as the plight of single-parent families and the rising cost of housekeeping, while the others singled out the economy and ecology (Szasz 1990, 994). As a final note on women's participation in Hungarian politics, I should mention that in the fall 1990 municipal elections for mayor of Budapest, both the SZDSZ and the FIDESZ identified their candidates, the former a man, the latter a woman; however, FIDESZ decided to withdraw its nominee, arguing that was the only way to ensure the success of the SZDSZ candidate. While the SZDSZ candidate, Gabor Demszky, did win a major

victory, this male-centered politicking nevertheless reinforces my argument.

22. One of the anonymous reviewers argues that "it bears mentioning that many people, including officials in different religious orders and institutions, disagree with the government's position regarding catechism in schools, and other issues at the heart of church-state relations." While it is true that within the MDF, the Christian Democrats, and the socialist parties there are so-called women's factions who do not agree with the rightist agenda concerning abortion, it is equally true that their voices are not powerful enough to counterbalance the situation at hand. Moreover, the main point in the current political discourse, as I argue here, is the reinforcement of a male-centered world view through a traditional romanticization of gender roles and sexuality after the abolition of Communist party control in Hungary. While postcommunism and postmodernism have not been compared adequately to my knowledge, the way in which they impinge upon the intersections of gender and politics, the representation of the "other" in the new political discourse, would, I think, deserve scholarly scrutiny; Compare, for example, Mascia-Lees, Sharpe, and Ballerino Cohen (1990).

23. It is quite remarkable the way in which the abortion debate has sprung up throughout the former East bloc countries. For example, as Bogdan Denitch remarks, in Croatia the ruling Croatian Democratic Union considers "abortions of *Croatian* women to be a crime against the nation" (1990, xvii). I might add here that similar developments have been taking place in Poland concerning women's reproductive rights. In the beginning of November 1990, the Polish legislature moved toward banning abortion, a political shift under heavy pressure from the Catholic church as well as Pope John Paul II (Engelberg 1990, 1, 15). In Romania, however, following the overthrow of the despised Ceauşescu regime, the ruling National Salvation Front "has abolished pronatalism, and thousands of abortions are being performed daily in Romanian hospitals" and "White babies available for adoption are scarce in both Western Europe and the United States, and would-be parents are flocking to Romania to find them" (Rothman 1990, 7). The issue of abortion is also a problematical one since German reunification, especially for East German women who must face the strict antiabortion law of the West German state. In an insightful article Celestine Bohlen, the *New York Times* correspondent, makes a convincing argument quite similar to mine concerning the close interrelationship between nationalism and sexuality when she writes: "In addition to economic shakedown, women face resurgent nationalist movements that advance the notion that the best place for women is at home, caring for the next generation of Hungarians, Slovaks, Serbs, Croats, or whatever national group is perceived to be in danger of being outnumbered or somehow diminished" (1990, E2).

References

Alter, P. 1989. *Nationalism.* New York: E. Arnold.

Anderson, B. 1983. *Imagined communities: Reflections on the origin and spread of nationalism.* London: Verso.

Ash, T. 1990. "Mitteleuropa?" *Daedalus* (Winter):1–21.

Attwood, L. 1986. "The new Soviet man and women—Soviet views on psychological sex differences." in *Soviet sisterhood: British feminists on women in the USSR*, ed. B. Holland. 160–172. London: Fourth Estate.

Berend, I. 1965. *Csepel tortenete*. Csepel: MSZMP.

Berend, I., and Ranki, G. 1985. *The Hungarian economy in the twentieth century*. London: Croom Helm

Berki, R. 1975. *Socialism*. New York: St. Martin's Press.

Bohlen, C. 1990. "East Europe's women struggle with new rules, and old ones." *New York Times* (November 25):E1–2.

Campeanu, P. 1988. *The genesis of the Stalinist social order*. Armonk: M. E. Sharpe.

Cornelius, B. 1990. "Women in the interwar populist movement: The Szeged youth." Unpublished paper presented at the twenty-second national convention of the American Association for the Advancement of Slavic Studies.

Denitch, B. 1974. "Sex and power in the Balkans." in *Women, culture and society*, eds. M. Rosaldo and L. Lamphere. 243–262. Stanford: Stanford University Press.

———. 1990. *Limits and possibilities: The crisis of Yugoslav socialism and state socialist systems*. Minneapolis: University of Minnesota Press.

Djilas, M. 1989. "The crisis of communism." *Telos* 80:116–121.

Dölling, I. 1989. "Culture and gender." in *The quality of life in the GDR*, eds. M. Rueschmeyer and C. Lemke. 117–143. Armonk: M. E. Sharpe.

Engelberg, S. 1990. "Abortion fight in Poland reveals qualms about church pressure." *New York Times* (November 6):1, 15.

Evans, R. 1987. *Comrades and sisters: Feminism, socialism and pacifism in Europe, 1870–1945*. New York: St. Martin's Press.

Farnsworth, B. 1980. "Communist feminism: Its synthesis and demise." in *Women, war and revolution*, eds. C. Berkin and C. Loiett. 90–110. New York: Holmes and Meier.

Fekete, G. 1989. "Anyak napi csokor—tovisekkel." *Hitel* (9):60.

Fel, E., and Hofer, T. 1968. *Proper peasants*. Chicago: Aldine.

Foucault, M. 1980. *The history of sexuality*. New York: Vintage Books.

Fulop-Miller, R. 1935. *Leaders, dreamers and rebels: An account of the great-mass-movements of history and of the wish-dreams that inspired them*. New York: Viking Press.

Gal, S. 1978. "Peasant men can't get wives: Language change and sex roles in a bilingual community." *Language in Society* (7):1–16.

Goodwin, B. 1984. "Economic and social innovation in utopia." in *Utopia*, eds. P. Alexander and R. Gill. 69–84. La Salle: Open Court Publishing.

Goody, J. 1990. *The oriental, the ancient, and the primitive: Systems of marriage and the family in the pre-industrial societies of Eurasia.* Cambridge: Cambridge University Press.

Gray, F. 1990. "Reflections: Soviet women." *New Yorker*, (February 19):48–80.

Hankiss, E. 1990. *East European alternatives.* New York: Oxford University Press.

H. Sas, J. 1984. *Noies nok ferfias ferfiak.* Budapest: Akademiai Kiado.

Heller, M. 1988. *Cogs in the wheel: The formation of the Soviet man.* New York: Alfred A. Knopf.

Hungarian Democratic Forum. 1989. "A Magyar demokrata forum programja." *Hitel* 10:51.

Inglis, K. 1989. "Men, women, and war memorials: Anzac Australia." in *Learning about women: Gender, politics, and power*, eds. K. Conway, S. Bourque, and J. Scott. 216–232. Ann Arbor: University of Michigan Press.

Jayawardena, K. 1986. *Feminism and nationalism in the third world.* London: Zed Books.

Kapferer, B. 1988. *Legends of people, myths of state.* Washington, DC: Smithsonian Institution Press.

Kedourie, E. 1966. *Nationalism.* London: Hutchinson.

Kikumura, A. 1986. *Through harsh winters.* Novato: Chandler & Sharp.

Kohn, H. 1966. *Nationalism in the Soviet Union.* New York: AMS Press.

Kolakowski, L. 1978. *Main currents in Marxism: Its rise, growth, and dissolution.* Oxford: Clarendon Press.

Kollontai, A. 1977. *Selected writings of Alexandra Kollontai*, trans. A. Holt. New York: W. W. Norton.

Kornai, J. 1982. *Growth, shortage, and efficiency: A macrodynamic model of socialist economy.* Oxford: Basil Blackwell.

KSH. 1990. *Magyar statisztikai zsebkonyv.* Budapest: KSH.

Kürti, L. 1990a. "Transylvania—a land beyond reason: Toward an anthropological analysis of a contested terrain." *Dialectical Anthropology* 14:21–52.

———. 1990b. "Red Csepel: Working youth in a socialist firm." *East European Quarterly* 23(4):445–468.

———. 1990c. "Hierarchy and workers' power in a Csepel factory." *Journal of Communist Studies* 6(2):60–79.

———. 1990d. "People vs. the state: Political rituals in contemporary Hungary." *Anthropology Today* 6(2):5–9.

Lamphere, L. 1986. "From working daughters to working mothers: Production and reproduction in an industrial community." *American Ethnologist* 13:118–130.

Luxemburg, R. 1970. *The Russian revolution and Leninism or Marxism?* Ann Arbor: University of Michigan Press.

Mascia-Lees , F., Sharpe, P., and Ballerino Cohen, C. 1990. "The postmodernist turn in anthropology: Cautions from a feminist perspective." *Signs* 15(11):7–33.

Mohas, L. 1990. *Ferfiak mellett maganyosan*. Budapest: Minerva.

Moore, H. 1988. *Feminism and anthropology*. Minneapolis: University of Minnesota Press.

Mork, L. 1990. "A hasam az enyem!" *Vilag* (February 8):20–21.

Morvay, J. 1956. *Asszonyok a nagycsaladban*. Budapest: Szirka.

Mosse, G. 1988. *Nationalism and sexuality: Middle class morality and sexual norms in modern Europe*. Madison: University of Wisconsin Press.

Reich, W. 1970. *The sexual revolution: Toward a self-governing character structure*. New York: Farrar, Straus & Giroux.

Rogers, B. 1980. *The domestication of women: Discrimination in developing society*. London: Kogan Page.

Ross, E., and Rapp, R. 1983. "Sex and society: A research note from social history and anthropology." in *Powers of desire: The politics of sexuality*, eds. A. Snitow, C. Stansell, and S. Thompson. 59–78. New York: New York Monthly Review Press.

Rothman, D., and Sheila, M. 1990. "How AIDS came to Romania." *New York Review of Books* (November 8):5–7.

Sandor, A. 1990. "Szuld meg ed add orokbe?" *168 Ora* 2(20):8–9.

Scott, H. 1974. *Does socialism liberate women?* Boston: Beacon Press.

Shlapentokh, V. 1988. "The Stakhanovite movement: Changing perceptions over fifty years." *Journal of Contemporary History* 23:259–276.

Simecka, M. 1984. "A world with utopias or without them?" in *Utopias*, eds. Alexander P. and R. Gill. 169–178. La Salle: Open Court Publishing.

Strathern, M. 1988. *The gender of the gift: Problems with women and problems with society in Melanesia*. Berkeley: University of California Press.

Szasz, A. 1990. "Honanyak civilen." *Talloz* (May 25):993–995.

Szelenyi, I. 1985. "The position of the intelligentsia in the class structure of state socialist societies." *Critique* 10–15:60–75.

Tucker, R. 1990. *Stalin in power: The revolution from above*. New York: W. W. Norton.

Volgyes, N., and Volgyes, I. 1977. *The liberated female: Life, work and sex in socialist Hungary*. Boulder: Westview Press.

Weeks, J. 1985. *Sexuality and its discontents: Meanings, myths and modern sexualities*. London: Routledge.

Wilczynski, J. 1982. *The economics of socialism, principles governing the operation of the centrally planned economies under the new system*. London: Georg Allen & Unwin.

Willis, P. 1981. *Learning to labour: How working class kids get working class jobs*. New York: Columbia University Press.

Zsuppan, F. 1990. "Rozsika Schwimmer and Hungarian feminism, 1904–1918." Unpublished paper presented at the twenty-second annual convention of the American Association for the Advancement of Slavic Studies.

Equality/Inequality: Contesting Female Personhood in the Process of Making Civil Society in Eastern Germany

HERMINE G. DE SOTO

THE DEVELOPMENT OF SOCIALIST THEORY

Although volumes of books need to be written to address the complex and paradoxical position of women in the development of socialist theory in relationship to the present revolution in Eastern Europe, in this chapter I will refer only to those propositions of classical writers that are pertinent to the focus of the problematic on gender equality and inequality in the socialist transformation process prior to recent social changes in Eastern Europe.

Karl Marx posited that the liberation and emancipation of individuals would be possible only if relations of class-based private property were replaced with socialist relations of production. Only then would women and men experience "the most natural relation of human being to human being" (Marx 1975, 229–346). While Marx concentrated on the general social evolution of "species-being," Engels attempted to formulate a theoretical framework for understanding the evolution of the family and of class, and the rise of social inequalities.

One important argument presented was that women's emancipation and equality were impossible as long as women were kept in the domestic sphere, and as long as marriages were merely bourgeois business marriages. In these bourgeois marriages, love between partners was replaced by economic concerns (i.e., the need for heirs to whom private property can be passed on through rules of inheritance). Also, adultery in such marriages was regarded as the male's exclusive right. Thus for Engels, such relations reproduce inequality. Working-class marriages, however, presented the possibility for equal relations, since such marriages were not based on the dominant cultural sanctions of business arrangements. But such marriages were exploited by public labor relations; thus working-class women could gain equality only if private-wage labor relations were changed into socialist labor relations. Under the changed conditions, women would be able to participate in the socialist large-scale production process, where profit was socialized in such a way that women would be freed from domestic work, and where they would be part of socialist society. For both Marx and Engels, equal partners under communism were not constrained by economic forces, hence each partner could freely enter or leave the particular marriage.

The introduction of socialist laws would allow bourgeois women to change their status from that of commodities, and they could at last enter the social welfare of the community as equals to men. The idea of woman as a commodity, or woman as an object, has received sophisticated analytic treatment by the feminist scholar Irigaray (1985a; 1985b). According to her analysis, the practice of depriving women of a subjective relationship and objectifying them into a relationship as a commodity is not bound to classes only, or to particular modes of production and their respective relations of production. Indeed, the evidence of anthropological studies suggests that in kinship-based societies in which the relations of production are based on predominantly collective property ownership and in which class relationships are absent, "access to resources and status is qualified and limited by age, sex, and kinship criteria" (Southall 1987, 182). In such societies, senior males' authority and prestige is based on the control and exchange of women. Meillassoux's (1978, 127–159) detailed ethnography of the Gouro of the Ivory Coast illustrates such relations, where not only women's labor but the labor of the future generation is valued and controlled in the exchange relations.[1]

The important point here is that the concept of equality as developed by Marx and Engels does not differentiate or isolate the problem of inequality between the sexes. Even though Marx developed a theoretical framework in which human nature could change within historically specific political and economic structures, Marx did not advance concepts for exploring issues of gender, sexuality, and race or for exploring late capitalist societies or socialist rational redistributive systems, as Konrád and Szelényi (1979) called the former socialist states of Eastern Europe. Marx's theory blindness to patriarchal tacit culture might be related to his preoccupation with concerns of class and equality. However, more serious concerns arise with Marx and Engels's theoretical position in that "they imagined communist society as necessarily equalitarian and harmonious [and] that they did not allow for the possibility that it [communism] could develop new forms of inequality and conflict" (Kulluk, this volume, p. 124). Returning to the theoretical debate on equality and women, August Bebel (1971) introduced a new feminist idea into the Marxist debate. He argued for a conceptual distinction between biological sex and what we today understand as culturally constructed gender behavior. He stressed that women's behavior needed to be examined within a capitalist social context in which men enjoy the most privileges. Because of that, women were denied equal access and were deprived of an economic base. They had to subordinate themselves when entering a marriage relationship. Furthermore, since men under capitalism entered marriage as a business relation, gender relations could only be altered by revolutionizing these relations. Women could only liberate themselves and determine their own financial situation in a socialist society in which they could participate in the labor process. Although sensitive to gender issues, Bebel essentially agreed with the earlier authors, thinking that equality for women could be achieved if women's—and not men's—behavior was altered.

Whereas Marx, Engels, and Bebel refrained from policy implementation, Lenin (1977) attempted to formulate policies for women in socialism as well as to continue the theoretical debate. Even though Lenin was aware of patriarchal cultural forms of domination, as he expressed succinctly in his cautionary remarks that "it is a far cry from equality in law to equality in life" (Lenin 1977, 61), he did not pursue this paradox further. Instead he focused on women's entry into the large-scale socialist economy. This limitation, as we will see, had severe consequences for theoretical development. For Lenin, women in nonsocialist society were oppressed in the domestic sphere, and freedom from such drudgery could only be achieved when women entered the socialist collective labor force. Not only would this politicize working women, it would also enhance their organizational skills. Additionally, such experience would help women to initiate their own liberation while simultaneously advancing the socialist revolution. A necessary step in this direction was the restructuring of the legal system, and a primary aim was to pass formal equality laws, particularly laws that would ease divorces, give equal rights to women, and provide equal status for children born out of wedlock. As Engels before him, Lenin saw women's entering the public workplace as the solution for altering equality at home. Thus new laws were geared to revolutionary changes: They advocated public dining rooms, nurseries, and kindergartens, as well as free public access to birth control (Buckley 1989, 26).

Even though Lenin promoted a large-scale socialist production assembly (in which women received equal rights to work and equal protection under the law), the question of inequality between sexes remained unchanged. Because of this, far-reaching paradoxes developed for women in socialist societies. Other problems arose because Lenin in his policy implementations relegated the woman question to the control of the socialist state and the party.

A major Marxist woman theorist and activist, Alexandra Kollontai (1982), expanded the theoretical attention to gender, sex, and sexism advanced by Bebel by examining the importance of socialism for women's liberation. For Kollontai, bourgeois women and working-class women had different class interests. Following Lenin's political strategy, she argued against separate women's organizations,[2] but she emphasized a need for legal equality. Such legal change should include labor laws that guaranteed both sexes in socialist society the equal right to work, social welfare programs, maternity leaves, civil marriages, divorce laws, and the legal right to keep one's surname.

Kollontai expanded the theoretical perspective further than Marx, Engels, Lenin, and Bebel and confronted the domestic sphere. For her, gender relations did not automatically change with legal equality. Like Lenin, she emphasized a need for communal kitchens, public dining areas, and public laundries; unlike Lenin, she argued for an end to housework under socialism. Such an end could be achieved by the creation of domestic jobs, which could be undertaken by members of either sex. Ahead of her time, Kollontai developed a theoretical link between sexuality and social relations, and she saw a primary need to deprivatize problems of sexuality so that it would be possible to confront male oppression, which hindered female self-expression and the reeducation of the psyche.[3] In a manner similar to that of Irigaray (1985b), Kollontai, by using different terminology, seems to point toward a female subjectivity that cannot develop within patriarchal structures. Kollontai's argument that the relationship of sex to housework is a political, not a private, issue raised Lenin's objection and she was finally isolated by the leading Bolsheviks of her time (Buckley 1989, 51–53).

Although Kollontai enhanced the theoretical perspective of women in socialism, she reproduced a class-reductionist position regarding equality as its solution. For her, only working-class women were actors for revolutionary change, since middle- and upper-class women would not be interested in identifying political and economic structures as sources of inequalities; rather, these women would blame men alone for their oppression. Recently two feminist scholars (having India in mind) pointed to the limitations of these positions:

> While it is true that upper class and caste women tend to share some of the privileges with their men, they nevertheless have no direct access to and control of the means of production. Women, therefore, have only a derived status or class-caste membership which is not equivalent to that of the male members. Besides patriarchal oppres-

sion, the sexual subordination, the familial duties in the form of child-rearing and care of the family members runs across class-caste situations, which tend to unite them with women of the peasant, working class and reinforces their alienation (Jayawardena and Kelkar 1989, 2124).

While Kollontai confronted inequality and called for legal equality, she did not press the issue of the domestic sphere and the restructuring of gender roles further. Thus she limited her awareness of the possibility that socialism could intensify unequal gender relations. Neglecting these issues meant that socialization practices would remain unproblematized, and that the very concept of equality would remain unlinked to equality in the family. If this problem was not critically assessed, neither power, authority, nor aggression between the sexes would be addressed. Thus sexism, oppression, discrimination, and violence could be reproduced in the "new" society. When such behavior was noticed at all, it was explained as leftovers from either feudal or capitalist relations of production.

The first phase of socialism—as seen in Marx, Engels, Lenin, Bebel, and Kollontai—was marked by theoretical and practical concerns about how to complete successfully its revolution with the help and participation of women. Even though striking achievements were made in favor of legal equality, Lenin's goal of politicizing the majority of women never materialized. With the entry of Stalin into political leadership, the theoretical debate on women's issues was halted, and pragmatic and economic collectivization and female labor power became the new concerns.

STALIN AND THE SOCIALIST RATIONAL REDISTRIBUTIVE MODEL

According to Konrád and Szelényi, socialist rational redistributive systems are based on "the coordination of economic and political power, by contrast with a free market economy where, for the first time in history, political and economic institutions are separated" (see De Soto 1983, 2).[4] And, in further contrast to market economies, "all redistributive systems, on the other hand, have in common the fact that the surplus product *and the legitimized right over its disposition* is not determined by economic means alone; its magnitude is the result of political decisions" (De Soto 1983, 2). In other words, the socialist redistributive system has a coordinated economy and political power. The authority in such systems to redistribute goods and surplus is legitimized through rational bureaucratic performances that are based on the power and knowledge of the officeholders. Surpluses in such economies are redistributed via political decisions. But how does the socialist redistributive model of economic integration respond to economic growth? It responds to a challenge to capitalism. This challenge is established by political means because the political goal is to catch up with the developed Western economies; however, this economic growth is seen as an external threat. Because of this, the rise of institutional authority and power is based on a noneconomic knowledge ethos toward the challenge.

In contrast, Western economies control economic growth, according to Konrád and Szelényi, "through an impersonal profit mechanism" (see De Soto 1983, 5) for expanding economic means. Konrád and Szelényi suggest that "if Weber is correct . . . [then] the core institution of a state socialist rational-redistributive economy is the nonmarket trade of labor [emphasis added]" (see De Soto 1983, 5), and it is this type of labor that allows an economy to be redistributive.

The above analysis implicitly suggests, then, that women's importance in such economies is first and foremost as laborers, and that policies regarding women's participation in large-scale industry are designed so that the reproduction of the labor supply is guaranteed for the system. If we examine Stalinist policies and ideologies in this way, his repressive power politics regarding women seem to have been successful in that it reproduced the labor necessary for the system. Stalin's entry into political leadership halted the theoretical debate on women's issues, and pragmatic and economic concerns of collectivization and female labor power became the new goals. To achieve these pragmatic goals, Stalin invented at different times certain ideological myths. One myth was that women's liberation had been completed. At another time, images of glorified, smiling women workers were presented. In the 1940s, the image shown of the socialist superwoman was of the woman who simultaneously fought successfully to achieve the goal of the redistributive economic plans and to oppose the internal as well as the external bourgeoisie. During this time, women were firmly integrated as laborers into the socialist redistributive system (Buckley 1989, 136).

WOMEN IN THE REDISTRIBUTIVE ECONOMY IN THE USSR AND THE GERMAN DEMOCRATIC REPUBLIC (GDR)

As suggested previously, the USSR under Stalin provides the model of a socialist rational redistributive system. Juxtaposing the conditions for women in the USSR with those in the GDR illuminates the relationship of the GDR to this model.

The question of legal equality and gender equality in the GDR reveals a structural development similar to that of the USSR redistributive system, with one major exception. As has been shown previously in this chapter, the socialist rational redistributive system was introduced almost forty years earlier into the Soviet Union. Therefore, women in the USSR had a much longer experience with the socialist system than did women in the GDR. In 1949 (during the Stalinist era in the USSR), the GDR received its first constitution in which legal equality (i.e., the right to work, equal pay for equal work, and social welfare securities for women, marriage, and the family) was a part. This constitution was modeled after the USSR's socialist rational redistributive system. Unlike Stalin, however, the GDR leaders did not close down the official women's organization (i.e., the Women's Democratic League [DFD]). The DFD was assigned responsibilities relating to women's equal rights, to equal pay for equal work, to the protection of married and single working mothers, and to childbearing, maternity grants, and prenatal and postnatal care (Kamenitsa 1991). However, the very fact that the DFD was placed under the umbrella of the party prevented the development of a more open debate on patriarchy, oppression, feminism, and women's self-determination (Einhorn 1981).

Even though politics for women were directed in part through the DFD, the organization made politics *for* women rather than *by* the women. Had it been the opposite, the authoritarian state of the redistributive system would have contradicted its own logic, since a rational socialist redistributive state cannot separate powers into political society and civil society (Gramsci 1971). In socialist states organizations are not independent negotiating agents of interest groups and mediators between political parties and the state; rather, socialist organizations are part of the official party, which represents in theory and in praxis the socialist state. In this way, the DFD carried out directions for women thought necessary for the reproduction of the system.

As under Stalin's rule, in the GDR during this time there was an analytic silence regarding contradictory developments of women's life in socialism. The party declared that equality had been achieved, and women—the workers or mothers—became officially idealized in the reconstruction phase of the socialist economy in the new state. During this phase, workers had to produce under repressive force in order to keep up the productivity quotas. In 1953, the year of Stalin's death, the repressive labor conditions erupted into an open worker resistance, which was forcefully defeated by the Soviet army.

Between 1953 and 1964, while Khrushchev attempted to de-Stalinize the USSR, women in the GDR became more firmly integrated into the industrial as well as the agricultural sectors, whose collectivization process was completed in 1960. As in the USSR, the GDR woman was "a superwoman, one who could successfully handle both family and career with the help of a beneficent state" (Cooper 1990, 60).

In the USSR, while Khrushchev, like Stalin before him, left unchallenged the old mythologies of women and equality, women nevertheless became politically important as allies for Khrushchev against the Stalinists' resistance (Buckley 1983, 159). Contrary to Lenin's vision, Khrushchev soon realized that the majority of women were not actively engaged in party politics. This discovery led Khrushchev to renew consideration of the question on women, which started to draw attention to women in the economy. Similar concerns were noted in the GDR state, which slowly started to improve labor and social security policies for working mothers. Soon the focus on such issues expanded to the domestic socialist paradox where women—the mothers—were found to be the major caretakers. This realization resulted in policy improvements for prenatal and postnatal care, improved pregnancy leaves, and expansion of creches and kindergartens.

The beginning of the Brezhnev era marked the first voicing in the USSR of official public concerns about the double burden of work that women had to endure. Additionally, because Soviet women over the years had used the strategies of birth control and divorce to reduce some of the work burden by decreasing the size of the family, demographic concerns arose about how the strategies of "the producers of the producers" (i.e., the procreative women) could be altered (Meillassoux 1978). This, in turn, redirected the focus to inquire again into the domestic sphere; this time, however, different policies were introduced to encourage research on gender roles, a process that continued up to the era of glasnost and perestroika. In spite of the growing demographic problem, GDR leaders declared in 1971 that gender equality had been satisfyingly accomplished, while everyday life experiences pointed to noticeable discrepancies.

GDR WOMEN BEFORE UNIFICATION

During the 1960s, women fiction writers were the first ones to cautiously address these discrepancies. In their novels, short stories, or essays about women's experiences in everyday life they linked the awakening female social consciousness to patriarchal structures. Even though no other official communication networks (i.e., radio, television, newspapers, and magazines) supported the writers' theme,[5] the rising demographic problem was noted officially by the state, and from the middle of the 1960s and up to 1982, the state found it necessary to encourage scientific gender studies and assessments of the social condition in the domestic sphere.

This research on gender roles and socialization not only revealed that gender-specific activities were reproduced at home, but that at the workplace, the contradiction between "public production" and "duties in the private service of the family" was not abolished (Dölling 1989, 30, 19). According to Nickel's studies (1989, 48–58), this development was linked in part to the historical socialization process in the GDR in which "gender-specific subjective abilities" were reproduced, resulting in different symbolic gender expressions in "language," "habit," and "spatial relations," and finally carried over into the workplace, where women more than men worked in "monotonous" and "simple technological jobs" (1989, 50). Numerous anthropological studies supported the findings.[6] In their independently conducted research on "the effects of the socialist reconstruction and articulation of gender roles in daily practice in contemporary Czechoslovakia, Hungary, Romania, and Yugoslavia" (Huseby-Darvas 1990, 385–388), "the research discoveries reveal, regardless of rural or urban workplaces, that in contrast to official claims, gender inequalities actually intensify during socialist transformation" (Huseby-Darvas 1990, 387).

The previously mentioned studies about everyday life experiences of GDR women before unification reveal something important: Working women have not been just passive victims. On the contrary, within the possibilities of constraints in a socialist rational redistributive economy, they have used their own cultural forms to resist hardship in the domestic as well as in the public sphere of work. While the domestic sphere, on the one hand, contributed to the double burden of work, on the other hand, it has been a preferred place for working women to relax through cooking, baking, crafts, book reading, listening to records, watching television, and chatting with friends or visiting relatives (Beyer 1990, 101–141). In a similar manner, the laws for abortion and easy divorce have given overworked women a possibility for planning, in part, their own personal space. Divorces have most often been initiated by women, and the statistical records suggest that the divorce rate in the GDR, measured on a world scale, is almost as high as the one in the United States, in the USSR, in Cuba, and in the United Kingdom. Other reports indicate that abortions doubled from 24,540 to 52,439 between 1960 and the 1980s. The reasons given by women for using these strategies are in part related to the high demands made on them at work and in the family and to the lack of forums for expressing an acceptance of female individuality (Beyer 1990, 109–110).

The decline in birthrates and the increase in divorces had caused new labor concerns for the redistributive state. Thus again, numerous welfare programs had been expanded in hopes of easing the double workload burden of women. Improvements in day-care centers, education, and health care had been made. Additionally, financial incentives had been granted for married and single mothers and their children. All in all, the same practices of improving welfare services geared to women continued up to the revolutionary year 1989 (Beyer 1990, 228–247).

While legal equality had provided women in the GDR with new social strategies, at the same time the strategies employed exposed the contradictory nature of the "socialist state." Being able to decide through available control practices their own reproductive rights and having access to easy legal divorce procedures have helped, on the one hand, to ease the double burden of work. Additionally, such strategies worked against social psychological constraints experienced in the family, where nurturing, caretaking, and the efficient management of the internal household remained mostly unquestioned and combined within the role of the mother. On the other hand, from the redistributive economical point of view, the decline of the birthrate, and thus a possible decline of labor power, hardly could have been intended by the state. In fact, such unintended developments could have proved, in time, critical to the economy. Thus, the state tried to reverse a labor shortage crisis by implementing over the years expanding social welfare programs for mothers and children. This process continued up to the fall of the Berlin Wall in 1989.

THE TRANSITION

Few people would have imagined that perestroika and glasnost introduced by Gorbachev would unleash a race for social change sweeping through Eastern Europe. Not only have redistributive state institutions been shaken apart but the central power structures of the authoritarian system have been confronted, contested, and finally uprooted by the peoples of Eastern Europe in various countries (with the USSR presenting a noticeably complex and paradoxical exception). Myriad women in Eastern Europe have collected, for at least the last forty years, similar experiences within the arrangement of "the economy of shortage" (Verdery 1991), in which

the intermediate space between state and households was cleansed of all independent organizations, anything not controlled by the state— the kinds of organizations that many refer to with the term "civil society." Trade unions, nationality councils, women's organizations, churches (where possible), social services, and all manner of other association were either attached to the state locked in a struggle of co-option with it, or placed under severe pressure. (16)

For Verdery (1991, 17), "the reconstruction of associations separate from the state is one of the most urgent tasks facing the peoples of eastern Europe," following the collapse of the socialist rational redistributive system.

In the GDR during the first phase of the revolution (1989) yet before unification in 1990, women organized independent women's groups, which were understood to be alternatives to the state-legitimized DFD. Within the transitional period in 1989, and after the opening up of the Berlin Wall, numerous other women's groups emerged and participated in the process of making civil society by declaring autonomy vis-à-vis the DFD. In a considerably short time (by December 1989), various groups initiated and founded a women's umbrella organization, the Independent Women's Association (Unabhängige Frauenverband [UFV]). Hoping to influence the future politics of the GDR in the newly gained civil space, those groups consciously drawing the boundaries of their movement within civil society began to identify themselves. Feminist themes have ranged from self-determination, consciousness-raising, self-discovery, and deconstruction of patriarchal models and coercion to free expression of needs and interests.

The UFV has defined itself as feminist in orientation and free of power. The organization acknowledges that while in the former GDR women and men lived under patriarchal structures, now a real democratization of society, in which women determine and form their own emancipation and equality, must be the aim.

Furthermore, all the needs of women (i.e., economic, political, symbolic, psychological, and spiritual) must be primary concerns and need to be voiced politically. Particularly important concerns of the league have been the needs of single parents, female senior citizens, foreign women, youth, and large families. Other tasks of the league have included a need for women-friendly spaces for communication and meetings: women's centers, women's houses, and women's cafes. Finally, the UFV has stood for a political struggle that would include both the rights of women in the FRG and a globally oriented solidarity with all democratic women's organizations. The movement has called for separation of powers of civil society from those of political society and advocates a sphere of democratic publicity. For further identity construction, the UFV has generated its own publications, newspapers, radio and television programs, cultural centers, independent women's studies programs, and research centers (Di Caprio 1990, 621–634).

Before the first East-West German election in 1990, women representatives of UFV participated in the political negotiation process at the roundtable, debating with other representatives of other parties and groups a possible third way for restructuring the GDR. The speed with which the Kohl government of the Federal Republic of Germany (FRG) pushed forward through national elections made the women of the UFV join with the newly founded East German Green party. Whether they did so because of hegemonic pressure or political inexperience with harsh electoral competition, or both, still is unclear. What we know is that for the East German women candidates, the election was a dismal failure. Politically, the women's initiatives and activism against the former dictatorial state were defeated, and they are presently becoming politically marginalized in the unified Germany (Kamenitsa 1991, 22).

Under the legal system of the FRG, East German women have lost most of their previously held rights, except the abortion law, which is presently fiercely contested. According to the research of a feminist West German legal scholar, the social welfare policies in the FRG are oriented not to individuals but to the patriarchal family. The policy of child care is based on privatization (i.e., where it is expected that women do the unpaid social work in the family). Labor laws support gender-segregated hidden male quotas, and two-thirds of the young women are unable to find vocational training jobs. Furthermore, East German women have entered a welfare state in which women "represent the largest group of those seeking employment" (Klein-Schönnefeld 1989, 2–22).

While in the former GDR, 90 percent of the women were integrated into the economy, today, entering the capitalist welfare state, the women fear losing their economic independence. With unification and its immediate economic restructuring, women have been among the first to be unemployed. A leading feminist summarized the concerns of many East German women, who fear losing their economic independence by being sent "back to the kitchen stove" (Merkel 1989, 30). While recent surveys have expressed that work is considered a *very important* need in life for women of all age groups in Eastern Germany and that the new job insecurity for many has resulted in serious expressions of anxiety (Fremery and Kupferschmied 1991), just a call from Western German social scientists for an awareness of the *different* needs of Eastern German women is not enough. Instead, as Gordon pointed out (with the capitalist welfare state in mind),

> the concept of "difference" does not capture what is at issue because it implies a pluralist multiplicity of stories that benignly coexist or interact; it may obscure relations of inequality, domination, and even exploitation among women. Women are not only divided by class,

race, and other "differences," but may enter into actual conflicts of interest with other women that directly affect their views on welfare policy (1990, 30).

Such conflicts might develop in the future if Eastern German women become further marginalized in the FRG welfare state. Given the fluidity of the present historical process and the contradictions embedded in the late capitalist welfare state, the possibility exists that women will contest future inequalities. It is in this context that the previously presented argument suggested that due to the logic of patriarchal and economic structures, neither the former rational socialist redistributive system nor the late capitalist one favors equality for women at the workplace and in the domestic sphere. However, whereas the former regime repressed human agency and women's contestations, the latter state has to refrain from such dictatorial procedures because the late capitalist welfare state's powers are limited vis-à-vis civil society.

As suggested in the theoretical development, especially in the ideas of Irigaray, Bebel, and Kollontai, these new forms of contestation and their concomitant call for subjectivity by women will be important areas for future research. For as Nickel wrote with regard to present and future developments, "One thing is certain: as we take off into the market economy conditions for women [again] are tougher than for most men" (1991, 99).

Notes

I wish to thank my colleagues at the Women's Studies Research Center at the University of Wisconsin-Madison for their intellectual support during the research seminar and the colloquia: Mary Ann Rossi, Barbara Burrell, Jane Berdes, Darunee Tan, and Rashmi Luthra. Special thanks are extended to Cyrena Pondrom, director of the Women's Studies Research Center for her institutional support and helpful suggestions.

1. The ethnographic evidence suggests that similar kinship-based organizations exist in pastoral economies (i.e., the Berbers, Beduin, Kurds, Afghans, and Kazaks). Other groups are also known from isolated geographical areas in Oceania and New Guinea. A detailed analysis of the kinship mode of production is provided in Aidan Southall's "Mode of production theory: The foraging mode of production and the kinship mode of production," in *Dialectical Anthropology*, 1987, vol. 12, no. 2, pp. 165–193.
2. In the first years of socialist transformation, Kollontai followed Lenin's opposition to the formation of an official women's organization. However, in 1919 the women's organization Zhenotdel began officially to work directly on women's issues. The Zhenotdel was subordinated to the party, and existed eleven years. The organization was dissolved under Stalin.

3. See Laszlo Kürti's excellent study in this volume ("The wingless eros of socialism: Nationalism and sexuality in Hungary") in which he discusses Kollontai's vision of sexuality for socialist women and men.

4. While studying in 1983 with Ivan Szelényi, I reanalyzed and compared three ethnographic studies applying Szelényi's concepts to the "socialist" rational redistributive economy in Hungary, Poland, and the "traditional" redistributive economy of the Gouro of the Ivory Coast.

5. K. Jankowsky, A. Larson-Thorisch, C. Love, and M. Silberman pointed out at the symposium Women Writing in the GDR in the fall of 1990 at the University of Wisconsin-Madison, German Department, that women authors in the GDR started to address gender inequalities in the 1960s and continued up to the late 1980s. Some of the women writers and their writing include Brigitte Reimann's *Ankunft im Alltag*; Christa Wolf's *Der geteilte Himmel*; Sarah Kirsch's *Landaufenthalt*; Irmtraud Morgner's *Leben und Abenteuer der Trobadora Beatriz nach Zeugnissen ihrer Spielfrau Laura*; Maxi Wander's *Guten Morgen Du Schöne: Frauen in der DDR*; and Christine Woltner's *Wie ich meine Unschuld verlor*.

6. The interested reader is directed to the *East European Quarterly*, 23, no. 4, January 1990, in which various anthropologists address the problem of gender relations in Eastern European countries prior to the fall of the Berlin Wall.

References

Arato, A. 1990. "Social movements and civil society in the Soviet Union." Unpublished manuscript, pp. 1–33.

Bebel, A. 1971. *Women under socialism*. New York: Schocken Books.

Beyer, M. 1990. *Frauenreport '90*, ed. Gunnar Winkler. Berlin: Verlag die Wirtschaft GmbH.

Buckley, M. 1989. *Women and ideology in the Soviet Union*. Ann Arbor: University of Michigan Press.

Cooper, B. 1990. "The truth about superwoman: Women in East Germany." *Michigan Feminist Studies* 5(fall):59–67.

De Soto, H. 1983. "Redistibutive systems in three communities: A comparative reanalysis." Unpublished manuscript (27 pp.), University of Wisconsin-Madison.

Di Caprio, L. 1990. "East German feminists: The Lila manifesto." *Feminist Studies* 16(3, fall): 621–635.

Dölling, J. 1989. "Culture and gender." in *The quality of life in the German Democratic Republic*, eds. M. Rueschemeyer and C. Lemke. New York: M. E. Sharpe.

Einhorn, B. 1981. "Socialist emancipation: The women's movement in the German Democratic Republic." *Women's Studies International Quarterly* 4(4):435–452.

Engels, F. 1975. "The origin of the family, private property, and the state."

in *Karl Marx and Friedrich Engels: Selected works.* 445–593. London: Lawrence and Wishart.

Fremery, U., and Kupferschmid, P. 1991. *Dokumentation: Frauen in den neuen Bundesländern im Prozess der deutschen Einigung.* Bonn: Pressereferat.

Gordon, L. 1990. *Women, the state, and welfare.* Madison: University of Wisconsin Press.

Gramsci, A. 1971. *Selections from the prison notebooks.* New York: International Publishers.

Huseby-Darvas, E. 1990. "Introduction." *East European Quarterly* 23(4, January):385–388.

Irigaray, L. 1985a. *This sex which is not one.* Ithaca: Cornell University Press.

———. 1985b. *Speculum of the other woman.* Ithaca: Cornell University Press.

Jayawardena, K., and Kelkar, G. 1989. "The left and feminism." *Economic and Political Weekly* (September 23):2123–2126.

Kamenitsa, L. 1991. "From socialism to pluralism: East German women and the new German politics." Paper (29 pp.) presented at the American Political Science Association, Chicago, April.

Klein-Schönefeld, S. 1989. "Female poverty on the interrelation of economic independence and the opportunity to claim human rights." Annual meeting of the Law and Society Association, University of Wisconsin-Madison, June 8–11.

Kollontai, A. 1982. *Ich habe viele Leben gelebt.* Berlin: Dietz Verlag.

Konrád, G., and Szelényi, I. 1979. *The intellectuals on the road to class power.* New York: Harcourt Brace Jovanovich.

Kulluk, F. 1992. "From the 'national question' to autogestion and perestroika: Controversies in theoretical and practical approaches to national(ist) movements." in *The curtain rises: Rethinking culture, ideology and the state in Eastern Europe,* eds. H. De Soto and D. Anderson. Humanities Press: (Forthcoming, here quoted from manuscript).

Lenin, V. 1977. *On the emancipation of women.* Moscow: Progress Publishers.

Marx, K. 1975. "Economic and philosophical manuscript of 1844." in *Karl Marx and Friedrich Engels: Selected works.* London: Lawrence and Wishart.

Meillassoux, C. 1978. "'The economy' in agricultural self-sustaining societies: A preliminary analysis." in *Relations of Production,* ed. D. Seddon. 127–159. London: Frank Cass.

Merkel, I. 1989. "Manifest für eine autonome Frauenbewegung." Das Argument, Zeitschrift für Philosophie und Sozialwissenschaften (180): 255–262.

Nickel, H. 1989. "Sex-role socialization in relationships as a function of the division of labor." in *The quality of life in the German Democratic Republic,* eds. M. Rueschemeyer and C. Lemke. New York: M. E. Sharpe.

Nickel, H. 1991. "Women in the GDR: Will renewal pass them by?" in *Women in German yearbook 6*, eds. J. Clausen and H. Caffert. New York: University Press of America.

Southall, A. 1987. "Mode of production theory: The foraging mode of production and the kinship mode of production." *Dialectical Anthropology* 12(2):165–193.

Verdery, K. 1991. "Ethnic relations, the 'economy of shortage,' and the transition in Eastern Europe." 1991 ASA conference, University of Cambridge, U.K., April 9–12.

The Spanish Route to Democracy: A Model for Eastern Europe in Transition?

ORIOL PI-SUNYER

When in the fall of 1989 I was invited to prepare the conference paper that proved to be the ancestor of this chapter, the situation in East-Central Europe was obviously in flux, but no one foresaw the rapidity of the change or the extent of the structural and conceptual transformations that have taken place and are still very much under way. If I was surprised, I found myself in good company, for it seems that virtually every evaluation of the Eastern European situation has been destined to be overtaken by the course and the pace of events.[1] We can probably all take to heart Timothy Garton Ash's (1990c, 325) words respecting his own prognoses and the problems of discussing what we cannot really know: "The events of 1989 in Eastern Europe, which for once deserved that over-used epithet 'revolutionary,' were a powerful argument for never again writing about the future. No one predicted them."

Granted, therefore, that it is not only difficult but even somewhat foolhardy to discuss a collection of sociopolitical orders (in several cases one hesitates to use the conventional term "states") that not only are undergoing change at an unprecedented pace but are also undertaking this journey in anything but synchrony or common direction, it still seems well worth the risk and the effort to venture comparisons with other polities in terminal crisis, especially if such a discussion can help mark some of the rough patches on the road to a more democratic system.

For several reasons, an examination of the Spanish transition would appear to be particularly salient. Most obviously, the end-of-regime scenarios have a good deal in common. At both ends of Europe one can document a long process of erosion of legitimacy (some would argue that legitimacy was always much more an official myth than a social reality) and growing problems of political control, including those occasioned by the rising militancy of class, ethnic, and nationality sectors.[2] These difficulties coincide with—and frequently reflect—systemic contradictions that are increasingly difficult to dissimulate. Again, in both situations, we have the emergence (or the reformulation) of not only a spectrum of counterregime movements and ideologies but opposition within, or on the margins of, the official political establishment. The similarities do not end here. It is most pertinent to observe that the time frames of crisis and reconstitution are sufficiently close to permit us to say that these are events of the same broad historical era played out within a shared conceptual cultural space.

What such a situation suggests is that to some degree—how much remains to be determined—these must be considered as *linked phenomena*, and not simply because of sequential ordering. In both East and West, regime opposition not only entailed a rejection of the system in place but the conceptualization of an alternative social and political arrangement, one generally rendered as "a normal European society" (Lewis 1988). Undoubtedly this model has many subtypes, but everyone, at least initially, seems to understand quite clearly what is meant by it—and conversely, what is not.

It is striking, if hardly unexpected, that in both Spain and Eastern Europe, intellectuals have played a similar role in expanding the cultural and political space available to opposition and dissent well prior to the terminal phases of the respective dictatorships. Fundamentally, this was accomplished by a relentless questioning of the regime's organizing myths and the structures of power that propagated them. A few years ago, I wrote (Pi-Sunyer 1987, 168) with reference to my work in the early 1970s that "what I was witness to in Catalonia was a distinct type of opposition politics not unlike what has been described for Central Europe. We find intellectuals playing a similar role and using a similar voice," and I went on to quote Garton Ash (1986, 47) on the special role of intellectuals in such settings, a role designed "to characterize and to shape . . . pressure from below. It is half description, half prescription. Its territory is the space between the state and the individual, between the power and the powerless." To sum up, even a cursory examination reveals quite striking similarities (there are also important differences that must be addressed) in both sets of events.

The idea that the Spanish example might function as a useful political model for societies in transition to democracy was originally proposed with reference to the democratization process in Latin America (Wiarda 1987) and only later applied to Eastern Europe as events there began to unfold.[3] But regardless of how we interpret such links and their direction (always an easier task in retrospect), the Spanish case forms part of a process that began two decades ago with the end of the last of the autocracies that ruled so much of Europe before the Second World War.

The redemocratization of Portugal and Spain are obviously not unrelated to similar processes in Greece, perhaps even in Turkey.

My own reading of the respective political and social situations is that although there is a great deal of cultural and institutional common ground between Spain and the Spanish-speaking countries of Latin America, the fit is actually better between Spain and Eastern Europe, in part at least because of similar devastating mid-century wars and painful postwar experiences. Thus, from the Spanish perspective, it seems reasonable to interpret Spain's Civil War (1936–1939) as the opening round of World War II in Europe. The war itself had an international dimension that continues to manifest itself in sundry ways. As a case in point, Petru Roman, the first prime minister of Romania installed after the fall of Ceauşescu, has a Spanish mother whom his late father met while fighting in Spain on the Republican side.[4] There are many such links between Spain and the countries of Eastern and Central Europe; furthermore, Spain has played a unique role (not always adequately recognized) in modern European memory. It is certainly the case that leaders from Eastern and Central Europe regularly cite the Spanish example as a model for both peaceful political transition and successful economic modernization. On a recent visit to Spain, Mikhail Gorbachev expressed "a specific interest respecting the relatively recent experience of your country's transition to democracy and a modern market economy" (*El País* [international edition], October 22, 1990; see also *New York Times*, October 27, 1990), a viewpoint echoed by Václav Havel (*El País* [international edition], December 17, 1990) on his official visit. Havel, it might be added, also made a special point of visiting Barcelona and conferring with Jordi Pujol, president of the Catalan government.

A good deal of this chapter is devoted to comparing similarities and differences, in context and in process, between the political transformation in Spain and what is now taking place in Eastern Europe. But as I have suggested, more is involved than a simple exercise in tracing out parallel, but essentially unrelated, developments. If a reasonable case can be argued that the redemocratization of Spain helped to stimulate change in the East, political events in Eastern Europe are today having a definite resonance in Spain, most obviously in the extent to which they have reinvigorated the debate on national self-determination. We shall return to these matters, but first it is necessary to have some understanding of the peculiarities of the Spanish transition and of the social and political burdens inherited from the antecedent regime. There are, I believe, useful lessons to be learned from such an examination.

THE REGIME

There are many different ways to describe the regime created by General Franco and the self-styled Nationalists in the aftermath of the Civil War. In several respects, it followed historical patterns of military dictatorship, but with a degree of repression that has no real parallel in modern Spanish history. It also, at least in its initial phases, borrowed the trappings (but not much of the substance) of fascism and nazism and, most definitely, it was a system of class domination that melded the interests of capital and the power of the bureaucratic-military apparatus. The political order was also inseparable from its founder, an element that helps explain both its almost forty-year duration and the fact that it had no real chance of surviving his demise. Finally, it was a complex political structure that changed over time, permitted some degree of within-system pluralism, and enshrined loyalty as the cardinal political virtue.

None of the above, however, adequately conveys the texture of the regime. To the degree that one can speak of a Francoist ideology, it was a strange and archaic amalgam of totalitarianism and Catholic corporatism. More than anything else, though, it has to be understood as a system of reaction and rejection: a rejection of the Spanish intellectual renaissance, which in the early decades of this century gave Spanish artists and thinkers an international reputation; a rejection of "alien" concepts and ideologies (everything from Marxism to psychoanalysis); and, in the political domain, a reaction against democratic institutions and procedures and the demands of minority nationalities. Spain, regime ideologues insisted, should be guided by "historic" virtues and precepts such as fervent Catholicism and the military spirit.

The regime's moral order, if one can speak of it as such, was characterized by enormous contradictions, perhaps the most evident being a highly traditional Catholic orthodoxy in tandem with a cult of technocracy and developmentalism. Official puritanism attempted, somehow, to coexist with the realities of profound class and economic disparities and, especially in the final phases of the regime, flagrant manifestations of greed and corruption. It is hardly surprising that the average Spaniard responded with biting cynicism and that, much as in Eastern Europe, antiregime humor emerged early as a mechanism of resistance available to all (Pi-Sunyer 1977). In retrospect, what people perhaps most remember about life under Franco is the sensation of claustrophobia or, as it was often expressed, how isolated, culturally, socially, and politically, they felt themselves to be from the rest of Europe.

Although long before the death of Franco (November 20, 1975), dissent, simple disassociation ("tuning out"), and increasing contacts with postwar Europe had sapped the ideological foundations of the system, this vacuum did not automatically translate into an administration in disarray; on the contrary, the pillars of the state, especially its key institutions of the bureaucracy, the police, and the military, remained in place and insisted that a viable transition was only possible with their full cooperation. One could, in fact, argue that these structures and institutions had actually increased in relative importance as the ideology became more threadbare and irrelevant. In the mid-1970s, there were not a few voices—and they did not all emanate from the political right—contending that given Spanish political and social realities, a peaceful transition absolutely required the incorporation or assimilation of these structures into a new democratic order.[5]

THE TRANSITION

The situation just outlined helps to explain one critical element of the transition: the relative ease with which the state/administration managed to empty itself of embarrassing ideological content. As indicated, this was a process that—with various ups and downs—had its origins deep in the history of the regime and goes some way in accounting for the system's longevity. With respect to the transition, this circumstance did much to frame the terms of reference: If "Francoism without Franco," as it was called at the time, was clearly not a political option after 1975, it is also true that no schema of political reform or renovation had much of a chance to prosper without at least the passive support of the state apparatus (Gunther, Sani, and Shabad 1988, 34–35; Carr and Fusi 1981, 207–217; Democracia 2000 1977, 184–187).

The political situation in the latter years of the Franco regime has to be examined—in fact, is only fully comprehensible—in the context of economic and social changes that had been under way for some time. Spain experienced a rapid (and in many respects, exceedingly short-sighted) phase of economic growth that took in most of the 1960s and came to halt only with the oil crisis of 1973–1974. Initially, this was almost a third-world type of development based on mass tourism (Spain became the premier tourist destination in Europe) and the export of labor to more prosperous countries.[6]

Two related migratory processes were destined to bring about an irreversible social transformation of the first magnitude. An *internal* rural-urban shift brought more than 3 million former peasants into burgeoning urban-industrial areas (primarily Catalonia, Madrid, and the Basque Country), while at the same time an *external* movement was responsible for the emigration of 1.5 million Spaniards to places of work in the European industrial core. By 1975, 8 percent of the labor force was working abroad (FOESSA 1970, 542–552; Gunther, Sani, and Shabad 1988, 24–27; García Fernandez 1965, 78–86).

These figures can be read in many different ways. Very obviously, they spell the demise of much of the old agrarian order, whether it be that based on peasant smallholding (especially the marginal farms) or the agrotown complexes of the South. In 1950, about half of the economically active population (and no doubt many who did not enter the statistics) worked on the land. By 1970, the figure was closer to 30 percent and falling (Del Campo 1975, 102), and writers began to speak of "rural depopulation" and of the "desert" surrounding Madrid (Nadal 1976, 253); today, about half this number are agriculturalists.

The rural exodus was a response to both push and pull factors, and most directly to the grinding poverty of many rural areas. Also, it is evident that without a major transfer of human resources from the countryside to the cities, there could have been no industrial takeoff. For most of this period—roughly from the early 1960s to the mid-1970s—Spain posted an economic growth rate on the order of 6 percent per annum, and while the benefits of the "Spanish economic miracle" were distributed very unevenly, Spanish society began increasingly to resemble its Western European neighbors in terms of a whole range of variables, including demography, styles of life, and social expectations. For example, it still comes as a surprise to many outsiders to learn that Spanish fertility rates (1.30 children per mother) are today among the lowest in the European Community (EC) and well below the figure for the United States (Riding 1990; World Bank 1989, 216–217).

These economic and social transformations were not so much the product of Spanish technocratic planning, as regime boosters insisted, as of cheap production costs (wages were initially very low) and the circumstance that the national economy was able in some measure to participate in a general Western European economic expansion, the tourism boom being the chief manifestation of this linkage. We should also not forget that the Spanish economy—not to mention the regime—benefited substantially from a whole series of grants and loans emanating from the U.S. bases agreement of 1953. What we need to keep in mind at this point is that the major economic and social transformation substantially antedated the political one. These shifts paralleled a change, gradual at first, in state economic philosophy from Fascist autarky (the local variant of the command economy, pretty much scrapped by the late 1950s) to a controlled neocapitalism and then to an increasingly deregulated market economy. By the time significant political change seemed realizable, a number of historical social and economic problems, such as the "agrarian question" (Malefakis 1970), had lost a good deal of their relative importance.

It was chiefly in the decade before the death of Franco that opposition political groups—a very broad spectrum indeed—reorganized themselves so as to be in a position to offer realistic platforms and to field slates of young and dynamic candidates in the event of the expected democratic opening. Political mobilization went together with, and often was virtually indistinguishable from, attempts to expand cultural horizons. Prior censorship had been abolished in 1966, leaving a great deal of ambiguity that could be, and was, manipulated for political purposes and in the interests of broadened cultural expression. By the end of the decade, there was a boom in publishing and developments in a number of other fields, including those in the very important realm of the cinema, a medium that lends itself particularly well to veiled opposition (Besas 1985; Hopewell 1986; Higginbotham 1988). It is reasonable to speak of this period as neither a dictatorship, as the term is generally understood, nor a democracy but as an in-between condition that Linz (1973, 219) has termed "semifreedom." This permitted some channels of expression and even a degree of alegal (as distinct from illegal) opposition. For dissidents and opponents, such an arrangement offered enticing opportunities but also posed the danger that a modicum of expressive freedom (relaxation of some controls over the press, the translation of foreign works, the toleration of some dissidence masked as "culture" or "folklore") might weaken resistance (Pi-Sunyer 1971).

The pressure for change, therefore, was strong, quite well organized, and came in sundry forms—political and cultural, internal and external. Internationally, it was obvious that only a Spain with democratic credentials—one without Franco—could hope to achieve the priceless reward of full membership in the community of Western democracies. As one of the editors of the Madrid daily *El País* was later to comment, "The Common Market always slammed its door in Franco's face every time he called. To join the Nine was to have regimes similar to theirs. Political problems were the main obstacle to our membership" (*New York Times*, May 21, 1980). Internally, the minimal demands articulated by the opposition called for the dismantling of the authoritarian state and the introduction of a multiparty system and representative government, as well as the legalization of labor unions and other measures designed to protect individual and group rights. It had also been evident for some time that the demands of minority nationalities, the Basques and Catalans in particular, would have to be addressed in any new democratic arrangement, although how those should be be met was—and remains—a hotly debated issue.

In summary, the ground for the transition to democracy had been cultivated for a long time, and the problems of a routinized, contradictory, and ideologically unpalatable system were more and more evident as the dictator entered his last and most protracted illness. The momentum for a rapid transition to democracy was initially resisted by the authorities, but pressure was too strong and the dismantling of the Franco regime was achieved within two years, first through the Law of Political Reform (December 1976), which defined the political playing field, and then through the general elections of June 1977 (the first democratic elections since the fateful year 1936). It is within this very short compass of time that the basic framework of the new political order was negotiated and put into place; virtually everything else that has occurred has been in the nature of fine tuning.

The major political and administrative problem that called for resolution was how to manage change in such a manner as to accomplish two seldom compatible goals: the maintenance of internal stability (including tranquility among the military) and the reintroduction of democratic institutions. The opposition and the administration opted for a formula that entailed political reform, but not an institutional break. In the words of Prime Minister Felipe González (1985, 5–6), "This transition—and this is the most significant feature in the case of Spain—was carried out without any sudden violation of established legality, and without a single day's institutional gap."

The redemocratization of Spain thus represented something quite singular in the way of political reordering. While the change has been real enough, it is, above all, a process that aims at the integration, rather than the peripheralization, of individuals and selected structures of the antecedent regime. Expressed differently, the last of the historic Fascist regimes has been displaced in the absence of internal revolution or external overthrow, and with something approaching a political consensus on the need to avoid too critical a scrutiny of the past, including the Civil War and the years of repression that followed it.

Most Spaniards, and most foreign observers, would give this transformation high marks. From the early 1980s to the present—and the fact that the system has lasted merits attention—the Spanish state has been changed from a dictatorship on the fringes of European society to a parliamentary democracy headed by a constitutional monarch. This democratization was conceived of as but one (although central and indispensable) part of a more general reordering of the political system aimed at transforming a unitary state with a long tradition of centralized control into what Spaniards term a "state of the autonomies," fundamentally a system of regional power-sharing. Spain is now organized into seventeen Autonomous Communities. Three of these—the Basque Country or Euzkadi, Catalonia, and Galicia—are recognized as "historic" in the sense that they had already achieved or voted for statutes of autonomy during the Second Republic (1931–1939). The other communities are a post-Franco development, although some of these areas are characterized by a certain tradition of particularism or had for some time manifested a desire for greater administrative decentralization.

I have argued elsewhere (Pi-Sunyer 1980; 1988) that on balance, the process of democratization has been much more successful than the parallel reallocation of power and resources from the center to the peripheries. The primary reason for this unsatisfactory outcome, I suspect, is that the majority culture continues to harbor Basques and Catalans; or looked at from a somewhat different angle, there is an extreme reaction of Spanish nationalism and the Spanish state in the face of minority political mobilization.

The unfinished agenda on the nationalities is undoubtedly the major unresolved political question in Spain today, and at least some of the blame for this situation devolves upon the particular model of transition, and the constraints that it imposed. But there have also been other consequential costs—political, social, and cultural—that often go inadequately examined. Obviously, a negotiated political change has entailed an "understanding" with powerful institutions from the earlier system. The military, for example, remains in a position of privilege, and Spain continues to field an army of some 285,000, one of the largest in Europe (*El País* [international edition], November 19, 1990). This circumstance brings with it *political* consequences since the military defines its mission as that of guarantor of national institutions and the territorial integrity of the state (that is to say, even the *possibility* of self-determination for the Basques or the Catalans is not to be contemplated). For fundamentally the same reasons, the model of the state, even in its current autonomic form, remains profoundly centralist—and this has little to do with the ideology of the party in power. Also, the very fact that the present socialist government is one of the longest lived in Western Europe probably goes some way in explaining its tendency to conflate state, nation, and administration, what many Spaniards, and by no means simply those on the periphery, refer to as its *prepotente*—i.e., authoritarian—instincts.

In a more general sense, the brokered transition has contributed to a strange cultural-political psychology, one of whose characteristics is the loss of historical memory, or what Antonio Bar (1981, 164) calls "the collective memory block." This phenomenon manifests itself in various ways: a tendency to treat the past with extreme caution; an unwillingness to come to terms with the civil war, its causes and its consequences; and a disinclination to examine the historical roots of the current system and its institutions.

Undoubtedly, these taboos are related to an element of complicity with the antecedent system, that is, with Francoism. Again, this complicity takes many forms. The privileged political status of the military derives directly from its central role as the bulwark of the old dictatorship, a role that makes a strange bedfellow to democracy. As a case in point, the imprisoned senior military officers who masterminded the failed coup of February 23, 1981—the reader will remember that the Spanish parliament was assaulted and its members held at gunpoint—continue to receive full pay and benefits while their junior colleagues have long been reintegrated into the military. As for the enlisted men who provided the muscle, a "gentlemen's agreement" guaranteed that they would never face prosecution.[7]

Other groups, individuals, and institutions, including the higher echelons of the bureaucracy and judiciary, inherited from the dictatorship are also accorded a similar type of privilege, although not always as explicitly. Of special significance—it comes close to functioning as a metaphor for the whole transition—is the contradictory place of the monarchy: On the one hand, it is obviously a system and an institution imposed on the Spanish people by the will of the dictator (there has never been a referendum on the form of government); on the other, few would deny the human and democratic qualities of a Juan Carlos, who has played such a critical role in consolidating the post-Franco democratization process. The issue, of course, is not really the crown or its bearer but the fact that the monarchy has been defined as falling outside the ambit of legitimate political debate and that, unfortunately, most public figures abide by this dictate (for a particularly negative assessment of the transition, see Pons Prades 1987).

If there is a reluctance to give much thought to a difficult and conflictive past, the present and the future tend to be conceptualized in the much more optimistic terms of Spain's European identity and its role in the EC. Again, the issue is not really Spain's place in Europe (although my sense is that the conventional Spanish view of Europe is decidedly anachronistic) but rather the fact that this place or membership is often taken to be a virtue in its own right. If nothing else, such a rush to be "European" is hardly likely to stimulate critical analysis of social and political issues, present or past. I am not implying that there is anything questionable or illegitimate about wanting to be counted as a full and active member of what Gorbachev (1987, 194–195) first called "The Common House of Europe," but simply that the *uses* of a particular European model of society (open, but also hegemonic; democratic, but also statist, etc.) can function to entrench sundry received views of state and society, and of Europe as a zone of privilege and exclusion (Stern 1989). To some degree at least, this European identity—often conceptualized as an assemblage of what are commonly referred to as "nation-states"—works to lend legitimacy to policies and ideological positions entrenching the cultural authority of the majority and the power of the state apparatus (Clark 1985; Pi-Sunyer 1986, 1988; Rudolph and Thompson 1990).

The above observation is as pertinent to matters of cultural politics as it is to issues of administrative authority (the two are often closely intertwined). At the risk of some simplification, it is reasonable to say that what we have is essentially a two-tier system in which the state and the dominant culture (generally glossed as "Castilian") are clearly privileged. As is also the case in other Western democracies, minority languages and cultures are not "persecuted" but rather made to feel their subordinate status. The proper niche for these entities, from the majority perspective, is the personal, the local, or the regional—arenas structurally different from the "national"—where the modern liberal state permits (even protects) the expression of cultural differences. This ordering reflects not only widely held ideas respecting the primacy of the state and its role in cultural affairs but also the common distinction between "public" and "private" domains and "civil" and "political" society. Perhaps it is sufficient to note here that in legal and constitutional terms, speakers of minority Spanish languages enjoy the *right* to use them but that all Spaniards have the *duty* to know Castilian ("Spanish" in this country), the majority language. Obviously, even in areas such as Catalonia where Catalan and Castilian are defined as co-official, one language is in fact more official than the other.

Essentially, what I have been describing is a particular type of political arena in which minority cultures and their institutions are constantly forced to define themselves in counterposition to the power of the state. This is not to say that the state is unaware of pressures from the peripheries, or that it refuses to take these pressures into account when formulating policy. Indeed, the most recent Spanish government reshuffle brought into the cabinet three Catalans, including those holding the portfolios of the vice-premier (the former minister of defense) and the symbolically important Ministry of Culture. Both Spanish and foreign commentators interpret this substantial Catalan representation as, among other things, a conscious effort to satisfy pressure from Catalonia (and, less directly, the Basque Country), and also as a maneuver designed to prepare the field for the 1992 general elections (*El País* [international edition], March 18, 1991; *The Economist*, March 16, 1991).

The situations described in the preceding paragraphs obviously have parallels elsewhere, including in several long-established democratic orders that continue to enshrine the power of the majority.[8]

To sum up, we can count on some fifteen years of political change in Spain, but no one should imagine that this transformation has been painless, or that all feel that a full measure of democracy has indeed been achieved. My own sense is that we still have what Spaniards sometimes term a "vigilated" (*vigilado*), or "provisional," democracy. Nevertheless, for all its shortcomings (and one reason I have discussed these is that they mostly go unexamined), the transition must be judged a relative success.

This success, however, is attributable only in part to formal political processes, while a good deal of the credit is due to other elements, the most important being a series of social, cultural, and economic transformations that did much to transform the character of Spanish society prior to the advent of democracy. As noted earlier, these changes were in substantial measure made possible by exogenous factors (chiefly the post–World War II Western European boom) and the fact that the social costs of economic restructuring were borne disproportionately by Spanish workers and peasants. Early industrialization involved large-scale population shifts and major economic dislocations (the recession of the late 1950s and the economic crisis of the mid-1970s); today the restructuring of the Spanish economy to fit the EC model includes such by-products as one of the highest unemployment rates in Western Europe (as high as 20 percent in 1987, 15 percent in the spring of 1992), a draconian process of industrial reconversion (some have termed it "Thatcherite socialism," others "supply-side socialism"), bouts of inflation, and substantial labor discontent (Benton 1990, Greenhouse 1989; Estefanía 1988; Riding 1989a, 1989b).

In the more strictly political sphere, although this too has an economic dimension, no overview can avoid at least passing mention of the Basque Homeland and Liberty (ETA) uprising in the Basque Country—one of the longest-running insurgencies in Europe. The situation in the Basque Country is complex and open to various interpretations, but at one level it is clear evidence that a substantial segment of the local population (and not simply those with arms in hand) strongly opposes the shape that the post-Franco political order has taken. All in all, the transformation of Spain from dictatorship to democracy has been less smooth, economically and politically and even culturally, than it appears from the outside. This is not to question the very evident truth that Spain in 1992 is, by all political measures, a very much better place than it was at the death of Franco, not to mention in the depths of the dictatorship. Similarly, no one need doubt that the quality of life enjoyed by the average Spaniard has improved dramatically in the course of a generation.[9] Also, the integration of Spain into Europe and its full membership in the EC has helped to anchor democracy and give Spaniards that sense of place that was long denied to them. But although we recognize all of this, it is equally necessary to insist that these gains have exacted a significant cost, a matter of some relevance as we turn our attention to Eastern Europe.

THE OTHER EUROPE

All anthropologists, as Appadurai (1986, 357) suggests, traffic in "otherness," a concept he links closely to place "and the tendency for places to become showcases for specific issues over time" (1986, 358; see also Herzfeld 1987, 1–7). I have been reminded of the significance of geographical loci and spatial contexts as events unfold in Eastern and Central Europe. On the one hand, it is a world that at times looks surprisingly familiar to someone who has worked in Southern Europe; on the other, I recognize that much of this almost palpable sense of the familiar may, in large measure, represent surface similarity. Appadurai's cautionary words point to the central fact that what anthropologists find in particular locations is very much mediated by expectations and the contingencies of theory. More specifically apropos Spain, I am particularly conscious of the extent to which anthropological interpretation has often been shackled by externally imposed theoretical constructs of polity, economy, and society (Pi-Sunyer 1974; 1987); it is understandable that I am wary of falling into a similar trap when discussing societies of which I have no firsthand knowledge.

The apparent familiarity of Eastern and Central European scenes is strongly reinforced when the post of observation is Spain and the images are transmitted courtesy of Spanish television and are seen in real time.[10] I am also sure that the déjà vu quality is increased by the presence of a Spanish audience ready to provide instant commentary. This sense of the known is not limited to major occurrences such as demonstrations (many older Spaniards have vivid memories of the popular actions that marked the end of the dictatorship) and elections, but encompasses many details: the way people dress, the inaccessibility of villages, the motor cars (to Spaniards, Trabants and other models seem like clones of the old "Seat 600"), the design of official architecture (remarkably similar in its triumphalism), even the stylistic forms that distinguish intellectual from functionary, country dweller from city dweller.

These are not, in the main, scenes that evoke the Spanish present, but rather the Spain of a generation or so ago: a time when much of the important political life took place "in clandestinity" (or barely out of it) or on the street, and a period when Spain was much poorer than it is today. The horse-drawn carts—driven by clearly identifiable "peasants"—on the country roads of Poland or Romania remind the rural viewer of a recent enough past, but a past nevertheless. Commentators are somewhat similarly drawn to pointing out affinities between the socioeconomic structures in Eastern Europe and those of a Spain in transition to democracy (Solé Tura 1990; Rivas 1990), and there is certainly, as noted earlier in this chapter, enough in common to warrant serious discussion.

Granted these similarities, some more substantial than others, there are also a number of major structural and sequential differences. Perhaps the most obvious of these is macropolitical. For all its history of poverty and dependency, for all its vulnerability and marginality, Spain is one of that handful of European countries, East and West, that has not been invaded, partitioned, occupied, or otherwise altered spatially since the end of the Napoleonic Wars.[11] This circumstance stands in the sharpest contrast to the situation in Central and Eastern Europe, where during the same period of time, the dominant political reality has been the competing power play of rival empires. Needless to say, the post–World War II "settlement" entrenched a new hegemony.

A number of important consequences emerge from this situation. Not least of these is the impression that those most basic conventional political markers, state frontiers, are anything but secure and permanent—witness the need to reassure Poland in the course of the two-plus-four German reunification negotiations and, more recently, the frictions in Czechoslovakia and the outright conflict in a disintegrating Yugoslavia. Emerging from the same historical experience is the geopolitical idea of a European center, encompassing the territories of Central Europe, articulated by a web of human and cultural exchange; in short, a Mitteleuropa that would once more play its rightful role as pivot, gatekeeper, interpreter, and intellectual crossroads (Garton Ash 1986; Judt 1990). The problem here is that there are bound to be various visions of Central Europe, and that the concept itself is not only open to different interpretations but by its nature excludes some states and nations and privileges others, a process of categorization that seemed to be very much on the mind of Henry A. Kissinger during a recent conference in Madrid. In his opinion, Poland, Hungary, and Czechoslovakia can be thought of as forming part of the European tradition and thus warrant our immediate attention and concern, while Romania and Bulgaria "belong to another world" and may have to wait decades before they develop the appropriate social and political institutions to put them in the same conceptual category (ABC [Madrid], July 19, 1990).

Finally, it warrants comment that one of the key components of political and cultural discourse in East Central Europe appears to be nostalgia in one form or another: the celebration of national myths and the remembrance of old injustices, even a certain historical wistfulness that would interpret the pre–World War I imperial order (now safely distant) as prosperous, tranquil, and free of much of the current ethnic strife.[12] I am not suggesting that nostalgia is an emotion unknown in Iberia, but that as a *political* force it is primarily associated with the residual extreme right, an element with minimal importance in today's political arena. Seen from the other side of Europe, the resurfacing of violent xenophobic and chauvinistic sentiments joined to a veneration of the past strikes an anachronistic—and frankly chilling—chord.

Quite clearly, comparisons between Spain and Eastern and Central Europe must take into account these differences in scale, history, and political and national composition that I have alluded to. Also, as noted earlier, political change in Spain came on the heels of extensive economic reordering and years of real growth.[13] This situation was not without its quota of problems—indeed, the contradictions inherent in fast economic development and slow political evolution fed discontent—but it meant that once the major political issues had been addressed (if hardly resolved), the economic integration of Spain into modern Europe was a reasonably feasible goal.

In contrast, the former Comecon states are, for the most part, saddled with remarkably impoverished and antiquated economies. Even if we allow for the difficulties inherent in comparing conditions in the early 1990s with those of the mid-1970s, it is hardly to be doubted that standards of living in Eastern and Central Europe are, generally speaking, much lower today than in Spain at the time of transition. Obviously, this poses a political problem since the incoming national directorates must attempt to satisfy two sets of demands—for a more democratic political system and for improved material conditions.

Some of the economic and social issues that had long helped to define Spanish society, such as the backwardness of rural life and the power of conservative elites in the countryside, find strange reflections in today's Central and Eastern Europe. In the Bulgarian elections, for example, the socialists (i.e., the renamed Communists) lost the cities to the Democratic Alliance but won the countryside. The Agrarian party, supposedly the party of peasant interests, managed no more than 8 percent of the vote. Given the current uncertainty, coupled with an actual drop in living standards, it is hardly surprising that most Eastern European farm-workers are more interested in holding on to their jobs and in the security of predictable arrangements with the landlord—the state—than in economic and social experimentation. As a recent report on East European farming points out, the conventional Western view "that the desire to own and farm private land is one of the most fundamental human instincts" is not shared by most of those who are employed in state and collective enterprises: "From the Baltic to the Black Sea, the peasants are not interested in taking their land back" ("East European Farming," *The Economist*, July 21, 1990). The rural situation is paralleled by employment patterns in other sectors of the economy. Thus Hungary, which abolished rigid state planning in 1968, still has an economy in which state-owned enterprises and cooperatives account for 85 percent of GDP. If nothing else, economies so structured have a built-in constituency with strong interests in maintaining the status quo. There are several other economic, cum-political considerations and comparisons that I can do no more than touch on. One of these is the heavy to substantial debt burden that most countries (especially Poland and the successor states of the former Soviet Union and Yugoslavia) are carrying, and the relationship of indebtedness to the size of internal markets and population.[14] Also, this accumulation of foreign debt is generally linked to several other highly deleterious factors, including strong inflationary pressures and the citizen's lack of confidence in the currency and the fiscal system—as has been so dramatically demonstrated in the former Soviet Union. In virtually every report of everyday life in Eastern Europe, one of the key characteristics of the local economies (some more, some less) is scarcity: Often, there is more disposable income than consumer goods to spend it on. Finally, note must be taken of the particular correlations of economic power that have emerged in this part of Europe. In the most simple terms, the end of Soviet hegemony has coincided with the emergence, in the course of the past two decades, of the German Federal Republic as the indisputable economic dynamo of Western Europe, a matter that carries both economic and political consequences. With Berlin now the capital of a unified Germany, this alone signals something of an eastern shift in Germany's political center of gravity. In short, one has to envisage an economically very powerful Germany surrounded by remarkably weakened neighbors on its eastern frontier.

Not much in this macroeconomic scenario particularly resembles the Spanish situation in the first decade of transition, although there are some interesting affinities respecting the geographic distribution of power and its effects. As noted earlier, Spain, together with Greece and Portugal, was granted full membership in the EC after it met, as set forth in the Treaty of Rome, the dual tests of democratic institutions and a market economy. Also, obviously, this Mediterranean cluster rounded out the European "West" in counterposition to the "East." The expansion of the club from nine to twelve members did not, however, confer economic equality, and it is still reasonable to speak of a "southern tier" of EC members that constitutes something of a periphery in relation to the wealthier core industrial societies.

It is with these considerations very much in mind, and remembering the considerable social costs incurred in restructuring the Spanish economy, that I ponder some of the models and constructs that have been proposed for the integration of Central and Eastern Europe into what is now being termed a "European economic space" (Larsson 1990; Monteira 1990). There is clearly substantial interest, particularly on the part of Czechoslovakia and Hungary, in joining the EC, but hardly in the near future, since all the economies are relatively backward (and would take years to be transformed into market-dominated systems). Furthermore, there is a long line of better-positioned candidates that will have precedence.[15] But apart from this, there seems to be a considerable reluctance to facilitate much in the way of EC expansion; the argument that was used to support Spanish, Portuguese, and Greek membership—that such association would help to cement democracy—is now seldom heard in Brussels.

It would appear that what is shaping up—there is talk of "concentric circles"—is a strangely Wallersteinian (1976) economic order with an EC "core," an EFTA "semiperiphery," and the other countries very much on the margins (Stern 1989; "The Making of a New Constellation," *The Economist*, August 4, 1990; "European Community," *The Economist*, July 7, 1990). This impression is reinforced by several other factors and elements.

Central and Eastern Europe, it seems, are increasingly being seen as a source of cheap labor, either in the countries of origin or in the form of immigrants to the developed West, the latter option at least in part designed to compensate for a slump in Western European birthrates (*New York Times*, July 22, 1990; August 5, 1990).[16] But the sheer magnitude of the potential immigrant wave—an exodus of some two million per annum from the former Soviet Union alone does not appear farfetched—is breeding something close to a seige mentality in some Western European countries. The early predictions (*New York Times*, May 17, 1990, August 1, 1990) that as Central and Eastern European societies shift to market economies, there is bound to be a heavy initial increase in unemployment have been proved only too correct. In many respects, Eastern Europe seems to be experiencing, with reference to Western Europe, a phenomenon remarkably similar to that of Mexico (and Latin America more generally) apropos the United States: As local economies break down or are dismantled, labor must increasingly seek employment in developed cores (Kearney 1986; 1991).

One can also reasonably expect—as happened in Spain—that the phasing out of centralized controls will lead to the growth of the informal sector, a shift that generally improves economic performance, but often at the price of a deregulated workplace and an unprotected work force (Benton 1990; see also Soto 1990). If we take all these factors together, it is hard to avoid the conclusion that, at least in the economic domain, no soft landing awaits the societies of Central and Eastern Europe. When we shift from the macroeconomic dimension to more strictly political considerations, the parallels between Spain and Central and Eastern Europe are often quite striking. The rapid dismantling of Soviet power, however we may assess its long-term consequences, has brought to the forefront the interests of a group of countries with a restored political sovereignty or a substantial measure of autonomy. Among the problems that need to be addressed by these polities is that of institutional continuity and a reasonably smooth political transition, desiderata that are all the more important if the economic prospects are clouded. All the evidence seems to point to a "pragmatic" approach, very much on the Spanish model. In the words of a *New York Times* (April 2, 1990) editorial, "Yesterday's dissidents need somehow to cohabit with their former oppressors, bearing in mind the admonition of Czechoslovakia's President, Vaclav Havel—that everyone in some sense was complicit with the old dictatorship." That this is in fact taking place is the theme of a recent essay by Garton Ash (1990b). He asks, "Former censors, former border guards, former apparatchiks, former secret policemen: What is to be done with them?" (1990b, 51). The answer is that, in the interests of efficiency and necessity, the best resolution is likely to be some type of continued civil service employment.

That this is a prudent policy goes without saying, and one can also make the case that all recent democratic restorations have taken much the same tack—not only in Spain but also in Argentina, Brazil, Chile, and Uruguay—and it very much appears that the South African transition now under way is bound to entail some closing of the books. Apart from reasons of prudence, one has to take into account that incoming administrations are understandably anxious to inherit a working state apparatus. This stress on the importance of governmental functions, and the fear of what some regard as "a dangerous leadership vacuum" (Szulc 1989), also signals an important shift in roles, perspectives, and procedures: The dissidents of yesterday are transformed into the government of today, while, at least on the part of many, there is a perception that not only are the "old structures" surviving but, as Hubinger and Lass (1991, 9) report with respect to Czechoslovakia, "the new ones are beginning to act like the old." As Victor Turner (1969) would have expressed it, communitas gives way to structure.

This is not to suggest that the processes outlined previously represent, as some would have it, an "end to ideology" or, for that matter, "the end of history." Those who proclaim the unabashed victory of economic and political liberalism fail, in their self-congratulation, to take into account several very important considerations, not the least being that much "of the advice now being offered the Central and Eastern European states proceeds from a view of the so-called capitalist or free-enterprise economies that bears no relation to their reality" (Galbraith 1990, 51). It is not only that advice—which is mostly what has been moving in an easterly direction—is cheap but that it often constitutes a sort of primitive ideology of how Western systems *should* work. Secondly, even when advice is more realistic, it tends to be decontextualized, thus failing to give sufficient weight to the fact that Western systems function reasonably well because they are underpinned and ameliorated by extensive social services, public controls, and adequate salaries. Finally, in the realm of priorities, there are other important issues besides effective problem-solving. Certainly, people in Central and Eastern Europe—as was also the case in Spain—yearn for a decent standard of living. But this fact is not to be taken as evidence that everything else is subordinate or insignificant. Issues of class and power have not disappeared from the agenda—and certainly not in Europe. The state and its functions, and also the premises and priorities of capitalism—what Havel (1990, 57) calls "the malignant pressures of technical civilization and the stupefying dictatorship of consumerism" —are not taken for granted everywhere, as is demonstrated by the substantial success of various contestatorial movements, including feminism and environmentalism.

Within this spectrum of social movements and political formations that remain very much alive, special note must be taken of a powerful ethnic and nationalist resurgence. Actually, one of the most revealing features of the two transitions is the serious challenge they pose to an assumption shared equally by Marxist theory and liberal ideology, namely, that nationalism is either dead or dying. What we are seeing in post-Communist Europe, as was also evident during the Spanish transition, is the reemergence of ethnic and national loyalties, particularly among subordinated groups. While this is not an altogether comfortable prospect—nationalisms, like state structures, do come in sundry forms, not all of them pleasant—one need not subscribe to the all-too-common interpretation that ethnic demands are inherently regressive and politically destabilizing. Just as there is little evidence that the state is "withering," granted the moves toward greater unity in Western Europe, the notion that ethnic and national collectivities are anachronistic holdovers seems equally erroneous. We may, as it has been suggested, be witnessing the Springtime of the Nations. It can reasonably be asked: Where, in fact, are the real nations of Europe? The way this question is answered will have a direct bearing on the future peace and tranquility of the whole continent.[17]

In conclusion, there would appear to be two significant political processes that emerge in the course of transition: the melding of old structures of power and new leadership, especially when privileged elements of the ancien régime (the military, the police, the bureaucracy) manage to take onto themselves the guardianship of order and administrative continuity; and the reemergence of a spectrum of minority demands for an increased say—in some cases not excluding self-determination—in the political process. If, on the one hand, the lesson is that state structures are very resistant, it is equally important to recognize that once political systems open up it becomes virtually impossible to promulgate only some types of reform, allow only some kinds of freedom.[18] If Europe in the decades to come does in fact move toward a greater degree of political integration, such an other-than-state system may function to better address regionalist and ethnonationalist concerns. In the interval, it would appear that conflicts between peoples are more likely than those between currently constituted states.

SPANISH POLITICS AND EASTERN EVENTS

A theme that I have tried to develop in this chapter is that the transformations that took place in Spain and that are currently under way in Central and Eastern Europe are, to some degree, linked events. If Spain can be said to have provided a ready-at-hand model of postdictatorship, some features of which could be emulated, it is equally true that influences have moved in the other direction as well. Since the summer of 1989, I have made four trips to Catalonia, where I found not only great interest in the news from Eastern Europe but also that these events were having a discernible effect on political and social discourses.

One consequence of an international environment in which the chances of a major European war seem remote has been the growing resistance of young Spanish men to serve their "wasted" year in military service. The *mili* has never been popular, and one of the evident problems faced by the socialist government is how to square its historical antimilitarism with a system of conscription. Conscientious objector status has been legalized, but this has not reduced the number of desertions. Almost 10 percent of the recruits from Barcelona now fail to report to their units, a figure many times higher than the 1.5 percent for the state as a whole. Desertions from military formations have also increased significantly, by some 70 percent overall since mid-1989 (*El País*, July 17, 1990; *New York Times*, October 5, 1989). My impression, based on several interviews with young people, is that this resistance to enlistment reflects both the perceived absurdity of military service and the influence of very powerful antimilitarist images received from Central and Eastern Europe, images that often show very ordinary people, mostly young, facing down the forces of reaction. I was also reminded several times that it was primarily students who confronted the tanks in Tiananmen.

This is not the whole story. My impression (very much in keeping with public opinion polls) is that the young are much more opposed to military service, and to military involvement in general, than are older people. The very substantial antiwar demonstrations that took place during the initial phases of the Gulf crisis were dominated by teenagers and young adults; they had little backing from the political establishment, from the Right or from the Left. What we may be seeing in Spain is the inception of a new political awareness spearheaded by the young. It is the young, after all, who face not only the prospects of conscription but greater risks of unemployment and other forms of margination. There are some parallels here with the situation in Central and Eastern Europe.

Discussion of a range of other issues has been stimulated by the changes taking place on the other side of the continent. As the full environmental costs of Communist-style industrial development are becoming more manifest, the impact of Spain's own development policies on the environment—including the emphasis on mass tourism—is coming under increasing scrutiny (*El País*, July 5, 1990). In a somewhat analogous way, the mounting realization that socialism in Eastern Europe typically entailed the subordination of women to male-dominated state and domestic structures has caused Spanish feminists to examine anew their own society—and to mobilize to protect victories that are far from consolidated (González Enríquez 1990).[19]

But undoubtedly, the most interesting development linked to changes in the East has been the revitalization of the debate on minority political rights. Both the Basque and Catalan parliaments have gone on record that their respective peoples have not renounced the right of self-determination, and this in turn has initiated intense debate and acrimony. During a formal military ceremony early in January 1990, King

Juan Carlos stressed that one of the missions of the military was to defend the "territorial integrity" of the state (*El País*, January 7, 1990), an indirect reference to the self-determination polemic. More ominously, three senior military commanders made declarations respecting the "indissoluble" unity of Spain. In such an environment, those in Catalonia who demonstrated the greatest discomfort were the leaders of the Catalan Socialist Party (PSC), a semi-autonomous entity allied to the governing Spanish Socialist Workers' Party (PSOE).[20] Thus, we find Pascual Maragall, the popular socialist mayor of Barcelona, claiming that the situation of Catalonia was in no sense comparable to that of Lithuania, and that consequently he did not "feel like a Lithuanian" (*Avui*, January 8, 1990), an opinion that generated several letters to the press from fellow Catalans who were not shy to claim that *they* indeed felt like Lithuanians, and for good reasons. Similarly, Raimon Obiols, first secretary of the party, gave a long interview denouncing violence, self-determination, separatism, and other evils and offered his opinion that in Spain "separatism would take us not to Lithuania, but to Albania" (*La Vanguardia*, January 12, 1990).

In contrast, many Catalans are of the opinion that comparisons with Eastern Europe are perfectly apt, perhaps especially now that the limitations inherent in the present Spanish political system are more evident than they were during the heady days of the early transition. Also, as several writers and editorialists have been quick to point out, Catalan nationalism, far from being "intolerant," "essentialist," and "parochial," has historically followed a progressive path, and not the least during the recent dictatorship (Porta Perales 1990; *Avui* [unsigned editorial], January 7, 1990; Porta 1990).

Not surprisingly, the leaders of independence-minded political parties have been making trips to Eastern Europe, and especially to the Baltic republics, stressing that the present composition of Spain is no more to be taken as "natural" than that of several other states, including the former Soviet Union (the matter is addressed in several reports and articles in the journal *Debat Nacionalista* [Barcelona]). If, nationalist authors argue, some ten one-time Soviet republics have opted for independence, and the current political and territorial order of such an established democracy as Canada appears far from immutable, it is difficult to insist that nationalism is a thing of the past. On the contrary, as several commentators observe, most of the countries on the world map owe their existence to the relatively recent disaggregation of imperial systems, from Ottoman to British and French.

Spain, as noted earlier, *is* different from much of Eastern and Central Europe, but mostly with respect to its neighbors and the antiquity of its frontiers; internally, there are strong centripetal pressures that have often been played down. Events in Eastern Europe are bound to stimulate further thought and action respecting the present political order, including serious consideration of options such as a much looser degree of state control in the framework of a common European political space—the "friendly union of friendly nations and democratic countries" that Havel (1990, 57) envisages.

Notes

1. Conscious that change in Eastern and Central Europe "had come at an incomprehensible speed," the editors of *Granta* chose to record the moment between "two histories: the one that existed before 9 November [the dismantling of the Berlin Wall], and the other one, still to be defined" (*Anonymous* 1990, 126). The editor of *Daedalus*, commenting on the problems of producing a special volume on Eastern Europe, notes that no issue of *Daedalus* "has been more difficult to bring to a satisfactory conclusion" because of "a year of extraordinary events, momentous and largely unanticipated" (Graubard 1990, i). These are pretty typical reactions. If 1989 was an *annus mirabilis*—hardly the firmest context for historical prediction—there is little evidence to suggest that major change is behind us.

2. On the surface, at least, the Soviet system seems to have been both more brittle and more long-lasting, although the Stalinist terror of the late 1930s may in part reflect a deep crisis in the state apparatus. In Francoist Spain, the internal regime crisis was gradual and cumulative. In their very different ways both the Franco regime and the Communist systems in Eastern and Central Europe claimed to have eliminated the underlying causes of conflicts between classes and between nationalities or ethnic groups.

3. See, especially, Alan Riding's reporting on Spain (1989a; 1989b). It is worth noting that in a relatively recent collection, the Spanish Prime Minister (González 1987) writes at length on Spain's new international role (Western Europe, Latin America, the Middle East) but does not raise the possibility of some influence on Eastern European events.

4. Many exiled Spaniards fought in different World War II Allied formations, while a division of Spanish volunteers fought for the Nazis on the Eastern front. The Spanish survivors of Nazi camps have recently been pressing the government, so far with little success, to make some official gesture honoring the Spanish victims of the Nazi system.

5. The distinction between the ideological foundations of the regime and the administrative structure of the state is not, in reality, always easy to make. We should keep in mind that Franco (very much a military traditionalist) never attempted to develop a mass party. The Spanish Fascist organization (Falange, later changed to the more innocuous Movimiento) soon became a patronage mechanism for state employment, especially the allocation of positions in the middle and lower echelons of the bureaucracy. As the political climate changed, officeholders increasingly identified themselves in terms of their state functions rather than their party membership.

6. Tourism grew from 1.26 million visitors in 1951 to 30 million in 1975. The

figure for 1989 is 54 million visitors—a statistic that needs to be considered in relation to a total Spanish population of 38.5 million (Promatora de Informaciones 1990, 364, 402).

7. It now appears that right-wing elements in the military were involved in several—perhaps as many as four—other plots, the most recent being a planned assassination of King Juan Carlos and Queen Sofia, the prime minister, and other members of the government during an Armed Forces Day parade in 1985 (*El País* [international edition], February 18, 1991, *New York Times*, March 3, 1991).

8. Needless to say, not all Western democracies are equally centralist and culturally intolerant. Switzerland has survived several hundred years as a functioning democracy combining three different cultures and four languages within one polity—and has done very well in the process. In contemporary Western Europe, hegemonic ideologies ("core national values," etc.) are also being used to frame the discourse on the status and place of Asian and African immigrants and their descendants.

9. Measures of comparative social well-being are notoriously hard to formulate. In this respect it is interesting to note that the United Nations's *Human Development Report 1990* gives Spain a higher "human development index" —essentially a measure of the quality of life—than it assigns to the United States (*Economist*, May 26, 1990).

10. Among the key developments I watched were the Romanian rebellions of December 1989 and early 1990 and events in the Baltic republics during the same time period. In the summer of 1990, the focus had changed to the impending reunification of Germany and events in Czechoslovakia.

11. The Spanish state frontiers are the same as those worked out in the Treaty of the Pyrenees in 1659 (Sahlins 1989). Only Gibraltar remains as a serious, but hardly dangerous, irredenta.

12. I do not take at face value speculations that the collapse of Eastern European communism may mean the return to power of sundry dethroned monarchs (Brooks-Baker 1990), but even serious historians (Deák 1990) are interpreting the institutions of the Austro-Hungarian Empire as remarkably beneficial, if hardly progressive. Strictly in terms of images, what I find remarkable about East Central Europe is the resurgence of religious (often linked to national) symbolism—saints, clerics, and crosses—that trigger a memory of what Spain was like more than a generation ago.

13. Some years ago (Pi-Sunyer 1974; Schneider, Schneider, and Hansen 1972) I debated the "reality" of this economic dimension and insisted that it was both real and politically important. For all the shortsightedness of post–World War II economic policies (problems that ranged from income distribution to environmental degradation), by the time Spain entered the European Community it could do so in at least some degree of equality.

14. Needless to say, population alone neither makes a country politically powerful nor assures it a substantial market for goods and services, as has been amply demonstrated by Ceauşescu's cruel and counterproductive pronatalist policies (Beck 1990). It is true, nevertheless, that the internal economies of most Central and Eastern European countries are small and underdeveloped in both relative and absolute terms. "Estimates of GNP or GDP vary widely. In 1990, the *Economist* (April 28) estimated the Soviet GDP per person at close to that of Portugal—one of Western Europe's poorest countries. The

same report put the USSR's GDP in the 'middle range' of what the journal still termed 'centrally planned economies.' There is little doubt that in the ensuing two years economic conditions in many of these lands have greatly deteriorated."

15. Fundamentally, the original political rationale for economic blocs (EC, EFTA, the socialist states of Eastern and Central Europe) has pretty well evaporated. EFTA countries, many of which did not join the EC because of policies of neutrality, are now much more eager to join. Turkey also applied (1987), and there is a cluster of small states (Cyprus, Malta, Iceland) that have expressed various degrees of interest. If to this list we add some of the countries of Eastern and Central Europe, the twelve could easily become the twenty-four.

16. Areas of possible expansion include automobile production (Greenhouse 1990) and tourism (see "Eastern Europe: The Test of Tourism" an extensive report in the *New York Times* travel section, July 22, 1990).

17. The issue of national and ethnic rights is complex and needs to be approached in a way that avoids sensationalism and the temptation to hold forth from a position of superiority. Even a cursory reading of Western press reports on Central and Eastern Europe indicates that ethnic processes are generally perceived as dangerous—terms like "conflict," "enmities," and "ancient divisions" are very common. The "Balkan" scenario is often applied uncritically.

18. That attempts, more or less successful, may be made to hobble minority participation and representation is another matter. The recent efforts on the part of Bulgarian parliamentarians to deny seats to ethnic Turks on the grounds that they were elected by a "movement" and not a "proper" political party, remind me of various strategies used to bar or limit the seating in the Cortes of some Basque and Catalan deputies. Outside the former Soviet Union and Yugoslavia, Bulgaria and Romania would appear to have the most critical minority problems, in very large measure because of the lack of flexibility on the part of the majority population and the state structures. Both countries, though, are now writing new constitutions and this offers an opportunity for minorities (in particular the Turkish minority in Bulgaria and the Hungarian one in Romania) to address pressing cultural and political issues. A system of regional autonomy, similar to that operating in Spain, would represent a great improvement.

19. The economic and political gains of Spanish women are for the most part recent, but not inconsiderable. They include a very substantial representation in the professions and the civil service and no less than seventy-two seats (12.5 percent) in the Cortes, the state parliament (*El País*, June 18, 1990; "Europe's Women," *Economist*, June 30, 1990).

20. This is not the place for a detailed analysis of the relationship of Catalan socialism to state-level parties. The autonomy of the Catalan Socialist Party (PSC) is certainly far from self-evident, yet Catalan votes (translated into Catalan Socialist Party seats) are absolutely indispensable for maintaining a government majority in Parliament. The recent cabinet reshuffle (three ministries now headed by PSC politicians) shows how central Catalonia looms in the strategies of power.

References

Anonymous, 1990. "The state of Europe [unsigned preface]." *Granta* 30:126.

Appadurai, A. 1986. "Theory in anthropology: Center and periphery." *Comparative Studies in Society and History* 28(2):356–361.

Bar, A. 1981. "Spain: A culture in transition." in *Spain: A culture in transition*, eds. S. Hoffmann and P. Kitromilides. 152–167. London: Allen & Unwin.

Beck, S. 1990. "What brought Romanians to revolt." Unpublished paper.

Benton, L. 1990. *Invisible factories*. Albany: SUNY Press.

Besas, P. 1985. *Behind the Spanish lens*. Denver: Arden Press.

Brooks-Baker, H. 1990. "Will blue blood succeed the red flag?" *New York Times*, February 17:27.

Carr, R., and Fusi, J. P. 1981. *Spain: Dictatorship to democracy*. London: Allen & Unwin.

Clark, R. P. 1985. "Dimensions of Basque political culture in post-Franco Spain." in *Basque politics: A case study in ethnic nationalism*, ed. W. A. Douglas. 217–269. Reno, NV: Associated Faculty Press.

Deák, I. 1990. *Beyond nationalism: A social and political history of the Habsburg officer corps, 1848–1918*. Oxford: Oxford University Press.

Del Campo, S. 1975. *Análisis de la población española*. Barcelona: Editorial Ariel.

Democracia 2000. 1977. *Primer año del posfranquismo*. Madrid: Pecosa.

De Soto, H. 1990. *The other path*. New York: Harper and Row.

Estefanía, J. 1988. "Los autores del 'milagro español'." *El País*, July 27:10.

FOESSA, F. 1970. *Informe sociológico sobre la situación social de españa*. Madrid: Editorial Euramérica.

Galbraith, J. K. 1990. "The rush to capitalism." *New York Review*, October 25:51.

García Fernandez, J. 1965. *La emigración exterior de España*. Barcelona: Ediciones Ariel.

Garton Ash, T. 1986. "Does central Europe exist?" *New York Review*, October 9:45–52.

———. 1990a. "Mitteleuropa?" *Daedalus* 119(1):1–2.

———. 1990b. "Eastern Europe: Après le déluge, nous." *New York Review*, August 16:51–57.

———. 1990c. *The uses of adversity, essays on the fate of central Europe*. New York: Vintage Books.

González Enríquez, C. 1990. "El sexismo que viene del este." *El País*, July 17:26.

González, F. 1985. Address by the Prime Minister at the Wilson Center, Washington, DC, September 27. Distributed by the Embassy of Spain.

———. 1987. "A new international role for a modernizing Spain." in *Spain in the 1980's*, eds. R. P. Clark and M. H. Haltzel. 179–190. Cambridge, MA: Ballinger.

Gorbachev, M. 1987. *Perestroika: New thinking for our country and the world.* New York: Harper and Row.

Graubard, S. R. 1990. "Preface to the issue." *Daedalus* 119(1):i–iv.

Greenhouse, S. R. 1989. "Spain's daring experiment in supply-side socialism." *New York Times*, February 13:D1.

———. 1990. "Fiat's thrust into Eastern Europe." *New York Times*, August 5:F1, F6.

Gunther, R., Sani, G., and Shabad, G. 1988. *Spain after Franco.* Berkeley: University of California Press.

Havel, V. 1990. "The return of Germany." *New York Review* (April 26):56–57.

Herzfeld. M. 1987. *Anthropology through the looking glass, critical ethnography in the margins of Europe.* Cambridge: Cambridge University Press.

Higginbotham, V. 1988. *Spanish film under Franco.* Austin: University of Texas Press.

Hopewell, J. 1986. *Out of the past: The Spanish cinema since Franco.* London: British Film Institute.

Hubinger, V., and Lass, A. 1991. "Memory and violence in the aftermath of the Czechoslovak 'velvet revolution.'" Unpublished paper.

Judt, T. 1990. "The rediscovery of central Europe." *Daedalus* 119(1):23–54.

Kearney, M. 1986. "From the invisible hand to visible feet: Anthropological studies of migration and development." *Annual Review of Anthropology* 15:331–361.

———. 1991. "Borders and boundaries of state and self at the end of empire." *Journal of Historical Sociology* 4(1):52–74.

Larsson, A. 1990. "Hacia un espacio económico Europeo." *El País*, July 19:10–11.

Lewis, F. 1988. "Oh, for a 'normal country.'" *New York Times*, October 12:A31.

Linz, J. J. 1973. "Opposition to and under an authoritarian regime: The case of Spain." in *Regimes and oppositions*, ed. R. A. Dahl. 171–259. New Haven: Yale University Press.

Malefakis, E. E. 1970. *Agrarian reform and peasant revolution in Spain.* New Haven: Yale University Press.

Monteira, F. 1990. "Entrevista con Jacques Delors." *El País*, July 19:1–2.

Nadal, J. 1976. *La población española (siglos XVI a XX).* Barcelona: Editorial Ariel.

Pi-Sunyer, O. 1971. "The maintenance of ethnic identity in Catalonia." in *The limits of integration: Ethnicity and nationalism in modern Europe*, ed. O. Pi-Sunyer, 111–146. Department of Anthropology Research Report, no. 9, Amherst, MA: University of Massachusetts.

———. 1974. "Elites and noncorporate groups in the European Mediterranean: A reconsideration of the catalan case." *Comparative Studies in Society and History* 16(1):117–131.

———. 1977. "Political humor in a dictatorial state: The case of Spain." *Ethnohistory* 24(2):179–190.

———. 1980. "Dimensions of catalan nationalisms." in *Nations without a state: Ethnic minorities in Western Europe*, ed. C. R. Foster. 101–115. New York: Praeger.

———. 1986. "The stalled transformation: Six years of the autonomy process in Catalonia." Program in Western European Studies Occasional Papers Series, no. 3, Amherst, MA: University of Massachusetts.

———. 1987. "Town, country and nation: studying culture and politics in Catalonia." *Anthropological Quarterly* 60(4):167–173.

———. 1988. "Catalan politics and Spanish democracy: An overview of a relationship." *Iberian Studies* 17(1–3):1–16.

Pons Prades, E. 1987. *Crónica negra de la transición española*. Barcelona: Plaza & Janes.

Porta, J. 1990. "Autodeterminació, democràcia i nacionalisme." *Avui*, January 10:13.

Porta Perales, M. 1990. "Ni síndrome nacionalista ni síndrome d'Estrocolm." *Avui*, January 20:9.

Promotora de Informaciones. 1990. *Anuario el país*. Madrid: Ediciones el País.

Riding, A. 1989a. "With Spain's prosperity comes a measure of pain." *New York Times*, October 15:1, 18.

———. 1989b. "Spain shifts towards the right edge of the socialist order." *New York Times*, November 5:E3.

———. 1990. "Western Europe, its births falling, wonders who'll do all the work." *New York Times*, June 22:1, 12.

Rivas, M. 1990. "La otra verdad de la otra Europa." *El País*, July 3:13.

Rudolph, J. R. Jr., and Thompson, R. J., eds. 1990. *Ethnoterritorial politics, policy, and the Western World*. Boulder, CO: Lynne Rienner.

Sahlins, P. 1989. *Boundaries, the making of France and Spain in the Pyrenees*. Berkeley: University of California Press.

Schneider, P., Schneider, J., and Hansen, E. 1972. "Modernization and development: The role of regional elites and noncorporate groups in the European Mediterranean." *Comparative Studies in Society and History* 14(3):328–350.

Solé Tura, J. 1990. "Ocho meses." *El País*, July 16:11.

Stern, F. 1989. "The common house of Europe." *New York Review*, December 7:6–10.

Szulc, T. 1989. "Is Eastern Europe ready?" *New York Times*, December 3:25.

Turner, V. 1969, *The ritual process*, Ithaca: Cornell University Press.

Wallerstein, I. 1976. *The modern world system*. New York: Academic Press.

Wiarda, H. J. 1987. "The significance for Latin America of the Spanish democratic transition." in *Spain in the 1980s: The democratic transition and a new international role*, eds. R. P. Clark and M. H. Haltzel, 157–178. Cambridge, MA: Ballinger.

World Bank. 1989. *World development report 1989*. New York: Oxford University Press.

Notes on the Contributors

DAVID G. ANDERSON is a doctoral candidate and Commonwealth scholar in the Department of Social Anthropology at the University of Cambridge, England. He has worked for several years in a Gwich'in community in Canada's Northwest Territories. His ongoing research and fieldwork are on social change among northern native peoples in Siberia.

SAM BECK is director of the Field and International Study Program at Cornell University. He is the coeditor of the *Anthropology of East Europe Review* and the coeditor of *Ethnicity and Nationalism in Southeastern Europe* (University of Amsterdam, 1981). He is the author of *Manny Almeida's Ringside Lounge: The Cape Verdian Struggle for Their Neighborhood* (Gavea-Brown, 1992). He has published on the relationship between uncollectivized peasants and the state under conditions of Romanian socialism, and on ethnicity, race, class, and the state. Currently he is researching the formation of civil society and its relationship to ethnicity in postrevolutionary Romania and in Austria since World War II.

TAHSIN CORAT is professor of political science at Carleton University in Ottawa, Canada. He teaches Western European politics and conducts research on knowledge-processing and the changing nature of the capitalist production system. He has published articles in *Parliamentary Affairs* and in *French Politics and Society of Harvard University*. He currently is working on a piece about the writings of the late Louis Althusser.

HERMINE G. DE SOTO is assistant scientist in anthropology at the Women's Studies and Women's Research Center at the University of Wisconsin-Madison. She is the editor of *Culture and Contradiction: Dialectics of Wealth, Power and Symbol* (Mellen Research University Press, 1992). Her previous research is forthcoming in *The Delayed Transformation: Experiences of Everyday Life in a Village in the Black Forest*. Presently her field research is on "contesting female personhood: comparison of east and west German legal cultures in the process of unification."

WILLIAM GRAF is professor of political science and chair of the Department of Political Studies at Guelph University in Guelph, Canada. His publications include *The Nigerian State* (Jas. Currey, 1988) and *The German Left Since 1945* (Oleander, 1976). His recent work is in *The Internationalization of the German Political Economy* (Macmillan, 1992). His current research focuses on the unification process in Germany and its relationship to the international political economy.

CHRISTOPHER HANN is university lecturer in social anthropology and fellow of Corpus Christi College in Cambridge, United Kingdom. He has carried out anthropological fieldwork in Poland and Hungary since 1975 and is also engaged in research in Turkey. In 1992 he will take up a professorhip of social anthropology at the University of Kent. His books include *Tazlar: A Village in Hungary* (Cambridge University Press, 1980); *A Village Without Solidarity: Polish Peasants in Years of Crises* (Yale University Press, 1985); *Market Economy and Civil Society in Hungary* (London F. Cass, 1990); and his latest book, *Tea and the Domestication of the Turkish State* (Eothen Press, 1990).

WILLIAM HANSEN is a freelance writer and scholar living in Hartford, Connecticut. He is coeditor of the acclaimed volume *The Soviet Bloc and the Third World: The Political Economy of East-West Relations* (Westview, 1989). He has also coedited articles on "Imperialism, Dependency and Social Class," and "Aid or Imperialism? West Germany in Sub-Saharan Africa." His contributions have appeared in *Monthly Review* and *Africa Today*. He has lectured at Boston University, Trinity College (Connecticut), and the University of Maryland. His current research is on Zimbabwe and on the state socialist countries of Eastern Europe.

ANATOLY M. KHAZANOV is professor of anthropology at the University of Wisconsin-Madison and of the Hebrew University in Jerusalem. He is a fellow of the British Academy and former senior member of the Academy of Sciences of the USSR. He is the author of seven books, including *The Nomads and the Outside World* (Cambridge University Press, 1984). His current research interests include pastoral nomadism, peoples of the Soviet Union, ethnicity, historical anthropology, and modernization.

DAVID A. KIDECKEL is professor of anthropology and chairperson of the Anthropology Department at Central Connecticut State University and coeditor of the *Anthropology of East Europe Review*. He is the author of *The Solitude of Collectivism: Romanian Villages to the Revolution and Beyond* (Cornell University Press, 1993). In his current research he considers the history and present nature of Eastern European conceptions of "East" and "West" and their role in shaping regional social relations and conflicts.

FAHRÜNNISA E. KULLUK is a doctoral candidate in sociology at the University of Wisconsin-Madison. She has conducted comparative research on the labor movement and new social movements in Western Europe 1960–1975 and their implications for the theories of class structure and social transformation. Her present research is on the legal, political, cultural, and psychological aspects of judicial decision-making in political asylum cases in Germany. In this context she has done extensive fieldwork all over the western part of Germany.

LASZLO KÜRTI is Postdoctoral Researcher in Anthropology at Rutgers University. He has carried out fieldwork in Hungary and Romania and is the author of various articles. Recently he was an observer during the national elections in Bulgaria. His current research interests include political economy, nationalism, gender, and the politics of representation.

CLAUDE A. MEILLASSOUX is directeur de recherche (1ère classe) at the Centre National de la Recherche Scientifique (CNRS) in Paris, France. He is the holder of the Silver Medal of the Centre National de la Recherche Scientifique, Paris 1984. He conducted fieldwork on the Ivory Coast, in Mali, Sénégal and Mozambique. Meillassoux is the author and coauthor of thirteen books. His latest book is *The Anthropology of Slavery: The Womb of Iron and Gold* (University of Chicago Press, 1992). In his current research he is working on a reappraisal of the theories of kinship and attempting a new approach to the topic.

ORIOL PI-SUNYER, a native of Barcelona, is professor of anthropology at the University of Massachusetts at Amherst. He has worked in Latin America and in Spain, and for the past two decades he has been studying the economic, political, and cultural transformations of the Spanish transition. His works include *Zamora: Change and Continuity in a Mexican Town; Humanity and Culture: Introduction to Anthropology* (coauthored); *The Limits of Integration: Ethnicity and Nationalism in Modern Europe;* and *Economic Development: The Cultural Context.*

BRIGITTE SCHULZ is professor of political science at Trinity College, Hartford, Connecticut. She is coeditor of the acclaimed volume *The Soviet Bloc and the Third World: The Political Economy of East-West Relations* (Westview, 1989). She has also coedited articles on "Imperialism, Dependency and Social Class" and "Aid or Imperialism? West Germany in Sub-Saharan Africa." Her recent research on the relationship of Eastern Germany to the third world is soon to be published. Her ongoing research is on the political economy of the former German Democratic Republic.

AIDAN W. SOUTHALL is emeritus professor of social anthropology at the University of Wisconsin-Madison. He is the past president of the American African Association and editor and author of several books, among them *The Alur* (Heffer and Sons, 1954) and *Urban Anthropology* (Oxford University Press, 1973). His research interests are in urban anthropology, political economy, peasantry, the segmentary state, religion, and kinship. His comprehensive urban research is forthcoming in *The City in Time and Space*.

DEJAN TRICKOVIC is a doctoral candidate at the New School for Social Research and adjunct professor at St. John's University in New York. He is a research associate of the Institute for Philosophy and Social Theory at the University of Belgrade. For his current research on language and discourse as the meeting point of anthropology, sociology, history, and philosophy, Trickovic received the Guggenheim Award. His present and future research focuses on social change in Eastern Europe, Yugoslavia, and pre-Aryan India, areas about which he has published in the United States and in the yearbook of the Institute for Philosophy and Social Theory, University of Belgrade.